Persecuted by MI5 Security Service

Volume One

Based on the website www.mi5.com

Copyright © Boleslaw Tadeusz Szocik 1996-2011

Foreword

This book of three volumes is written by the author of website www.mi5.com based on material presented in that site. Because the site is multimedia and the book is not, the website is to be regarded as the definitive and dynamic entity.

It tells the story of my persecution by a criminal gang of evil Security Service homosexuals since June 1990 who have employed the full resources of the British Establishment in their pursuit of just one man. They are doing so for reasons of their own sexual satisfaction, as proven by the Masturbating MI5 Agent who was caught on video on 1/September/2000. The amorous Security Service agents have made rape threats against me and followed that up with a death threat which they conspired to carry out on 17/November/2001, unsuccessfully.

Coupled with the evil of MI5 is the uselessness and greed of the English lawyers I have employed to bring this matter to court. The firm of Bates Wells Braithwaite refused to present the case to any court or tribunal and emphasized the necessity of "Save You Money", taking £ 30,909.99 from me without even initiating a substantive legal case. They frittered the money away purely on technicalities, that being in their eyes the surest way of "Save You Money". MI5 labelled BWB's solicitor Lawrie Simanowitz "Heidi Fleiss", a Jewish prostitute, for his greed and corruption.

Contents

Foreword 2

Summary of Szocik's Complaint vs MI5 8

Website Homepage 13

Frequently Asked Questions 16

    Introduction 16

    Who Knows About It? 17

    The BBC, Television and Radio 17

    Capital Radio - Chris Tarrant 18

    Abuse in Set-up Situations and in Public 19

    Why the Security Services? 20

    MI5: The Cost of Running the Campaign 21

    MI5: Methods and Tactics 22

    MI5: Bugging and Counter-Surveillance 23

    How and Why did it Start? 24

    My Response to the Harassment 24

    Bernard Levin expresses his views 25

    Harassment at Work 27

    Purpose in Publicizing, and Censorship 27

    Why won't the British Police Put a Stop to it? 28

Site Map 29

Revision History 29

Peter Krüger's article 35

Iain Hotchkies' Medical Viewpoint 40

Toronto Freenet Supports Free Speech 43

Commendations 44

Usenet Discussion Archive 45

    Introduction 45

    "BBC's Hidden Shame" 4/5/95 46

    "A doubting Thomas is heard" 9/5/95 48

    "Recognition by Strangers is Normal" 12/5/95 51

    "Truth or Troll?" 13/5/95 54

    "Let it go" 1/8/95 57

    "But why?" 2/8/95 61

"Surveillance methods" 5/8/95 68

"Stand up for Free Speech" 14/8/95 70

"Troubling Censorship Issues" 20/8/95 71

"Options" 21/9/95 72

"Question and Answer" 27/9/95 75

"Watch Out, Forger About" 27/9/95 79

"Grievous Bodily Harm" 2/10/95 81

"Do they fear truth?" 3/10/95 84

"A new Kafka?" 3/10/95 86

"Dihydrocodeine" 26/11/95 87

"Flight or fight" 7/1/96 90

"Jeff Rooker MP" 5/3/96 92

"Email Cruelty" 11/3/96 95

"Shoot to Kill" 4/4/96 96

"Leant On" 7/4/96 98

"Stasi" 21/4/96 101

"Fitted up" 26/4/96 102

"Bernard Levin" 1/6/96 105

"alt.fan.mike-corley" 6/6/96 106

"Old_500" 5/7/96 107

"Silly-billy" 6/7/96 109

"BBC+ITN=MI5" 23/7/96 111

"Latest technology" 31/7/96 113

Just too crazy 30/9/96 114

Usual targets of such abuse 10/10/96 116

"Excellent web page" 19/10/96 117

WTGROMT 18/11/96 119

No Justice 20/11/96 120

David Hepworth (1) 26/2/97 122

Striking out action 10/3/97 125

I am being ignored 17/4/97 129

Continuing Silence 9/5/97 134

Victor Lewis-Smith 9/5/97 135

David Hepworth (2) 16/5/97 137

Evidence 139
    Overview 139
    Dimbleby / John Major, April 1997 140
    Channel Four TV News - 12/Feb/1999 141
    Nicholas Witchell - 10/April/1999 142
    Jealous Gay British Agents Masturbating Outside Window 143
    Blair Press Conference - 13/January/2003 145
    Blair's speech to Labour Conference - 13/March/2004 145
    Postscript to Blair 146
    Life is so hard 147
    GLR-David Hepworth (21/Feb/1997) 148
    GLR-David Hepworth (9/May/1997) 149
    Foxy's Showtime on Capital FM 25/11/98 7.35pm 150
    Virgin Radio-Johnny Boy (21/August/1998) 151
    Virgin Radio-Johnny Boy (19/June/1999) 152
    POSK Cafe - 2/Feb/1998 153
    BA984 LHR->TXL 13/June/1998 154
    Battersea Library 29/3/99 155
    Royal Festival Hall 15/4/99 156
    Balham - LT bus (8/July/1999) 157
    Clapham South (17/Feb/2000) 158
    Clapham Junction (6/May/2000) 159
    Balham High Road (3/Nov/2000) 160
    Crescent Grove, Clapham Common (2/Dec/2000) 161
    MI5 Deathsquad in Florida (17/Nov/2001) 163
    Why hasn't this been revealed yet? 166
    Virgin Radio-Jon Holmes (4-5/Jan/2002) 167
    Balham Hill Post Office (14/Nov/2002) 169
    Eclipse pub in Balham (20/Dec/2002) 171
    Barbican Library - 6/Feb/2003 172
    Eurostar Waterloo - 18/Apr/2003 174
    Clapham South (25/Oct/2003) 175
    Clapham South (27/09/2005) 176
    Clapham South (Sept/2005) 178

Clapham Junction (4/10/2005) 181

Mikey Peck - Bald Wanker (14/Nov/2005) 182

MI5 Crank Call (10/Jan/2008) 183

Fanatic's Fare for the Common Man 184

Private Eye, 23 Oct 1992 188

Articles faxed to, and Faxes received from, British organisations 190

Introduction to the Sent Faxes webpages 192

Faxes Sent to British Diplomatic/Legal logs 193

Faxes Sent to British Media logs 199

Faxes Sent to British Parliament logs 213

MI5 Persecution: How Could It Be True? 220

MI5 Persecution: "Why do you think MI5 are responsible?" 222

MI5 Persecution: "Why would they be doing this to you, sir?" 225

MI5 Persecution: .net Magazine Applauds my Website 228

MI5 Persecution : BBC Newscasters Spying on my Home 230

MI5 Persecution : How to Identify the Persecutors 233

MI5 Persecution : Browse Website www.five.org.uk 235

Comparing the MI5 Persecution with German "Final Solution" 239

MI5 Waste Taxpayer Millions on Pointless Hate-Campaign 243

Four Years of "MI5 Persecution" Posts on Internet Newsgroups 246

MI5 Persecution: BBC Newscasters Lie & Deny They're Watching Me 250

MI5 Persecution: Molestation during Travel 254

MI5 are Afraid to Admit They're Behind the Persecution 258

MI5 Persecution: No Justice for the Victims of MI5 262

MI5 Have Systematically Destroyed My Life 266

MI5 Persecution: Harassment through the Radio 271

Three Years of "MI5 Persecution" Faxes 274

MI5 Want Me to Send You these Faxes 278

Faxes Sent to US Congress logs 282

Introduction to Received Faxes from Parliament 2006 291

Faxes Sent to Parliament 2007 300

My Complaints 307

Overview 307

Jeffrey Gordon Solicitors 308

Ottawa Civic Hospital and Alan Holdsworth	314
My First Summons against BBC	316
My Second Summons against BBC	323
A letter from MI5	329
Security Service Tribunal Denies	330
Interception of Communications Tribunal Denies	331
Gagged by BBC Ariel's editor	332
Eye Say, and Lord Gnome Answers	334
Bindman and Partners, Solicitors	336
Counter-surveillance sweep by Nationwide Investigations Group	342
Home Office MI5 Liaison won't comment	344
Communications with Security Service Tribunal in 1999	345
Charing Cross police, March 1999	352
Correspondence with Keith Hill MP, 1997-99	356
Data Protection application to Keith Hill MP, 2002	362
Eye Say, 2002	364
Orange County Sheriff's Office 2006	370
Orlando Police Department 2006	373
Bugsweep by Steadman's team	379
Eye Say, 2006-07	385
BBC Ariel accepts my MindControl Torture advert	387

Summary of Szocik's Complaint vs MI5

- MI5 has been stalking me for twenty years since June 1990 almost continuously. My home at 45 Englewood Road has been under surveillance from the outset for video and audio, every room. They have broken up my friendships and manipulated all three places of work (CSA, OCTS, AIT) so that I lost two of those and suffered a mental breakdown at the third due to abuse.
- They tried to kill me in November/2001, of which I have evidence since they made a tangible written threat immediately prior, and I have an audio recording of what they were shouting during.
- They set the British media on me from the outset in 1990, with interactive reactions from radio and TV presenters; in other words, TV news presenters look into my home while they read the news, and they react immediately to what they see inside my home.
- This article summarises material which is described in detail on website www.mi5.com These occurrences have been discussed on Internet newsgroups from 1995 onwards. MI5 had their own man (Paul Janik) on newsgroups in the late 1990s.
- There was frequent abuse in public on streets and transport, everywhere I go; UK, Canada, France, USA, Poland. Currently I wear a minidisc recorder and carry a camera to record faces, so this has reduced. However MI5 have shouted from the front of the house through the windows while I am in the upstairs front room.
- I didn't figure out until 1995 that it was MI5 doing these things. Previously I had thought it might be private detectives. Tam's suggestion to tribunal president in November/2003 that MI5 would claim a Serious Crime exemption is a key admission, because it means that MI5 has admitted some responsibility.
- I have brought legal cases against MI5 before the Security Service Tribunal, the Information Commissioner, the Information Tribunal, Orlando Federal Court, the Investigatory Powers Tribunal and also the European Court of Human Rights, which is still in progress. All the other cases failed.

Intrusive Surveillance

Started in June/1990 when I was completing an MSc at Imperial College, having graduated from Cambridge (Selwyn College) the previous year; I think someone at Cambridge may have set them on me, but MI5 haven't said who it was. I was unpopular with some people in my college, and it may have started from there.

First events were "interactive watching" by TV newscasters (BBC/ITN) in summer 1990, when they made clear they could see what was happening inside my home. In June/1990 Sue Carpenter (ITN) saw my mother bring an apple into the room for me, and laughed. Similar occurrences through summer of 1990 until I sold my portable TV and stopped watching TV entirely.

MI5 have made clear they have 24/7 electronic video and audio surveillance of every room in my home using some sort of electronic bugging. They repeat words which are said in my home, and they got my "friends" (Andrzej Choroszewski) to parrot words and laugh at what had been happening in my house. They got work colleagues (OCTS) to similarly repeat words from my home; MI5 also in 1992 bugged the house of Mrs Bielan (in her seventies, family friend) and they got Ian Cunningham (OCTS) to repeat sarcastically a comment about "ironing" from her house.

Media Harassment

MI5 get TV/radio presenters to say particular phrases, and words with subtext. They also make "interactive watching" where the TV/radio presenter can see or is told what is happening inside my house. This has been going on throughout the 20-year period, but particularly in the early 1990s. Currently I do not watch TV or listen to the radio because it is hurtful. They also got some newspapers to write about me, for example Bernard Levin of the Times (see website).

There are two incidents recorded on my website in the Evidence area "Nicholas Witchell - 10/4/1999" and "Channel 4 News - 12/2/1999" which I can be sure fall into the "interactive watching" category. Understandably when I watch TV and record the program, then TV presenters are circumspect in their behaviour. In the early 1990s when I wasn't recording anything, they were unsubtle.

Malcolm Kennedy (Liberty's client) reports that there is a method whereby MI5 tell TV/radio presenters what to say to "wind up" their viewers/listeners. My case is a more extreme development because from June/1990 they were directly looking into my home while they read the news.

Interference with Employment

In 1991-1997 I worked for three companies; CSA 1991, OCTS 1992-94, AIT 1994-97. MI5 interfered with all three companies. CSA was a little company with one manager Brian Hunt who was being egged on by MI5 to bully me. He kept saying "shit" and I kept crying. Eventually CSA fired me.

OCTS (Oxford Computer Group) was a company of 30 people of whom about half knew MI5 were abusing me. Applications manager Steve Mitchell kept abusing me and repeating what MI5 told him to say from their surveillance of my home in London and rented accommodation in Oxford, and again I kept crying, which spurred them on to attack me. Mitchell and his sidekick Slater attacked me particularly viciously and constantly in autumn 1992, as a result of which I had a psychotic breakdown and went to hospital as an outpatient in November/1992. There I was placed on antipsychotic medication which I have had to take for 18 years because MI5 have constantly attacked me throughout the period.

Mid-1994 I emigrated to Canada to try to escape from the persecutors. They followed me and managed to recreate the same conditions (abuse on street, abuse through friends and in the workplace) in Ottawa. In particular they got co-workers at AIT Corp to parrot words. I was made redundant from AIT in 1997, at which point I took disability pension, which I have been on for 12 years.

Complaints on Internet newsgroups

From 1995 I complained on internet newsgroups about MI5's activities, the purpose being to expose their activites so they would cease. I first made these complaints anonymously. MI5 had their person Paul Janik on the newsgroups, who encouraged me to complain to Security Service Tribunal in early 1997. Immediately after MI5 had received my complaint from SST, their man Janik published my name, address and phone number on internet newsgroups, the intent clearly being to silence me. Obviously the SST found against me, as they have for every single other complaint.

I also tried to sue the BBC for the newscaster spying, which got nowhere; Michael Buerk and Martyn Lewis categorically told their employers that interactive spying was not taking place, and consequently the BBC's lawyers lied to the court. There is a substantial website at www.mi5.com detailing my complaints. I have also tried to complain by sending many thousands of faxes, of which half went to the British Parliament (see website) which only brought a lot of complaints; ultimately the Police phoned to threaten me that imprisonment would result unless the faxes ceased. My elected representative Keith Hill MP (Labour - Streatham) has refused to help, and told me he was "unable to remember" whether he contacted the Police for them to stop my faxed complaints.

I have tried to complain to UK Police three times, in 1995 to Clapham police station, in 1999 when contacted by Charing Cross police, and in 2000 when contacted about the faxes. Each time they have refused to accept my complaint; I think it is improbable that they would progress this type of complaint.

Canada 1994-98

MI5 recreated the "abuse by public" aspect in Ottawa in 1994-98. They kept getting people to shout obscenities particularly "prostitute" and similar words. Similarly in London shouted the same words. Most of these occurrences I deleted because I did not think I could admit that people had shouted these words at me. However a few (15 or 20) I still have on minidisc recording.

In the part of Ottawa where I lived (Byward market) there was a nightclub directly opposite my window, where late at night youths would shout "prostitute, schizophrenic" and similar words.

There is a particular MI5 agent whom I have seen several times. I saw him on a KLM flight from Ottawa to London in 1995; at Ottawa's Civic Hospital in 1996, where he loudly announced his name to be "Tad" to which the doctor said "but your name is Alan X" where the X sounded like Holdsworth; at Ottawa airport in June/1998 where he was pacing to and fro in a menacing manner; at a cinema in Streatham (London); and at Abbeville Road, Clapham on 10/Dec/2001 when I went to post the SAR letter to MI5. He seems to have a sidekick, a small black haired man, whom I saw a couple of times.

USA 1999-2001

In 1999 I went to Florida, living first in Miami then Orlando. MI5 continued to attack me while I was in Orlando. There seems a significant sexual element in their abuse towards me; in summer/2000 they made several incidents of public masturbation, and on 1/September/2000 a Brtish agent masturbated publicly outside the window (see website video). In autumn 2001 they were placing their people in the basement bar of the residence (Post Parkside), to make the usual words of "schizophrenic, prostitute" etc. On one occasion their person said "I was raped". I was worried they would try to break into my apartment. I bought a Glock-17 pistol in October/2001, and then a Colt 45 calibre pistol in early November for self defence. Also MI5's stalking depended on my being defenceless, and I thought if I were to present a defence then they might leave me alone.

MI5 reacted by trying to kill me on 17/November/2001. I was on the 9th floor in my apartment, they placed approx 7 men in the park in front of the building. You can hear for yourself what the men were shouting; "I am not a whore", "I don't wanna shoot people" etc. They had made a public death threat on 11/Nov/2001 on "uk.misc" group, which said;

From: "Boil Grapes" <fake@dontreply.net>
Newsgroups: uk.misc
Subject: Test
Date: Sun, 11 Nov 2001 18:12:59 +0000
Message-ID: <87rpn7.8153$ny6.8332847@news.dial.pipex.com>

They say that when a man with a 45 meets a man with a rifle,
the man with the pistol is a dead man.

Let's see if that's true.

It was not until early next year that I understood properly the enormity of had happened. The newsgroup death threat and group of men outside shouting matched; in retrospect you can see they were trying to force me to attack them with a pistol, and when I approached them, they would shoot me with a rifle.

A recording exists of this incident of 18 minutes; the group of men shout sexual obscenities, death threats and other abuse; the words have been verified by Mr Ginsberg of Professional Audio Laboratories, Inc. (www.proaudiolabs.com)

London Dec/2001-present

I returned to London in December/2001 and MI5 immediately verbally attacked me every time I left the house. I have several incidents recorded on minidisc from Dec/2001. I then made a data protection request to MI5, and an appeal to Information Tribunal in May/2002. MI5 have continued to follow me and verbally attack me throughout this period. In July/2003 in south France with my mother, group of young men said "shit shit", then "we might do it by accident, but not deliberately", "kurwa" which means they were considering staging an accident; it also reflected what I had said recently. In February/2004 in New York "you're a liar I will fuck your ass", group of four middle aged men near hotel, also man at La Guardia airport "I will fuck his ass". British intelligence prefer to incite other races to make actual threats.

Information Tribunal case

In Dec/2001 I made a data protection subject access request to MI5, to which they made a minimal response some months later, admitting a communication between themselves and SST in 1997 (which obviously I knew about already). I tried to bring a legal action under the Data Protection Act to the Information Tribunal, under s28(6) of the Act, which would have meant MI5 giving data they held on me to the Tribunal; then the Tribunal would decide whether or not it was of National Security relevance and had to be kept secret, or whether it could be disclosed without harm to national security.

I thought hiring lawyers would strengthen my case, so in November/2002 I instructed solicitors Bates Wells Braithwaite (www.bwbllp.com) and barrister Tim Pitt-Payne (11 King's Bench Walk) and as a result there were two hearings, in June/2003 and Nov/2003. Unfortunately BWB's solicitor Simanowitz chose to conduct the case purely on the technical paperwork point of whether "proceedings" existed as required by the Act; he kept insisting the priority was to "Save You Money"; and as a result the hearings were without mention of the complaint substance, which was that MI5 had tried to kill me in Nov/2001. Barrister Pitt-Payne openly and corruptly favoured the opposition particularly at the Nov/2003 hearing; the result was £ 20,000 spent without any result and without even being able to tell the Tribunal the complaint material.

However the tribunal president was able to extract an admission from MI5's barrister Tam that MI5 were conducting some sort of activities against me; and Tam tried to suggest a serious crime exemption instead of National Security, which is propaganda because when compared against their activities it is irrelevant.

There have been interferences between BWB and myself; letters have been "lost in the post"; while I have waited in BWB's waiting room a man outside shouted the usual sexual obscenities; MI5 have tried to create a meme "get your money back" which would sever the relationship; they have induced children to shout "Heidi Fleiss" which is a Jewish prostitute in reference to BWB's solicitor Simanowitz.

I am trying to bring a case to the Tribunal which will include mention of the complaint.

Current activities

Currently (Feb/2010) MI5 are inflicting a technological mindreading/ telepathy while at home as of approx 10/Oct/2005, and some sort of inflicted sound/electronic ventriloquism which is at home and also follows me when I go somewhere; it bypasses earphones and is directly inflicted on the ears or on the brain. I have some evidence of this, but it is mostly impossible to record; therefore their agents obsessively and incessantly shout obscene sexual abuse. They also tried in autumn 2005 to set the neighbours against us; also they follow me around London of which there is some evidence.

I would previously never have believed it was possible to read a person's thoughts as has been happening to me since 2005; but that is clearly happening now so I have had to modify my view. I have written a transcript of their methods and some of what they have said.

In 2008 I brought a case against MI5 to the Investigatory Powers Tribunal, which they investigated by asking MI5 whether my claims were meritorious. Of course MI5 answered they were not, and IPT answered in August 2009 that they had made no determination in my favour, as in almost every other case. There is no appeal in the UK legal system from a decision of IPT, so I have recently brought an application to the European Court of Human Rights agains MI5 based on IPT's decision.

Website Homepage

Thames House on Millbank, the London headquarters of the Security Service

Newsgroup members join in the discussion

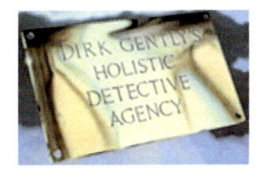

Peter Krüger writes about "Dirk Gently on the Toronto Case".

Hotchkies FAQ: Looking at it from a medical viewpoint, proving that medicine isn't much use for dealing with real life persecution.

Accolades for the Web Site
Read what people said about this web site.

Visitor count: 494970 since August 11, 1996

Persecuted by the Security Service

Since June 1990 the British security service MI5 has waged a campaign of harassment against a UK citizen, through the broadcast and print media, verbal abuse at work, and molestation in public and during travel.

Despite widespread knowledge of the campaign in the UK and discussion of its characteristics on Usenet for over fifteen years, it continues today both in Britain and North America. Its cause and basis is xenophobia on the basis of the genetic accident of mental illness, coupled with discrimination against an inferior "foreigner" whom they condemn as "not up to British Standards". *If this is your first visit to this site, please read the FAQ first. Feel free to contact the author with any questions.*

- Frequently Asked Questions article outlines the parameters of the persecution. Who is involved, and why? What technical and social means do they employ? What response have I made, and why has

Free Speech Online
Blue Ribbon Campaign

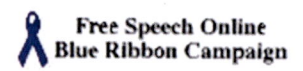

Toronto Freenet supports free speech

Intelligence agency sources on the Web

Intelligence Watch Report covers intelligence agencies around the world.

kim-spy
Korea WebWeekly kim-spy Intelligence and Counter-Intelligence link page.

Lobster Journal publishes research on the intelligence community.

Cryptome

Cryptome is an online source of intelligence related material.

MI5 has a website, too, but you should prepare yourself for some serious "alternative reality" if you plan to visit it.

their campaign yet to be exposed?

- The UK Security Services which are believed to be behind it all. *Domestic security* is the province of MI5 while the *secret intelligence service* MI6 combats foes (and its former employees) on foreign shores.

- Usenet archive chronicling the (sometimes very enthusiastic) exchanges which have taken place on UK-local newsgroups since May 1995.

- Quite a lot of evidence has been recorded. Although none of it is particularly conclusive, by presenting it I hope to explain what I understand from some television and radio programmes. Most of the "clinching" material was aired in 1990-92, and no recordings exist now, which is quite unfortunate.

In September 2000, British Intelligence organised an agent to perform an amorous expression outside the window, which was promptly recorded on my video camera. The instance was one of a series, and clarifies a particularly troubling sexual aspect of the personalities of the MI5 "stalkers".

On 17/Nov/2001 MI5 attempted to kill me as evidenced on an audio recording. Obviously they failed, and the legal system has yet to deal with their activity. In August 2005 MI5 started a programme of MindControl Torture which has continued ever since, consisting of mind reading and silent obscene verbal abuse "direct to skull", of which I have acquired some evidence.

- My complaints to the BBC and MI5 (via the Security Service Tribunal and Interception of Communications Tribunal), and their response to my challenges, are recorded here. Basically they deny everything, they have put their denials (mostly - Buerk and Lewis refused) in writing, and I don't believe them. Part of the website also documents media coverage of my campaign to expose the persecution.

- Faxed articles to, and responses from British organisations including Parliament and UK media. Over 24,259 faxes in all were sent from 1998 to 2000. Their aim was to boot discussion of the persecution into the public domain, and that aim was not accomplished.

- I have been keeping notes of the persecution while it has been happening, and various random items can be found in the harassment area of the website.

- There are several areas of legal documents on this website, namely SAR for the Subject Access Request to MI5, IC for communications with the Information Commissioner in 2001-02, SAR for the SAR to Investigatory Powers Tribunal, IT2002 for communications with Information Tribunal in 2002, and not least Orlando Lawsuit for the legal action against MI5's attempt to kill me in Nov/2001.

- In 2002 I instructed solicitors Bates Wells Braithwaite to bring the substantive case before the Information Tribunal. They readily seized my money and turned it into a game of pure legal technicalities, because as their solicitor Simanowitz was keen to point out, the main objective was to "Save You Money". MI5 used small children to label Simanowitz as "Heidi Fleiss", a Jewish prostitute. You can read the whole sorry story on these pages. They never did any constructive work for me; they ruined two Information Tribunal hearings; they charged me over £ 30,000 and they tried to kill off my case due to my alleged incapacity, despite the numerous statements of capacity from many doctors.

You may find the Site Map and Revision History page helpful in navigating the webpages.

This website is designed for Windows using IE7. I recommend you install the TIFF viewer alternatiff to read multipage documents, and download QuickTime from Apple's website to experience multimedia content unless this is installed already.

Contact the author by feedback

Frequently Asked Questions

> *Exposing a Campaign of Persecution by the Security Services*
>
> Since June 1990, a Secret Campaign of Persecution has been Waged by the British Security Service against a UK Citizen. The Harassment is widely known about within the UK, yet there exists an Omerta suppressing its Publication.

Introduction

In June 1990 a horrifying campaign of harassment was initiated in London by what are believed to be elements of the security services. The harassment has continued for twenty years, starting from the broadcast and print media, and encompassing abuse through set-up situations and by people in public places. It has been brought to the attention of the police and they are aware what is happening, but are not taking any action to prevent it.

The harassment has several faces; in the broadcast and print media, people in the world of television know there is a conspiracy to spy, BBC newsreaders peek while reading the news, radio presenters interject abusive remarks in their commentary. "Set-up" situations have been organised, frequently during travel, with people briefed on what they are to say and in what manner. In public, people throw abuse in the knowledge that their cowardice will not be challenged. At a previous workplace, employers perpetrated verbal sexual harassment and repeated verbatim things said at my home and accommodation.

You may think while reading this that it could be a "troll", a humorous invention for the amusement of its author. It isn't; the enumeration of verifiable events (even if those events are difficult to check) should prove that. You may also think that it's close to the symptoms of psychiatric illness and can be explained in those terms. But the reason this type of harassment was started in the first place is because those initiating planned to simulate the symptoms of illness; any complaint of harassment would be seen at first glance as indicative of psychiatric illness and "treated" accordingly. The fact that so many people now have a good idea of the truth makes it difficult for that position to be maintained.

Who Knows About It?

Many people know, both in the establishment and media, and among the general public. Despite an absence of its target from the UK for more than two years, the echoes of paranoia can still be heard loud and clear from across the water. When it started in 1990, the only people who knew were those in BBC television who were spying on my home, and a few radio broadcasters. There were a few cases of public harassment, but very little compared to the situation that developed a couple of years later.

The list today includes BBC TV staff (newsreaders such as Martyn Lewis, Michael Buerk, Nicholas Witchell), people from radio stations such as Chris Tarrant of Capital and Radio 1 DJs, people in the print media, but also many people in the general public. All united in a conspiracy which breaks the laws which the UK does have regarding harassment, and all completely uncaring for any semblance of decency or elementary respect for individual rights.

The British police (obviously) do know the nature of the harassment and in all probability the identity of those behind it. Some time ago I made a complaint to my local police station in London, without positive result. The UK police are failing in their duty to see the law enforced in not checking the abuse.

The BBC, Television and Radio

The first incident in June 1990 was when a newsreader made what seemed to be a reaction to something which had happened in my home, and out of context of what they were reading. My first reaction was disbelief; nothing of the sort had ever happened before, the idea that such a thing could occur had not crossed my mind, yet there was no doubt of what had just taken place. My disbelief eroded as this recurred time after time. Besides the news, offenders included shows such as Crimewatch (!), Newsnight, and "entertainment" shows. There seems to be very little moral understanding among the people who make these programmes; they just assume they will never be caught, so they carry on without a thought for the illegality or amorality of what they do. The only time I ever heard a word raised in doubt was by Paxman being interviewed by someone else (I think by Clive Anderson) back in 1990; referring to the "watching" he said it troubled him, and when asked by the host what you could do about it, replied "Well, you could just switch it off" (meaning the surveillance monitor in the studio). He clearly didn't let his doubts stand in the way of continued surreptitious spying from his own or other people's shows, though.

Now you're convinced this is a troll, aren't you? This story has been the subject of much debate on the uk.* Usenet newsgroups for over a year, and some readers believe it to be an invention (it has even been suggested that a group of psychology students are responsible!), others think it symptomatic of a derangement of the author, and a few give it credence. Quite a few people do know part or all of the story already, so this text will fill in the gaps in their knowledge. For the rest, what may persuade you of the third possibility is that some of the incidents detailed are checkable against any archives of radio and TV programmes that exist; that the incidents involve named people (even if those hiding in the shadows have not made their identity or affiliations evident), and those people may be persuaded to come out with the truth; and that the campaign of harassment is continuing today both in the UK and on the American continent, in a none-too-secret fashion; by its nature the significant risk of exposure increases with time.

On several occasions people said to my face that harassment from the TV was happening. On the first day I worked in Oxford, I spent the evening in the local pub with the company's technical director Ian, and Phil, another employee. Ian made a few references to me and said to Phil, as if in an aside, "Is he the bloke who's been on TV?" to which Phil replied, "Yes, I think so".

I made a number of efforts to find the bugs, without success; last year we employed professional counter-surveillance people to scan for bugs (see later) again without result. In autumn 1990 I disposed of my TV and watched virtually no television for the next three years. But harassment from TV stations has gone on for over six years and continues to this day. This is something that many people obviously know is happening; yet the TV staff have the morality of paedophiles, that because they're getting away with it they feel no wrong.

Other people who were involved in the abuse in 1990 were DJs on BBC radio stations, notably disc jockeys from Radio 1 and other stations (see the following section). Again, since they don't have sense in the first place they can't be expect to have the moral sense not to be part of criminal harassment.

Capital Radio - Chris Tarrant

Capital Radio DJs have been "in on it" from the start. One of the first things I heard in the summer of 1990 was from a Capital DJ who said, "If he listens to Capital then he can't be all bad" (supportive, you see. We're not bastards). Much of what came over the radio in 1990 is now so far away the precise details have been obliterated by time. No diary was kept of the details, and although archives if they exist may give pointers, the ambiguity of what broadcasters said would leave that open to re-interpretation.

In spring 1994, Chris Tarrant on his Capital morning show made an aside to someone else in the studio, about a person he didn't identify. He said, "You know this bloke? He says we're trying to kill him. We should be done for attempted manslaughter".

That mirrored something I had said a day or two before. What Tarrant said was understood by the staff member in the studio he was saying it to; they said, "Oh no, don't say that" to Tarrant. If any archives exist of the morning show (probably unlikely) then it could be found there; what he said was so out of context that he would be very hard put to find an explanation. A couple of days later, someone at the site where I was working repeated the remark although in a different way; they said there had been people in a computer room when automatic fire extinguishers went off and those people were "thinking of suing for attempted manslaughter".

Finally, this isn't confined to the established radio stations. In 1990 after I had listened to a pirate radio station in South London for about half an hour, there was an audible phone call in the background, followed by total silence for a few moments, then shrieks of laughter. "So what are we supposed to say now? Deadly torture? He's going to talk to us now, isn't he?", which meant that they could hear what I would say in my room.

Abuse in Set-up Situations and in Public

Strangers in the street have recognized me on sight many times, and shown awareness of the current thread of abuse. To give you one example, in 1992 I was seriously ill, and a manager at work somewhat humorously said that "it wasn't fair" that people were bullying me. A few days later, I attended for the first time a clinic in London as an outpatient, and on my way out was accosted by someone who asked if "they had paid my fare", with emphasis on the word "fare". He repeated the word several times in this different context; that they should have paid my "fare", each time emphasizing the word.

For two and a half years from the time their harassment started until November 1992 I refused to see a psychiatrist, because I reasoned that I was not ill of my own action or fault, but through the stress caused by harassment, and that a lessening of the illness would have to be consequent to a removal of its immediate cause, in other words a cessation of harassment. I also reasoned that since they were taunting me with jokes about mental illness, if I were to seek treatment then the abusers would think that they had "won" and been proved "right". Remember, the constant theme of any persecution is, "we must destroy you because you're X", whether X is a racial or other attribute. In this case the X was "we persecute you because you have brain disease". The similarity of this logic to Nazi attitudes to the mentally ill is striking.

The same manager who'd said "it wasn't fair" asked me in winter 1992 why I didn't seek help from a psychiatrist; was it, he asked, because "they would think they had won" if I sought treatment? That was something I'd never said at work... again, taken separately it proves nothing, but many such things over a period of months proves conclusively that people in the company knew what was going on, and in quite a lot of detail.

Usually harassment in public lacks the level of finesse of "paying your fare". Most people's imagination does not go beyond moronic parroting of the current term of denigration. That is not surprising given the average level of the abusers; if they do not have the intelligence to distinguish wrong from right then neither will they have the capacity for anything other than mindless repetition of a monosyllabic term calculated to fit into their minds.

The first incidents of verbal assault in public were in again in the summer of 1990, although they increased in frequency and venom with time. In July 1990 the first public incident occurred on a tube train on the Northern line. Two men and their girlfriends recognised me; the women sprang to my defence, saying "He looks perfectly normal, he doesn't look ill". Their boyfriends of course knew better, and followed the party line; one of them made reference to an "operation", apparently to work at the tube station but implicitly to a visit that I had made to hospital a couple of weeks previously.

In August 1990 going home from college, soon after getting on a tube train at Gloucester Road I was followed by a group of four youths, who started a chant of abuse. That they were targeting me was confirmed by other people in the carriage, one of whom asked the other "who are they going on at, is it the bloke who just got on?" to which the second replied "yes, I think so". I was tempted to reply, but as in every other instance the abusers are enabled in their cowardice by physically outnumbering the abused; any confrontation would result in my being beaten up, followed by a complaint to the police that "he attacked us", and of course he's ill, so he must have been imagining that we were getting at him. Shitty, aren't they?

But the shittiness of the four youths on the tube train is as nothing compared to the episode on the National Express coach to Dover in the summer of 1992. While going on holiday to the Continent I was verbally set upon by a couple travelling sitting a few rows behind. The boy did the talking, his female companion contributing only a continuous empty giggling noise. He spoke loudly to ensure other people on the coach heard, always about "they" and "this bloke" but never naming either the abusers or the person he was talking about. He said "they" had "found somebody from his school, and he was always really stressed at school". They must have dug deep to find enemies there; perhaps someone who dropped out of school, someone who didn't do too well later, who was jealous and keen to get their own back? The boy also said "he was in a bed and breakfast for only one night and they got him". By a not unexpected coincidence I had been in a B&B in Oxford a week previously, which had been booked from work; other things lead me to the conclusion that the company's offices were bugged for most of the 2 1/2 years that I was there, so "they" would have known a room in the B&B had been booked. (But I'll bet "they" didn't tell the company's managers their offices were bugged, did they?).

After a few minutes of this I went back to where they were sitting and asked where they were travelling. The boy named a village in France, and the girl's giggling suddenly ceased; presumably it permeated to her brain cell what the purpose of the boy's abuse was.

This and other set-up situations are obviously calculated to provoke a direct confrontation which would bring in the police, with the abusers claiming that they were the ones attacked. Again in 1992, outside the house where I was living in Oxford I was physically attacked by someone - not punched, just grabbed by the coat, with some verbals thrown in for good measure. That was something the people at work shouldn't have known about... but soon after a couple of people were talking right in front of me about, "I heard he was attacked". The UK police have a responsibility for preventing assault occurring, but they do not seem to take any interest in meeting that responsibility. I suppose their attitude is that harassment does not come within their remit unless it involves physical assault, and they will only become involved once that happens. That is of course quite the wrong attitude for them to take, but as I now understand, the police investigate only the crime they wish to investigate; if they do not take your complaints seriously then there is nothing you can do to make them take action.

Why the Security Services?

You may ask, why do I think the "they" referred to are the security services? Is there any evidence that there is a single source, as opposed to a loosely based "whispering campaign" amongst many people? Even if there is a single source, is there any evidence that "they" are professional "buggers" as opposed to amateurs, or perhaps people working for a privately funded organization?

a) As to the question of a single source versus something more fragmented; it is quite obvious that there is a single source from the way the campaign has been carried out. Since things have been repeated verbatim which were said in my home, there must be one group which does the watching and listening. Since on several occasions (mainly during travel) people have been planted in close proximity and rehearsed in what they were to say, it follows that someone must have done the planning for that, and again a single source is indicated.

b) So why couldn't it be amateurs? Why couldn't it be a private organisation, for example a private detective agency paid to manage the campaign and undertake the technical aspects? Some detective agencies are unscrupulous as has been proved on the occasions in the past when they've been exposed or caught; they too can have access to the bugging technology deployed; and there are reported cases of MI5 paying private eyes to do their dirty work (against peace campaigners and similar enemies of the state) on the understanding that if they were caught then they could deny all knowledge. Why couldn't that be the case?

The main factor pointing to direct security service involvement (as opposed to amateurs or MI5 proxies) is the breadth of their access to the media in particular, and the fact that the television companies are so involved in the campaign. The BBC would not directly invade someone's home themselves, since it would not be within their remit to allocate personnel or financial resources to do so. An organisation of their stature would not take part in a campaign set up by private sources. The only people they would take material from would be the security services, presumably on the assumption that if the cat ever flew out of the bag yowling it would be MI5 who would take the consequences.

State sponsorship for these acts of psychological terrorism is also indicated by duration; support for over six years for a team of three or four people would be beyond the means and will of most private sources. The viciousness of the slanders and personal denigration also points to MI5; they traditionally "protect" the British state from politicians of the wrong hue by character assassination, and in this case are using their tried and tested methods to murder with words an enemy they have invented for themselves.

And there are precedents. Diana and Hewitt were alleged to have been filmed "at it" by an Army intelligence team which had operated in Northern Ireland, these allegations were made by someone called Jones who had been on the team. His statements were denied by the defence establishment who tried to character-assassinate by describing him as the "Jones twins". Funny how if you tell the truth, then you must be ill, isn't it? Thought only communists behaved like that?

Hewitt later said that he'd been spoken to by someone in the army who revealed the existence of videotapes of him and Diana, and that the tapes would be published if any attempt was made by them to resume their association.

MI5: The Cost of Running the Campaign

Here's what a couple of other people on Usenet (uk.misc) had to say regarding the cost of running such an operation...

```
PO: >Have some sense, grow up and smell reality. What you are talking about
PO: >would take loads of planning, tens of thousands of pounds and lots of
PO: >people involved in the planning, execution and maintenance of it. You
```

PO: >must have a very high opinion of yourself to think you are worth it.

```
PM: >But why? And why you? Do you realize how much it would cost to keep
PM: >one person under continuous surveillance for five years? Think about
PM: >all the man/hours. Say they _just_ allocated a two man team and a
PM: >supervisor. OK., Supervisor's salary, say, £30,000 a year. Two men,
PM: >£20,000 a year each. But they'd need to work in shifts -- so it would
PM: >be six men at £20,000 (which with on-costs would work out at more like
PM: >£30,000 to the employer.)
PM: >
PM: >So, we're talking £30,000 x 6. £180,000. plus say, £40,000 for the
PM: >supervisor. £220,000. Then you've got the hardware involved. And
PM: >any transcription that needs doing. You don't think the 'Big Boss'
PM: >would listen to hours and hours of tapes, do you.
PM: >
PM: >So, all in all, you couldn't actually do the job for much less than
PM: >a quarter million a year. Over five years. What are you doing that makes
PM: >it worth the while of the state to spend over one and a quarter million
PM: >on you?
```

Those are pretty much the sort of calculations that went through my head once I stopped to consider what it must be costing them to run this operation. The partial answer is, there have been periods when the intensity has been greater, and times when little has happened. In fact, for much of 1993 and the first half of 1994, very little happened. Although I don't think that was for reasons of money - if they can tap into the taxpayer they're not going to be short of resources, are they?

The more complete answer is in the enormity of what they're doing. Relative to the cost to British pride of seeing their country humiliated for the persecution of their own citizens, isn't is worth the cost of four or five people to try to bring things to a close in the manner they would wish? To the government a million or two is quite honestly nothing - if they can convince themselves of the necessity of what they're doing, resources will not be the limiting factor.

MI5: Methods and Tactics

They deliberately set out to harass in a way that would resemble the symptoms of schizophrenia, so that any report of the harassment would be taken as indicating mental illness and "treated" accordingly. They never show their own faces; they only work through proxies, in the media, among the public, and by manipulating people in the workplace. Since they do not declare their identity there is no evidence to initiate legal action against the security services or anyone else. The only people you can prosecute are the proxies and they will deny knowledge of any conspiracy.

By repeatedly humiliating and abusing the victim, they induced mental illness. This is the worst form of human rights violation: making any statement of the harassment appear to be symptomatic of the illness which they cause through the harassment. That this can happen, and people collude by silence, is absolutely horrifying.

From the beginning in June 1990 they set a pattern of harassment which they have followed without change for the last twenty years. They paint me as a "threat" to which people must "react" (shades of Nazi persecution methods), while simultaneously portraying their hate campaign on which they have spent millions of pounds of taxpayers' money as a "joke".

The MI5 that breaks the law with the silent complicity of the police is the same agency that is now seeking a role in the fight against crime. Perhaps the real joke is the proposed involvement in the implementation of justice of an organisation which commits criminal acts with secrecy and disinterest for the legal process.

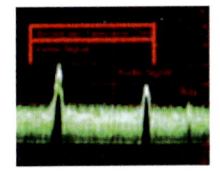

MI5: Bugging and Counter-Surveillance

```
PO: >Did you ever look for the bugs in your house ? If not, why not ? I mean if
PO: >I thought that was happening to me, I'd search the place from top to bottom,
PO: >I mean I live there I would know if anything was out of place. If I was
PO: >really suspicious, I would call in one of those bug detection teams which
PO: >have those machines that pick up the transmitted radio waves. This
PO: >reminds me of BUGS, that new programme on BBC1 on
```

That's exactly what we did. We went to a competent, professional detective agency in London, paid them over 400 quid to debug our house. They used scanner devices which go to over 1 GHz and would pick up any nearby transmitter in that range, they also checked the phones and found nothing... but if the tap was at the exchange, then they wouldn't find anything, would they?

```
CS: >Doesn't this suggest to you that there are, in fact, no bugs to be found?
```

You can assume that they've done this sort of thing to other people in more "serious" cases, where they would know the targets would suspect the presence of electronic surveillance. So they will have developed techniques and devices which are not readily detectable either by visual inspection or by electronic means. What those techniques might be, I couldn't guess.

In this case, the existence of bugging devices was clear from the beginning, and they "rubbed it in" with what was said by the boy on the coach. It was almost as if they wanted counter-surveillance people to be called in, who they knew would fail to detect the bugging devices, causing loss of credibility to the other things I would have to say relating to the harassment.

I did all the things someone in my situation would do to try to find the bugs. In addition to calling in professional help using electronic counter-surveillance, I made a close visual inspection of electrical equipment, plus any points where audio or video surveillance devices might have been concealed. Of course, I found nothing. Normal surveillance "mini-cameras" are quite noticeable and require visible supporting circuitry. It seems to me the best place to put a small video surveillance device would be additional to a piece of electronic equipment such as a TV or video. It would be necessary to physically break in to a property to fit such a device.

How and Why did it Start?

The harassment didn't start by itself, so someone must have been there at the outset to give it a firm push and set the "animals" after me. It looks as if I was set up in June 1990, and the timing indicates someone from university was responsible.

```
>One thing which has been missing from this discussion is this simple
>prognosis: that maybe he is right and that, despite his admitted
>mental condition, there really is a campaign against him organised by
>now-influential ex-students of his university.
```

In May or June 1990, Alan Freeman on Radio 1 read out a letter from someone who had known me for a few years, who wrote of the one who "wore out his welcome with random precision" (from the Pink Floyd song). Freeman went on to say to the writer "that's a hell of a letter you wrote there". The indication is strongly that people I had parted from soon before nursed a grudge against me and were trying to cause trouble for me.

The suggestion is that Freeman might have shown the letter to other people, and things could have snowballed from there. Right from the start the real source (security services presumed) didn't announce themselves as the origin, but let the "talkers", the radio DJs, believe that they were the originators. Think about it; if you announce, "we're MI5 and we have a campaign against this bloke" then people might not go along with it; but if you say, "everyone else is getting at this bloke because he 'deserves' it" then people will join in with fewer qualms.

```
>Why would "they" wish to assassinate your character?
```

It's the classic case of hitting a cripple to prove you're stronger. Why would the security services expend hundreds of thousands of pounds and more than six years of manpower to try to kill a British citizen? Because they are motivated by people who knew me at university and feel personal animosity; because they knew me to be emotionally weak, and it is in the nature of bullies to prey on those known to be weak; and because they can rely on the complicity of the establishment, which the security services manipulate and derive funding from. This is England's biggest humiliation today, and the British security services are intent on preventing their humiliation becoming reality by continuing their campaign of attempted murder to suppress the truth from becoming public.

My Response to the Harassment

My first reaction in 1990/91 was to assume that if I broke contact then they would not be able to follow and would lose interest. So I did the things that have been suggested by other people; I sold my television, stopped listening to the radio and tried to withdraw away from the sources of abuse as much as possible. I reasoned that they must have more important things to deal with and that normal people would simply leave me alone if it were made difficult for them to continue their harassment.

I reckoned without the sheer vindictiveness of the abusers. They did not let up but instead "got to" people around me, mainly people at work, to do their dirty work for them. I went to see my GP, who refused to believe what he was being told, and refused to direct me on to anyone who could be of practical assistance. It was not until three years had passed that the GP admitted the matter was outside his competence and suggested going to the police.

In the summer of 1994 we called in counter-surveillance experts from a private detective agency to sweep our house and telephone for bugging devices. They conducted a thorough search and found nothing; but as noted above, since the existence of surveillance was being forced in my face by the harassers, you would expect them to have taken the possibility of a counter-surveillance sweep into account when planning the type of devices to be employed.

In Easter 1995 I made a complaint to my local Police station in London, but the police have not expressed any intention to do anything about the continuing harassment ("we're not saying it's happening and we're not saying it isn't happening" were the words used). I think the officer I spoke to at Easter wasn't aware of it happening, although other members of the police force obviously do know.

From May 1995 until the present time the matter has been discussed in a lot of detail on the Usenet (Internet) "uk.misc" newsgroup. That discussion has given birth to the article which you are now reading. My hopes in posting to Usenet were that wider publicizing would discourage the security services from continuing their harassment, and "draw people out" into concurring with the truth of what was being said. Neither of those have followed, but the discussion has served a purpose in allowing this structured report to be created.

THE TIMES

Bernard Levin expresses his views

The article of which part is reproduced below was penned by Bernard Levin for the Features section of the Times on 21 September 1991. To my mind, it described the situation at the time and in particular a recent meeting with a friend, during which I for the first time admitted to someone other than my GP that I had been subjected to a conspiracy of harassment over the previous year and a half.

```
There is a madman running loose about London, called David Campbell; I have no reason
to believe that he is violent, but he should certainly be approached with caution.
You may know him by the curious glitter in his eyes and a persistent trembling of his
hands; if that does not suffice, you will find him attempting to thrust no fewer than
48 books into your arms, all hardbacks, with a promise that, if you should return to
the same meeting-place next year, he will heave another 80 at you.

If, by now, the police have arrived and are keeping a close watch on him, you may
feel sufficiently emboldened to examine the books. The jackets are a model of
uncluttered typography, elegantly and simply laid out; there is an unobtrusive
colophon of a rising sun, probably not picked at random. Gaining confidence - the
lunatic is smiling by now, and the policemen, who know about such things, have
significantly removed their helmets - you could do worse than take the jacket off the
first book in the pile. The only word possible to describe the binding is sumptuous;
```

real cloth in a glorious shade of dark green, with the title and author in black and gold on the spine.

Look at it more closely; your eyes do not deceive you - it truly does have real top-bands and tail-bands, in yellow, and, for good measure, a silk marker ribbon in a lighter green. The paper is cream-wove and acid-free, and the book is sewn, not glued.

Throughout the encounter, I should have mentioned, our loony has been chattering away, although what he is trying to say is almost impossible to understand; after a time, however, he becomes sufficiently coherent to make clear that he is trying to sell the books to you. Well, now, such quality in bookmaking today can only be for collectors' limited editions at a fearsome price - £30, £40, £50?

No, no, he says, the glitter more powerful than ever and the trembling of his hands rapidly spreading throughout his entire body; no, no - the books are priced variously at £7, £8 or £9, with the top price £12.

At this, the policemen understandably put their helmets back on; one of them draws his truncheon and the other can be heard summoning reinforcements on his walkie-talkie. The madman bursts into tears, and swears it is all true.

And it is.

David Campbell has acquired the entire rights to the whole of the Everyman's Library, which died a lingering and shameful death a decade or so ago, and he proposes to start it all over again - 48 volumes this September and 80 more next year, in editions I have described, at the prices specified. He proposes to launch his amazing venture simultaneously in Britain and the United States, with the massive firepower of Random Century at his back in this country, and the dashing cavalry of Knopf across the water, and no one who loves literature and courage will forbear to cheer.

At the time this article was written I had believed for some time that columnists in the Times and other journalists had been making references to my situation. Nothing unusual about this you may think, plenty of people have the same sort of ideas and obviously the papers aren't writing about them, so why should my beliefs not be as false as those of others?

What makes this article so extraordinary is that three or four days immediately preceding its publication, I had a meeting with a friend, during the course of which we discussed the media persecution, and in particular that by Times columnists. It seemed to me, reading the article by Levin in Saturday's paper, that he was describing in some detail his "artist's impression" of that meeting. Most telling are the final sentences, when he writes, "The madman bursts into tears, and swears it is all true. And it is." Although I did not "burst into tears" (he seems to be using a bit of poetic licence and exaggerating) I did try hard to convince my friend that it was all true; and I am able to concur with Mr Levin, because, of course, it is.

At the beginning of the piece Levin reveals a fear of being attacked by the "irrational" subject of his story, saying "I have no reason to believe that he is violent, but he should certainly be approached with caution". This goes back to the xenophobic propaganda of "defence" against a "threat" which was seen at the very beginning of the harassment. The impression of a "madman running loose" who needs to be controlled through an agency which assigns to itself the mantle of the "police" is also one which had been expressed elsewhere.

In the final paragraph of this extract, his reference to Everyman's Library as having "died a lingering and shameful death a decade or so ago" shows clearly what sort of conclusion they wish to their campaign. They want a permanent solution, and as they are prevented from achieving that solution directly, they waste significant resources on methods which have been repeatedly shown to be ineffective for such a purpose.

Harassment at Work

Once I stopped watching television and listening to the radio at the end of 1990, "they" had to find other ways of committing abuses. So they took what must be for them a tried and tested route; they get at you by subversion of those around you. Since they wouldn't be able to do that with my family or friends, that meant getting at people in the workplace to be their mouthpieces and do their dirty work for them.

They supplied my employers in Oxford with details from what was going on in my private life, and what I and other people had said at my home and accommodation in Oxford. So people at work repeated verbatim words which had been said in my home, and repeated what I'd been doing recently. Often the most trivial things, the ones from your domestic life, are the ones which hurt most. One manager in particular at Oxford continuously abused me for ten months with verbal sexual abuse, swearing, and threats to terminate my employment. After ten months I was forced to seek psychiatric help and start taking medication, and was away from work for two months. I spoke later with a solicitor about what had happened at that company; he advised it was only possible to take action if you had left the company as a result of harassment, and such an action would have to be started very soon after leaving.

Abuse at work is comparable to that elsewhere in that tangible evidence is difficult to produce, and the abusers will always have their denials ready when challenged. And even if a court accepts what you say happened, it still remains to prove that abuse causes the type of breakdown I had at the end of 1992. In a recent case before a British court, a former member of the Army brought a case against others who had maltreated him ten years previously. Although the court accepted that abuse had occurred, it did not agree that depressive illness necessarily followed, and denied justice to the plaintiff.

Purpose in Publicizing, and Censorship

The postings to uk.misc newsgroup generated a very defensive reaction from Usenet readers in the UK. So much so, that they tried strenuously to suppress what was being said, both by breaking the rules of netiquette in their responses on the forum, and directly by action to revoke the account from which the postings were issued.

Yet the postings were within the normal boundaries of behaviour for uk.misc, and other less partisan spectators did not see justice in the censorship which was effected, as the following excerpt shows;

Karen Lofstrom (lofstrom@lava.net) wrote

```
>It does seem that the frequency and the size of his posts are
>approaching net abuse.  However, IMHO, they aren't quite there yet.  If
>his postmaster were to act in this instance, it would raise troubling
```

```
>censorship issues.
```

The inescapable conclusion of the censorship effected on the uk.* newsgroups is that the British are intent on their wrongdoing remaining concealed, and therefore seek to subvert and suppress freedom of speech, not only in their own country where the media shows xenophobic bias and bile against all perceived enemies within and without, but also in other countries which have their own statutes to guarantee the basic human right of free speech.

It is absolutely necessary to bring their hate campaign out into the open where it can be placed under scrutiny and the harassers seen for what they are. That is the only way of making it impossible for the security services to carry it out. There is a wider dimension, though. Xenophobia as demonstrated by British people and institutions over the last few years belongs to the same stable as racial hatred. In one case, two youths on a Tube train made that racism explicit by referring to their victim as a "soft toy, not up to British Standards". Doubtless others victimize partly on the basis of race (isn't it odd that they chose to torment someone who is not ethnically English?) while expressing their abuse in terms of another genetic attribute, namely mental illness. All xenophobia on a genetic basis is wrong, but while racial insults are illegal, abusing the mentally ill is neither against the law nor subject to similar condemnation when it is exposed.

Why won't the British Police Put a Stop to it?

The British police obviously do know what is taking place. Besides my interpretations of what individual officers have said which forces that conclusion, it would be inconceivable for them to be unaware of something on this scale.

If they know, then they will know that the abusers have broken laws in the UK and abroad. Recently the UK introduced laws against electronic spying which carry a penalty of several years jail if caught. If the police know illegal harassment is taking place, and do nothing about it, then they are failing in their responsibilities.

In Easter 1995 I went into the local police station in London and spoke to an officer about the harassment against me. But I couldn't provide tangible evidence; what people said, in many cases years ago, is beyond proof, and without something to support my statements I cannot expect a police officer to take the complaint seriously.

The current situation with regard to the police is not one which allows a breakthrough in dealing with the problem. On the one hand, most individual officers at a local police station may not know about the ongoing assaults, so a complaint at that level will not yield results. Yet the police as an organisation do know of the harassment, and they must be aware that a complaint has been made at a police station. So it is clearly their duty to take preventative action against the continuing molestation, but because the criminals are operating on behalf of a state agency, the police are not carrying out their duty.

Site Map

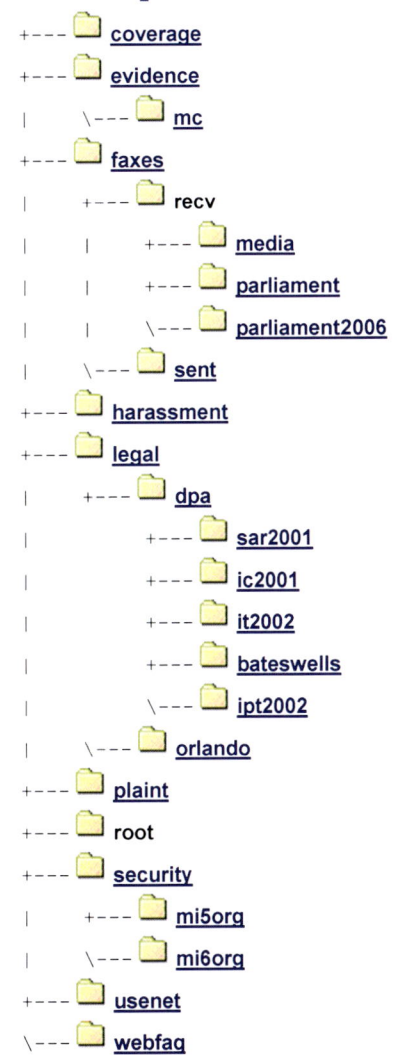

```
+--- 📁 coverage
+--- 📁 evidence
|    \--- 📁 mc
+--- 📁 faxes
|    +--- 📁 recv
|    |    +--- 📁 media
|    |    +--- 📁 parliament
|    |    \--- 📁 parliament2006
|    \--- 📁 sent
+--- 📁 harassment
+--- 📁 legal
|    +--- 📁 dpa
|    |    +--- 📁 sar2001
|    |    +--- 📁 ic2001
|    |    +--- 📁 it2002
|    |    +--- 📁 bateswells
|    |    \--- 📁 ipt2002
|    \--- 📁 orlando
+--- 📁 plaint
+--- 📁 root
+--- 📁 security
|    +--- 📁 mi5org
|    \--- 📁 mi6org
+--- 📁 usenet
\--- 📁 webfaq
```

The purpose of the hierarchical sitemap above is for clarity in the structure of this website. All webpages linked from the above diagram are also reachable from the site's main page.

Revision History

The website change history was started with 2004.04 updates, and its purpose is to allow the returning browser to view only those areas which have been revised since their last visit.

2004.04 /plaint/#eyesay

Eye Say, 2002
In 2002 I placed an entire year's worth of advertising with Private Eye magazine classifieds, in the Eye Say column. The aim was, as usual, to send the constant reality of MI5 Persecution into the public domain - since MI5 insist that everyone know how clever they are in ruining my life, getting the media to attack me, and trying to physically harm me, then I insist everyone know about their actions also. However, when you describe the illegal actions of the English Stasi to English people, the response is rigid silence.

2004.07 /evidence/#blair04a

Blair Conferences, Jan.03/Mar.04
British prime minister Blair got chatty at a no. 10 press conference in January 2003 with his friend ITN newscaster Jon Snow. Blair seemed to be having doubts as to the integrity of the intelligence services.

At the Labour conference in March 2004, Blair spoke of the terrorism, "We will not defeat it by hoping it will leave us alone or by hiding away", words I had recently spoken of the MI5 persecution.

2005.06 mi5.com

www.mi5.com
This website, which was previously located only at URL www.five.org.uk, is now to be found also at www.mi5.com.

2005.06 /evidence/#eurostar

Waterloo Eurostar, 18.Apr.2003
During a trip to Paris at Waterloo station, a group of men laughed and made a term of MI5's abuse which seemed targeted at a friend of mine, at a time when MI5 was actively trying to harm my friendships.

2005.06 /evidence/#egirl

Clapham South, 25.Oct.2003
Near my home, returning in the evening, a girl passed me and spoke into her cellphone, "listen I thought I was committing suicide". This was one of numerous incidents created by MI5, of which some were instructions to kill myself.

2005.09 /evidence/#sept27

Clapham South, 27.Sep.2005
In September/2005 I again tried to bring a complaint against MI5, on the grounds of their trying to kill me on 17/November/2001. They responded with a massive volume of verbal abuse, particularly repetition of electronically recorded phrases, and they tried to set the neighbours against us, to a degree they had not previously attempted. They also followed me around and

shrieked obscenities, again to a level previously unseen.

2005.12   /evidence/#croom

Clapham South, Sep.2005
I recorded a number of clips in late September/2005 directed at my house in Clapham. Some of these apparently were technologically inflicted, and preliminary to what may perhaps have been 'mind control' from mid October/2005. The purpose of MI5's activities was to silence any complaint of their behaviour.

2006.01   /evidence/#deathsquad

MI5 Deathsquad in Florida, 17.Nov.2001
MI5 conspired to kill me in Florida on 17/November/2001, the actual attempt being carried out by a group of men who shouted outside the apartment building where I was living. Unusually their attempt was captured on an audio recording.

2006.02   /evidence/#mikeycp

Clapham South, 14.Nov.2005
Our terraced house is next to an English family whose live-at-home son Mikey has been swearing through the wall for many years, on instructions from Security Service. One such instance is recorded on this webpage.

2006.02   /evidence/#claphs

Clapham Junction, 4.Oct.2005
I went to Clapham Junction and Clapham Common, where MI5 employed numerous resources to cope with an incipient complaint against their behaviour. Particularly blatant incidents are shown on this page. Shortly after this there began a "mind control" exercise which is still ongoing as of Feb/06; whereby MI5 are able to read the contents of my mind, and write to my mind using "thought insertion"; which constitutes torture.

2006.04   /faxes/fslusacongress.htm

Faxes Sent to US Congress, 2004-2006
During Sept/20004 to April/2006 I sent numerous faxes to the US Congress in Washington D.C. containing the FAQ article about the MI5 persecution.

2006.04   /coverage/#lobster05

Lobster magazine, Winter/2005 issue
In late 2005 I wrote to Robin Ramsay, Lobster's editor, with a summary of my complaint and evidence of MI5 having tried to kill me in November/2001.

2006.11   /evidence/mc/mc.htm

MindControl Torture, from August/2005
Beginning August 2005, MI5 tortured me using mindcontrol direct to skull methods, reading my mind and inflicting voices and thoughts, of which I have acquired some evidence. Their purpose was to force my suicide in order to stop the MI5 Persecution from being made public.

2006.12   /plaint/#ocso

Orange County Sheriff's Office 2006
In late 2006 I belatedly complained to OCSO about the Masturbating MI5 Agent from 1/September/2000 after having been motivated by seeing the HollaBackNYC website which shows videos of sex predators in action.

2006.12   /faxes/recv/parliament2006/faxrp.htm

Received Faxes from Parliament 2006
During 2006 I sent numerous faxes to the British Parliament, as ever with the aim of forcing the MI5 Persecution into the public domain. Again that aim was not accomplished, and the Westminster politicians complained bitterly about the cost of ink for printing out my faxes.

2007.02   /plaint/#steadman

Bugsweep by Steadman's team
In April 2006 competent TSCM specialist Nick Steadman swept my house for bugs, and found nothing.

2007.05   /legal/dpa/ipt/ipt2002.htm

Subject Access Request to IPT in 2002
I made a data protection request to the Investigatory Powers Tribunal, which returned minimal data.

2007.05   /legal/dpa/sar2001/sar2001.htm

Subject Access Request to MI5 in 2001
I made a Subject Access Request to MI5 in 2001, in response to which they mentioned an exchange of correspondence between themselves and the Security Service Tribunal in 1997.

2007.05   /faxes/fsluk2007.htm

Faxes Sent to Parliament 2007
During Feb/March 2007 I sent faxes to Parliament which attracted the attention of the Metropolitan Police "Fixated Threat Assessment Centre".

2007.07   /harassment/harassment.htm

Harassment Notes

Various notes on the harassment I have suffered from MI5 from 1990 onwards.

2007.07   plaint/#eyesay2006

Eye Say, 2006-07
Advertising in Private Eye in 2006-07, mostly about the attempted killing of Nov/2001.

2007.08   /orlando/orlando.htm

Lawsuit against MI5
Florida Lawsuit againt MI5 for assault/attempted murder of Nov/2001.

2007.10   /legal/dpa/ic2001/ic2001.htm

Communications with Information Commissioner in 2001-02
Simultaneously with the SAR to MI5 I was communicating with the Information Commissioner regarding a Request for Assessment.

2007.11   /legal/dpa/it2002/it2002.htm

Communications with Information Tribunal in 2002
In 2002 I appealed to the Information Tribunal, initially as a litigant in person. After a few months the appeal was taken over by lawyers.

2008.01   /evidence/#crank

MI5 Crank Call, 10.Jan.2008
MI5 made crank phone calls to my house at 4am and 5am, from an Englishman pretending to be an American Jew.

2008.02   /coverage/#opera

Persecution Opera, Sep/2007
Performed 19-21 Sep 2007 at the South Bank Centre.

2008.02   /evidence/mc/#tent

Shielded Tent, Nov/2007
It didn't stop the mindcontrol.

2008.03   /plaint/#ariel08

Advertising in BBC Ariel magazine, 2008
Accepted but unproductive.

2008.06   /coverage/#fun

FUN magazine 2008
Ben Freeman's article.

2008.06   /coverage/#moscow

Moscow News
James Scott is intimidated by MI5 in Russia.

2008.06   /plaint/#opd

Orlando Police Department 2006
I complained about MI5's attempt to kill me in Nov/2001.

2008.07   /legal/dpa/bateswells/bwb.htm

Bates Wells Braithwaite Solicitors
In 2002 I instructed Bates Wells Braithwaite whose "Heidi Fleiss" prostitute Simanowitz kept insisting the priority was to "Save You Money" while avoiding the material case.

Peter Krüger's article

```
From: flames@flames.cityscape.co.uk (Peter Krüger)
Newsgroups: uk.misc,uk.media
Subject: Dick Gentle On The Toronto Case 2/2     (Long)
Date: Tue Oct 24 14:51:57 1995
```

Dirk Gentle On The Toronto Case.

Dirk was on the West Coast when he got the call. An old friend at the Toronto police department thought he would like to fly up and take a look at a homicide which had occurred the previous evening. He decided to skip the last day at the World Holistics conference and take the next plane out of San Francisco.

The flight was bad; Dirk had been hit on the back of the head by the Newspaper trolley, the drinks trolley, the dinner trolley and now the gift trolley. When the hostesses weren't trying to tear his arm off they pestered him to stop leaning into the aisle - ignoring the fact that the guy next to him was taking up one and a half seats. Air Canada used to be the flight which was so good you just didn't wanna get off - on this occasion Dirk would be glad to see the back of the plane and the over sized alternative comedian wedged into the window seat.

After breathing in a couple of lungfulls of crisp Canadian air Dirk took a taxi into town. There was a small group of demonstrators outside the MacDonalds and the taxi driver insisted on stopping on the opposite side of the street. 'Don't Eat Meat' the placards read and the demonstrators chanted. A couple of policemen where stopping the crowd entering the restaurant itself - one held up his arm and challenged Dirk. A wave of the fax he had been sent and the policeman pushed open the door.

There were few customers in the restaurant. Not surprising really with a demonstration going on outside, half the dining area roped off with tape and a dead body seated at one of the tables. 'Mr Gently sir' the officer in charge called out as he peeled one end of the tape off a column 'We were told not to touch anything til' you got here'.

The body of the man slumped awkwardly in a chair. Then even a dead body would start getting uncomfortable in a MacDonalds chair after twenty minutes - and this one had been there for at least eighteen hours. Two back legs and the tail of a cat hung out of the man's gaping mouth. Dirk turned to the officer, 'I suppose you are going to tell me this is the darndest thing you ever saw?'

'Ain't this the darnd...'. The officer seemed annoyed that Dirk had second guessed him. 'We're removing the body in a few minutes, so if you can get through as quick as possible'

'Many people eat cats in fast food restaurants?' Dirk asked and without waiting for an answer leant over the table to pick up an untouched burger. 'And what's this?' he asked waving it in front of the officers face.

'It's a Vedgie Burger' The waitress, who was cleaning one of the adjacent tables, shouted across. She walked over to Dirk. 'We started doing them because of that lot out there' she nodded towards the protesters who were pressing there faces against the windows 'They're called Linda McCartney Vedgie burgers - ever heard of them?'

Dirk suddenly felt faint, perhaps a combination of hunger and jet lag. 'This is deja vu all over again' he thought to himself. He glanced at policemen - at the badge on his shoulder 'OPD' but this wasn't Ontario this was Toronto. OPD - Officially Pronounced Dead. It dawned on Dirk what was happening, he knew what he would see if he looked out of the window. Sure enough, there it was, the Volkswagen Beetle parked across the road - number plate 28IF - 28 IF Paul McCartney had lived. And amongst the lyrics of the song blaring out into the restaurant he could pick out the words 'I buried Paul'. Now it was though Dirk was viewing the whole scene though a TV screen. This was conspiracy. Not -a- conspiracy, or -the- conspiracy, but just plain conspiracy.

'You look faint - are you OK mister? The waitress asked.

Dirk shook his head 'Probably a bit hungry' Then to economise on dialogue took out a pack of cigarettes and held it out towards the girl. She was about to take one but Dirk snatched the pack away, held it up to his mouth and drew out two cigarettes. He lit both then passed one of them to the girl. It was the closest he had come to a sexual encounter in three months.

'Want a Burger?' the waitress asked.

Dirk looked down at the Vedgie Burger on the table. 'No thanks - just a plate of fries'

The waitress walked away and Dirk looked around the room. Apart from a family seated in the far corner there was only one other person in the restaurant - and he wasn't eating. The guy was about mid twenties and had straggling, shoulder length hair. On the table in front of him were lots of pieces of paper cut into squares. Every so often he would pick up a camcorder and pan it around the room and then, when he was finished, speak into a microphone which was attached to a tape recorder. Dirk walked over to where the man was sitting.

The small pieces of paper had paragraphs of text written on them and were stuck to the top of table with blobs of mustard. Lines had been drawn, some solid some dotted, on the table top with a marker pen. The lines ran from one piece of paper to another.

'What are the lines for?' Dirk asked, realising straight away that 'What the hell are you doing?' would be more appropriate.

'You see' The man replied nervously 'The dotted lines are weak links and the solid lines are strong links. The dotted lines are things which are happening in the rest of the world and the solid lines are things which are happening to me. Now you see I draw over a dotted line, replacing it with a solid line, when I can link something back to me. Like this' The pen squeaked over the Formica and before Dirk could interrupt the man added. 'You see I lost my short term memory and, as a consequence have a very short attention span. I write down, record and film everything then put it all together later'

'So' Dirk interrupted. 'You filmed what happened here?'

'Yes, yes, it's here on this tape' The man pushed the cassette across the table. On the label the words 'Grassy Knoll' had been crossed through and replaced with 'MacDonalds'.

Suddenly the man sprung from his seat. Dirk turned and saw that the body was being removed on a stretcher. As it passed the man picked a small object off the edge of the stretcher itself. 'This is important' he said, laying a blood stained bullet on one of the small pieces of paper on the table.

Suddenly the room was filled with a deafening throbbing sound as a Black Helicopter landed in the street outside. Two men in United Nations uniforms got out and collected the stretcher. Back at the table the long haired man was replacing all the dotted lines with solid ones. Dirk panicked and began to walk backwards at some speed. Barging through the swing doors he stumbled into the kitchen, tripped and felt himself sink slowly into a large vat.

'The guys fallen into the batter' Dick heard someone shout before he sunk below the surface. He came to sitting in a chair with the batter solidifying all over his body. He surveyed the room through two eye-holes someone had cut. Suddenly the chair on which he was sitting was picked up carried through the restaurant and out of the building. As the chair was being lifted and put into the back of a van, Dirk caught a glimpse of the waitress following him. 'Your fries mister, your plate o...'.

The doors of the van shut and Dirk tried desperately to steady himself as it sped across town. Eventually the doors flew open and Dirk was flung into the road at which point the solidified batter shattered and set him free. Standing up he found himself outside the international departures terminal of Toronto airport.

In the departure lounge Dirk had time to reflect on the day's events. He had got caught up in the conspiracy theories and the haphazard welding together of pieces of irrelevant information. It was time to catch the person who was operating the bizarre cognitive engine which appeared in front of him like a fairground mirror, distorting any flaw it could find in his own, fragile, map of the real world.

Dirk leant into the aisle of the plane as it took off for London. The oversized person next to him swung his arms violently as he complained about every thing from the supper in a plastic tray to the state of British politics. With a shaven head and a badly fitting suit the man looked as though he could have worked behind the reception desk of the Kremlin. However when he spoke he did so in a Liverpudlian accent. 'Me I blame the Con-serv-a-tive government, me. The Tour-rees. That-cher. Me. They need a good kicking' He jerked his feet forward and struck the seat in front with his Doc Martins. 'With these. Me Doc Martins. Doctor Martin's, Doctor Martin's, Doctor Martin's Booots!' The phrase was now being sung over and over again as the man writhed in his seat and clicked his fingers.

Dirk looked down at the boots and thought of the reaction most people used to deal with the paranoids at the end of the wire. A nice quick kick. 'Oi nutter - get some therapy'. This is the easy way out and perhaps the safest. After all there you are sat, alone, in front of the screen. No body language between you some paranoid. No way of telling if he really is some gibbering psycho. Look at it too long and you be drawn in. Fall into the tangled database of weird links with him. Who knows he may be watching you, reassembling and linking your experiences with his. How sure are you of you own cognitive threads. After all cognition is only a bug fix for a neurological system which was designed in a hurry - it's abused by everyone from politicians to advertisers. If people really can convince each other that a bottle of washing up liquid is as exciting as an orgasm using just television God knows what they can do with a computer. Better to avoid the risk. A swift kick. After all if you're Homophobic you put the boot in because you are scared of any ambiguity in your own sexuality - why not be Nutterphobic as well.

Although Dirk would have liked to devoted time to tracking the culprit down he decided to let it rest. The Internet changed over the next twenty odd years. A lot of the people who used it went out and got lives. And those who already had lives burnt them away. The number of users had dwindled after someone had invented a C++ program, with truth as a variable, to deal handle politics and government. Dirk had already retired from finding old ladies cats with the help of obscure science when he got another call from Toronto.

It was 4th March 2025 when he booked onto the Air Canada flight from Heathrow. The silver haired woman in the seat next to him painted bright red lipstick around her mouth. 'Of course it was no surprise to be offered the job after Claire Raynor retired' she sneered' After all I used to be a psychiatric nurse... Now if Blokes had periods they would understand...'

Dirk leant out in the aisle. 'Three overweight alternative comedians in as many decades' he thought to himself.

By chance the taxi ride to Toronto mental hospital took him past the MacDonalds - where the whole thing had started. Of course it was barely recognisable having become a Church Of Scientology Vedgie Bar. Police in riot gear kept the two sets of demonstrators apart. Dirk didn't really know what to expect when he got to the hospital. The girl at the reception desk directed him to a row of chairs in a wide well lit corridor. There was a strong smell of disinfectant, the furniture and the carpets were immaculately clean and behind the rows of teak veneer doors the 'nutters' were all safely locked away. For some reason Dirk started thinking about CompuServe forums.

A tall blond woman in a white coat approached. 'Mr Gentle, I assume'

'Yes' Dirk replied shaking her by the hand. 'You're the nurse who...'

'Doctor' She interrupted, 'Doctor Killfile' She led Dirk across the corridor towards one of the doors then stopped with her hand resting on the handle. 'Now you know about this person don't you?' and after Dirk nodded she continued 'Don't tell him anything about yourself - don't let him get into you head. If he does he'll screw it up'

The door opened to reveal a frail man sitting in from of a TV screen. He had a keyboard on his lap and next to the television was a computer screen. Dirk glanced at the walls of the room and remembered that his settee at home need upholstering. The nurse left the room and the man looked up 'So you come to my daughters wedding and ask me to kill a man' he said in a dry cackling voice. 'Look' he continued, pointing at the screen, 'I know that man. They're talking about me now - listen'. The man stared at Dirk. 'What's your name? Are you one of my friends from the Internet? - Are the lambs still screaming Dirk?'

Dirk, at first recoiled in horror, then felt a sense of anti climax. So this is what they hyped up to superstar status on the back of their own fears of madness. Dirk was reminded of the film 'A day on The Beach' where a submarine had set off to search a post nuclear World to track down a signal coming from a remote military base - only to find it was being sent by a Coke bottle half balanced on a Morse tapper. Outside the room the nurse waited for him. Because his nicotine craving had returned - and to avoid an awkward piece of dialogue -Dirk turned to her and asked . 'Patch?'

'Sure' she replied, smile lines appearing beside her eyes.

Dirk took two nicotine patches from his wallet the first of which he stuck onto the inside of his arm. Stepping closer to Doctor Killfile he opened her white coat and slid his hand into the opening at the front of her dress. He pressed the patch onto her leg as close to the top of her inner thigh as he dare. She took a deep breath and then slowly breathed out. 'What Bogart could have done with these things' Dirk thought to himself.

'Is he crazy?' Dirk asked tilting his head back to towards the door.

'Who knows' Doctor Killfile replied 'We let him type away. He sees something on the TV in the morning and it keeps him busy all day. What he types doesn't go anywhere it just stays on a mainframe in the basement. It can be read by anyone else in the building but that's it. We got them all in here conspiracy theorists, racists, nationalists. They've created a world within a world really...' Her voice trailed away and she stared down the corridor for a while then added 'So long are two things are different neither will come to be in the other and so become at once both one and two.'

Dirk gave her a puzzled look 'You mean their brains are fried?'

'Fried?' Killfile smiled at Dirk 'No that was Plato'. Then the smile fell from her face. 'You must remember, mister, plate o...'

(With apologise to Douglas Adams - Long Dark Teatime Of The Soul.)

Peter Kruger
----
http://www.gold.net/flames/
flames@flames.cityscape.co.uk

Iain Hotchkies' Medical Viewpoint

```
From: iain@hotch.demon.co.uk (Iain L M Hotchkies)
Newsgroups: uk.misc,uk.legal,uk.politics,uk.media,soc.culture.british
Subject: Corley FAQ (v0.1)
Reply-To: iain@hotch.demon.co.uk
Date: Sat May  4 19:30:34 1996

Mike Corley FAQ
version 0.1
first edition 5th May 1996
last updated 5th May 1996
Iain L M Hotchkies iain@hotch.demon.co.uk

Mike Corley is a 'net personality' who has been active on the following
newsgroups (uk.misc,uk.legal,uk.politics,uk.media,soc.culture.british)
since....? Well, at least as far back as the summer of 1995.

He posts long tracts, the tone of which approximates that which one might
expect from a reasonably intelligent paranoid schizophrenic.

No details are known of Mike's 'real' personal life or background. Once
would presume that he came from a reasonable family and was reasonably
well educated before the first symptoms of schizophrenia began.

Schizophrenia: Clinical features (from the Oxford Textbook of Psychiatry,
2nd Edition)

The acute syndrome

Some of the main clinical features are illustrated by a short description
of a patient. A previously healthy 20-year-old male student had been
behaving in an increasingly odd way. At times he appeared angry and told
his friends that he was being persecuted; at other times he was seen to be
laughing to himself for no apparent reason. For several months he had
seemed increasingly preoccupied with his own thoughts. His academic work
had deteriorated. When interviewed, he was restless and awkward. He
described hearing voices commenting on his actions and abusing him. He
said he believed that the police had conspired with his university
teachers to harm his brain with poisonous gases and take away his
thoughts. He also believed that other people could read his thoughts.

This case history illustrates the following common features of acute
schizophrenia: prominent persecutory ideas with accompanying
hallucinations; gradual social withdrawal and impaired performance at
work; and the odd idea that other people can read one's thoughts.

In appearance and behaviour some patients with acute schizophrenia are
entirely normal. Others seem awkward in their social behaviour,
preoccupied and withdrawn, or otherwise odd. Some patients smile or laugh
without obvious reason. Some appear to be constantly perplexed. Some are
restless and noisy, or show sudden andunexpected changes of behaviour.
Others retire from company, spending a long time in their rooms, perhaps
lying immobile on the bed apparently preoccupied in thought.

The speech often reflects an underlying thought disorder. In the early
stages, there is vagueness in the patient's talk that makes it difficult
to grasp his meaning. Some patients have difficulty in dealing with
abstract ideas (a phenomenon called concrete thinking). Other patients
become preoccupied with vague pseudoscientific or mystical ideas.
```

When the disturbance is more severe two characteristic kinds of abnormality may occur. Disorders of the stream of thought include pressure of thought, poverty of thought, and thought blocking. Thought withdrawal (the conviction that one's thoughts have been taken away) is sometimes classified as a disorder of the stream of thought, but it is more usefully considered as a form of delusion.

Loosening of association denotes a lack of connection between ideas. This may be detected in illogical thinking (knight's move') or talking past the point (Vorbeireden). In the severest form of loosening the structure and coherence of thinking is lost, so that utterances are jumbled (word salad or verbigeration). Some patients use ordinary words in unusual ways (paraphrasias or metonyms), and a few coin new words (neologisms).

Abnormalities of mood are common, and of three main kinds. First, there may be sustained abnormalities of mood such as anxiety, depression, irritability, or euphoria. Secondly, there may be blunting of affect, sometimes known as flattening of affect. Essentially this is sustained emotional indifference or diminution of emotional response. Thirdly, there is incongruity of affect. Here the emotion is not necessarily diminished, but it is not in keeping with the mood that would ordinarily be expected. For example, a patient may laugh when told about a bereavement. This third abnormality is often said to be highly characteristic of schizophrenia, but different interviewers often disagree about its presence.

Auditory hallucinations are among the most frequent symptoms. They may take the form of noises, music, single words, brief phrases, or whole conversations. They may be unobtrusive or so severe as to cause great distress. Some voices seem to give commands to the patient. Some patients hear their own thoughts apparently spoken out loud either as they think them (Gedankenlautwerden) or immediately afterwards (echo de la pensee). Some voices seem to discuss the patient in the third person. Others comment on his actions. As described later, these last three symptoms have particular diagnostic value.

Visual hallucinations are less frequent and usually occur with other kinds of hallucination. Tactile, olfactory, gustatory, and somatichallucinations are reported by some patients; they are often interpreted in a delusional way, for example hallucinatory sensations in the lower abdomen are attributed to unwanted sexual interference by a persecutor.

Delusions are characteristic. Primary delusions are infrequent, and difficult to identify with certainty. Delusions may originate against a background of so-called primary delusional mood - Wahnstimmung. Persecutory delusions are common, but not specific to schizophrenia. Less common but of greater diagnostic value are delusions of reference and of control, and delusions about the possession of thought. The latter are delusions that thoughts are being inserted into or withdrawn from one's mind, or broadcast' to other people.

In acute schizophrenia orientation is normal. Impairment of attention and concentration is common, and may produce apparent difficulties in remembering, though memory is not impaired. So-called experiences result from illness, but usually ascribe them to the malevolent actions of other people. This lack of insight is often accompanied by unwillingness to accept treatment.

Schizophrenic patients do not necessarily experience all these symptoms. The clinical picture is variable, as described later in this chapter. The table below lists the most frequent symptoms found in one large survey.

The most frequent symptoms of acute schizophrenia (World Health Organization 1973)

Symptom	Frequency (%)
Lack of insight	97
Auditory hallucinations	74
Ideas of reference	70
Suspiciousness	66
Flatness of affect	66
Voices speaking to the patient	65
Delusional mood	64
Delusions of persecution	64
Thought alienation	52
Thoughts spoken aloud	50

Various theories exist about Mike Corley:

1) he exists and is disturbed and has net access and for reasons uncertain spams a selected number of newsgroups on a regular basis - if you are reading this FAQ then you will almost certainly have seen one of his posts.

2) Mike Corley is a 'virtual schizophrenic'. Mike displays the relevant features so well that some people think he may be a construction of one or more people with intimate knowledge of mental illness and the mentally ill. Perhaps they wish to monitor the effects on the internet of the posts of a schizophrenic. Moving into X-Files territory a bit, ourselves, here.

Mike's posts attract different responses:

1) cruel, humourous, dismissive posts from those who've seen his posts many times and have become generally irritated by his behaviour while accepting that he probably has a mental illness.

2) posts from Corley-newbies - those who have come across relateviely few of Mike's posts. These may be humorouous or disbelieving.

3) posts from people who have been sucked in (for one reason or another) into Mike's Wild & Wacky World (TM)

That's enough for now.

comments, suggestions, additions, corrections to iain@hotch.demon.co.uk

Toronto Freenet Supports Free Speech

Despite an orchestrated campaign of attempted censorship by UK-resident newsgroup readers, TFN did not bow to demands for a suppression of freedom of speech. TFN general policy on the matter is as follows;

Draft Policy on Account Deactivations due to News Group Postings
News group postings occasionally take the form of a message which goes against the "topic" of the conference. For example, a derogatory message about Canadians in the soc.culture.canada.

Members of such news groups then may send a message to the system administrators asking that a user's account be terminated because of such posting.

The Toronto Free-Net Board of Directors has taken the position that the only postings that will get a person's account terminated is material that is illegal under Canadian law. Otherwise, the Toronto Free-Net will not take any action.

Freenet Executive Director Mike Anderson had this to say regarding the continued attempts of a minority of usenet participants to have my account on his system deactivated;

The TFN's policy is not to take action against members unless they contravene the Criminal Code of Canada, or engage in practices such as forgery, attacks against other computer systems or mailbombing.

Mr. Corley, while possibly being very annoying, has not contravened the TFN's policies. The TFN believes strongly in freedom of expression, while recognizing that the price for such freedom may be a high signal-to-noise ratio in Usenet.

If Mr. Corley breaks the law, we will take action -- until then, he has the same rights as any TFN member to post to Usenet newsgroups. Actions such as mailbombing the TFN in protest will be met by strong complaints to the originating site's postmaster. The best defense against unwanted postings may be simply be to ignore them and deny the poster an audience.

TFN Executive Director Toronto, Ont CANADA

Personally, I find it gratifying that my contributions to usenet discussion are recognized as being conducive to a high signal-to-noise ratio by their quality and thoughtfulness.

Commendations

```
From: aalgha@zen.sunderland.ac.uk (gillian.hardy)
Newsgroups: uk.misc,uk.legal,uk.politics,uk.politics.misc,uk.media
Subject: Re: Read About "MI5 Persecution" on the Web!
Date: Mon May 13 21:27:26 1996


: In article <Dr5sDI.50x.0.bloor@torfree.net>, bu765@torfree.net wrote:

: |> This site is now running brilliantly. It will be updated with new
information regarding this case and is well worth including in your
bookmark file.

For my sins I had a look and it's quite good actually.  Nicely set out and
presented.  Didn't read it though, having read the rants a million times
before.  By the way, anyone noticed Chris Tarrant looking at you funny
during Man O Man yet?  Thought not...

Gillian
-------------------------------
From: franco@elea.demon.co.uk (Francis Devonshire)
Newsgroups: uk.misc,uk.legal,uk.politics,uk.politics.misc,uk.media
Subject: Re: Read About "MI5 Persecution" on the Web!
Reply-To: franco@elea.demon.co.uk
Date: Tue May 14 19:17:26 1996


In message <4na2d0$dho@leofric.coventry.ac.uk> Stephen Hopkins wrote:

:Yes, I have to be honest: that page is one of the best examples of how to
present a long document on the Web that I've seen. Hopefully, frames will
become more and more prevalent and this style of presentation will become
the norm for long documents such as that.

My html thingy doesnt seem to do frames so all I got was a blank page.
Then again, maybe someone, somewhere doesn't want me to read it.

BTW does 'troll' bring to mind a fishing lure (ie you are American), or an
ogre type thing (ie you are European). I much prefer the image of the
latter.

| Francis Devonshire                    Titchfield, Hampshire, United Kingdom

Newsgroups: uk.misc,uk.legal,uk.politics.misc,soc.culture.british
From: duncan@yc.estec.esa.nl (Duncan Gibson)
Subject: Re: MI5 Persecution: Bugging
Date: Wed Jun 12 06:46:41 1996


Mike Corley <bu765@torfree.net> wrote:
> Read about the MI5 Persecution on the Web

Now, whatever you might think about the content, this is a very well
designed and presented web page (if you use Netscape to look at it anyway
- Mosaic couldn't handle it).
--
Duncan Gibson, ESTEC/YCV, Postbus 299, 2200AG Noordwijk, The Netherlands
Tel: +31 71 5654013    Fax: +31 71 5656142   Email: duncan@yc.estec.esa.nl
```

Usenet Discussion Archive

Introduction

The first shots in the Usenet campaign were fired on Thursday, 4 May 1995 with a posting to alt.conspiracy entitled "BBC's Hidden Shame". The more interesting articles from the ensuing war of words (which took place mostly on the uk-local groups) are archived here in date order.

The discussion has been more energetic at some times than others; at the time of writing (July 1997) two years of posts have not resulted in either an admission from the guilty parties or solid evidence coming to light. Discussion on the newsgroups has all but petered out, although with the short attention-span of Usenet a resumption of posts could occur at any time.

If you haven't read the FAQ yet then you should have a look at that before browsing these posts.

"BBC's Hidden Shame" 4/5/95
The first mention on the Internet of the "BBC Newsreaders Conspiracy".

Date: Thu May 4 18:27:24 1995
Newsgroups: alt.conspiracy
Subject: BBC's Hidden Shame

Remember the two-way televisions in George Orwell's 1984?
The ones which watched you back? Which you could never get
rid of, only the sound could be turned down?

Well the country which brought Orwell into the world has
made his nightmare follow into the world after him.
Since 1990 the British have been waging war against one of
their own citizens using surveillance to invade privacy
and a campaign of abuse in the transmitted media in
their efforts to humiliate their "victim".

And the most remarkable thing about it is that what they
do is not even illegal - the UK has no laws to protect
the privacy of its citizens, nor does it proscribe
harassment or abuse except in the case of racial abuse.

A lot of people in England know this to be going on,
yet so far they have maintained perfect "omerta";
not a sound, not a squeak has escaped into the English
press, and for all the covert harassment absolutely
nothing has come out into the public domain.

Have the British gone mad? I think we should be told.

From: "Mr.B" <dgb01@stir.ac.uk>
Newsgroups: alt.conspiracy
Subject: Re: BBC's Hidden Shame
Date: Mon May 8 05:32:13 1995

Mmmm.

Who, exactly is this victim you're talking about?

First up, Britain or the UK (not 'England' - England is
a part of Britain, like Kansas is a part of the USA) does
have laws that protect the individual from harassement -
you can't just threaten people willy nilly. There are laws
against that. And if someone lies about you in the press
or tv then you have recourse to libel/slander etc. laws.

True, Britain has no 'privacy' laws as such, but isn't that
a good thing? As of this moment, the govt. are considering
a privacy law, but it is unlikely to succeed. Why? Because any
such law would benefit the priviledged and those in power.
Privacy laws, while supposedly protecting the individual, help
those in power hide their mistakes/scandals. They stop the press

etc. investigating. Privacy laws are undemocratic - they prevent
the people from keeping an eye on govt.

And stop looking for some kinda conspiracy in the British
press. It's hardly perfect, but your notion that they don't
cover/campaign against press legislation, harrassment,
discrimination, human rights etc. is plain wrong. You've never
seen a British paper in yr life.

You clearly have a specific case/individual in mind. Speak up!
The thought police aren't coming round just yet.

Douglas.

Date: Mon May 8 19:21:28 1995
Newsgroups: alt.conspiracy
Subject: Re: BBC's Hidden Shame

Confession time - the victim is/was me (except my name isn't
Corley, but that's irrelevant). What happened was not threats;
just invasion of privacy, in a partiicularly flagrant and
shocking way, in a way which most people would consider to
constitute harassment.

You know there's a particular category of person with mental
illness to whom TV and radio "talk", ie they feel the broadcast
is directed at them in particular? This happpened to me,
quite some time ago in the UK (I'm originally from London,
so I've seen plenty of British media print and other).
They invaded my home with their bugs, they repeated what I
was saying in the privacy of my home, and they laughed that it
was "so funny", that I was impotent and could not even communicate
what was going on. Who did this? Our friends on BBC television,
our friends in ITN, last but not least our friends in Capital
Radio in London and on Radio 1.

How did they do this? I'll give you an example. About a year ago,
I was listening to Chris Tarrant (Capital Radio DJ among other
pursuits) on his radio morning show, when he said, talking about
someone he didn't identify, "you know this bloke? he says we're
trying to kill him. We should be done for attempted manslaughter"
which mirrored something I had said a day or two before
(I'm not paranoid, honest!). Now that got broadcast to the whole
of London - if any recordings are kept of the shows then it'll be
there.

"A doubting Thomas is heard" 9/5/95
The stock reaction of the unbeliever (until they find out it really is true).

From: pao1@ukc.ac.uk (P.A.Orrock)
Newsgroups: uk.misc
Subject: Re: BBC's Hidden Shame
Reply-To: pao1@ukc.ac.uk (P.A.Orrock)
Date: Tue May 9 05:54:20 1995

>have laws that protect the individual from harassement -
>you can't just threaten people willy nilly. There are laws
>against that. And if someone lies about you in the press
>or tv then you have recourse to libel/slander etc. laws.

Yup, agreed

>True, Britain has no 'privacy' laws as such, but isn't that
>a good thing? As of this moment, the govt. are considering
>a privacy law, but it is unlikely to succeed. Why? Because any
>such law would benefit the priviledged and those in power.
>Privacy laws, while supposedly protecting the individual, help
>those in power hide their mistakes/scandals. They stop the press
>etc. investigating. Privacy laws are undemocratic - they prevent
>the people from keeping an eye on govt.

Agreed again.

>Douglas.

I am slightly confused here as to who is writing what. this just seems to
be an amalgam of posts and replies posted to here to keep the thread going.

>Confession time - the victim is/was me (except my name isn't
>Corley, but that's irrelevant). What happened was not threats;
>just invasion of privacy, in a partiicularly flagrant and
>shocking way, in a way which most people would consider to
>constitute harassment.

>You know there's a particular category of person with mental
>illness to whom TV and radio "talk", ie they feel the broadcast
>is directed at them in particular? This happpened to me,

You mean the category where they think that everyone is after them ? that
one ? So lets get this straight you know you are paranoid and you think
that they are out to get you ? Uh huh, try putting the two together and
see what you come up with.

>quite some time ago in the UK (I'm originally from London
>so I've seen plenty of British media print and other).
>They invaded my home with their bugs, they repeated what I
>was saying in the privacy of my home, and they laughed that it
>was "so funny", that I was impotent and could not even communicate
>what was going on. Who did this? Our friends on BBC television,
>our friends in ITN, last but not least our friends in Capital
>Radio in London and on Radio 1.

Oh yeah, I can see it now. All of them banding together, in a united
effort against one man. So ITN, the BBC, and Capital all decide to sit
round the table and they come up with idea of breaking into someones
house, putting bugs everywhere, listening in to his conversation, and
shoving it out on the news everyday. This someone has nothing to do with
politics, or business, or entertainment, just an ordinary Joe Bloggs who
seems to be extremely paranoid.

Have some sense, grow up and smell reality. What you are talking about
would take loads of planning, tens of thousands of pounds and lots of
people involved in the planning, execution and maintenance of it. You
must have a very high opinion of yourself to think you are worth it.

>How did they do this? I'll give you an example. About a year ago,
>I was listening to Chris Tarrant (Capital Radio DJ among other
>pursuits) on his radio morning show, when he said, talking about
>someone he didn't identify, "you know this bloke? he says we're
>trying to kill him. We should be done for attempted manslaughter"
>which mirrored something I had said a day or two before
>(I'm not paranoid, honest!). Now that got broadcast to the whole
>of London - if any recordings are kept of the shows then it'll be
>there.

Of course you are not paranoid, just slightly mad. Did you ever look for
the bugs in your house ? If not, why not ? I mean if I thought that was
happening to me, I'd search the place from top to bottom, I mean I live
there I would know if anything was out of place. If I was really
paranoid, whoops I mean suspicious, I would call in one of those bug
detection teams which have those machines that pick up the transmitted
radio waves. This reminds me of BUGS, that new programme on BBC1 on
saturdays which is all about this kind of stuff, but, shown as a drama /
thriller. I suppose thats based on you as well is it ?

>is that there is a conspiracy in Britain, that it encompasses the
>broadcast media, and there is no way of breaking the conspiracy.
>The people who are involved in it will not open up.

What a load of jolly hollyhocks, I would say something else but,
apparently students are not allowed to swear on newsgroups in case it
damages the reputation of the university or some such jolly hollyhocks.

This guy is extremely paranoid to suggest that the entire British media
is after him in such a big way. He gives no real reason as to why they
are after him, just that he suffers/suffered from a slight mental
disorder, could it be paranoia perhaps ?? No surely not.

I put it to the house that he has never recovered from this mental
disorder, lets come out with it and call it paranoia, and thinks everyone
is after him. Remember just because you aren't paranoid, doesn't mean
they aren't after you.

This guy has a serious problem to suggest that the media would go to such
lengths just to single out and ridicule one person. I mean apart from
anything else, we (the listening masses) wouldn't be interested unless
it concerned the royal family, politicians or showbiz personalities. e.g.

the camillagate tapes. I would think that almost everyone, no matter how
much they went on about infringements of privacy read the transcripts with
interest. I really don't think that Joe Bloggs ordinary guy or paranoid
nutter would have the same appeal. Well actually I dunno. :)

Regards,

Paul.

--

 Paul Orrock, Websurfer wannabe, http://www.idiscover.co.uk/paul/home.html
 PC Consultant and HTML freelance Writer, http://www.idiscover.co.uk/paul/
===
   Diplomacy is the art of saying "nice doggy" until you can find a rock.

"Recognition by Strangers is Normal" 12/5/95
Claire Speed describes how being recognised by total strangers is just run-of-the-mill.

From: speedc@cs.man.ac.uk (C Speed)
Newsgroups: uk.misc
Subject: Re: BBC's Hidden Shame
Date: Fri May 12 04:34:26 1995

>Yes, I realize that. But after five years I think I can tell the difference
>between reality and unreality. Look, in the part of London where I used
>to live, I went back there over Easter, and I got recognized walking
>down the street by people I had never seen before. That's happened
>quite a few times and I am at a complete loss to explain it.

That is what happens in big cities. Hell, it scared me to death when I first
started working in Manchester. People keep talking to me on the streets,
even if its just to say hello, and I've no idea who they are. This happens
to most people, don't worry about it.

>>paranoid, whoops I mean suspicious, I would call in one of those bug
>>detection teams which have those machines that pick up the transmitted

>That's exactly what we did. We went to a competent, professional detective
>agency in London, paid them over 400 quid to debug our house. They found
>nothing.

Doesn't this suggest to you that there are, in fact, no bugs to be found?

>Over Easter I went to the police in London, telling them basically
>what I've posted here. I don't think you'll be surprised to learn
>that I didn't get very far; they asked "why would they be doing this to
>you in particular?" and the answer "they are because they are" doesn't
>go very far.

Exactly. All you have offered so far as proof of your harrassment by these
people is:

    1) Someone on radio said something that you had recently said
and
    2) People on the streets seem to recognise you.

These are both perfectly normal occurences and happen to lots of people every
day so it is unsurprising that people here, and the police, are not taking
you seriously.

Trying to always keep an open mind about things I would say that one of three
things is likely.

Either there is a lot more to this that you are not telling us, or you are
messing about or you have some genuine delusions. I'd like to think that in
two of the three cases you would find some real support here, but it seems
unlikely I'm afraid.

Claire

```
****************************************************************
*  "And though we say all information should be free it is not.      *
*   Information is power and currency of the virtual world we inhabit."   *
****************************************************************
*  C.Speed  -  <speedc@cs.man.ac.uk>  <http://www.cs.man.ac.uk/~speedc/>   *
****************************************************************
```

Date: Fri May 12 17:41:49 1995
Newsgroups: uk.misc
Subject: Re: BBC's Hidden Shame

>That is what happens in big cities. Hell, it scared me to death when I first
>started working in Manchester. People keep talking to me on the streets,
>even if its just to say hello, and I've no idea who they are. This happens
>to most people, don't worry about it.

The key is the pattern, or a change in the pattern. I've lived in London
almost all my life, and just walking around the streets, I never got
hassled by anybody. All of a sudden, people start harassing you,
throwing abuse at you, behaving as if they know you personally, as
if they've seen you before somewhere. I read in the papers that this
happens to Colin Stagg and people like that Eastenders actress, but
they've had their picture in the paperes, so that is understandable.
In a couple of cases people have even known my name - when I was in
London over Easter I was walking down Shaftesbury avenue in the
West End when somebody (no idea who they were, just some bloke with
his girlfriend) called me by name - quite clearly, and my name is
distinctive. This also happened once about four 1/2 years ago, onn
the tube - some blokes I had never seen started chanting my name
and a term of abuse.

It's the pattern which convinces me there's something to it - and
would convince any impartial abserver who could see things tyhrough
my eyes.

>Doesn't this suggest to you that there are, in fact, no bugs to be found?

There's a little story behjjind this. First iof all, in 1992 I worked
for a company where the people made clear they knew what was going on,
first of all directly (the very first evening I was there I went out to
the pub with them and the Technical Directpor said to another guy,
"is this the bloke who's been on TV?" "yeah, I think so") and also
indirectly, by rep[peating stuff I was saying at home in London and
in my rented accomodation there (I moved several times in the course of
1992 and they followed me each time). Now, if "they" (the buggers)
knew their bugs could be found easily, they wouldn;'t be keen to make
their existence known, would they?

Also, in summer 1992 I went on a trip abroad to Europe by coach, and
on the way out there were a couple a little younger than myself on the coach
a bloke and hius girlfriend. He said things about some bloke who was
never named, who sounded exactly like me - and he made explicitly

clear that our house was bugged, and that a neighrbours house was
bugged (and at work they'd been rep[earting what was said at the
neighbours, so this looks like independent corroboration).
They also said stuff like "at school he was always really streesed,
they found someone from his school and he was a real psycho"
and that "he was in a B&B for one night and they got him", dead right
again, I had been in B&B for once night a few days before this trip
and weatching the news again got a reaction from the newsreader.

"Truth or Troll?" 13/5/95

Could it all be a troll by psychology students? Why would anyone want to persecute you?

Date: Sat May 13 21:41:57 1995
Newsgroups: rec.arts.tv.uk
Subject: Re: BBC's Hidden Shame

>:some pirate radio station in London in 1991, started listening to
>
>Conclusive proof if ever I heard it.
>
>Of course you were the only person in the office in the whole of Britain

Yeah, but this is the point. Each incident is easily and automatically deniable along the lines you're taking. But when this happens every time, and when you get independent corroboration from other people, then there's no escaping it. For example, immediately after I lost my job in 91 I went into the local garage to get some work done on the car, and one of the blokes there said to the other, "so what do you think of it then? it's getting killed on the radio isn't it"
Now again, you look at that and no proff; you can ask them what they're referring to and they can say they're talking about something else.

>I know you may be a little paranoid, but I suggest you sit down
>and work out rationally what possible reason anyone off television,
>or radio would have for listening to your conversations. After all
>it must be hard enough to present a show to millions of people
>without the added burden of watching and listening to a single
>person and slipping their phrases into the programme.

These presenters are clever people. They wouldn't be presenters if they weren't - they're easily capable of reacting to an individual in this way.

What possible reason? I guess because they think it's amusing to do so. They know that if you ever tell anybody, without being able to show any evidence, then the reaction you'll get from just about anybody will be the one you're showing now.

I realize there are loads of people in England and elsewhere with the sort of thoughts I've described in these postings; and almost all impartial observers would say that nothing other than an go after their private conversations (if they did it to me then I can do it to them, it's a questions of technical competence and money). If you were lucky, you might be able to entrap them into admission. You could of course harass or threaten them back (any coppers reading this?) but that would be illegal and might get a result quite different to the one you're trying to achieve. Of course, it might come out of its own accord given time - if so many people know, if they have an escape valve in their "subtext" through the media, will it not cease to be at a covert level, given time? Surely it is in my interest for it to become overt, since the transgressions at this time are on their side and not on mine?

Thoughts? There must be some way of breaking the secrecy. This
isn't the first time in human history that a conspiracy has taken
place on this scale, but the truth tends to out. The situation
now is they think they';re "winning" hence have little stimulus
to change the rules - if they started seeing themselves "losing"
things could change drastically.

==

From: amh15@cus.cam.ac.uk (Alan Hart)
Newsgroups: uk.misc
Subject: Re: BBC's Hidden Shame
Date: Sun May 14 09:59:54 1995

: Thoughts? There must be some way of breaking the secrecy. This
: isn't the first time in human history that a conspiracy has taken
: place on this scale, but the truth tends to out. The situation
: now is they think they';re "winning" hence have little stimulus
: to change the rules - if they started seeing themselves "losing"
: things could change drastically.

Mike, if that is your name,

I'm going to try to rationalise what you're telling us. I can think of three
possible explanations for what you are experiencing.

One is that there _is_ a conspiracy against you. As a previous writer said,
though, a lot of these programmes are taped, so it really isn't possible in
some of the cases you've named. Further, why were no bugs found in your
house? Finally, unless you are a political figure or someone else in the
public eye, why would anyone bother? People like me (and I assume you) are
small fry; our contribution to society is likely to be minor. Why would
anyone spend so much money and effort on you?

Another possibility is that you are developing some kind of paranoia. There's
no stigma attached to this; we're all paranoid to some extent, although
perhaps not to the extent that a doctor would call us paranoid. I think
paranoia is quite a straightforward explanation here - you really do believe
that all these things are aimed at you; you see people everywhere trying to
get at you. Logic suggests that this cannot really be the case.

The third possibility is that not even you really believe any of this, and
that this is a "troll". I'm not sure I believe this possibility, but it's
possible.

Anyway, if you want to be sure that you're _not_ going mad, I'd go and see
your G.P. if I were you. If you don't trust him/her, why not see someone
recommended by a person you can trust? If you don't trust anyone any more,
don't you think it's time you got help?

Alan

Alan Hart - amh15@cam.ac.uk - Cambridge University, UK - +44 1223 515460
 "How many letters are there in the alphabet - is it 27?" - J.R. Histed
----

From: Ian Preece <ianp@dktower.demon.co.uk>
Newsgroups: uk.misc
Subject: Re: BBC's Hidden Shame
Reply-To: ianp@dktower.demon.co.uk
Date: Sun May 14 14:58:08 1995

In article <3p52cq$rsl@lyra.csx.cam.ac.uk>
        amh15@cus.cam.ac.uk "Alan Hart" writes:

> The third possibility is that not even you really believe any of this, and
> that this is a "troll". I'm not sure I believe this possibility, but it's
> possible.

For a troll, the posts are remarkably well-informed on paranoid
behaviour.. you'd need to be one, or be reasonably well-informed on the
subject to sustain the tale... which lead me to my theory...*ahem*...:

An extension to possibility 3 (Number 3.5, perhaps?) is that the original
poster may be somehting like a psychology student writing a term paper
on the net community's reactions to this tale. (Now, there's paranoia
for you! Not only are they listening to/watching us, they're writing
reports about us too...:-)

More likely, though, is that the poster is genuinely in need of professional
help (he has intimated as much, himself) and, as such, he should be encouraged
to seek it.

regards,
IanP
--

Ian Preece   ianp@dktower.demon.co.uk

IT Project Specialist   Ideas for Hire

"Let it go" 1/8/95

Why not let it go, and try to forget about it? Because, unfortunately, they won't let me.

From: speedc@cs.man.ac.uk (C Speed)
Newsgroups: uk.misc
Date: Tue Aug 1 10:23:46 1995

>OK, so instead of my posting the same tedious stuff every day,
>why don't you actually read the contents, and make a meaningful
>reply? Something more constructive than those silly little
>jokes about paranoia perhaps? Like what objectively can you do
>to break the conspiracy open, if one exists :-) ? If somebody
>did it to you, what would you do?

But we've *done* that. I certainly have at least. Way back when you
originally started posting and your posts were neither tediously repetitve
nor stupidly long.

But whenever anyone makes any good suggestions you ignore them and start
posting from the begining again. You don't want us to help you - so what do
you want? If you really wanted help you would listen to peoples suggestions
and respond to them. Is this just an attention thing?
But I'll try again, because I'm a fool like that.

>o Tell people about it, go to the police / legal services
>   Done that; those around me either don't believe me, or they
>"sort of" believe but can't do anything about it. As for going
>to the police; I did, over Easter. Discouraging. They must be
>familiar with the occasional person walking into a station with
>this sort of story. "If a psychiatrist says you're imagining
>it, then that's what it is".

You haven't yet given any examples of anything concrete to suggest that this
is really happening to you. This, I would imagine, will be the stumbling
block for the police. How can they possibly help you when your only evidence
is a jumbled mess of TV presenters saying things that could be construed as
answers to your comments and the 'feeling' that people are talking about you
and watching you?

I seem to recall that last time this was being discussed someone asked if you
had been to see a psychiatrist about this - after all if this is really
happening then you have can only benefit from being given a clean bill of
health. I don't recall an answer.

>   I also went to a firm of solicitors; again, very
>discouraging. Put bluntly, they can't deal with cases where the
>perpetrators aren't well-defined and the existence of the crime
>itself is unprovable.

Well how could they? Who would you sue? The country?

>o   so if that option is out, what's left? well, there's the
>"do nothing" option. To some extent this option works. They've
>spent a lot of money and ultimately achieved nothing except to

>force me out of the country - which has been an own goal for
>them, since now they can't do what they were doing in the UK.
>Expenditure of further resources would feed the pockets of
>their greedy contractors, but is a waste of money as far as the
>employing organization is concerned.

So you are no longer in the uk? And this is not happening anymore?

Then let it go. Just leave it alone and get on with your life. Its just not worth it. There is nothing you can do to prove that this happened whether it did or did not. So forget it. Go and explore the net - when people aren't spamming it with useless repetitve posts there's a lot of interesting and worthwhile things out there to see and do. Likewise real life (I'm told *&).

>completely conventional, I have a good academic and work
>record. Until all this started, I had no mental health
>problems; the diagnosis of illness was only after 2 1/2 years
>of abuse. If they did this to me, they could do this to
>absolutely any British citizen. If this stuff gets out, it
>won't be me that has to worry - it'll be them. They take a
>normal person, lie about him, demonise him, try to force him
>into killing himself - and this is in a country where the rule
>of law applies?

If this gets out then *that* will be the time to bring your claims to the foreground.

The only thing ruining your life right now is you, Mike. And the only thing that will make your life any better now is also you. So go and make your life better and show them that they failed.

Claire

```
********************************************************************
*  "And though we say all information should be free it is not.      *
*    Information is power and currency of the virtual world we inhabit."   *
********************************************************************
*  C.Speed - <speedc@cs.man.ac.uk>  <http://www.cs.man.ac.uk/~speedc/>  *
********************************************************************
```

==

>But we've *done* that. I certainly have at least. Way back when you
>originally started posting and your posts were neither tediously repetitve
>nor stupidly long.

Once again we're running into a brick wall. The reason I started posting was because I couldn't figure out a way out of the situation, and thought that saying it out into the open would provide a catalyst for one of those "in the know" (there are plenty in this category, and it's a fair bet that some of them are reading this) to speak up.

It hasn't worked, yet. A little more aggressive shit-stirring (excuse expletive) might do the trick. Perhaps Usenet posting is the wrong arena for this sort of activity; although obviously it does have the advantage of rapid feedback.

Thing is, for people to open up, you would have to provide them with a
reason why it would be in their interest to do so. There's no obvious way
of doing that; to get thinking people to incriminate themselves when they're
safe in denying all knowledge is not a trick I can figure out how to do.

>But whenever anyone makes any good suggestions you ignore them and start
>posting from the begining again. You don't want us to help you - so what do
>you want? If you really wanted help you would listen to peoples suggestions
>and respond to them. Is this just an attention thing?
>But I'll try again, because I'm a fool like that.

A "good" suggestion would be one which had the effect of halting the
persecution, which so far hasn't happened. If you make a "good" suggestion then
damn right I'll stop posting - because then I won't have to.

>You haven't yet given any examples of anything concrete to suggest that this
>is really happening to you. This, I would imagine, will be the stumbling
>block for the police. How can they possibly help you when your only evidence
>is a jumbled mess of TV presenters saying things that could be construed as
>answers to your comments and the 'feeling' that people are talking about you
>and watching you?

Because, as said previously, concrete proof does not exist. If it existed then
I wouldn't be talking to you - if it could be proved, or if those doing it
could be found, they wouldn't be able to continue.

What's happened is all conversation. You can't prove conversation, not without
a tape recorder, and even then you would have to prove that what they meant
corresponded to what you understood.

The psychopath who manages the Applics group at my previous employers
played little word games, not only with me but with at least one other
person in the group; words which rhyme with swear words, words which are
ambiguous, eg "bent", words which rhyme with wank, "sheet" rhymes with shit,
end (how was your weak end? being the standard salutation on a Monday morning).
Sounds childish, most people would easily tell him to fuck off; except to people
with predisposition to depression and the inability to express themselves
(this was before I started taking medication), that sort of nastiness is
not bearable. After ten months of this I was so ill I was crying constantly,
eventually I went into hospital and started on medication. Somebody else he
did this to (over a year later!) got so depressed he took an overdose of
pills, had to go on antidepressants and left.

And where does the "concrete proof" of this trouble exist? NOWHERE. Even
if you had physical evidence, even if you had the presence of mind to
record what was said, how could you prove what he actually meant by what
he was saying? In some cases of harassment you can prove what was done,
because it's undeniable. But when the harassment is done with any presence
of mind whatsoever, it becomes difficult. In the case of the wider harassment,
the people doing it obviously know what they're about - they must have done
similar things to other people before in one form or another, and they know
what they can get away with, they know what the police will do nothing about.

>I seem to recall that last time this was being discussed someone asked if you
>had been to see a psychiatrist about this - after all if this is really
>happening then you have can only benefit from being given a clean bill of

>health. I don't recall an answer.

Yes. The reply was of the "neither confirm nor deny" variety. Not much else they can say, is there?

>Well how could they? Who would you sue? The country?

Hmmm, now there's a thought... :-)

>If this gets out then *that* will be the time to bring your claims to the
>foreground.

Wrong way round. It won't get out unless I do something to bring that about; remember, it isn't in THEIR interest for THEIR criminality to be exposed. Yelling loudly on Usenet might nudge things along in the right direction.

>The only thing ruining your life right now is you, Mike. And the only thing
>that will make your life any better now is also you. So go and make your
>life better and show them that they failed.

Ignoring them would be bliss, but it's not a winning strategy.

There are going to be more of these posts. Sorry. That's the way it is.

"But why?" 2/8/95
Why would the British establishment expend significant resources on such small fry?

From: peter@petermc.demon.co.uk (Peter McDermott)
Newsgroups: soc.culture.british
Date: Wed Aug 2 13:11:34 1995

>Very unstructured, no proof whatsoever. So why should anyone
>take it seriously? If I said to you, "my next door neighbour eats
>babies", how much credibility would you attach to that?

Well, cos it's true. I was hoping that someone "in the know" would appear and make some self-revealing comments, but that hasn't happened. Everyone's keeping quiet. What a pity.

>>This is an agglomeration of articles and replies previously
>>posted to Usenet, so it's a bit hard to read. This posting
>>describes a campaign of character assassination initiated

>Who's character is being assassinated? It isn't clear from the post.
>Are we talking about Grenville Janner? I thought he was a spook
>himself? He's certainly able to hold his own on the issue you cite.

Mine, mainly. The reason for putting that episode at the top of the posting is that they tried to kill two birds with one stone at the Beck trial - they simultaneously put words into the mouth of their invented "witness" to smear Janner, and repeated exactly, word-for-word, stuff which had been said by and about me.

That was the only occasion (the only one recognizable to me, anyway) when they went after another target at the same time. And it's quite lucky they did that - because it could give some pointers to who they might be.

Presumably there are people still around who were involved in that trial, and know what happened. Beck might be dead, but the "witness" would still be around, as would Beck's solicitor.

>>by a group of people or agency within the UK. Although
>>they have never presented their identity, you can draw
>>your own conclusions on that point. There aren't many
>>people with the technical resources and contacts in
>>society to make feasible the sort of deliberate attack
>>on an individual which is described in this article.
>
>There aren't _any_ as far as I am aware.

I'm afraid there are.

>>The most disturbing part of the whole episode is the
>>participation of British institutions and their members, fully
>>comprehending what they do, in what is an act of attempted
>>murder against a British citizen.

>
>The whole society, in fact. From the top to the bottom. They
>wouldn't be trying to tell you to kill yourself by any chance,
>would they?

You got it. I'm a popular guy.

>>After the trial Janner said that "now he knew what it felt like
>>to be a victim of Beck's"; but, it wasn't Beck who set up the
>>attempted character assassination on Janner; the fact that they
>>took a side-swipe with their verbatim repetition shows
>>where the real source is to be found.
>
>The newspapers?

Well, your guess is as good as mine. But what newspaper would
send a team after someone for five years? I don't think so,
somehow. Of course they could, but it wouldn't be in their
commercial interest.

You'd have to look at a corporate entity which would indulge in
activity of this type, and the nature of the contacts they have
narrows down the search.

>>The goons behind the molestation are lower than the paedophiles
>>they use to convey their propaganda - they use the same
>>strategy of covert abuse, but there is nobody to check their
>>actions, or to bring these criminals to justice.
>
>Ummm.. Janner is a Barrister, a journalist who writes on a wide
>variety of issues, and a long-standing Labour MP. If he's unjustly
>smeared, he's more that capable of setting the record straight.

Janner blamed Beck for the invention. He didn't say anything about
it having any other origin. Even had he suspected any other source,
he could hardly have pointed the finger without some evidence.

>You say that the media is making similar allegations about you in
>relation to this issue? So, you're accused of child abuse, amd
>the allegation was reported in the media, I assume.

I've been accused of many things although that wasn't one of them.
Most of them have been yelled in my face by people on the street
in London at some time or other. Bit difficult to misinterpret
when that happens.

>What exact;y are they saying about you? (Respond here please. I'm
>leaving the UK tomorrow, so I can't read e-mail.)

It changes with time. Every so often, they sing a new song;
so at one point the allegation was homosexuality, at another
is was low intelligence, then it degenerated into sexual abuse.

<snip>

>>They invaded my home with their bugs, they repeated what I

>>was saying in the privacy of my home, and they laughed that it
>>was "so funny", that I was impotent and could not even communicate
>>what was going on. Who did this? Our friends on BBC television,
>>our friends in ITN, last but not least our friends in Capital
>>Radio in London and on Radio 1.
>
>How do you know this? Just from what you hear on the radio?

I can't remember if this was mentioned in the "regular" posting,
but on a few occasions they set me up with people nearby to talk
about me, or more correctly, to talk about somebody who
(in their minds) "resembles" me, with actually naming me.

One such occasion was a coach trip to Europe in June 1992.
The "set up" comprised a guy talking to a vacant giggling female
about "this bloke", who was never named. Apparently "they"
(also never named) "found somebody from his school",
"they" "got" him at his house and at a neighbours, and at
a B&B where their target was for one night.

Apart from that, yeah, from "what I hear on the radio". And
from what I see on TV. (I wouldn't be doing my job as a
mentally ill person properly if the TV and radio weren't
talking to me, now, would I?)

>>Oh yeah, I can see it now. All of them banding together, in a united
>>effort against one man. So ITN, the BBC, and Capital all decide to sit
>>round the table and they come up with idea of breaking into someones
>>house, putting bugs everywhere, listening in to his conversation, and
>>shoving it out on the news everyday.
>
>But why would they do this? What possible reason would they have?

But why get at anybody? Victimisation is the pastime practised against
other people; as the scorpion said to the frog, "it's in my nature".

>Are you aware that what you describe is also a common symptom of people
>who are suffering from a psychiatric illness? Have you been to your
>doctor and told him about this? Did he prescribe any medication? Have
>you been taking it, or have you stopped?

Yes, Yes, and Yes respectively. Still taking it. Doing quite well actually.

>>This someone has nothing to do with
>>politics, or business, or entertainment, just an ordinary Joe Bloggs who
>>seems to be extremely paranoid.
>
>Usually a clinical symptom rather than proof of a conspiracy in such
>matters.

>>How did they do this? I'll give you an example. About a year ago,
>>I was listening to Chris Tarrant (Capital Radio DJ among other
>>pursuits) on his radio morning show, when he said, talking about
>>someone he didn't identify, "you know this bloke? he says we're
>>trying to kill him. We should be done for attempted manslaughter"
>>which mirrored something I had said a day or two before.

>>Now that got broadcast to the whole of London - if any recordings
>>are kept of the shows then it'll be there.
>
>And this is supposed to mean... what? Chris Tarrant is in on this plot
>to kill you? It sure sounds like a joke to me. When you start to get
>ill, the mind often makes connections that seem logical and lucid to
>you, but do not to the rest of the world. This is one of those connections.
>They are usually known as delusions.

This is the problem, and there doesn't seem to be any way around it.
If a clearly sane person reported this persecution, you might believe
him, but probably you'd tell him to go see a doctor to "verify his
sanity". If someone with the illness of which you could argue these
things to be symptomatic says these things, again, you might believe
him, but it would be unlikely - the easiest route is the one you are
taking in the above paragraph. The only way I can convince you of what
I am saying is by giving precise details of what, when, how - and for
most of that stuff is based solely on memory.

To prove it would require an admission from somebody, or else hard
proof in the shape of physical evidence such as tape recordings.
Of course, I don't have that.

>The idea of a "pattern", and the notion that if anyone could look
>through your eyes they would see the same thing is very indicative of
>the onset of a psychiatric illness. Schizophrenia and manic depression
>have similar symptoms. I'm not trying to be disrespectful here.
>This may be an illness and it can be managed by the use of medication.
>If it _isn't_ treated, it can lead to terrible tragic consequences.

I'm quite aware what the symptoms would be, and that the reality
corresponds to those symptoms.

But if anything, that is an argument which could convince you of
the truth of what I'm saying. If they deliberately set out to
simulate the symptoms of schizophrenia - in other words, if they
know through observation that their target is either suffering
from the illness, or is on the borderline and could be pushed in
with an appropriate stimulus, then they can feel safe in what
they do, since once you are registered as suffering from the
illness, people will assign less credibility to assertions that
persecution is based in reality.

That this can happen, and people collude by silence, is absolutely
horrifying. It is all the more horrifying that it can happen in a
country such as Britain which has no history of repression.
Perhaps its happening in the UK is due to the arrogant assumption
of moral superiority on the part of those in the media and others
involved - we won the last war and we can keep harping on about
German and Japanese war crimes, so we can do whatever we like and
we'll be right, up to and including destroying the lives of our
citizens (as long as we're not caught doing it).

>>That is the level it's at - basically they show they're listening
>>to what you're saying at home, they show they're listening to you
>>listening to them

>
>But why? And why you? Do you realize how much it would cost to keep
>one person under continuous surveillance for five years? Think about
>all the man/hours. Say they _just_ allocated a two man team and a
>supervisor. OK., Supervisor's salary, say, £30,000 a year. Two men,
>£20,000 a year each. But they'd need to work in shifts -- so it would
>be six men at £20,000 (which with on-costs would work out at more like
>£30,000 to the employer.)
>
>So, we're talking £30,000 x 6. £180,000. plus say, £40,000 for the
>supervisor. £220,000. Then you've got the hardware involved. And
>any transcription that needs doing. You don't think the 'Big Boss'
>would listen to hours and hours of tapes, do you.
>
>So, all in all, you couldn't actually do the job for much less than
>a quarter million a year. Over five years. What are you doing that makes
>it worth the while of the state to spend over one and a quarter million
>on you?

Those are pretty much the sort of calculations that went through my
head once I stopped to consider what it must be costing them to
run this little operation.

The partial answer is, there have been periods when the intensity has
been greater, and times when little has happened. In fact, for much
of 1993 and the first half of 1994, very little happened. Although
I don't think that was for reasons of money - if they can tap into
the taxpayer they're not going to be short of resources, are they?

The more complete answer is in the enormity of what they're doing.
When countries kill their own people, as a rule, they get found
out and all hell breaks loose. This isn't some para shooting
Irish teenagers in the back. This is something which permeates
English society, which they are ALL responsible for, and which
they cannot escape responsibility for.

Relative to the cost to British pride of seeing their country
humiliated for the persecution of their own defenceless citizens,
isn't is worth the cost of four or five people to try to bring
things to a close in the manner they would wish? To the
government a million or two is quite honestly nothing - if they
can convince themselves of the necessity of what they're doing,
money is not going to be the limiting factor.

>>What possible reason? I guess because they think it's amusing to do
>>so.
>
>What? Spend a quarter mil. a year to amuse themselves? And why not
>change every now and again? Why keep watching you? (Unless you _are_
>doing something, and I don't think you are, though you may have some
>deep, dark secret in your past.)

See the above.

==

>>I'm going to try to rationalise what you're telling us. I can think of three
>>possible explanations for what you are experiencing.

>>Another possibility is that you are developing some kind of paranoia. There's
>>no stigma attached to this; we're all paranoid to some extent, although
>>perhaps not to the extent that a doctor would call us paranoid. I think
>>paranoia is quite a straightforward explanation here - you really do believe
>>that all these things are aimed at you; you see people everywhere trying to
>>get at you. Logic suggests that this cannot really be the case.

>I think the evidence leans towards this explanation myself. Why not
>try soc.support.depression and see what some of the people there have
>to say about this? Just to get some more perspective on your perspective,
>so to speak?

Sure, it "leans" towards it. But please at least admit there is a
POSSIBILITY of it being very real. And once you've done that, can
you come up with some thoughts on methods of proof? I may be missing something
in my assessment - there may be a way of proving it, in the face of non-
cooperation from the "players".

>>>Finally, unless you are a political figure or someone else in the
>>>public eye, why would anyone bother?
>>
>>Yes, this gets me. I think the answer is that I was set up by
>>someone. I was very aware when this started back in 1990 that I
>>was being painted as a "threat" to which people had to "react"
>
>Who by and what for?

I think I know who set me up. I don't know the mechanics of how it happened.
What for? I just have the feeling this may be part of the "cock-up"
theory of history - you know, somebody talks to someone, who bumps into
someone else and tells him, "by the way there's this bloke...." and
the whole thing escalates.

The alternative explanation is that someone who knew me personally may
have been in on it from the beginning, giving a good push to get things
going. I don't really want to think about that possibility, though.

>>There is a dichotomy in attitudes between the majority of people
>>who don't know what is going on, and the few who do. Most would
>>Those who don't know react in the way people have reacted to these
>>postings. Those who are "in on it" mainly treat it as a joke;
>>after all, we have the power, he can't do anything, so it's funny,
>>isn't it? The bloke can't even control his own mind without medicine.

>You think that "they" are employing some sort of mind control technology
>as well as the bugging? Can you expand on this a little?

That isn't what I meant. Without drugs, I cannot exclude the illness
from my brain. Therefore I am not in control of my mind unless I
take medication.

The medicine they give you isn't perfect, but at least it prevents the
grosser discomforts, and makes you look fairly normal to the rest of

the planet.

>>There is an absence of morality in their abuse of power - yet
>>since they are "winning" they are able to disregard it.

>When you say "winning", winning what? What is their aim? Just to have a
>laugh at your expense? It sounds like a terrible lot of time and trouble
>to go to...

Society spends many millions of pounds on films, on theatre, on
entertainment. You send packs of journalists after the royals, to
ferret out insalubrious details of peoples private lives.

And so here we have Concentration Camp entertainment, persecution
for amusement. If they get caught, it'll be "it was his fault,
we were doing it for the good of society", or perhaps "it wasn't us",
the trademark until now.

It's really sad what you're doing to your country with this. Sooner or
later, the truth will out; sooner or later, you will have to face up
to what you've done, and the excuses we've heard up til now aren't
going to cut it.

>>That is
>>the attitude the police are bound to take - they must see other
>>people with symptoms similar to mine, and in most cases those
>>people will be suffering from delusions.

>So why do you feel that you are somehow different?

Because a lot of (to put it nicely) independent corroboration
has come my way.

>>One of the aims of these postings has been to change the rules of
>>the game - if lots more people "know" (even if they don't believe
>>what they're told) then there is less secrecy.

>Well, I hope it makes you feel better and more secure. However it
>pans out, it's an awful state to be in. You have my deepest sympathy.

It's actually very useful to have a public forum in which to discuss
these things. It would be even more useful if someone could consider
what has been said, and think of a way of verifying it.

>Best wishes.
>
>--
>peter@petermc.demon.co.uk   joker and degrader!

Thanks for your posting.

"Surveillance methods" 5/8/95
The type of surveillance technology that might be employed.

From: Pamela Willoughby <pjw31@willouby.demon.co.uk>
Newsgroups: uk.misc
Date: Sat, 05 Aug 1995 18:08:32 GMT
Organization: Myorganisation
Lines: 15
Message-ID: <142297143wnr@willouby.demon.co.uk>

>Hmmm, strange eh.
>I mentioned all this goings on to my boyfriend, who works for the
>British intelligence service, and he assures me this sort of thing
>never goes on.. not ever...honest.
>Though he said the name was familiar...

it does go on, although it's an open question who does it.

Some time ago there were press reports of an Army intelligence person
called Jones who claimed Diana and Hewitt had been photographed in a
compromising position... he said he'd been doing this as part of an
Army unit which had previously operated in Northern Ireland.

Then Hewitt said he'd been told the same thing by some Army people,
and that they were threatening to release the tapes unless they
curtailed their liaison... as per usual everyone denied everything,
painted Jones as the "Jones twins" - not very original in how
they deal with their perceived enemies, are they?

You have to wonder how they manage to achieve this sort of
surveillance though. Audio you can understand, it's possible to put
a microphone through the wall, and apparently there exist devices
which will retrieve sound from a laser beam bounced off a window -
sounds sci-fi, but there's a well known surveillance electronics
company in London which sells these things.

But how would you get video out of a room, unless you had actual
physical access in order to plant a device for pickup? We're not
talking about looking in from afar, but an actual device within
the room. You could either drill through the wall and shove a
pickup through; or you could supply a trojan device with a hidden
pickup inside; but most likely, you would have to physically break
into your target room to plant a camera. That's not an infeasible
option; all it means is having your target(s) watched to make sure
they're not in the vicinity, then you negotiate any locks on the
property and find a suitable receptacle for your device.

The next question is how they defeat the usual methods of counter-
surveillance. We had private detectives carry out a "sweep" of
every room and the telephone line. They found nothing. That
indicates at least four possibilities that I can think of;
(this is all guesswork BTW, and probably fanciful guesswork
at that!)

1) no bugs (pull the other one)

2) radio-transmitting devices which can be controlled from an external source, ie you can instruct them to switch off when you detect a counter-surveillance sweep taking place

3) hard-wired devices; probe microphones or whatever they're called, things you poke through the wall

4) passive surveillance devices; so you bounce laser or radio waves off a suitable reflecting surface (again, sounds far-fetched but such things may apparently exist).

5) there is a fifth possibility, that the PI's didn't detect an actual transmitting device; there are technologies specifically designed to avoid detection, eg frequency hopping and suchlike. But how much sophistication could you build in to a device which would have to be small enough to be physically concealable?

I guess the real question is to find out who is ultimately behind these "goings on". And if the "great and good" (or the better known, at any rate) can't protect themselves, what hope is there for the rest of us?

"Stand up for Free Speech" 14/8/95
The Censoring Tendency loses a battle.

From: rji@cheetah.inmos.co.uk (Richard Ingram)
Newsgroups: uk.misc
Date: Mon Aug 14 10:08:32 1995

Some cencorship loving bore wrote :

> In article <GEVANS.95Aug14094119@mvagusta.uk.tele.nokia.fi> gevans@mvagusta.uk.tele.nokia.fi (Gareth Evans) writes:
>
>   His sysadmin is also next to useless, and has not replied to my request or
>   even acknowledged it. Maybe this person *is* a sysadmin?
>
> He's not. It seems the public access site he uses has got no proper
> management over its users. Here's a copy of a reply I got from a
> complaint I made. [After returning every one of Corley's postings to

[snip a large pile of winging complaining drivel]

Geez what a bunch of tossers you all are - you don't like someones postings so you try and get him evicted from the net, why not just use a kill file - you DONT have to read his posts/threads now do you ?

Why is it the net is getting populated by the biggest bunch of self absorbed little Hitlers ? You don't like someones posts so you bloody complain or mail bomb them - grow up you bunch of fucking sad gits !

Richard.

"Troubling Censorship Issues" 20/8/95

There is no harassment on Usenet. It's all in the readers' minds. (What makes them think they're being persecuted?)

Fred Read (postmaster@foxhouse.demon.co.uk) wrote:

: He posts this drivel every week or so to a number of groups that
: I subscribe to and nothing seems to stop him. *ALL* of his posts
: are off topic and unwelcome to the groups he posts to.

: We have complained about him to his postmaster on at least four
: previous occasions and he still posts the same crap. As his SP
: seem unwilling, or unable, to do anything about him, we were
: windering if there was anything you could do?

If he is not actively using tactics to avoid or sabotage killfiles
(posting from various systems, forging, massive crossposting to create
cross-newsgroup flame wars) then it should be quite easy to killfile
him.

It does seem that the frequency and the size of his posts are
approaching net abuse. However, IMHO, they aren't quite there yet. If
his postmaster were to act in this instance, it would raise troubling
censorship issues.

--
Karen Lofstrom   lofstrom@lava.net

    "Adventures for those of the inadmissable kind,
     with no follow through."
          --- a flaming bonzo beckwithian idiot

"Options" 21/9/95
How would you react if your television sprouted eyes and ears?

From: john heelan <john@lorca.demon.co.uk>
Newsgroups: uk.misc,alt.current-events.net-abuse,alt.journalism
Subject: Re: CENSORHSIP IS IMMORAL, UNJUST AND WRONG
Date: Thu, 21 Sep 95 19:17:30 GMT
Organization: (Private)
Lines: 65
Message-ID: <811711050snz@lorca.demon.co.uk>
References: <DF8DMu.Dqu.0.bloor@torfree.net> <43qpdh$iki@news3.digex.net>
Reply-To: john@lorca.demon.co.uk
X-NNTP-Posting-Host: lorca.demon.co.uk
X-Newsreader: Demon Internet Simple News v1.29

You have to admit that Mike is persistent and obviously feels deeply that he is being hounded by the "Security Services" and there is a Conspiracy out to get him personally. If that is true, then we should be concerned; if he is just paranoid, then we should empathise with his sickness. What we should not do is to invite censorship....that just could be implicitly joining in the putative Conspiracy.

Let's look at Mike's potential options (and the alleged responses he has received):

> 1. Complain to the Police: (their alleged response
> "Don't be silly, Sir"; Mike's rationale "They are part
> of the Conspiracy")
>

I don't think the police as an organisation are part of it. They're certainly not the source.

The officer I spoke to at Easter clearly didn't know anything about it. And that was at my local police station in London - if anyone in the police knew you would think the people at your local cop shop would.

A couple of years ago I had to go into the station after a motoring infraction, the guy I spoke to then said something about "brain like a computer sir" which my suspicions latched on to - (I'm alleged to be a programmer as some people reading this know) - but as per the usual "can';t prove nuthin" and you ask yourself if you're just being stupid suspecting on the basis of a straw

> 2. Complain to a Member of Parliament (Mike's rationale: "Can't
> because they are part of the Conspiracy")
>

I could do that actually. But he would probably tell me to go see the police, for which see above.

> 3. Make it visible through the UK Press. (Mike's rationale:

> "Can't because they are part of the Conspiracy")
>

They are actually. There's a difference though in the way journalists
react to this stuff when they're "got to" by the security service.

This is completely giving the game away, but the trouble originally
started with my reading into stuff that was being written by Times
columnists, in particular our antagonistic friend Mr Levin.
But you see that some journalists are taking part in the conspiracy and
others are only doing it because their puppet masters have been feeding
them information which they can't allow themselves to ignore. The
security services have their hooks into the UK media, this case shows
that very explicitly. You also see how things get gradualkly wqorse with
a particular journalist; a couple of weeks ago Peter Tory in the Express
was writing about "nerds seeking their revenge on him through the Net",
guess what that was about.

>   4. Complain to the UK Security Services. (Mike's rationale: "Can't
>   because they ARE the Cnspiracy")
>

Quis custodiet ipsos custodes? If the fascist Gestapo bastards plot to
see you dead then who's going to deal with it? Not the security
services, that's for sure.

>   5. Make it visible through Internet: (Mike has done this
>   suvccessfully; but any gainsayers are "part of the Conspiracy".
>

I don;t think you';re part of the consipracy if you refuse to believe or
email the postmaster. Those who do know are keeping their silence.

>   6. Complain to the Canadian National and State Governments. (Has
>   Mike done this yet ?)
>

No. It's a UK problem so that's where it should be dealt with. The
perpetrators are UK residents, are unidentified, and would be difficult
to deal with through the Canadian courts.

Ditto the police in Canada, ditto the press - it isn't their problem,
it's caused by UK people against someone from the UK. Of course Canadian
laws are being broken relating to harassment and "stalking" which do not
exist in the UK, but the Canadian police do not have a very good record
of enforcing those laws anyway.

>   7. Complain to the Canadian Security Services (Has Mike done this
>   yet ?)
>
>   8. Complain to the Canadian Press. (Has Mike done this yet ?)
>

I think if they didn't knoiw, they'd just think you were having
delusions; and if they did, then they would side with the people with the
power, the smiling English people with their knives out.

Remember, nobody uis going to side with the person who has less power in
a copfrontation. The team over here in Canada have the resources of their
organization behind them, other broadcasters etc in the UK would have
influence with their counterparts in Canada; after all, this was once a
British colony, there is still a feeling of "looking up to" the UK among
many Canadians, so if a team of security services arrives from the UK
with apparently limitless resources to pursue their target,   people
over here will forget anything they ever knew about basic human rights
and go along with what they are told to do and how they are told to behave.

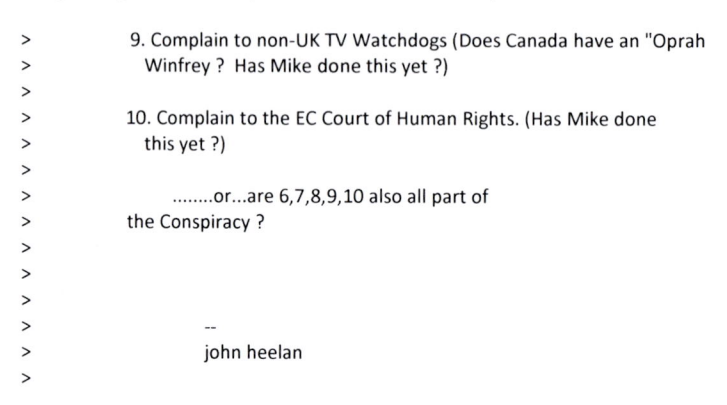

> 	9. Complain to non-UK TV Watchdogs (Does Canada have an "Oprah
> 	 Winfrey ? Has Mike done this yet ?)
>
> 	10. Complain to the EC Court of Human Rights. (Has Mike done
> 	 this yet ?)
>
> 	 ....or...are 6,7,8,9,10 also all part of
> 	the Conspiracy ?
>
>
>
> 	 --
> 	 john heelan
>

"Question and Answer" 27/9/95
Who, what, where, and how? Why would they?

In article <DFGxnF.Cr8.0.bloor@torfree.net>
          bu765@torfree.net "Mike Corley" writes:

>>> ##: There were also a few other things said at the trial
>>> ##: relating to this which I won't repeat here; it was in the papers
>>> ##: at the time anyway. This quote and others said by and about this
>>> ##: witness were repeating things that had been said by and about
>>> ##: me at around that time.

>   When, where and by whom ? Let's have some details
>   that can be checked.

I'm not going to repeat them. They're hurtful to me because they contained abuse that was
directed against me by someone else at the time and which got picked up and thrown again
in the trial. It is a matter of record but I won't repeat it here.

>>> PM: >Who's character is being assassinated? It isn't clear from the post.
>>> PM: >Are we talking about Grenville Janner? I thought he was a spook
>>> PM: >himself? He's certainly able to hold his own on the issue you cite.

>>> ##: Mine, mainly. The reason for putting that episode at the top
>>> ##: of the posting is that they tried to kill two birds with one stone
>>> ##: at the Beck trial - they simultaneously put words into the mouth
>>> ##: of their invented "witness" to smear Janner, and repeated exactly,
>>> ##: word-for-word, stuff which had been said by and about me.

>   Why would "they" wish to assassinate your character?

Well, let's put it this way - just because this is the first time it's happened in this way,
from these people, on this scale, doesn't mean that it hasn't happened before, on a lesser
scale. At university there were people who quite overtly hated me and would have wished
something nasty to happen to me. Because of where I went making the wrong sort of enemies
is pretty deadly.

"They" would wish to assassinate my character because it had all been done before, and
because they knew I would not be able to react in any other way than I'd reacted previously.

>>> ##: They invaded my home with their bugs, they repeated what I
>>> ##: was saying in the privacy of my home, and they laughed that it
>>> ##: was "so funny", that I was impotent and could not even communicate
>>> ##: what was going on. Who did this? Our friends on BBC television,
>>> ##: our friends in ITN, last but not least our friends in Capital
>>> ##: Radio in London and on Radio 1.

>   Please give details of when, where and by whom these
>   comments were made, so that they can be checked.

This was four, five years ago... sorry, I don't remember. I can remember individual incidents,
words which were repeated by different people at different times in different locations.

Around the end of 1992 Private Eye rtan a front-cover with John and Norma Major, with
the title "Major's support lowest ever" and John saying to Norma "Come back norma" on the

front cover. What can you read in to that? Not a lot, seems like standard fare for PE.
The first time I saw it I was in the pub with some people from work. One was expressing doubts
to the other (let's call the first one Simon, shall we? and the second one Phil?) about
whether what was going on was right. Phil's answer was that if Private Eye was doing it
then it must be ok, "they're usually right".

A few days later, again near work, there were some students laughing in the street,
"Were you COMING BACK later? But I thought you said you were COMING BACK ha ha ha?"
Play on words, you see. Not very nice, either. I had start medication soon afterwards.
Clever people, these chaps who think up PE titles. Just slightly lacking in any
sense of morality.

>>> ##: How did they do this? I'll give you an example. About a year ago,
>>> ##: I was listening to Chris Tarrant (Capital Radio DJ among other
>>> ##: pursuits) on his radio morning show, when he said, talking about
>>> ##: someone he didn't identify, "you know this bloke? he says we're
>>> ##: trying to kill him. We should be done for attempted manslaughter"
>>> ##: which mirrored something I had said a day or two before.
>>> ##: Now that got broadcast to the whole of London - if any recordings
>>> ##: are kept of the shows then it'll be there.

>>>>>> What was the date of the broadcast ?
>>>>>> Out of 2 million plus listeners, why should you be
>>>>>> the only one that Tarrant was allegedly referring to ?

Sometyime in spring 1994. I can't remember the date, I heard the broadcast in the
car - I was going into the office from London that day and just happened to snap
on the radio, and hey presto! Mr Tarrant gives us the benefit of his excellent
understanding.

>>> ##: That's exactly what we did. We went to a competent, professional
>>> ##: detective agency in London, paid them over 400 quid to debug our house.
>>> ##: They found nothing.

>>>>>> What was the name of the detective agency and their
>>>>>> address ?

I don't see why I should tell you that, but they're in Yellow Pages; they're
a well-established outfit.

>>> PM: >What? Spend a quarter mil. a year to amuse themselves? And why not
>>> PM: >change every now and again? Why keep watching you? (Unless you _are_
>>> PM: >doing something, and I don't think you are, though you may have some
>>> PM: >deep, dark secret in your past.)
>>>
>>> ##: See the above.

>>>>>> Is there a deep dark secret in your past ?

Apart from "it's all happened before in a different way", no.

>>> ##: In a couple of cases people have even known my name - when I was in
>>> ##: London over Easter somebody (no idea who they were, just some bloke with

>>> ##: his girlfriend) called me by name - quite clearly, and my name is

>>> ##: distinctive.

> Is your name truly Mike Corley, or are you using it as
> an alias ?

It's an alias. I'm not English by ethnic origin. If someone manages to pronounce
my name as well as that guy did then they must have been really trying.

>>> ##: There's a little story behind this. First of all, in 1992 I worked
>>> ##: for a company where the people made clear they knew what was going on,
>>> ##: first of all directly (the very first evening I was there I went out to
>>> ##: the pub with them and the Technical Director said to another guy,
>>> ##: "is this the bloke who's been on TV?" "yeah, I think so")

> Have you appeared, or been reported by name on TV ?
> When, where and by whom ?

No. Never. Not directly.

>>> ##: Also, in summer 1992 I went on a trip abroad to Europe by coach,

> What was the name of the coach company and your date
> of departure ?

It was a national express coach. At dover we boarded a ferry for Holland somewhere.
The company that organized the trip went out of business some time ago, so they won't
have records of passengers - so we can't get any corroboration from anyone else
that way. We tried all that last summer, ran into a brick wall.

The other thing is in summer 1992 I was visibly ill, so other people in the
party might remember that more than anyone getting at me on the coach trip.

>>> ##: >>Yes, this gets me. I think the answer is that I was set up by
>>> ##: >>someone. I was very aware when this started back in 1990 that I
>>> ##: >>was being painted as a "threat" to which people had to "react"

> Why were you being painted as a "threat"; is this related
> to a "deep,dark, secret" ?

Aaaarrrrgh. I think I should make clear that that's their created justification
rather than the real reason. They started harassing first and then came up with the
reasons for it.

>>>
>>> ##: I think I know who set me up.

> Who ?

Someone who knew me some time ago. Someone who would have been able to talk this
little campaign into existence.

>>> ##: The bloke can't even control his own mind without medicine.

> Is this true ? What is the medication and dosage ?

Yes, I'm afraid so. Sulpiride, 200mg a day. It's designed to stop people coming up with the sort of ideas you've heard here for the last few weeks. Give him a higher dose!!

In the long term it causes tardive dyskinesia, tardive dementia and general nasty stuff to your brain. So it's three years of sulpiride talking to you here.

>--
>john heelan

"Watch Out, Forger About" 27/9/95
A forged post to reduce my credibility! Who could have done that?

From: ray@ultimate-tech.com (Ray Dunn)
Newsgroups: uk.misc,soc.culture.british
Subject: Re: An apology from Mike Corley
Date: Wed Sep 27 14:20:36 1995

In referenced article, David Wooding says...
>Well, Mike Corley might or might not have written the apologies, but I
>think not. I thought the following line both witty and imaginative.
>
>>>It was the razor blades stuffed down between the keys that told me.

Corley himself denies posting this "apology", but I'm impressed if it
is a forgery.

Here's the header of my received email. It looks very genuine except
for the fact that postings to newsgroups are directed through demon's
mail to news gateway, which is strange.

Also the message id is <m0sxbx2-000JEeC@bloor.torfree.net> which seems
to be in a different format from previous Corley postings, e.g.
<DFJJB3.6Ft.0.bloor@torfree.net>

The mail seems to have been received directly from mail.torfree.net.

One way of telling for sure would be if anyone on the recipient list
contacted torfree, but did not publish any complaints on the newsgroups
- he would not have had access to their address in that case.

>Received: from SpoolDir by ULTIMATE (Mercury 1.20); 26 Sep 95 12:00:14
+0500
>Return-path: <bu765@torfree.net>
>Received: from mail.torfree.net by smtp.ultimate-tech.com (Mercury
1.20);
>   26 Sep 95 12:00:04 +0500
>Received: from bloor.torfree.net ([199.71.188.18]) by mail.torfree.net
>   (/\==/\ Smail3.1.28.1 #28.6; 16-jun-94)
>   via sendmail with smtp id <m0sxbyy-000LXSC@mail.torfree.net>
>   for <ray@ultimate-tech.com>; Tue, 26 Sep 95 11:31 EDT
>Received: from torfree.net by bloor.torfree.net with smtp
>   (Smail3.1.28.1 #6) id m0sxbx2-000JEeC; Tue, 26 Sep 95 11:29 EDT
>Message-Id: <m0sxbx2-000JEeC@bloor.torfree.net>
>Apparently-To: bu765@torfree.net, snail@objmedia.demon.co.uk,
>   ray@ultimate-tech.com, Frank@acclaim.demon.co.uk,
>   p.marshall@axion.bt.co.uk, me93jrb@brunel.ac.uk,   >
mikeh@mordor.com,
>   michael@everyman.demon.co.uk, tim@xara.co.uk,
>   Alan.Holmes@brunel.ac.uk, uk.misc@news.demon.co.uk,
>   uk-misc@news.demon.co.uk, uk-media@news.demon.co.uk,
>   uk.media@news.demon.co.uk, uk.legal@news.demon.co.uk,
>   uk-legal@news.demon.co.uk, alt-conspiracy@news.demon.co.uk,
>   alt.conspiracy@news.demon.co.uk,

> soc.culture.british@news.demon.co.uk,
> soc-culture-british@news.demon.co.uk,
> soc-culture-canada@news.demon.co.uk,
> soc.culture.canada@news.demon.co.uk
>Newsgroups: uk.misc, uk.media, soc.culture.british,
soc.culture.canada, uk.legal, alt.conspiracy
>From: bu765@torfree.net (Mike Corley)
>Subject: Oops! Sorry!
>Organization: Toronto Free-Net
>X-Newsreader: TIN [version 1.2 PL2]
>Date: Thu, 26 Sep 1995 01:23:45 GMT
>Lines: 27
>X-PMFLAGS: 33554560

--

Ray Dunn (opinions are my own) | Phone: (514) 938 9050
Montreal | Phax : (514) 938 5225
ray@ultimate-tech.com | Home : (514) 630 3749

"Grievous Bodily Harm" 2/10/95

Fascinating, and quite believable, even. If they have this power, then they will surely use it.

From: jeibisch@revolver.demon.co.uk (James Eibisch)
Newsgroups: uk.misc,soc.culture.british,uk.politics,uk.media,rec.arts.tv.uk.misc
Subject: Re: Auntie gets it in the emails
Reply-To: jeibisch@revolver.demon.co.uk
Date: Mon Oct 2 19:44:19 1995

lig0007@queens-belfast.ac.uk (TOM OATES) wrote:

>However, I'm pleased to say that, in the past couple of days, Mike Corley has
>stopped doing it and he appears (I say this cautiously) to be acting more
>reasonably. True, his postings are still based on paranoid delusions.
>However, so long as he doesn't go back to his old practices of multiple,
>identical, unreadable postings, I'm sure that most people on this newsgroup
>are willing to put up with him.

Time to come out of the woodwork of this thread (or variations thereof)...

I find it annoying that discussion of Mike's situation is spread over multiple threads - it makes it hard to follow, and especially to follow up. If it could be consolidated into one thread on relevant newsgroups (I'm reading this on uk.media btw).

I'm a little surprised with the volume of abuse Mike has received, but believe strongly in freedom of speech if such a thing were to exist, which clearly includes abuse as much as anything.

One thing which has been missing from this discussion is this simple prognosis: that maybe Mike is right and that, despite his admitted mental condition, there really is a campaign against him organised by now-influential ex-students of his university.

Does anyone remember the TV series GBH, a fictional account of security service and governmental power games? Fictional, certainly, but one of the most powerful pieces of TV drama I've seen in many years, fascinating and quite believable, even.

The fact is, as Mike has pointed out (oh, so many times :-), that the security services _do_ have the influence, contacts, resources, and time to conduct such a campaign of surveillance and even psychological terror if they so chose. If they have this power, then they will surely use it

We still don't have all the facts from Mike, and the most pertinent here I think would be about his time at university - the people who took against him, the ringleaders. We need to know far more about Mike: his political and social affiliations, put in context with his univeristy years, the enemies he made, the reasons people ganged up on him at the very early stages.

I don't subscribe to conspiracy theories generally, but I know there is far more that goes on in the universities, old boy's clubs, civil and secret services and Parliament than is ever made public.

Mike, I leave it to you to construct a _single_ thread in a relevant newsgroup about this topic and keep to this thread to give us new information and answer questions about your situation. Ignore the 'Mike Corley is a nutter' posts unless they are relevant.

Give us more detail. Who knows? It may be true, stranger things have happened.

```
               _
James Eibisch   ('v')    N : E : T : A : D : E : L : I : C : A
Reading, U.K.   (,_,)    http://metro.turnpike.net/J/jeibisch/
         =======
```

Tue, 03 Oct 1995 04:01:34   uk.misc   Thread   3 of 14
Lines 58   Re: Auntie gets it in the emails   Respno 16 of 16
J.J.Smith@ftel.co.uk   John J Smith at Fujitsu Telecommunications Europe Ltd

In article <812677261.12841@revolver.demon.co.uk>,
James Eibisch <jeibisch@revolver.demon.co.uk> wrote:
>lig0007@queens-belfast.ac.uk (TOM OATES) wrote:

>One thing which has been missing from this discussion is this simple
>prognosis: that maybe Mike is right and that, despite his admitted
>mental condition, there really is a campaign against him organised by
>now-influential ex-students of his university.

We're trying to find this out on uk.misc. He's posted some *new* *huge*
replies (which I'd have to give up my day job to reply to), detailing
some things like:

   a) Mike Corley is *not* his real name
   b) Exactly what the "abuse" is (it seems be such things, as taking
   completely unrelated newspaper articles, striving to make them a
   disgusting insult, then redirecting against himself).
   c) How he came to the conclusion.

I think he's doing rather better nowadays..

>Does anyone remember the TV series GBH, a fictional account of security
>service and governmental power games? Fictional, certainly, but one of
>the most powerful pieces of TV drama I've seen in many years,
>fascinating and quite believable, even.

This would be a point, apart from the fact that this was directed against
someone of political importance. I don't believe Mike is...

>The fact is, as Mike has pointed out (oh, so many times :-), that the
>security services _do_ have the influence, contacts, resources, and time
>to conduct such a campaign of surveillance and even psychological terror
>if they so chose. If they have this power, then they will surely use it
>at some point against some people.

It appears he has formed the Security Service conclusion, because they

are the only ones capable of doing it. A "searching for an enemy capable
of it".

>We still don't have all the facts from Mike, and the most pertinent here
>I think would be about his time at university - the people who took
>against him, the ringleaders. We need to know far more about Mike: his
>political and social affiliations, put in context with his univeristy
>years, the enemies he made, the reasons people ganged up on him at the
>very early stages.

I'm beginning to think that we never will get all the facts from Mike. We
may, however, get enough...

>Mike, I leave it to you to construct a _single_ thread in a relevant
>newsgroup about this topic and keep to this thread to give us new
>information and answer questions about your situation. Ignore the 'Mike
>Corley is a nutter' posts unless they are relevant.

Uk.misc, me boy...

    Smid

===

From: flames@flames.cityscape.co.uk (Peter Kr|ger)
Newsgroups: uk.misc,soc.culture.british,uk.media,uk.politics,alt.politics.british,alt.conspiracy
Subject: Re: What it's like to be watched by the security services
Date: Tue Oct 3 15:41:54 1995

In article <44rrrh$t6v@news.ox.ac.uk>, idaniel@jesus.ox.ac.uk (Illtud Daniel) says:

>
>And what do you mean when you state that the symptoms are too
>'textbook'? Are the textbooks wrong?

I think what is meant by 'textbook' is that some of the symptoms
of 'illness' displayed in the posts seem to have been lifted from
textbooks describing mental instability and personality disorders.

I must admit I haven't seen Mike's postings before has he only just
started posting again?

Peter Kruger
----
http://www.gold.net/flames/
flames@flames.cityscape.co.uk

"Do they fear truth?" 3/10/95
They must fear the truth: they've been covering up and lying for six years.

From: flames@flames.cityscape.co.uk (Peter Krüger)
Newsgroups: uk.misc,soc.culture.british,uk.politics,alt.politics.british
Subject: Re: What it's like to be watched by the security services
Date: 3 Oct 1995 15:38:20 GMT
Organization: Steinkrug Publications
Lines: 66
Message-ID: <44rldc$nrm@news.cityscape.co.uk>
References: <DFus24.HxB.0.bloor@torfree.net>
NNTP-Posting-Host: aa040.du.pipex.com
X-Newsreader: WinVN 0.92.6+

In article <DFus24.HxB.0.bloor@torfree.net>, bu765@torfree.net (Mike Corley) says:
>
>It completely mystifies me how it can be done. One night in June 1992 I
>was in a bed-and-breakfast in Oxford (some hard facts now, you'll be
>bored of the generalisations). I booked the B&B from the office phone.
>So if they had the office bugged, or the phone system bugged, they could
>have heard the call.

If it was as late as 1992 then there was already a system available to
feed digital video out of a domestic TV via the mains. Each raster of
video was preceded by a sixteen bit address which identified the
television set. All that was needed was a decoder box plugged into the
mains somewhere between your room and the grid transformer. The signal
was decoded and then fed down to the phone line. They probably
even had a PC which enabled them to see the picture as well. By 1992 the
technology had moved on from slowscan to near real time video with the
advent of devices from Brooktree and Harris etc.

>the newsreader reacted. Breathed deeply, as if in psychological relief.

Maybe, or perhaps as if in:-

sci.psychology.announce
sci.psychology.consciousness
sci.psychology.journals.psyche
sci.psychology.journals.psycoloquy
sci.psychology.misc
sci.psychology.personality
sci.psychology.psychotherapy
sci.psychology.research
sci.psychology.theory

>I can't describe to you what goes through your mind when you know
>someone on TV is "seeing" you the viewer.

You're doing OK so far.

>Your instinct is to switch the TV off, to change channel,

Not much point unless you switch off the TV at the mains

>like an ostrich,

Looks like Ostrich farming is going to catch on in the UK as you may have seen in some of the other uk newsgroups

>The one time I did directly ask someone in the company who knew what was
>going on, first he spewed wool about, "well we have to think what is
>reality and what is proof anyway", then went into barefaced denial liar
>mode. It opens your eyes, if they can't say out loud what they keep
>saying in a disguised fashion, they must fear exposure, they must fear
>the truth.

wool_ barefaced_ denial_ liar_ eyes_ fashion_ fear_ exposure,

How is your mother these days Mike?

And BTW - How is the thesis coming along?

Peter Kruger
----
http://www.gold.net/flames/
flames@flames.cityscape.co.uk

"A new Kafka?" 3/10/95
Publish and be damned (but I'm damned already).

Newsgroups: uk.misc,soc.culture.british,uk.media,uk.politics
From: jackson@soldev.tti.com (Dick Jackson)
Subject: Re: What it's like to be watched by the security services
Message-ID: <1995Oct13.225312.6514@ttinews.tti.com>
Sender: usenet@ttinews.tti.com (Usenet Admin)
Nntp-Posting-Host: soldev
Organization: Citicorp-TTI at Santa Monica (CA) by the Sea
References: <DFy9tB.3JK.0.bloor@torfree.net> <813188298snz129.os2.7@blackcat.demon.co.uk> <DGE7uJ.8tF.0.bloor@torfree.net>
Date: Fri, 13 Oct 1995 22:53:12 GMT
Lines: 34

In article <DGE7uJ.8tF.0.bloor@torfree.net> bu765@torfree.net (Mike Corley) writes:
>
>Strangers in the street have recognized me on sight many times, and shown
>awareness of the current thread of abuse. To give you one example, in 1992
>I was seriously ill, and a manager at work somewhat humouroursly said that
>"it wasn't fair" that people were bullying me. A few days later, I
>attended for the first time a clinic in London as an outpatient, and on my
>way out was accosted by someone who asked if "they had paid my fare", with
>emphasis on the word "fare". He repeated the word several times in this
>different context; that they should have paid my "fare", each time
>emphasising the word.
>
>For two and a half years from the time their harassment started until
>November 1992 I refused to see a psychiatrist, because I reasoned that I
>was not ill of my own action or fault, but through the stress caused by
>harassment, and that a lessening of the illness would have to be
>consequent to a removal of its immediate cause, in other words a cessation
>of harassment. I also reasoned that since they were taunting me with jokes
>about mental illness, if I were to seek treatment then the abusers would
>think that they had "won" and been proved "right".

<I've deleted a lot, but I think this gives the idea>

I have so far not contributed to this tread, it has been unpleasant
in my opinion. However, I was struck by the resemblance of the above
passages to the writing of Franz Kafka.

Viz. while from an objective viewpoint it seems to refer to a abnormal
world, in a strange way it does resonate strongly at other levels.

Mr. Corley, have you tried to write for publication? I honestly think
it might lead somewhere positive.

Dick Jackson (serious for a change and expecting to get beaten up)

"Dihydrocodeine" 26/11/95
You'd have to be taking something pretty lethal to act like this.

From: michaelm@easynet.co.uk (michaelm@easynet.co.uk)
Newsgroups: uk.misc,uk.media,uk.politics,alt.politics.british,alt.radio.uk
Subject: Re: Britain's Shame (repost)
Date: Sun, 26 Nov 1995 09:19:13 GMT
Organization: ------------
Lines: 89
Message-ID: <817374781.20251@michaelm.easynet.co.uk>
References: <DIM34L.755.0.bloor@torfree.net>
NNTP-Posting-Host: michaelm.easynet.co.uk
X-NNTP-Posting-Host: michaelm.easynet.co.uk
X-Newsreader: Forte Free Agent 1.0.82

bu765@torfree.net (Mike Corblymee) wrote:

| In June 1990 a horrifying campaign of harassment was initiated in London by
| what are believed to be elements of the security services. The harassment has
| continued for over five years, starting from the broadcast and print media,
| and encompassing abuse through set-up situations and by people in public
| places. It has been brought to the attention of the police and they are aware
| what is happening, but are not taking any action to prevent it.

<whopping great snip of 884 lines>

corley, you puzzle me!

i've narrowed your possible motives down to one or more of the following:

1) you work on behalf of the british government with a hidden agenda of furthering the largely right wing (most to hide) censorship brigade's cause, "a drug-crazed psycho posting dangerous nonsense - how very very sad - but in the public interest,we must act." draft internet (censorship) bills rolling off hm govt's banders at this very moment, I don't doubt it!

2) you work for the daily mail which has started to feel the "internet pinch" as it suddenly clicks in the chronically adled minds of yet more and more of their readers - that shudder-inducing realisation that the entire editorial staff at the mail are scaremongering, imbecilic, blood-leeching , totalitarian twats - can any else sense a coordinated campaign on its way ??- "Mail urges (their) government to act - internet safety endangered by uncontrolled surfing lunatics - boys hands blown off by internet maniacs - net porn responsible for 392323rd rape " .net porn responsible for 392324th rape " .net porn responsible for 392325th rape " .net porn responsible for 392326th rape " .net porn responsible for 392327th rape " net porn responsible for 392328th rape " .net porn responsible for 392329th rape " <yawn> .net porn responsible for 392330th rape " .net porn responsible for 392331st rape " .net porn responsible for 392332nd rape " net porn responsible for 392333rd rape " <yawn> .net porn responsible for 392334th rape " .net porn responsible for 392335th rape " .net porn responsible for 392336th rape " .net porn responsible for 392337th rape " net porn responsible for 392338th rape " etcetera, straight from the old nag's mouth..

lee-potter (and english), take particular note.. (how ever you two common ********* managed to avoid encarceration for what was, quite evidently,wilful contempt of court in the regina v taylforth & knights case, is frankly beyond me.. those dreaded and now all too familiar words "endemic corruption" were muttered by at least one Q.C.

>3) you (at least) believe there's (some) substance to your claim(s) and you
>have a genuine axe to grind. If so, bloody well go for it, but scrape the
>heavy layer of steaming dung off the top (that's assuming you're even
>capable of distinguishing fantasy from reality.)

4) you (as an email address) are serving as some bizarre "educational" programme orchestrated by the psychiatric industry - ever keen to justify enforced electrical lobotomies, electroshock and dwugs .All poised for the echo? - "corley frigging well needs lobotomising"

5) you're just clinically insane with absolutely no comprehension or insight into the consequences you will possibly face as a result of repeatedly posting what, certainly on the face of it, looks like complete and utter bullshit.

6) you're some weirdo prankster(s) - probably a group of student psychiatrists having a cheap crack whilst high as kites on pilfered dihydrocodeine.

7) You are infact working for the ss yourself, gauging public awareness of the extent and methods of bugging - infinity transmitters, microwave surveillance devices, satellite tracking equipment, 'chipping' of black crims, say no more.

8) You're fuelling the central usenet administration committee, who, it is believed, are keen to see the introduction of a wide-reaching framework of self-created powers relating to posting cancellation. (see the 'son of RFC1036')

my bet's on (5) - but just fuck off corley- irritate the lard-arsed canucks instead. The cia's financing of "professor" cameron's brain-washing experiments in montreal.. would be a good starting point ... or perhaps "professor" watts and his widely admired masterful double eye-jabbing trick - a couple of wallops with an icepick. such a waste of perfectly edible four year old hispanics !!!!.. Perhaps the old marylebone rd posse could fill us in with a few more facts on this one...?? You are all on the .net now ????? A very warm welcome :-) ... christmas rapidly approaching..
>business booming?? Do we all get a look in at flotation ??!!

==

From: Gulliver <kst2co@herts.ac.uk>
Newsgroups: uk.misc,uk.media,uk.politics,alt.politics.british,alt.radio.uk
Subject: Re: Britain's Shame (repost)
Date: Sun, 26 Nov 1995 18:25:32 +0000
Organization: University of Hertfordshire
Lines: 12
Message-ID: <Pine.SUN.3.91.951126182156.16879B-100000@altair.herts.ac.uk>
References: <DIM34L.755.0.bloor@torfree.net> <817343873snz@objmedia.demon.co.uk>

NNTP-Posting-Host: altair.herts.ac.uk
Mime-Version: 1.0
Content-Type: TEXT/PLAIN; charset=US-ASCII
In-Reply-To: <817343873snz@objmedia.demon.co.uk>

Actually, upon thinking about Mike's story it reminds me of someone I
heard about who suffered from a persecution copmlex. He was an immigrant
from some Eastern Bloc country who believed that 30 years after he
emigrated the KGB were still after him. He would blame them if he
had difficulty unlocking his car for instance (he reckoned they were
putting something into the locks!).

Something is very wrong, probably in Mike's head but what the hell,
loonies make life more fun!
--
Angus Gulliver

===

Subject: Castrate the depraved MI5 buggers now
Newsgroups: uk.misc
Organization: Toronto Free-Net

>Something is very wrong, probably in Mike's head but what the hell,
>loonies make life more fun!

Something is very wrong when the security services abandon their usual
target of politicians and the well-known, to pursue the hitherto unknown
nonentities such as myself.

>corley, you puzzle me!

Why? Because of my pathological truthfulness?

>3) you (at least) believe there's (some) substance to your claim(s) and you
>have a genuine axe to grind. If so, bloody well go for it, but scrape the
>heavy layer of steaming dung off the top (that's assuming you're even
>capable of distinguishing fantasy from reality.)

Bloody well go for it I will.

I think the "standard spiel" is quite studded with facts actually.
There's plenty of "meat" there if the appropriate people can be motivated
to get their act together and pursue the case.

>my bet's on (5) - but just fuck off corley- irritate the lard-arsed canucks
>instead. The cia's financing of "professor" cameron's brain-washing

the lard-arsed canucks (?) are irritating me, but you don't want to hear
about that

>business booming?? Do we all get a look in at flotation ??!!

"Flight or fight" 7/1/96

What would you do if an MI5 agent started abusing you aboard a British Airways jet?

From: huge@axalotl.demon.co.uk (Hugh Davies)
Newsgroups: uk.misc
Subject: Re: persecution rant (re-post)
Reply-To: huge@axalotl.demon.co.uk
Date: Sun Jan 7 04:43:41 1996

Yo, Mike, Happy New Year! Haven't you killed yourself yet?

In article <DKMIs5.158.0.bloor@torfree.net>, bu765@torfree.net (Mike Corley) wri
>For anyone who hasn't yet read this,

There is no-one in the known Universe who hasn't read this at least 5 times.

>and really really wants to then here

No-one wants to read it, Mike. It's drivel.

>is the article that was posted last year in this newsgroup....

Over and over and over and over and over and over and over and over again....
--
Regards,

Huge.

===

Subject: persecution rant (re-post)
Newsgroups: uk.misc
Organization: Toronto Free-Net
Summary:
Keywords:

>Yo, Mike, Happy New Year! Haven't you killed yourself yet?

But I can't, you see then I wouldn't know how things would turn out
("we're only doing this because we don't know how it's all going to end"
- logic error in line 100)

>There is no-one in the known Universe who hasn't read this at least 5 times.

It doesn't seem to have done a whole lot of good since the good old
persecution stuff is still going on. Over Christmas I was flying BA and
got hassled by a couple of people on the flight (sounds like something
you've heard before, doesn't it?). All the usual stuff about the town I'd
been staying, "he doesn't know who we are", self-justification that we're
doing it because he's a "nutter" etc. Real friendly like. Also a fairly
obvious wind-up and attempt to get some reaction. I think they're trying
quite hard to get a reaction.

If I hit someone on a flight over the Atlantic, am I actually breaking any laws, and if so whose? Is a BA aircraft British territory subject to British laws while it's in mid-flight? It is really tempting to "reply" and that's obviously what they want, so who am I to refuse a blow to the head for people who ask for it so consistently?

"Jeff Rooker MP" 5/3/96
Jeff Rooker won't help, and now he's forgotten he ever spoke to me.

From: rael@midnight.org (Rael A. Fenchurch)
Newsgroups: uk.misc,uk.politics,uk.media,uk.legal,alt.politics.british
Subject: Re: Persecution in the U.K.
Date: Tue Mar 5 04:37:52 1996

Mike,

>"go away" replies, and one from a Labour MP saying he was aware of my situation
>but wouldn't help me because he regarded me as the "bad guy". Gee thanks, they
>do this and then offload the shame they should feel onto you by telling you "oh
>but it's your fault". It's a mad world.

Do you happen to have a copy of this MPs letter? After all, a scanned
copy of it would lend great weight to your case here. At the moment,
you've offered us nothing in the way of evidence, which is one of the
main reasons we all think you've truly gone fishing. So?

Rael...

--- Rael A. Fenchurch (rael@midnight.org, http://www.midnight.org/rael/) ---
---   "I don't think compassion's the language of our time"   ---
---   "Doubt or Die" ---

===

From: Andy Howard <andy@kiss100.demon.co.uk>
Newsgroups: uk.misc,uk.politics,uk.media,uk.legal,alt.politics.british
Subject: Re: Persecution in the U.K.
Reply-To: andy@kiss100.demon.co.uk
Date: Tue Mar 5 06:06:15 1996

In article: <DnrMsq.239.0.bloor@torfree.net> bu765@torfree.net (Mike Corley) wr
I got a few
> "go away" replies, and one from a Labour MP saying he was aware of my situatio
> but wouldn't help me because he regarded me as the "bad guy".

Which Labour MP Mike?
>
--

| Andy Howard   EMail andy@kiss100.demon.co.uk |
| My opinions, not my employer's (Jolly nice people though they are). |
| If my employers shared my opinions... Well, frankly I'd be amazed |

===

Subject: Re: Persecution in the U.K.
Newsgroups: uk.misc,uk.politics,uk.media,uk.legal,alt.politics.british,soc.culture.br$

Followup-To: uk.misc,uk.politics,uk.media,uk.legal,alt.politics.british,soc.culture.b$
References: <DnFtLs.E37.0.bloor@torfree.net> <4h45nq$87o_002@leeds.ac.uk> <4h6gkbivc
Organization: Toronto Free-Net
Distribution:

Mike Corley (bu765@torfree.net) wrote:
: >Do you happen to have a copy of this MPs letter? After all, a scanned
: >copy of it would lend great weight to your case here. At the moment,
: >you've offered us nothing in the way of evidence, which is one of the
: >main reasons we all think you've truly gone fishing. So?

: The letter was by email, not on paper. (In addition to snail-mailing, I
: emailed all the relevant addresses I could find.) I'll see if I can find
: it, I keep a record of most of this correspondence so I may still have it.

I'm afraid I don't have a copy of the correspondence. In future I will keep
useful letters, so with luck there may be a "next time".

The MP was Jeff Rooker, Labour MP. Having looked again at the Labour web page I
find he doesn't have an address listed, but I have a record of his address as
having been jeff.rooker@geo2.poptel.org.uk. I don't know where I got the
address from. I'm so disorganised!

==

Newsgroups: uk.misc,uk.politics,uk.media,uk.legal,alt.politics.british
From: J.J.Smith@ftel.co.uk (John J Smith)
Subject: Re: Persecution in the U.K.
X-Nntp-Posting-Host: death-on-the-rock.ftel.co.uk
Message-ID: <Dnw49L.D1H@ftel.co.uk>
Sender: smid@death-on-the-rock.ftel.co.uk (RFC931)
Organization: Fujitsu Telecommunications Europe Ltd
References: <DnFtLs.E37.0.bloor@torfree.net> <DnrMsq.239.0.bloor@torfree.net>
<Dnsrnu.Jr1.0.bloor@torfree.net> <DntKEo.86E.0.bloor@torfree.net>
Date: Thu, 7 Mar 1996 09:12:56 GMT
Lines: 54

In article <DntKEo.86E.0.bloor@torfree.net>,
Mike Corley <bu765@torfree.net> wrote:
>Mike Corley (bu765@torfree.net) wrote:
>: >Do you happen to have a copy of this MPs letter? After all, a scanned
>: >copy of it would lend great weight to your case here. At the moment,
>: >you've offered us nothing in the way of evidence, which is one of the
>: >main reasons we all think you've truly gone fishing. So?
>
>: The letter was by email, not on paper. (In addition to snail-mailing, I
>: emailed all the relevant addresses I could find.) I'll see if I can find
>: it, I keep a record of most of this correspondence so I may still have it.
>
>I'm afraid I don't have a copy of the correspondence. In future I will keep
>useful letters, so with luck there may be a "next time".

Don't believe you. Because that might be proof, and we just *cant* have that.

>The MP was Jeff Rooker, Labour MP. Having looked again at the Labour web page I
>find he doesn't have an address listed, but I have a record of his address as

>having been jeff.rooker@geo2.poptel.org.uk. I don't know where I got the
>address from. I'm so disorganised!

I did Email this MP yesterday. This is what I wrote:

Smid>I am sorry to bother you, but there is a person with a known
Smid>personality disorder on the internet usenet, claiming that you
Smid>as an MP have backed up his claims that he is being persecuted
Smid>by MI5.

Smid>His name is Mike Corely, and posts from canada (email address
Smid>available if you require).
Smid>
Smid>He claims that you have told him that his claims that the
Smid>"television is watching him", are justified, yet cannot find the
Smid>email in which he did so..

Smid>I'd be interested in what you have said to him, because we have
Smid>had a long term battle to convince him that he really is schizophrenic
Smid>and that Chris Tarrent, MI5 and Martin Lewis from News On Ten are
Smid>persecuting him... If you do have the original Email, then that'd
Smid>be nice...

Smid>If you nothing of this subject, it would not suprise me, however.

His reply, surpise, suprise was:

MP>No idea what you are on about. I am getting really sick of some of
MP>the junk on E mail.   I just dump it so he may have contacted
MP>but as to an answer I 've better things to do.

Your move, Mike.

    Smid

"Email Cruelty" 11/3/96
Accomplishing what the Luftwaffe couldn't do to the Mile End Road.

From: D.S.Toube@qmw.ac.uk (David Toube)
Newsgroups: uk.misc,uk.politics,uk.legal,uk.media,soc.culture.british
Subject: Re: Why Censorship Must Not Be Allowed on Uk.*
Reply-To: D.S.Toube@qmw.ac.uk
Date: Mon Mar 11 11:47:13 1996

A OSHINEYE <TA5330@QMWCC7.qmw.ac.uk> wrote:

:D.S.Toube@qmw.ac.uk (David Toube) wrote:
:>I would also be very pleased if Mike Corley would not mailbomb me
:>via my university account with messages entitled 'This Is What
:>You Get For Censorship', thus closing down the entire college
:>email system.
:>
:>Although it does not personally inconvenience me, it is rather
:>dull for the college.

:When did this happen? BTW you can always use Pegasus Mail to send all
:email from Corley's address back to him and see how he likes it.
:--Ade
:
This weekend. The result, Mike Corley will be gratified to hear,
was that all users of the college system were prevented from
using email.

I suspect that there is no stopping Mike Corley. If mail is
automatically returned to him, he will return it back to you
tenfold. If he is thrown off his account, as he surely will be,
he will find another one.

I do not care whether Mike Corley has an email account or not. It
is a matter of supreme indifference to me whether his fanciful
account of persecution is aired or not. If he thinks that he has
been persecuted by M15 and Chris Tarrant, then that is a matter
for him. But there is a world of difference between repeatedly
spamming usenet - which is unacceptable - and setting up a Web
Site containing his post, which is entirely acceptable. Then it
will be possible to choose whether or not to partake of his
fantasy.

However although I would not like to see the censorship of posts
because they demonstrate evidence of mental illness, I suspect
that Mike Corley will inevitably be censored by his ISP following
a number of complaints of usenet abuse and mailbombing.

David Toube
Lecturer in Law
QMW, University of London

"Shoot to Kill" 4/4/96
So why didn't they just shoot you dead? It would have been a lot cheaper.

Newsgroups: uk.misc,uk.politics,alt.politics.british,soc.culture.british
From: jbaker@pobox.com (Jill Baker)
Subject: Re: MI5 Persecution: How and Why Did it Start?
Reply-To: jbaker@pobox.com
Date: Thu Apr 4 05:03:01 1996

jbaker@pobox.com (Jill Baker) wrote:

>bu765@torfree.net (Mike Corley) wrote:

>>Why would
>>the security services expend hundreds of thousands of pounds and more than fiv

>>years of manpower to try to kill a British citizen? Because ...

>So why didn't they just shoot you dead?
>It would have been a lot cheaper.

Please make the effort to respond to this point Mike.
It was a serious question.

      Jill   (my opinions are entirely my own, no-one else's)

==

Subject: Re: MI5 Persecution: How and Why Did it Start?
Newsgroups: uk.misc,uk.politics,alt.politics.british,soc.culture.british
Followup-To: uk.misc,uk.politics,alt.politics.british,soc.culture.british
References: <Dp5IAr.1EB.0.bloor@torfree.net>
Organization: Toronto Free-Net
Distribution:

jbaker@pobox.com (Jill Baker) wrote:

>bu765@torfree.net (Mike Corley) wrote:

>>Why would
>>the security services expend hundreds of thousands of pounds and more
than fiv
>>years of manpower to try to kill a British citizen? Because ...

>So why didn't they just shoot you dead?
>It would have been a lot cheaper.

I think there are two reasons nobody has taken physical action as opposed
to verbal;

a) A lot of people "know". Perhaps you the reader might not know, but
lots of people in the media etc do. Remember, I was born in the UK and
lived there until a couple of years ago. I don't think these people would

condone state-sponsored murder of someone who might be seen on a good day as one of their own.

b) Rather than doind anything directly, they're going for spying, verbal harassment, media harassment, every form of persecution short of the physical. Because as soon as anything turns physical, the police become involved; and unless it turns physical, the police can shrug and say 'not our problem'.

So they persecute you and try to get you to react, either by hitting one of them (in which case I clearly find myself in the wrong as far as the police are concerned), or by trying to harm myself (in which case they can pretend they weren't responsible).

It's a pretty unproductive form of harassment actually, because if you don't react then they're wasting they're time. Or perhaps they're just cheap bullies and trying to wreck someone's life, without any ulterior motive?

"Leant On" 7/4/96

The Police probably realise that if they looked into this, they would be leant on hard.

From: Green <Green@guidion.demon.co.uk>
Newsgroups: uk.misc,uk.politics,alt.politics.british,soc.culture.british
Subject: Re: MI5 Persecution: Why Aren't the British Police Doing Their Job?
Reply-To: Green@guidion.demon.co.uk
Date: Sun Apr 7 21:13:30 1996

In article <DpIE0r.736.0.bloor@torfree.net>
    bu765@torfree.net "Mike Corley" writes:

> Last Easter (1995) I went into the local police station in London and spoke to
> an officer about the harassment against me. But I couldn't provide tangible
> evidence; what people said, in many cases years ago, is beyond proof, and
> without something to support my statements I cannot expect a police officer to
> take the complaint seriously.

This in itself dos not suggest that the police have it in for you.
The old bill operates on extremely tight spending limits forced on
them by that pillock Michael Howard, and without evidence, they
often have higher priorities than chasing something that cannot go
to court.

I doubt that the police are actually being leant on, but they probably
realise that if they looked into this, they would be leant on hard.
The met always stays away from anything that looks like it has Defence,
Security or secret service interest already, because they realise that
they are below these government agencies in the general pecking order.

This attitude was made clear in a TV show where a left wing comedian
heckled some aristocratic Tory candidate in a local election. The
police officer gave the comic a ticking off, even though you could see
that this young copper sympathised with the comedian, and regarded
the Tory as an upper-crust wanker. He said, and I quote "I'm giving you
the ticking off and not him because he's a Lord and I'm a Police Constable."

If I walked into my local nick and complained that MI5 were snooping on me,
they would show me the door without even looking at my evidence, because
that bored desk seargant with only five years to go before he retires
doesn't want to start fucking about with somebody who has incurred the
wrath of Stella Rimington. He would rather deal with the lost dogs and
driving licence producers, eat his cheese and pickle sandwiches and piss
off home at the end of his shift than have some high ranking spook having
a go at his boss and getting him a bollocking.

In short, you have earned much sympathy but little surprise. Just remember
that saying about the enemy of your enemies.

Have a nice day.

*** QUOTE OF THE DAY*******************
* You have just read the opinons of :   * "Common sense is merely the set *
*   * of prejudices a person acquires*

Subject: Re: MI5 Persecution: Why Aren't the British Police Doing Their Job?
Newsgroups: uk.misc,uk.politics,alt.politics.british,soc.culture.british
Followup-To: uk.misc,uk.politics,alt.politics.british,soc.culture.british
References: <DpIE0r.736.0.bloor@torfree.net>
Organization: Toronto Free-Net
Distribution:

>This in itself dos not suggest that the police have it in for you.
>The old bill operates on extremely tight spending limits forced on
>them by that pillock Michael Howard, and without evidence, they
>often have higher priorities than chasing something that cannot go
>to court.

I think the police know well what's going on. It is up to them to do
something about it. They know I've made a complaint at a police station.
I could probably do more to try to help myself (I think someone suggested
making a written complaint to the chief constable) but even then I nthink
they would not take action.

>
>I doubt that the police are actually being leant on, but they probably
>realise that if they looked into this, they would be leant on hard.
>The met always stays away from anything that looks like it has Defence,
>Security or secret service interest already, because they realise that
>they are below these government agencies in the general pecking order.
>
So we have a situation where the security service breaks the law,
everyone knows MI5 breaks the law, and the police won't investigate
crimes that would otherwise earn a jail sentence.

Oh good, I'm really glad the UK is a democracy. (<sarcasm>, for those of
you who didn't catch that)

>If I walked into my local nick and complained that MI5 were snooping on me,
>they would show me the door without even looking at my evidence, because
>that bored desk seargant with only five years to go before he retires
>doesn't want to start fucking about with somebody who has incurred the
>wrath of Stella Rimington. He would rather deal with the lost dogs and
>driving licence producers, eat his cheese and pickle sandwiches and piss
>off home at the end of his shift than have some high ranking spook having
>a go at his boss and getting him a bollocking.

In this case I think it is 'high-ranking' police officers who are aware
of the persecution, they know a complaint has been made, and they're
doing nothing. What is more, I don't think there is anything I can do
that would make them take action, both because they may be being 'leant
on' and through the wider view that it could be deleterious to the state
to have a persecution by state organs exposed.

They're wrong in taking that point of view, because sooner or later this
will all out anyway, and they it will be n years of police inaction
(n>=6) that will be questioned.

>
>In short, you have earned much sympathy but little surprise. Just remember
>that saying about the enemy of your enemies.
>
>Have a nice day.

"Stasi" 21/4/96

They infiltrate organisations, people's jobs and lives. They operate almost like a cancer.

Subject: Chief Constable Alderson Condemns "Stasi" MI5
Newsgroups:uk.misc,uk.politics,uk.media,uk.legal,soc.culture.british
Organization: Toronto Free-Net
Summary:
Keywords:

John Alderson, former Chief Constable of Devon and Cornwall, had the following to say about the expansion of the Security Service's powers, in a recent magazine article;

"It is fatal to let the secret service into the area of ordinary crime. MI5 is not under the same restraints as the police. They infiltrate organisations, people's jobs and lives. They operate almost like a cancer."

"At the moment the acorn of a Stasi [the former East German communists' secret service] has been planted. It is there for future governments to build on."

The message is clear. Criminal subversion and criminal harassment by an unpoliced minority not subject to the law, "infiltration of people's jobs and lives" is with us today.

"Fitted up" 26/4/96

They "fitted me up" in such a way that what they did would resemble the symptoms of schizophrenia.

Subject: Re: MI5? Please can someone explain what's going on here?
Newsgroups: uk.misc
References: <4l1khm$4cn@utopia.hacktic.nl> <4l2lhj$6h6@bignews.shef.ac.uk>
Organization: Toronto Free-Net
Distribution:

David Stretch (dds@leicester.ac.uk) wrote:
: In article <19960418.000817.55@hotch.hotch.demon.co.uk>,
: Iain L M Hotchkies <iain@hotch.demon.co.uk> wrote:
: >The (remote) possibility remains that 'Mike Corley' is either
: >not schizophrenic (but is 'pretending' to be so) or 'he' is
: >a product of a number of persons (?psychology students).

: Given other ways in which I have seen people exploit some of The Internet's
: capabilities to disrupt or indulge in sophistry, or to exploit a medium
: that resembles speech without the non-verbal and intonation cues, etc
: as a means of denigrating others, I question your use, albeit in quotes,
: of the word "remote". I'm not saying it isn't remote and therefore it is
: great, I'm just saying that I don't think we can easily classify it as
: remote, moderate, or great.

I think you can build up quite a good picture based on what someone says
and on their posting patterns. I don't think "The Internet" (capitals, no
less) is as opaque a medium as you make it out to be.

: It is not easy to determine the validity of all information on The
: Internet without making use of extra supplementary information.

: We do have the problem, pointed out by someone else, of the possibly
: "too perfect" textbook characteristics of what is being posted.

I explained that one, but I don't mind explaining it again (you don't
mind having it explained again to you, do you now?). The reason my
"symptoms" are such a perfect fit to the textbook is because the people
causing the campaign "fitted me up" in such a way that what they did
would resemble the symptoms of schizophrenia. Hence TV, radio, other
media, people in the streets etc. By a fortunate coincidence (for them)
these mthods of harassment are the ones which offer easiest channels of
access (for them).

It's really quite neat. All it takes is for people to start believing
that the "symptoms" aren't symptoms but reality, though, and the house of
cards collapses in a heap. And there are _lots_ of people now who knoiw
full well what has gone on.

: If harrassment by email, etc, has happened by someone out of the country,
: can a complaint be made that results in arrest or whatever upon that
: person's entry into the country? An interesting point which Mike may be
: able to inform us about, as he's said he will be in the UK in a few weeks
: time.

Picture the scene at the airport;
"I arrest you for being Mike Corley and mailbombing people"

"But my name isn't Corley. Who he? Mailbombing isn't illegal is it? You'd have to lock up a lot of people if sending annoying email was a crime"

"Er....."

: --
: David Stretch: Greenwood Institute of Child Health, Univ. of Leicester, UK.
: dds@leicester.ac.uk   Phone:+44 (0)116-254-6100   Fax:+44 (0)116-254-4127
==

: context-free parts of articles, conversations and things-on-the-TV and
: assume they are meant for you. Mike, this is called paranoia.

But that's the way real abuse works, too. People interject words and phrases into what they say which they know will have meaning for the listener.

And sometimes, they make it obvious. The very first evening of my job in Oxford, we went for a drink with the technical director, and a couple of other employees. The TD said in an "as-if" aside to one of the others, "Is this the bloke who's been on TV?" (he said it directly in front of me, and obviously meant mke to hear him saying it). The other person replied, "Yes, I think so".

I think the subtext of what the TD said was "Why are they bothering with him? He's so insignificant, why would they possibly want to spend the resources going after him and putting all that expensive technology in his home, when there must be much better targets?". The Technical Director was given to sometimes disrespecting people, you see, and in my case he couldn't see the point of anyone expending money on harassing me.

==

Subject: Re: Treatment of Schizophrenia
Newsgroups: uk.misc,uk.legal,uk.politics,alt.politics.british
Followup-To: uk.misc,uk.legal,uk.politics,alt.politics.british
References: <153321Z22041996@anon.penet.fi> <4lge6r$p00@news.ox.ac.uk>
Organization: Toronto Free-Net
Distribution:

Illtud Daniel (idaniel@jesus.ox.ac.uk) wrote:
: Probably 'cos you come across as reasoned & articulate, it's a pity
: about the other stuff :)

Veracity is so unreasonable.

: >>pps. You should still see a doc again Mike.
: >
: >Doing so. Trouble is, all this mental-illness stuff provides camouflage
: >for the harassment, which is real. It alows people who otherwise would
: >consider the harassment seriously to disregard it. It makes conversations
: >with a lawyer or police brief when otherwise it would merit discussion.

: The point is that there are two possibilities happening here-

: 1. There's a large conspiracy of people out to get you, for no
:   other reason than that they have the means to do so, and that
:   it involves a lot of the Media & a proportion of the public

: 2. You (who admit to having some headspace problems) are suffering
:   from acute paranoid schizophrenia.

: Possibility #1 is _possible_, but would be unprecendented (OTOH,
: how would we know?), unfeasible, and many other things beginning
: with _un_ which I can't think of at the moment. Besides, if there
. was something going on, chances are some of us here would know
: about it, and I'm convinced that nobody does.

"Unprecedented" hits the nail on the head. It _is_ unprecedented, but we
have only just reached the technical stage at which it is feasible, and
we know video-spying is done to other people (NB the Diana-Hewitt
episode) and is a routine tool of security agencies.

Perhaps what is unprecedented is not the technical side, but the social
manipulation of many people by a concealed element in what other
countries would be called the secret police. The most disturbing element
is the degree to which people allow themselves to be unquestioningly
manipulated by an evil element within the state.

"Bernard Levin" 1/6/96
The Times columnist fears a "madman running loose about London".

Subject: Re: "FANATIC'S FARE FOR THE COMMON MAN"
Newsgroups: uk.misc,uk.media,uk.legal,uk.politics.misc
Followup-To: uk.misc,uk.media,uk.legal,uk.politics.misc
References: <Ds0L1o.BMF.0.bloor@torfree.net> <ADCF291096681F4E@cara.demon.co.uk>
Organization: Toronto Free-Net
Distribution:

Peter Ceresole (peter@cara.demon.co.uk) wrote:
: In article <Ds0L1o.BMF.0.bloor@torfree.net>,
: bu765@torfree.net (Mike Corley) quoted a typical, overblown Bernard Levin
: piece, which sounds exactly like any number of other pieces by Levin over
: the past thirty years.

: He then goes on to draw an anguished parallel with a totally unrelated
: incident that had happened between him and a friend a few days earlier.

It is in the same style as his other pieces, but it's so close to what actually happened a few days previously, that it's completely reasonable to assume that someone told Levin about the meeting, hammed it up a little bit and motivated him to write that article.

Look at the parallels;

1. "madman running loose about London"

2. it's about a meeting which took place recently

3. the police are called (he must be controlled, however much that consumes in resources)

4. he might be violent, approach with caution, yes we're laughing but really we're afraid of him, or is it perhaps our own propaganda that we're letting manipulate us

5. he "bursts into tears, and swears it's all true - and it is" a very exaggerated impression of the conclusion of that meeting

Don't worry if you don't believe me, neither my friend to whom I explained this nor my GP believe me either (until the friend found out otherwise!). If someone just presented this to you as I am presenting it now then I wouldn't find it credible (most likely), so it's not until you actually find out it's true that you can find it credible. And by then it's too late, because they've got you in their trap and explained how "funny" the abuse is.

"alt.fan.mike-corley" 6/6/96

A newsgroup for pugilistic underdogs.

From: richard@musicians-net.co.uk (Richard Fairhurst)
Newsgroups: uk.misc,uk.media,uk.legal,uk.politics.misc
Subject: A Mike Corley newsgroup?
Date: Thu Jun 6 05:02:17 1996

In article <2520@osiris.win-uk.net>, burridge@osiris.win-uk.net (Paul Burridge) wrote:

> In article <833844951snz@eloka.demon.co.uk>, Owen Lewis
> (oml@eloka.demon.co.uk) writes [re: Mike Corley]:
> >To be honest, having made the mistake of reading his magnum opus twice
> >(like many forms of discomfort, one is prone to repeat the experience to
> >confirm that it really is a bad as one thought), I read nothing he writes
> >but am tempted by some of the sub-threads that develop.
>
> I made the grave error of showing one of his masterpieces to my
> mother, together with some of the (less than respectful) responses
> to it. Regrettably, she is now addicted to the Corley saga, is
> very much an admirer of him (viewing him as a pugilistic underdog
> deserving of great admiration) and I have to waste reams of paper
> printing all this bilge out every other day, for her delecation.

Given that Mr Corley clearly holds a certain fascination for some people, and that his website, although "informative", isn't exactly ideal for encouraging discussion of the sort that we all enjoy so much (including Mike himself, by the look of things), would anyone be up for a Mike Corley newsgroup - uk.fan.mike-corley, alt.fan.mike-corley, whatever? (Sorry, I'm not very well up on these things.)

This would be a perfect place for Mike to post his writings, and perhaps the occasional "look at the ...mike-corley newsgroup" posting in uk.misc and so on would be accepted in place of the current cross-posts.

--

Richard Fairhurst (assistant editor, Keyboard Review)
"I am the vine: and you are the branches"

"Old_500" 5/7/96
Big Ears talks to himself about a "man who knows".

From: box6565@embankment.com (Old_500)
Newsgroups: uk.misc
Subject: Dear Mike Corley
Followup-To: uk.legal,uk.misc
Date: Fri, 05 Jul 1996 15:41:16 GMT
Organization: XYz
Lines: 55
Message-ID: <31dd3788.8481134@news.dircon.co.uk>
NNTP-Posting-Host: gw1-073.pool.dircon.co.uk
X-Newsreader: Forte Agent .99e/16.227

==

Subject: Now we tell the truth as it really is
Newsgroups: uk.misc
Organization: Toronto Free-Net
Summary:
Keywords:

:AND a second posting which appeared in uk.legal on 5th July 1996 (isn't Mr
:Corley popular ?)

>   Dear Mike,

>   I've just spoken to a man who knows and he has told me you
>   have never ever been a target.

>   My man knows because he once wrote a report on you after
>   you made complaints.

Come off it "Big Ears", if you're going to pretend someone else is giving me
advice then at least get one of your fellow coppers to write it so that it
isn't obviously written in the same style as your posts.

Also both your post and the one you're pretending isn't yours were posted from
pipex via news.dircon.co.uk, viz:

YOURS;

From: BigEars@technocom.com (Big Ears.)
Message-ID: <31ddacfe.7445797@news.dircon.co.uk>
NNTP-Posting-Host: gw5-072.pool.dircon.co.uk

"NOT YOURS";

From: box6565@embankment.com (Old_500)
Message-ID: <31dd3788.8481134@news.dircon.co.uk>
NNTP-Posting-Host: gw1-073.pool.dircon.co.uk

:NCIS leaks and most policemen regard it as unaccountable and occasionally
:insecure. M Howard promises to make NCIS publicly accountable.

You know a lot about what policemen think, don't you?

"Silly-billy" 6/7/96
Baseless allegations. Escalated to extreme. Flame!

From: Mike_Corley_Fan_Club@Nut_house.org (Old_500)
Newsgroups: uk.misc,uk.legal,uk.media,alt.radio.uk,rec.arts.tv.uk.misc
Subject: MC Exposed as a Fraud
Date: Sat, 06 Jul 1996 17:01:05 GMT
Organization: Anti-Nuts Inc.
Lines: 33
Message-ID: <31de9b91.11926469@news.dircon.co.uk>
References: <Du4Lql.32o.0.bloor@torfree.net>
NNTP-Posting-Host: gw5-055.pool.dircon.co.uk
X-Newsreader: Forte Agent .99e/16.227

Sad, confused and emotional disturbed Mike Corley wrote:

> { snip }

Because he has made himself into a martyr and now he finds it impossible to back down. Mike's big secret has now been exposed. He made everything up.

Every time Mike makes allegations against the police, MI5, Tom-Dick-and-Harry etc. those organisations have taken people off vitally important work to ascertain whether or not there was any substance in Mike's ranting allegations.

When I'm told by someone who really does know such things that there was never any plot to get Mike then I trust that person sufficiently enough to accept his word.

The problem is Mike has escalated matters to an extreme level and like many silly billys he will find it impossible to give up all his self created crap and to live a normal life. After all what can Mike do now this crap has been exposed as untrue ? What new cause can Mike dedicate himself to ? (Some might read that as: who else can Mike now start upsetting ?)

So Mike write to John Major, c/o the Private Secretary, 10 Downing Street, London SW1A 2AA and ask the Prime Minister to help you. I'd normally disclose his fax numbers but if I did that you might jam up the lines with abusive postings just like you do here on Usenet.

Is anyone interested in joining with me to do a mass e-mailing of protests to Anon Penet and to Toronto Free Net in an attempt to flood their computer systems thus forcing them to seriously consider pulling the plug on Mike ? I'm not sure but is my proposal called a "flame" ?
==
From: BigEars@technocom.com (Big Ears.)
Newsgroups: uk.misc,uk.legal,uk.media,alt.radio.uk,rec.arts.tv.uk.misc
Subject: Re: MC Exposed as a Fraud
Date: Sat Jul 6 17:34:46 1996

John Youles commented:

> I've found that torfree.net don't respond, perhaps if they got a high
> enough number of complaints they might take notice. See their web pages

> for email addresses.

Perhaps we should give Mike 7 days from today (6 July 96) to come to his senses and they start a massive multiple E-mailing campaign to Toronto Free Net. If all us victims send multiple copies of E-mails to the right addresses in Toronto then perhaps the Canadians will begin to get the appropriate message.

Copy e-mailed to Mike, just so he knows what is coming if he persists.

Big Ears.   Posted to uk.misc
==
Please think of the people sleeping in shop doorways every night
==

Subject: I'm wasting MI5's time! I should be arrested!
Newsgroups: uk.misc,uk.legal,rec.arts.tv.uk.misc,alt.journalism,alt.journalism.print,$
Organization: Toronto Free-Net
Summary:
Keywords:

It's such a pity that the Security Service has no powers of arrest. How are they supposed to implement a proper secret police state without the ability to snatch Joe Citizen off the street whenever they feel like it?

"Old_500" aka "Big Ears" aka "PC Plod" wrote:
>Every time Mike makes allegations against the police, MI5,
>Tom-Dick-and-Harry etc. those organisations have taken people off vitally
>important work to ascertain whether or not there was any substance in Mike's
>ranting allegations.

I see. So they're not wasting six years of manpower to persecute you. They're wasting six years of manpower to prove I'm _not_ being persecuted.

I wish I was clever enough to think of something like that. I really, really do.

>When I'm told by someone who really does know such things that there was
>never any plot to get Mike then I trust that person sufficiently enough to
>accept his word.

Come on "Big Ears", why don't you admit that you made this posting? This is exactly the same line you were feeding me a few months ago. The posts are from the same news server, it's even the same newsreading software (Forte Agent .99e/16.227).

I'm afraid that if you friend "in the know" denied the existence of a plot then he was being, as they say, economical with the truth. Judging by the extreme reaction in London in May, and the panic you're showing now, as well as the replay post yesterday, I would say that things are hotting up again. But for you this time, not for me. I am out of harm's way, and there is very little you can do as long as I stay out of the UK.

"BBC+ITN=MI5" 23/7/96
MI5 buy into the media.

Newsgroups: uk.misc,alt.radio.uk,uk.media,alt.politics.british,uk.legal
From: bu765@torfree.net (Mike Corley)
Subject: MI5 Buy into the Media
Message-ID: <Dv0p34.73.0.bloor@torfree.net>
Organization: Toronto Free-Net
X-Newsreader: TIN [version 1.2 PL2]
References: <Pine.OSF.3.91.960716155603.6898A-100000@ermine.ox.ac.uk>
Date: Tue, 23 Jul 1996 22:28:15 GMT

Peter Harding (harding@ermine.ox.ac.uk) wrote:
: I was at speakers' corner on Sunday. There was one chap who was bellowing
: about something or other, I don't know what, but one thing he said to
: someone caught my ear:

: "BBC, MI5, same thing."

Can't disagree with that sentiment.

Wasn't it documented that MI5 sometimes "bought" journalists and broadcasters? I remember reading a report by some jouralist who had been offered an extra tax-free income by MI5 to become their covert mouthpiece, and had refused.

Bet you lots of others didn't refuse. Why do you think MI5 have such easy access to the BBC and media? Because they're directly paying them off, that's why.

==

Tue, 23 Jul 1996 20:01:15   uk.misc   Thread 20 of 25
Lines 17   Re: MI5 Buy into the Media   No responses
Iain@cummings.demon.co.uk   Iain Cummings at Fish!

In article <Dv0p34.73.0.bloor@torfree.net>, Mike Corley
<bu765@torfree.net> writes
>
>Wasn't it documented that MI5 sometimes "bought" journalists and broadcasters?
>I remember reading a report by some jouralist who had been offered an extra
>tax-free income by MI5 to become their covert mouthpiece, and had refused.
>
>
It was Jon Snow of Channel 4.
--
Iain C*mmings - iain@cummings.demon.co.uk
VISIT THE FEARFUL WORLD OF JIMMY McNULTY - VIOLENT NUTTER!
This web-site is not suitable for mature prudes.
http://www.geocities.com/SunsetStrip/7433/

==

> : >mouthpiece, and had refused.
> :
> : It was Jon Snow of Channel 4.
>

> Was it reported in any of the papers?

It has been reported several times. The most recent was in Private Eye,
a few months back. As I recall they also wanted information from him;
journalists would be a natural choice for members of the Security Service
and the Secret Intelligence Service for information sources.

> It might be interesting to see what he had to say regarding their
> attempt to recruit him.

He was most concerned that many others would have accepted such an
offer. However, we can probably make an educated guess as to some of
those who accepted: Nigel West (Rupert Allason, MP) and Chapman Pincher
would come near to the top of the list.

--

\/ David Boothroyd. Socialist and election analyst. Omne ignotum pro magnifico.
British Elections and Politics at http://www.qmw.ac.uk/~laws/election/home.html
I wish I was in North Dakota. Next General Election must be before 22nd May '97
The House of Commons now : C 324, Lab 272, L Dem 25, UU 9, PC 4, SDLP 4, SNP 4,
UDUP 3, Ind 1, Ind UU 1, Spkrs 4. Government majority = 1. Telephone Tate 6125.

"Latest technology" 31/7/96
What private detectives use to spy on people.

From: Jon <Jon@jongru.demon.co.uk>
Newsgroups: uk.misc,uk.legal,uk.politics.misc,alt.politics.british,uk.media
Subject: Surveillance
Date: Wed, 31 Jul 1996 23:20:19 +0100
Organization: -
Lines: 29
Distribution: world
Message-ID: <wIznBGAjw9$xEwTw@jongru.demon.co.uk>
References: <105319Z26071996@anon.penet.fi> <4tfo1f$rvc@morgana.netcom.net.uk>
NNTP-Posting-Host: jongru.demon.co.uk
X-NNTP-Posting-Host: jongru.demon.co.uk
MIME-Version: 1.0
X-Newsreader: Turnpike Version 1.34 <nQyLm4IxRmtU60uHtPa$08ppe9>

In article <4tfo1f$rvc@morgana.netcom.net.uk>, "B.Jury" <bj2@ukc.ac.uk> writes
>an410901@anon.penet.fi wrote:
>> ... Normal surveillance
>>"mini-cameras" are quite noticeable and require visible supporting
>>circuitry. It seems to me the best place to put a small video surveillance
>>device would be additional to a piece of electronic equipment such as a TV
>>or video.
>
>I would imagine it is quite easy to compleatly hida a camera, even in
>a familar enviroment, such as a persons home. You only need a hole the
>size of a pin hole, for the camera to see through.

This is true. I frequently employ private detectives to spy on people
(there's a good reason for this and I'll tell you if you guess
correctly) and one such detective showed me the latest technology only
last week. A small rucksack. One strap of the rucksack has a tiny hole
in it that you wouldn't notice unless someone pointed to it. That's the
camera: the wires lead into the rucksack itself where there is a video
tape recorder little bigger than a Walkman. I don't know if that's what
Roger Cook uses but it certainly explains why it is that the subject can
look straight into the lens and not realise (s)he's being filmed. Now, I
say "latest technology" and I think that's the technology that the
police use as well as the retired police who become private detectives,
but no doubt the security services have far more sophisticated
equipment.

--
Jon

Just too crazy 30/9/96
So crazy it must be true.

Subject: Re: Is MI5 persecuting Mike Corley?
Newsgroups: uk.politics.misc,uk.net,uk.misc,uk.legal
Followup-To: uk.politics.misc,uk.net,uk.misc,uk.legal
References: <NEWTNews.843523097.30215.apascoe@apascoe.patrol.i-way.co.uk> <DyADyG.8IK$
Organization: Toronto Free-Net
Distribution:

wooding@cf.ac.uk wrote:
: In article <NEWTNews.843523097.30215.apascoe@apascoe.patrol.i-way.co.uk> apascoe@pa$
: >   In summary, for there to be a serious possibility that Mike
: >Corley's allegations are true, there needs to be evidence of two
: >things. Firstly, there must be evidence of subversive activity on
: >his part. Secondly, there needs to be evidence of MI5 taking
: >measures to counter this subversive activity, in proportion to the
: >magnitude of the threat posed. Upon reading Mike Corley's posts,

: Alan,

: What about the following scenario? MI5 conducts "experiments" including
: field trials of novel surveillance methods. Say there was a "research
: project" underway to see just how invasive a surveillance of an
: individual could be. Perhaps it wasn't research, perhaps it was for
: training of novice personnel. Either way, there is a sizeable risk of
: detection. In order to minimise the consequences of this, you choose
: someone who is out of the public eye, and if possible someone whose
: credibility is already damaged - by diagnosis of schizophrenia, for example.
: This will facilitate the "plausible denial" if something goes wrong.

: I think this would be closer to Mike's theory.

: Mike, if you are reading, please don't post the story again. Anyone can
: read it at [snip] if they are interested. Also, don't
: think that I actually *believe* the above. On cost alone, it is extremely
: unlikely to be true, and some elements of the story (people in the media
: being "in on it") are just too crazy (though I can see how the paranoia
: builds to the extent that you can see "them" everywhere).

My argument is that the fact that it's so totally crazy is what makes it so
plausible and so hard to prove.

I shall continue to try to find ways to kick down the house of cards. Because
it is a brittle structure. It only needs one person to corroborate, and then
it's all over.

: P.S. Anyone else ever thought of "what-ifs" along the same lines? I
: remember as a boy daydreaming that maybe I was the focus of national
: attention in a "let's follow the life of one person from life to
: death" study - that while I was out or in bed there were programmes on
: the television about my life so far, etc. It makes for a good fiction,

Perhaps MI5 have become victims of their own paranoia. Their agency has been
thought of as acting disreputably, so when their decision arrives, they don't

think twice about breaking the law. Whereas say CSIS (the Canadian equivalent) is at pains to point out how it would never ever do anything in contravention of the law, and how it is strictly controlled in what it does and how it does it.

If this matter does ever make it into the public gaze, then it won't just be a few individuals in the media or security service who'll get hit. The UK is supposed to be a civilized democratic country (East Germany called themselves a democracy and they had the Stasi, but anyway). In a civilized country these things shouldn't be happening - and it is ultimately Parliament and the government who are answerable for not imposing sufficient restraints and accountability on those who are supposed to be ensuring security for citizens, not jeopardising it.

Usual targets of such abuse 10/10/96
Usually this type of 'hidden abuse' is racial.

Subject: Re: MI5 says "Kill Yourself"
Newsgroups: uk.misc,uk.legal,uk.politics.misc,uk.media
References: <zlsiida.4248.3258FE24@fs1.mcc.ac.uk> <53eeev$cmg@axalotl.demon.co.uk> <5$
Organization: Toronto Free-Net
Distribution:

iain@hotch.demon.co.uk (Iain L M Hotchkies) wrote:
>Indeed. If you've ever had a 'conversation' with someone suffering
>from florid schizophrenia, you'll know how difficult it can be to
>'argue' with them.

I don't have florid symptoms. But I'm in a difficult situation, because those
people who don't know, aren't going to believe, and those who do, they just go
along with the crowd. It's never a good idea to go against the grain, and the
grain here is defined by interests in the establishment and the media. Even
people who could say out loud what was happening won't, because then there's a
risk that they'll be seen as traitors and ostracised.

Usually this type of 'hidden abuse' is racial and targetted at a racial
minority within a country. You keep the minorities out of the good jobs, but
you don't admit discrimination exists. It happens everywhere, not just in
Britain. The persecution that is going on now is in reality a refined form of
racism. Instead of "nigger" it's "nutter", and abusing the mentally ill is
still socially acceptable today. In 50 years it might not be, but today there
isn't any social or legal sanction against it.

So really they've refined racial harassment down to a minority of one. The
words may be different, but the methods are the same.

"Excellent web page" 19/10/96
"Definite waste of talent" says the crowd.

From: Chris Lawton <chrisla@ti.com>
Subject: Re: MI5 persecution ;; Cost of the Harassment
Message-ID: <325A3DA6.3447@ti.com>
Date: Tue, 8 Oct 1996 11:40:22 GMT
Reply-To: chrisla@ti.com

DANIEL ROBERT HOLDSWORTH wrote:
>
> In article <3262b4fc.14638885@192.168.2.1>,
> stevea@castlsys.demon.co.uk.no.spam.thanx (Steve A) writes:
> :On 4 Oct 1996 13:19:16 +0100, drh92@aber.ac.uk (DANIEL ROBERT
> :HOLDSWORTH) wrote:
> :
> :>
> :> Oh NO!
> :>
> :> Not here too.
> :>
> :> This MI5 persecution thread's been doing the rounds of UK.MISC for ages;
> :> it concerns some paranoid loony who thinks that MI5 are out to get him.
> :>
> :> They're not; everyone else on that newsgroup IS.
> :>
> :> Killfile the moron NOW!
> :

Bit sad really, the guy (must be the same one) has an excellent web
page. Definite waste of talent.
PS: I am NOT disclosing his URL.

> The man's been changing his anon remailer address periodically, too.
>
> Why on earth he does I don't know; he's in serious danger of creating some
> real enemies, apart from the phantoms his sadly deranged mind has created.
>
....
From: nuala@mimir.com (Nuala Fahey)
Subject: Re: MI5 persecution // BBC TV and Radio
Date: 4 Oct 1996 16:03:24 +0100
Message-ID: <5338vs$hrc@freyja.mimir.com>

Simon Lord <simonl@hrmconsult.co.uk> wrote:

>I expect he will soon be seen in uk.out.to.lunch

Considering he spammed it far and wide (well, at least to alt.angst and
alt.folklore.urban which I saw and each of those included other groups
in the Newsgroups line) I doubt he'll be seen anywhere for long. Using
the xs4all remailer doesn't really help if you post the url to a
web site which makes it clear who you are.

Nuala, who thinks that the sad thing is he used frames much better than many sites done by supposedly 'sane' people.

--

Out of the ash I rise/With my red hair/And I eat men like air - Plath
You were everything to me/For twenty minutes/
Now I'd rather you would leave - Baby Chaos

....

Date: Sat, 19 Oct 1996 01:36:26 +0100
From: mike.monty@zetnet.co.uk
To: bu765@torfree.net
Subject: Praise

Hi,
Totally excellent page. Although I am a little confused whi is being percecuted?

Cheers Michael

mike.monty@zetnet.co.uk
....

WTGROMT 18/11/96

"Well that's got rid of me then" (perhaps, perhaps not!)

Subject: Re: MIKE AND THE DOWNFALL OF UK.LEGAL
Newsgroups: uk.misc,uk.legal,uk.politics.misc,uk.media
Followup-To: uk.misc,uk.legal,uk.politics.misc,uk.media
References: <DytvBE.9J.0.bloor@torfree.net> <Dzt3oG.EE2.0.bloor@torfree.net> <54q3pd$$
Organization: Toronto Free-Net
Distribution: world

J.J.Smith@ftel.co.uk (John J Smith) wrote:
>Actually, I see uk.misc as a source of occasional interesting information,
>and I like jokes. Some people can laugh, you see.
>
>And as for you spams, exactly how much good have they done so far?

Not much. I thought they might, but the realization has arrived that this
particular avenue of exploration is at a dead end.

WTGROMT (well that's got rid of me then!)
....
Subject: Re: MIKE AND THE DOWNFALL OF UK.LEGAL
From: wooding@cf.ac.uk ()
Date: 1996/11/04
Message-Id: <E0CFFH.1J9@cf.ac.uk>
X-Nntp-Posting-Host: thor.cf.ac.uk
Sender: news@cf.ac.uk (Usenet News user)
References: <DzuwML.F4o.0.bloor@torfree.net> <DzzBs1.n3v@ftel.co.uk> <E05GoF.Ku.0.bloor@torfree.net>
Organization: University of Wales College at Cardiff
Newsgroups: uk.misc,uk.legal,uk.politics.misc,uk.media

In article <E05GoF.Ku.0.bloor@torfree.net> bu765@torfree.net (Mike Corley) writes:
>J.J.Smith@ftel.co.uk (John J Smith) wrote:
>>Actually, I see uk.misc as a source of occasional interesting information,
>>and I like jokes. Some people can laugh, you see.
>>
>>And as for you spams, exactly how much good have they done so far?
>
>Not much. I thought they might, but the realization has arrived that this
>particular avenue of exploration is at a dead end.

Oh please let this be true and not just another wind-up!

>WTGROMT (well that's got rid of me then!)

Mike, without the spamming I'm sure you are welcome to stay around, being
one of the colourful "characters" of uk.misc.

Have a custard cream.

Dave.
....

No Justice 20/11/96
No Justice for those with mental illness.

(sent 20/11/96)
Subject: No Justice for those with mental illness
Newsgroups: uk.misc,uk.legal
Organization: Toronto Free-Net
Summary:
Keywords:

Well, the "legal option" has just foundered on the rock of lawyers refusing to deal with me on the grounds that my perception of harassment must be due to the disease.

So we're back to square one again, the same place we were two years ago.

Now perhaps one of our uk.legal participants can clarify this point. To me it seems illogical that lawyers should have the final say on whether you are allowed to proceed with a civil case or not. Is there a default mechanism or agency for cases such as mine where it is difficult to find a solicitor to represent you? What exactly is the "official Solicitor"? What is it possible to do if you can't find a lawyer to represent you?

A chance to get a useful response out of the uk newsgroups! perhaps they can be good for something else besides spamming.
....

Represent yourself....like the defendants in the McLibel trial.
you will need to read some law..but you CAN legally represent yourself I believe.
Mike W.
....
From: burridge@osiris.win-uk.net (Paul Burridge)

Yes, a lot of people do this nowadays. Saves on legal fees too. Lots of reading up required first, though.

-- Paul
....
(posted 30/11/96 from bu765)

Subject: Re: No Justice for those with mental illness
Newsgroups: uk.misc,uk.legal
Followup-To: uk.misc,uk.legal
References: <E173G8.1oy.0.bloor@torfree.net> <5711vp$tfu@newton.cc.rl.ac.uk> <3311@os$
Organization: Toronto Free-Net
Distribution:

burridge@osiris.win-uk.net (Paul Burridge) wrote:
>>Represent yourself....like the defendants in the McLibel trial.
>>you will need to read some law..but you CAN legally represent yourself I
>>believe.
>>Mike W.
>

>Yes, a lot of people do this nowadays. Saves on legal fees too. Lots
>of reading up required first, though.

What can I do to get competent legal help though? If the case is on the face of it so bizarre that no solicitor would represent me or talk to me, then surely there must be a default mechanism? What is the "official Solicitor" that's been mentioned?
....

All you need do is go to a good library & read up about it - that's what the McLibel 2 did.

--
                Ban Everything or Ban Nothing !
http://www.mahayana.demon.co.uk/   ISO 1386-C compliant .sig
     All words written in the above posting are my opinions
....

David Hepworth (1) 26/2/97
The "Absolute Obscene" Mr Hepworth on GLR radio.

Subject: "Absolute Obscene" David Hepworth (GLR)
Newsgroups: uk.misc,uk.legal,alt.radio.uk,uk.media,uk.media.radio.misc
Organization: Toronto Free-Net
Summary:
Keywords:

Last night (21/Feb/97), I was listening to BBC GLR. You have to understand that I was listening by stealth. Back in 1990 I used to have Capital blaring out of the speakers all over the garden ("if he listens to Capital then he can't be all bad", thanks ever so much). But now I listen on my walkman on headphones with the volume turned right down. It could not possibly be overheard by any listening device, no matter how sensitive, because sound does not carry from the headphones.

Yet somehow they are still able to tell which station I am listening to on the walkman. And last night, I bravely tuned to GLR 94.9FM at around 8.45pm. Everything went well for the first half hour or so. The DJ (today GLR told me it was David Hepworth) had a "rock star spelling competition" (how do you spell Shakespear's Sister?), no trouble there. I was recording the show onto tape just in case anything unpleasant happened, as I had reason to think it might.

Around 9.10pm, it did. Here, precisely, is what Hepworth said after the song "Come Around" by the Muttonbirds (I have this on tape, and at some point will be posting the audio on my website);

"New album's called 'Envy of Angels', that comes out soon, that's the single that's already out, I would imagine, that's 'Come Around', the Muttonbirds, er, coming up after this, we got the rock-and-roll A-level, we have, I assume, Brian do we have an embarrassment of prizes in there, we do, don't we, (EMPHASIS) absolute obscene (END-EMPHASIS) amounts of prizes, there will no doubt be a riot at the back door", and that's, er, A-level coming up after this"

The key phrases in what he said are, "EMBARRASSMENT of prizes", and what he himself emphasized verbally, "ABSOLUTE OBSCENE amount of prizes". It is my belief (based on content and tone of voice) that when he spoke these phrases he knew I was listening, and that the phrases refer directly to my situation. The "EMBARRASSMENT" is the embarrassment he and other media people would feel at having their wrongdoing exposed; the "ABSOLUTE OBSCENE" (which he verbally emphasized) described the disgusting sexual abuse which the harassers have been throwing at me.

Needless to say, I can't prove this is what he meant, although this has happened enough times that it's hard not to recognise it when you see it. But I shall be sending him a copy of this explanation. We'll see what he has to say for himself.
....
Subject: Re: "Absolute Obscene" David Hepworth (GLR)
Newsgroups: uk.misc,uk.legal,alt.radio.uk,uk.media,uk.media.radio.misc
Followup-To: uk.misc,uk.legal,alt.radio.uk,uk.media,uk.media.radio.misc
References: <E60IAy.CL5.0.bloor@torfree.net> <330f2bac.2665181@nntp.best.com> <331372$
Organization: Toronto Free-Net

Distribution:

Anthony@dircon.co.uk-antispam (Anthony) wrote:

>Greg W wrote:
>
>> On Sat, 22 Feb 1997 16:11:22 GMT, bu765@torfree.net (Mike Corley)
>> wrote:
>>
>> >Last night (21/Feb/97), I was listening to BBC GLR. You have to understand that
>> >I was listening by stealth. Back in 1990 I used to have Capital blaring out of

[snip]

>> huh?
>
>I can't understand it myself. Can anyone else help us ?

I will try to explain with greater clarity.

I am prone to have ideas of "interactive watching" by people on TV, and "interactive listening" by people on the radio; which means as I listen to their programme, they are aware that I am listening (because my home is spied on, and those doing the spying phone up the radio station and tell them that I am listening to them), and they then interject nasty remarks in what they say. This is what I believe may have happened on Friday night with GLR, and what I was trying to explain in my article.

It's happened before with other radio stations, most worryingly when I am listening quietly on my walkman as happened on Friday. This time, the interjected words were "embarrassment" and "absolute obscene". The "absolute obscene" referred to the abuse which is currently being directed at me.

I hope that's a little clearer.
....
From: simon@star-one.org.uk (Simon Gray)

Facility thusly:

~ huh?

Just because you need to read it twice in order to understand it, is that any reason to inflict it on the rest of us again ?

--
 '2% of people *do*, 98% of people wish they *had*' - David Fanshawe
http://www.mahayana.demon.co.uk/   Read Flatland !
....
Mike, try playing a cassette in your walkman. There is no way they can reach you then. HTH

--
Don Whybrow - Correct email address: don@whybrow.demon.co.uk
....

Mike Corley wrote:

> .... This time, the
> interjected words were "embarrassment" and "absolute obscene". The "absolute
> obscene" referred to the abuse which is currently being directed at me.

But it is possible that those two sets of interjected words could have
validly referred to something else.

> I hope that's a little clearer.

Thank you, it is a bit clearer.

Posted in uk.legal by Anthony@dircon.co.uk
....
Simon Rushton <Simon@ppushers.demon.co.uk> wrote:
>Some people, new to this group, may not realise the Mike is our resident
>Paranoid Schizophrenic. This is not a joke, it is serious. He has
>already admitted stopping taking prescribed drugs for his condition.

Though I have to say I've never heard one as obscure as that, even
from Mike. How he can believe a rubbish trail for a crap competition
is directed at him is beyond me!
He's sent a copy of the post to the jock, too. I hope he doesn't read
it out.

--
The John Shuttleworth Homepage:
It's just an Austin Ambassador of a site!
http://www.steviep.demon.co.uk/shuttle.htm

Striking out action 10/3/97
"Scandalous, Frivolous or Vexatious".

Subject: "Scandalous, Frivolous or Vexatious"
Newsgroups: uk.misc,uk.legal
Organization: Toronto Free-Net
Summary:
Keywords:

A couple of weeks ago I issued a summons against the BBC in my local county court, for the tort of private nuisance caused by the spying by their newsreaders on my home. My argument was that their spying had prevented me watching the news at home, and therefore interfered with my normal use of my home.

The BBC's Litigation Dept at White City have replied not with a defence, but with an application for my claim to be struck out because;

(a) it discloses no reasonable cause of action; and/or
(b) it is scandalous, frivolous or vexatious.

Their application will be heard next week. They have not made any affidavit in support of their application, nor have they given particulars as to why they consider my summons to be unarguable in law, which would be a necessary condition for there to be no reasonable cause of action.

I am more worried about point (b). Allegations are scandalous (says Stuart Sime's book) if they impute dishonesty against another party; which my allegations do, against the BBC's newsreaders. As for frivolous or vexatious, I think that will be up to me to make a good argument for the effect the BBC's spying has had on my life, and up to the district judge's opinion of my case.

Apparently seeking to have a claim struck out in this way is common practice when the plaintiff is a litigant-in-person. Even if it is struck out, there is always the opportunity to appeal. I think we could be in for a fight next week.
....
Sun, 02 Mar 1997 20:38:59   uk.legal   Thread 52 of 54
Lines 13   Re: "Scandalous, Frivolous or Vexatious"   Respno 1 of 1
Kate@carterce.demon.co.uk   KKKKatie

In article <NQoVQiAnHgGzEwl3@solicit.demon.co.uk>
        andy@solicit.demon.co.uk "Andrew Nichols" writes:

> Well, that'll liven up the dear old District Judge. Almost worth taking
> the day off to see how Mike fares.

almost worth taking a day off to see if he exists

Kate
--
Just back from the US - you've got to love a country that puts
        "Vertical Clearance Impeded" for "Low Bridge"
....
Subject: Re: "Scandalous, Frivolous or Vexatious"
Newsgroups: uk.misc,uk.legal

References: <E6FEFJ.IE7.0.bloor@torfree.net> <NQoVQiAnHgGzEwl3@solicit.demon.co.uk><8$
Organization: Toronto Free-Net
Distribution:

burridge@osiris.win-uk.net (Paul Burridge) wrote:
>Almost worthwhile taking the day off to go and punch him in the
>face for all abuse he's given us on these groups. Which court is it?

Thank you for your kind thought.

I'm not telling you which court it is. I don't want to be hounded by irate
uk-miscreants!

As for raising eyebrows, the member of staff who took the summons form didn't
change their facial expression at all. Seen it all before, no doubt.
....
In article <857597450snz@adams.demon.co.uk>,
Derek Tidman <Derek@adams.demon.co.uk> wrote:
>In article <E6JAxt.EFK.0.bloor@torfree.net>
>   bu765@torfree.net "Mike Corley" writes:
>
>-I'm not telling you which court it is. I don't want to be hounded by irate
>-uk-miscreants!
>-
>-As for raising eyebrows, the member of staff who took the summons form didn't
>-change their facial expression at all. Seen it all before, no doubt.
>
>Take no notice Mike, some people are like that. I hope
>you finally get this matter into court.

I'm not so fond of the threats of violence against the persistent (yet
quiet for a bit, and probably soon to restart..) spammer that is Mike
Corley. Yet, encouraging the fantasies of the mentally ill isn't
exactly healthy either. Do you go up to homeless mad people as say
things like: "They're coming to get you", or "Look out behind you?".

            Smid
....
Quite the contary Mike. Your recent posts have been no problem. By
explaining things rationally, and not spamming us, you have made more
friends than you know.

I hope that you sort out your problem, sincerely.
--
****
I'm Alan Packer and I move in a very mysterious way. If replying to me
....
In article <857686006snz@adams.demon.co.uk>,
Derek Tidman <Derek@adams.demon.co.uk> wrote:
>In article <5fmdc7gga1@ftel.ftel.co.uk>
>   J.J.Smith@ftel.co.uk "John J Smith" writes:
>
>I think it's good for Mike to vent his anger and frustration on
>these two newsgroups. Consider it to be part of your duty to
>the community in general.

Yep. Just not, the, I think 180 posts, one week, when his illness
got really bad. Oh yeah, and there was only three real posts,
just repeated 60 times.

>Mike does a first class job of drawing out the real personality
>of the person hiding behind a node name. The way people react
>to Mike gives it all away.

Erm, explain this rather dubious statement.

>As for you. Don't you think it's a trifle condescending to refer
>to people as mad. I know they are homeless and without internet
>access, but maybe they are just eccentric.

Congratulations. This is my first real flame for about a year.

I try to control my anger when I come across another uninformed
naive idiot on usenet, but sometimes it goes free. We've had Corley
for well over three years now, and his constant spams of various degrees
have killed a couple of usenet groups I really rather lied. uk.media,
to name but one. I gets my goat to read another useless fucker
thinking he is a harmless eccentric.

Mike is mentally ill. He is unwilling to deal with it. He seems to
think that uk.misc is some sort of forum that MI5 reads. And it
should be avenged. He's mailbombed a large quantity of people,
because they opposed his spamming.

> 1. He thinks MI5 watches him through his television
> 2. He thinks all references to mad people, refer to him
> 3. He thinks all people shouting, are shouting at him.
> 4. He's been diagnosed as mentally ill, just not a paranoid schizophrenic.
> 5. He gives not a shit about any newsgroups he abuses.
> 6. He goes through quiet periods, then _very_ nasty periods.
> 7. All evidence of this great conspiracy is laughable, to say the least.
> 8. He gives internet/usenet a bad name to the media. Including mailbombing Chris Tarrant and faxing various celebrities.

I do not condescend to him. I actually know what he does, and has done
in the past, and am frankly not too respectful of him. He can be openly
referred to as "mad" because he is. Let's check my mailbox saves:

Repost of when I thought I'd seen the last of loopy mike:

>>J.J.Smith@ftel.co.uk (John J Smith) wrote:
>>Actually, I see uk.misc as a source of occasional interesting information,
>>and I like jokes. Some people can laugh, you see.
>>
>>And as for you spams, exactly how much good have they done so far?
>
>Not much. I thought they might, but the realization has arrived that this
>particular avenue of exploration is at a dead end.
>
>WTGROMT (well that's got rid of me then!)

Have you actually visited his web page, and read the massive conspiracy that is supposed to be against him? Apparently MI5 watch him, but for no reason. They do it for a laugh. Because they can. It costs them a lot of money, but they still do it. Reality is but a memory for this man.

>Anyway I understood the UKMTC members upset Mike Corely , but
>I could be wrong.

Heaven forbid.

       Smid
....
From: burridge@osiris.win-uk.net (Paul Burridge)

In article <33207CAA.1097@sos.bangor.ac.yuk>, David Roberts (oss108@sos.bangor.ac.yuk) writes:
>Derek Tidman wrote:
>
>> Anyway I understood the UKMTC members upset Mike Corely , but
>> I could be wrong.
>
>There was a pitched battle between MC and "the artist formerly
>known as Big Ears" but that was before the UMTC by which time
>MC had seen the light and stopped spamming.

He hadn't seen the light at all. His level of spamming had got to such outrageous proportions that we had to mount a concerted attempt to get his account(s) closed. The reason for the lack of spam lately is that Mike has been furiously swotting up on Law so he can bring an action as a LIP against the BBC (all solicitors having quite rightly and honourably declined to act for him). When this course of action is exhausted without result, I confidently predict that we will once again be the innocent victims of his ire and the spamming will commence again.
....

I am being ignored 17/4/97
They won't react when they know they're being recorded.

Subject: I am being ignored
Newsgroups: uk.misc,uk.legal
Organization: Toronto Free-Net
Summary:
Keywords:

Something mildly unusual is happening. Nobody has been getting at me for the last couple of weeks. Best of all, about three weeks ago I bought a video recorder to try to get some evidence from the News etc, and despite having watched Martyn Lewis, Michael Buerk and the whole lot of them, not one of them has said anything to me in the last three weeks. And I have been listening to and recording Capital, with no ill effect. All in all, I am being comprehensively ignored.

Of course, I should have video-taped the news programmes back in 1990/91/92 (and even 93) when it was still all going on. Anthony Johnsson (casually name-drop to stick the knife in) will tell you how intelligent a person I am, yet I didn't have the good sense to record the programmes at the time, and it's a bit late now.

Today another avenue of exploration closed when my second summons against the BBC was struck out (basically through lack of evidence), and an order was made by the district judge saying that I could not sue John Birt again without the express permission of the court. She explained that this was for my own good, to save me the summons fees. Costs were not awarded though (the BBC didn't even really seek costs), and I am free to sue anyone else I take a shine to.
....
It is not that you are being ignored.... it is just that as your mental health improves, so your paranoia eases.

OR...

The dark forces are gathering strength for the final battle with you...

Seriously though, it's nice to see you back - cos as long as they are persecuting you, I can relax knowing they haven't got time to bother me!

Harry
--
Harry Adams
harry@smcat.com
http://www.smcat.com
....
From: burridge@osiris.win-uk.net (Paul Burridge)

Great news! Keep taking the tablets.
....
(posted 11/apr/1997, re Neil Long at 8.35pm Capital Radio)

Subject: Re: I am being ignored

Newsgroups: uk.misc,uk.legal
Followup-To: uk.misc,uk.legal
References: <E8HKJw.LIK.0.bloor@torfree.net>
Organization: Toronto Free-Net
Distribution:

Mike Corley (bu765@torfree.net) wrote:

[unreasonable optimism snipped]

Well, that didn't last very long, did it?

Capital Radio this evening approx 8.35pm, Neil Long's programme a few moments
after I switched to it (I am listening to it as I type this). The following
spouted from his mouth;

"want to see Jacko in town? what a gig it's going to be, that guy is amazing,
and PSYCHOTIC, but amazing on stage, 0171-4200958, on stage he's a MADMAN but
he's wonderful"

God, I am so tired of this. It's been going on for seven years. When's it going
to stop?

I have the above extract on tape. When I get around to it I will post it, and
the Hepworth snippet, as audio files on the website. Of course, all the
doubting Thomases and Smids can carry on doubting, because the mere fact that
moments after switching on the DJ starts talking about "psychotic", that's not
proof is it?

I wrote an aggrieved letter to Chris Tarrant at Capital and sent it off today,
copied to Richard Park, Group Director of Programmes. I suppose they'll just
lie as usual. Bastards, basically.
....
The solution is surely to not have a TV, video, radio or telephone in
the house, Mike. That way they can't be used to watch you.

Dave
--
dave@ llondel.demon.co.uk
Any advice above is worth what I paid for it.
....
Subject: Re: I am being ignored
Newsgroups: uk.misc,uk.legal
References: <E8HKJw.LIK.0.bloor@torfree.net> <E8HpM1.608.0.bloor@torfree.net> <860893$
Organization: Toronto Free-Net
Distribution:

"Dave {Reply address in.sig}" <noone@llondel.demon.co.uk> wrote:
>The solution is surely to not have a TV, video, radio or telephone in
>the house, Mike. That way they can't be used to watch you.

No. I tried that strategy in 1990/91 when I sold my television and stopped
listening to the radio. It didn't work because they got at me through
co-workers and eventually the general public.

The solution is to gather evidence by recording everything, and then complain

or sue if possible. I wish I'd recorded it all five or six years ago, then I
might be more successful in a legal action now.
....
Did anyone else watch the X-Files on Sky last night (Sunday 13th April) and
recognise Mike's symptons in the chap with the tattoo? It was quite
interesting to see someone responding in precisely the same way, picking up
on individual words and phrases in ordinary sentences and applying parts to
themselves as though they were intended.

Not a pleasant ending though. You take care, Mike, and keep taking the
medication. uk.misc just wouldn't be the same without you now.

Claire
--
****
* Claire Speed   [ENTX] * Network & Operations Unit, Manchester Computing *
* Dial-up, ISDN, TICTAC * C.Speed@mcc.ac.uk http://www.mcc.ac.uk/Claire/ *
****
....
>moments after switching on the DJ starts talking about "psychotic", that's not
>proof is it?

No, it isn't, but you knew that anyway.

Mike, how is it that you think that this can't be a coincidence because
it happened 'moments' after you switched on the radio? Haven't you just
told us that you haven't heard a thing for two weeks? Going two weeks
watching TV & listening to the radio without a reference to 'mad', 'crazy'
or 'loony' is quite an acheivement, especially given the trashy radio you
seem to prefer.

I've just spent a lot of the weekend trying to keep a manic depressive
under control, so that she doesn't have to go back into hospital and
lose the last few months' memories to ECT. One thing I've noticed is
that manic depressives almost seek to foster their fantasies, they
enjoy the control and the high. You seem to be the same - you refuse
to answer the points put to you that explain away what you call persecution
totally - do you have the courage of your convictions to reply to this?
Or do you enjoy the attention your illness brings you?

--
Illtud Daniel   idaniel@jesus.ox.ac.uk
-see Twin Town-   -Buy Apollo 440-
....
Mike Corley wrote:

> Something mildly unusual is happening. Nobody has been getting at me for the
> last couple of weeks.

Do please tell the *truth*. It has been longer than *2* weeks as I'm sure
you have noticed, hasn't it ?

Well I claim responsibility for the absence of persecution. When I rang
John Major's personal private secretary, not the personal political one or

any of the others in the same office, and I said you would vote for the
Conservative Party at the General Election the secretary said Johnny would
be so happy and as a sign of gratitude he rang-up the Head of MI5 and told
them to save money for tax cuts by abandoning forthwith their campaign
against you. Consequently MI5 and MI6 have been able to redeploy urgently
needed resources (i.e. manpower and telecoms interceptions) against an
international band of (*****censored*****).

On behalf of the law-abiding and decent citizens in the British islands, I
would like to sincerely thank you for your invaluable contribution to
crime fighting by your instrumental achievement in releasing badly needed
and very scarce MI5 and MI6 resources.

Many thanks,

> Best of all, about three weeks ago I bought a video recorder to try to get some
> evidence from the News etc, and despite having watched Martyn Lewis, Michael
> Buerk and the whole lot of them, not one of them has said anything to me in the
> last three weeks. And I have been listening to and recording Capital, with no ill
> effect. All in all, I am being comprehensively ignored.

Please don't forget it is National Election time and the news broadcasts
at 21:00 on BBC1 are preoccupied with British politics.

> Of course, I should have video-taped the news programmes back in 1990/91/92
> (and even 93) when it was still all going on.

Any particular date in mind ? I have a few in the library. You can also
purchase copies from the BBC on 0181-743 8000 (central switchboard).

> Anthony Johnsson (casually name-drop to stick the knife in) will tell you how intelligent
> a person I am, yet I didn't have the good sense to record the programmes at the time,
> and it's a bit late now.

Perhaps it is for the best. Now that it is all over, you can return to
Canada. Did you manage to get your Canadian citizenship ? What did your
contracts at MI5 say about you becoming Canadian ? You never did mention
the name of your MI5 liaison officer nor of any of the others.

> Today another avenue of exploration closed when my second summons against the
> BBC was struck out (basically through lack of evidence), and an order was made
> by the district judge saying that I could not sue John Birt again without the
> express permission of the court. She explained that this was for my own good,
> to save me the summons fees. Costs were not awarded though (the BBC didn't even
> really seek costs), and I am free to sue anyone else I take a shine to.

That's true. But as it is now all over there is no need to worry about
the past. MI5 said your file has been removed from the Registry and put
in a burn-bag so there is nothing left for anyone ever to find.

By the way, what was the URL of your famous Corley web site ?
....
Subject: Re: I am being ignored
Newsgroups: uk.misc,uk.legal
Followup-To: uk.misc,uk.legal
References: <E8HKJw.LIK.0.bloor@torfree.net> <E8HpM1.608.0.bloor@torfree.net> <5it60e$

Organization: Toronto Free-Net
Distribution:

Illtud Daniel (idaniel@jesus.ox.ac.uk) wrote:
: Iain L M Hotchkies <iain@hotch.demon.co.uk.spam-free.zone> wrote:
: >Illtud Daniel typed:
: >
: >> You seem to be the same - you refuse
: >> to answer the points put to you that explain away what you call persecution
: >> totally - do you have the courage of your convictions to reply to this?
: >> Or do you enjoy the attention your illness brings you?

I have to admit that it is actually mildly amusing to have newsreaders watching you, although it is tiresome after a bit. I am currently in an interesting situation, because after my lawsuits against them I think the BBC newscasters have stopped watching me entirely; I also think that ITN, in particular John Suchet, *are* still watching but they're being subtle about it (his blink pattern followed mine).

Being called nasty words is quite horrible though, and seems gratuitous; what do they gain by it, except to exercise their sadism?

: >I think we all ought to remember that schizophrenia is a
: >psychosis, and as such, unless you are American and believe
: >that *anything* can be dealt with through counselling and/or
: >psychotherapy, will not respond to this type of treatment.

: Tell me about it. My friend is now unhappily resident in Warneford
: mental health unit, or whatever they call psychiatric hospitals nowardays.

I've never been in a hospital as an in-patient, ever. I think I've been very lucky in that regard.

: Having said that, one should seek to disabuse even psychotics of their
: delusions.

The medicines haven't made any difference to my ideas. They obviously make a difference in the emotional impact and reaction.
....
>I've never been in a hospital as an in-patient, ever. I think I've been very
>lucky in that regard.

You have. They're not pleasant atmospheres, especially the secure wings, which have more in common with prisons ('airlock' doors, list of 'banned' articles, continuous observation). They have to be that way, unfortunately.

--
Illtud Daniel   idaniel@jesus.ox.ac.uk
-see Twin Town-   -Buy Apollo 440-
....

Continuing Silence 9/5/97
Admittedly I am recording every moment, but still.

Subject: The Continuing Silence
Newsgroups: uk.misc
Organization: Toronto Free-Net

The silence continues. I am enjoying listening to Radio 4 without any ill effects whatsoever. Admittedly I am recording every moment, but still. Even better, I have fished out a recording from ITN last year which at the time I was convinced had been about me, and on re-seeing it I am now convinced it is not about me at all.

But that is not to disclaim all the many "live incidents" that have happened. Everything written on my website is true. For the newcomers, its URL (as seen in the Observer and Private Eye) is

[snip]
....
Mike Corley wrote:
>
> The silence continues. I am enjoying listening to Radio 4 without any ill
> effects whatsoever.

Already the New Labour govt improves the quality of life of the populace!
--
To reply by email you must delete the trailing x from the To: field
Why not drop by my web page sometime? http://www.man.ac.uk/~zlsiida
Manchester's cheapest poker game still needs more players - drop me
a line if interested, or if you know another game that I might like.
....
From: David Roberts <oss108@sos.bangor.ac.yuk>

Mike, you're a ray of sunshine on a cold and miserable day.
Long may the silence continue.

David
--
***************==================***************
   Right that's enough junk mail.
   If you really want to e-mail me,
   remove the y from my address
....
>better, I have fished out a recording from ITN last year which at the time I
>was convinced had been about me, and on re-seeing it I am now convinced it is
>not about me at all.

You've cheered me up with this news, Mike. Seriously. The last sentence suggests that your health is improving, and you are beginning to become pragmatic, in some way...

Take a deep breath, and look to the future. I wish you well.
         Smid

Victor Lewis-Smith 9/5/97
Is he writing about me? His webmaster says he isn't.

Victor Lewis-Smith has broken the silence in his TV review column "Goon and best forgotten" in the Evening Standard (on Thursday 8/May). He said, "If I sound paranoid, that's probably because I once worked there. Eventually, I had to leave because they were all trying to kill me but, for sheer pathological hatred of the Corporation, I couldn't hold a candle to Spike Milligan".

I take this to be about me, because recently I wrote to both the BBC and Capital Radio, saying "I believe the current purpose of the harassment is to force me to kill myself to prevent the harassers, yourselves included, from being brought to justice, and last year there were several incidents of people shouting 'suicide' at me, which would appear to corroborate that view." I think VLS's words about the BBC "all trying to kill me" shows he has seen or heard of what I sent to the BBC or Capital.

Nasty eh? I believe that VLS or his mates read this newsgroup. I wonder how he would explain his article?
....
Date: Fri, 9 May 1997 23:11:40 +0000 (GMT)
From: Webmaster for Victor <vls@bbcradio.demon.co.uk>
To: Mike Corley <bu765@freenet.toronto.on.ca>
Subject: Re: paranoia

Dear Mike,

Victor's not writing about you.

Yours,

John Hayward-Warburton
Victor's Webmaster
....
For some reason, I don't quite believe you. It's just too close a match.
....
In article <E9xG0x.Gtr.0.bloor@torfree.net>,
Mike Corley <bu765@torfree.net> wrote:
>Victor Lewis-Smith has broken the silence in his TV review column "Goon and
>best forgotten" in the Evening Standard (on Thursday 8/May). He said, "If I
>sound paranoid, that's probably because I once worked there. Eventually, I had
>to leave because they were all trying to kill me but, for sheer pathological
>hatred of the Corporation, I couldn't hold a candle to Spike Milligan".

Erm, Mike, I'm a bit of a fan of Victor Lewis-Smith, ever since his days of "BuyGones". I must admit, he often likes to play the flawed lunatic evil nasty person. He's been doing it for years, with prank calls, far before your illness. Its his act. He wouldn't be VLS without it.

He doesn't like the "Goons" either. It isn't about you.

>I take this to be about me, because recently I wrote to both the BBC and
>Capital Radio, saying "I believe the current purpose of the harassment is to
>force me to kill myself to prevent the harassers, yourselves included, from
>being brought to justice, and last year there were several incidents of people

>shouting 'suicide' at me, which would appear to corroborate that view." I think
>VLS's words about the BBC "all trying to kill me" shows he has seen or heard of
>what I sent to the BBC or Capital.

I don't think Victor Lewis-Smith has worked for the BBC (or Capital) for
several years (1994 was the last time...), so the connection, is paranoia
here.

Personally, I believe VLS as a person of reasonable integrity, who wouldn't
give a fuck about you...

>Nasty eh? I believe that VLS or his mates read this newsgroup. I wonder how he
>would explain his article?

Keep up the medication, not as many people read this newsgroup as you think,
even though you are now incorporating that into your illness.

Victor? Are you there?

    Smid
....

David Hepworth (2) 16/5/97
It's an "Absolute Embarrassment" of prizes this evening.

Subject: David Hepworth (GLR) is taking the piss
Newsgroups: uk.misc
Organization: Toronto Free-Net
Summary:
Keywords:

>Last night (21/Feb/97), I was listening to BBC GLR. You have to understand that
>I was listening by stealth. Back in 1990 I used to have Capital blaring out of

Not much changes. Today I was listening again to David Hepworth's show on GLR, having more or less waded in on it by accident. Here is the exchange;

David: "we have executive drivetime, we have Brian in charge of the prize cupboard. Brian it's not a bad prize cupboard this week is it?"

Brian: "no David it's an absolute (EMPHASIS) embarrassment (END-EMPHASIS) of prizes this evening" (laughter)

David: "what have we got?"

Brian: "well in my left hand alone we've got that .... Gary Clale, I don't know if you remember him obviously still alive and kicking...."

David: "Rock and roll spelling test is your first opportunity to take advantage of this embarrassment of prizes"

What do I read into this exchange? The laughter after the word "embarrassment" shows they're aware of the last complaint I made on usenet (copied by snail-mail to them). The "left hand" business is I think a coded way of calling me a w***er (the term would be better applied to Brian and David).

I have a tape of this exchange, and will eventually get around to posting it on the website.
....
Subject: Re: David Hepworth (GLR) is taking the piss
Newsgroups: uk.misc
References: <E9xMvw.4H2.0.bloor@torfree.net>
Organization: Toronto Free-Net
Distribution: uk

I don't understand. Why has nobody replied to this post? You keep on asking for evidence, then I present you with something that looks very much like evidence, and everybody just ignores it. OK I haven't posted the actual sound extract, and it still isn't proof.

Perhaps everybody just finds it all too boring and dull. Should I start spamming again from one of those nice anonymous remailers to wake everyone up? Now there's a thought.
....
Mike Corley <bu765@torfree.net> wrote:
>I don't understand. Why has nobody replied to this post?

Cos you don't reply to our points - you're ignoring us, why shouldn't we ignore you?

>You keep on asking for evidence, then I present you with something
>that looks very much like evidence,

No you don't, you post something which could _never_, _ever_ be construed as referring to yourself. Can't you see it? No, of course you can't, you've an illness.

>Perhaps everybody just finds it all too boring and dull. Should I start
>spamming again from one of those nice anonymous remailers to wake everyone up?
>Now there's a thought.

And I see you've started. Give it a rest, Mike, unless you're prepared to enter into proper discussion.

--
Illtud Daniel   idaniel@jesus.ox.ac.uk
-see Twin Town-   -Buy Apollo 440-

....

>Mike Corley <bu765@torfree.net> wrote:
>>I don't understand. Why has nobody replied to this post?

Never read it. Repost?

        Smid

....
In article <5lhg3i$ete@news.ox.ac.uk>,
Illtud Daniel <idaniel@jesus.ox.ac.uk> wrote:
>[reposted]
>
>>Brian: "no David it's an absolute (EMPHASIS) embarrassment (END-EMPHASIS) of
>>prizes this evening" (laughter)

Uh-Uh. He's on for a bad attack, if he's singling out words which are apparently attacking him. He previously restricted himself to just dialog about the mentally ill.

TAKE YOUR MEDICATION MIKE.

        Smid

....

Evidence

Overview

In the video section of this part of the website, we have MPEG-4 clips of Jon Snow of ITN in action, also interviews with Ken Clarke and John Major of the ousted Tory regime. These are embedded in the page using QuickTime. While each audio/video clip is coded to automatically download the QuickTime player, you may find it helpful to download QuickTime from Apple's website before you start viewing the media files, if you do not have it installed already. There is also video of an MI5 agent masturbating publicly in Winter Park, Florida in September 2000, which is very helpful in explaining the obsessive motivation of homosexual British Intelligence operatives in pursuing me all over the globe.

Note that each item is awarded a rating of the confidence I feel that it is directed at me, expressed as a percentage. Items with 50% or more are probably about me; 100% indicates a "dead cert".

In audio we have MP3 files of harassment at work in Canada in late 1996, also GLR's David Hepworth not even trying to pretend that he isn't getting at me, and a snippet of Capital. There is also a recording of MI5 trying to kill me in Orlando, Florida in 2001. The newspapers section contains an article by Bernard Levin on his encounter with a madman who "bursts into tears, and swears it is all true - and it is".

I have added several recordings of abuse "in public". By Sept/1998 I had seven minidiscs of such recordings, unfortunately containing mostly very nasty sexual slanders which I will not be publishing on this website. The recordings were made on a Sony Minidisc Walkman MZ-R30, which I purchased in Canada in July/1997, with ECM-T140 microphone. After both the MZ-R30 and the microphone reached the end of their lives, in June/2001 I purchased as replacement an MZ-R900 walkman with ECM-T145 mono microphone. As of 2006 I have kept up to date with the latest Sony minidisc technology and microphones.

Share and Enjoy! I hope you enjoy partaking in my "delusions" which have been recorded with high fidelity digital equipment and presented for your listening pleasure. (Unless you are a richly compensated and medically- or legally-"correct" doctor or lawyer, you will have understood that the last sentence contained irony.)

In 2006 I added a further area to Evidence to describe the MindControl Torture which MI5 had inflicted on me, beginning August 2005, using American technology and the same US law enforcement personnel who had tried to kill me in November 2001. I have been keeping a detailed record of what they told me, and their methods and activities.

Dimbleby / John Major, April 1997

Certainty level: 90%

Dimbleby interviews John Major during the election campaign. Here is the exchange, regarding Neil Hamilton, the "sleazy" Tory candidate;

```
Dimbleby: "It's a direct quotation from what he said to Sir Gordon Downey
and what he said to his local newspaper, the Knutsford Guardian".
Major: "Well, heaven forfend that I should doubt what the Knutsford
Guardian actually said"
Dimbleby: "Well I should hope so"
Major: "Absolutely, it would be quite unforgivable to doubt the Knutsford
Guardian".
```

What I find in this segment is an assonance between "Knutsford" and "Nut" or "Nuts". I think Dimbleby deliberately invents the play on words, and says it clearly enough for Major to pick it up and repeat it. You can gauge Dimbleby's intent from his facial expression of false honesty when he uses the words "Knutsford Guardian"; and Major's reaction follows from his recognition of Dimbleby's intent; Major smiles and says it would be "unforgivable to doubt the Knutsford Guardian". These are much clearer on the original video than on this Quicktime clip.

Channel Four TV News - 12/Feb/1999

Certainty level: 100%

I am positively, utterly, completely sure this item is about me. It's a bit subtle so the objective reader might not understand my certainty. Here is what happened. I was watching Channel Four News with Jon Snow, on the day Clinton "got off" (as it were) in the Monica-gate scandal. Snow said;

```
"[and we're anticipating that the President himself will make his] first
comments after the trial in which he has now been cleared at around half-
past seven. So we'll have more on the historic judgment, we'll also be
considering [starts smiling] the winners and losers in this whole sorry
saga. Now further doubts have been...."
```

When Snow said "half-past seven", I looked at the clock on the mantelpiece above the TV. Snow saw my glance, and in reaction to my glance at the clock, smiled. I think he was smiling at what he perceived as my self-importance.

Usually when newscasters or radio presenters laugh at me, there is an excuse for their laughter; usually they manage to find some reason for my being "funny"; their amusement is blamed on me; it is my "fault" they are laughing. And so it was with this instance; Jon Snow thought it was funny that I should be so interested in seeing Clinton, and his half-smile while reading the words "winners and losers" expresses that.

I wrote to Snow at ITN shortly after this broadcast to ask him about his behaviour; of course, he didn't reply.

Nicholas Witchell - 10/April/1999

Certainty level: 100%

This clip is of Nicholas Witchell reading the BBC2 evening news at 7pm on Saturday 10 April 1999. You have to understand that the psychopaths of the Security Service consider their abuse of me to be "so funny"; and central to their persecution of me is their inducement of their "bought journalists" like the BBC's Nicholas Witchell to laugh at me on television.

So in this clip we see Witchell smirking and grinning while he reads the news. Only part of the news broadcast is shown in the clip; preceding it, Witchell's upper lip quivers in mirth for several minutes, until his entire mouth twists into the uncontrollable smile shown in this clip, through the excuse of a weak non-joke about sports fixtures.

Jealous Gay British Agents Masturbating Outside Window

Certainty level: 100%

This video clip portrays a quite certain case of unpleasant MI5 harassment; because of context, surrounding events, not just this one happening. It's the first time an MI5 agent has been caught on video, and, presumably to their chagrin, their paid agent is either engaging in an onanistic practice, or, more probably, pretending to do so, in order to carry out an act of harassment.

The background is as follows. In late June 2000 I had posted the following message to Usenet, about MI5's making obscene noises at me on several recent occasions;

```
>From: bu765@torfree.net (Mike Corley)
>Subject: relax, don't do it (mi5 again)
>Date: 22 Jun 2000 00:00:00 GMT
>
>you will recall that a couple of weeks ago I was supposing what MI5 were
>doing with their 'single'handed' posting antics at 2am
>
>exciting stuff
>
>so about a week ago someone rings me up at home.... 'is that Emmanuel
>Goldstein?' then he phones back the following day and goes 'huaaaagh' on
>the phone before dropping the handset in excitement
>
>and a day or two later, just coming out of our house to put something in
>the rubbish bin, a pair of blokes over the other side of the road, again
>start making orgasmic noises
>
>I'm not paranoid enough to record minidisc when I pop out for a few
>seconds...... but perhaps I should be
```

The video clip, which was captured on 1/September/2000, is the culmination of that thread of harassment. You have to understand that MI5's abuse is in threads; they choose a topic, and then continue with it for months and years. Sometimes they drop a topic, usually to be replaced by a worse one, and you never hear of it again.

If the person in the video clip were not an MI5 agent, then he would deserve privacy, despite carrying out a real or feigned act in a public place. But I am 100% sure, because of context, that this man was one of their operatives, which removes any consideration of privacy from his act, which was carried out as an act of sexual harassment and power. He is facing away and cannot be clearly identified from this clip. I've never seen this man before or since, but that is true of most other such incidents.

I found it very worrying that British Intelligence should have sent a man to masturbate outside my window in 2000. My initial reaction was one of disgust, with a rapid realisation that here was an opportunity to catch one of them in the act, so I grabbed my Sony videocamera and began filming. But when men masturbate while thinking of another man, it is difficult to escape the conclusion that the MI5 agents are aggressive homosexuals and were carrying out an aggressively gay activity. They have frequently expressed their homosexuality in other ways, particularly over the mindcontrol which occurred from August 2005 onwards where the "Obscene English Pig" person is obviously a violent homosexual as evidenced by his constant forced sexual abuse. Truly there is something very wrong with the British Security Service, that instead of defending the national security which is supposed to be their job, they engage in what may be accurately described as homosexual fantasising about other men, and gay stalking and gay rape over the mindcontrol. Homosexuality is a uniquely English vice, because other countries do not practice it as an instrument of power to the same extent; for example, the Americans on the mindcontrol gave me very little sexual abuse, whereas that was the specialty of the English agents.

In 2006 I complained to Orange County Sheriff's Office about the Masturbating MI5 Agent, because the incident had occurred within their jurisdiction. An account of my complaint and their response can be seen by following this link.

Blair Press Conference - 13/January/2003

Certainty level: 50%

In January 2003 I was watching a number 10 Press Conference on the American CSPAN TV channel, when I heard Blair say the following;

```
This discussion began against the background of sanctions eroding, of us
being unable to be sure that we really were preventing Saddam acquiring
these weapons and of intelligence to the British Security Services. Now
people can have their own view of the British intelligence services but I
happen to believe they do a good job and I don't think they would be
advising me this if they weren't doing it honestly and properly.
```

The quote was later obtained from the following webpage; http://www.number-10.gov.uk/output/Page3005.asp

What the above statement appears to be is an affirmation of Blair's belief that British Intelligence carries out its job as it should. But if you look beyond the veneer, and at the subtext, the meaning is the opposite. The phrase "Now people can have their own view of the British intelligence services" subtly expresses doubt which the speaker claims to imply will be dismissed in what follows; but in the original broadcast Blair has been answering questions from his friend Jon Snow of C4news, who as readers will know is a frequent watcher of events inside my home, while at the same time claiming to be cynical of Security Services; and my guess is that it is Snow's claimed cynicism of MI5 that Blair is referring to.

Blair goes on to say "I happen to believe they do a good job and I don't think they would be advising me this if they weren't doing it honestly and properly." The meaning is in the subtext; "happen to believe they do a good job" immediately followed by the negation "I don't"; and "they weren't doing it honestly and properly". This is about as near as a current Prime Minister can get to making this type of statement. Again the question is whether Blair's disbelief in the intelligence services is in general, or particular to my case; and because he was talking during the press conference to Jon Snow, who looks into my home while he reads the news, there may be some part of the latter. This is perhaps a tenuous connection to make, hence its mere evens probability of relevance.

Blair's speech to Labour Conference - 13/March/2004

Certainty level: 50%

British PM Tony Blair made a speech to Labour Party Conference in Manchester on Saturday 13 March 2004. It was mentioned in an American news website, which quoted part of it. During the speech he said;

```
and it is terrorism designed to strike at the very heart of our way of
life, our democracy our freedom and the rule of law. We will not defeat it
by hoping it will leave us alone or by hiding away. We must be prepared
for them to strike whenever and however they can.
```

The relevant words in his speech are "hoping it will leave us alone or by hiding away". I had for some time been going round the house saying "why can't they just leave me alone", and as people know, I had for some years been attempting to hide away in north America, without much luck, since MI5 invariably found me and resumed their usual peculiar activities. I don't watch TV for obvious reasons, and I only saw this excerpt because it was quoted on the US news site.

It's an evens bet that the quoted phrase is relevant. I'd guess that Blair would not be so rash as to himself have created the deliberate reference in his speech, and his facial expression discloses nothing but earnestness - so whoever his speechwriter was, may have made the reference without informing him of its true meaning. Even so, it's of uncertain relevance, hence its mere 50% rating.

However if my supposition is accurate, then the consequences for Blair's office are horrendous. The conference speech was on March 13, two days after the Madrid train bombings had killed 200 people. In creating a secretly amusing "troll", Blair's speechwriter would be urinating on the memories of hundreds of dead Spaniards. Security Service's usual "neither confirm nor deny (but covertly giggle)" policy would be incorrect for such a purpose.

Postscript to Blair

The above two items may be tenuous, but what happened after they were published is not. This webpage was created in July/2004 and soon after Blair came on the radio news sounding very annoyed. He made remarks apparently about Eurosceptics, where the subtext was clearly about my case. Blair was clearly trying to decide whether to use the word 'lunacy' and instead settled for 'extreme foolishness'. He didn't disclose anything as to the accuracy of the first two items on this page, but was obviously aware of them. Unfortunately I do not have a recording of his remarks.

Life is so hard

Certainty level: 100%

This relates to harassment at my workplace in Canada. Yes, "they" had their claws into my employers in North America, it doesn't just happen in England, it happens here as well.

During the second half of 1996, at work, I was sitting near a co-worker whom we shall call Mark Lee (we can, because that's his name). This guy occasionally came out with words and phrases that made me think that "they" had got to him and were supplying him with information about my home life (not social life please note, because of course I don't actually have a social life here).

During November 1996 I tried to catch him in the act of saying something "meaningful", a difficult exercise because as soon as he saw a tape recorder, he shut up completely, except for times when he knew he would be out of range of the walkman. (Note that the quality of this recording is not very good; I was just using a four-year-old tape walkman with a cheap microphone, quite low-tech).

During the evening of 12 November 1996, at home in my apartment (flat to you UK-ers), I said "life is so hard, and then you die". A nihilistic, negative thing to say, but quite distinctive. The following day, 13 November, Mark said loudly, "life is so hard eh, and then you die" followed by loud laughter.

In my book the precise repetition of the words makes this incident a 100% certainty. You, the reader, may differ, but then living in a free country allows each of us to have our own opinions, doesn't it?

GLR-David Hepworth (21/Feb/1997)

Certainty level: 80%

I was listening to BBC Greater London Radio (GLR) by stealth, ie. on my walkman with headphones, with the sound turned right down, to prevent anyone from hearing what I was listening to. Yet somehow "they" are still able to tell what station I am listening to on the walkman. After half an hour or so listening to GLR, DJ David Hepworth came out with this;

```
"I assume Brian, do we have an embarrassment of prizes in there, we do,
don't we, absolute obscene amounts of prizes, there will no doubt be a
riot at the back door, and that's A-level coming up after this"
```

The key phrases in what he said are, "EMBARRASSMENT of prizes", and what he himself emphasised verbally, "ABSOLUTE OBSCENE amount of prizes". It is my belief (based on content and tone of voice) that when he spoke these phrases he knew I was listening, and that the phrases refer directly to my situation. The "EMBARRASSMENT" is the embarrassment he and other media people would feel at having their wrongdoing exposed; the "ABSOLUTE OBSCENE" (which he verbally emphasised) described the disgusting sexual abuse which the harassers have been throwing at me.

Of course, I can't prove that this is what he meant, although this has happened enough times that it's hard not to recognise it when you see it. I sent David Hepworth a copy of this explanation, with the results listed in a subsequent item (David Hepworth 9/May/1997).

GLR-David Hepworth (9/May/1997)

Certainty level: 100%

This time I deliberately listened to Hepworth with the sound turned up on the radio, to try to get a reaction. Sure enough, he and his cronies reacted;

David: "we have executive drivetime, and we have Brian in charge of the prize cupboard. Brian it's not a bad prize cupboard this week is it?"

Brian: "no David in fact it's an absolute (EMPHASIS) embarrassment (END-EMPHASIS) of prizes this evening" (laughter)

David: "what have we got?"

Brian: "well in my left hand alone we've got that .... Gary Clale, I don't know if you remember him obviously still alive and kicking.... and that's just in my left hand"

David: "So it's certainly worth competing. Rock and roll spelling test is your first opportunity to take advantage of this embarrassment of prizes"

What I "read into" this item should again be quite obvious. Remember, I sent off a letter of complaint to Hepworth after his spying activity during the previous show. Here the emphasis on "absolute embarrassment" of prizes shows he knows this is a "key" phrase.

It might be interesting to try to talk to DJs like Hepworth and ask them what they get out of abusing their listeners. But if you challenge them directly, they show their true colour (yellow) by either not answering the challenge, or by denying that harassment has taken place.

Foxy's Showtime on Capital FM 25/11/98 7.35pm

Certainty level: 100%

This one, I can say with absolute certainty, is about me. It was recorded on my Sony Recording Walkman on the evening of Wednesday 25 November 1998. It doesn't mention me by name, so the objective observer might have trouble understanding why I'm so sure it's about me. I'm sure, because the harassment had restarted over the period when this piece was broadcast, and what Capital transmitted would have been in context with events at the time. (Sorry if that explanation is somewhat opaque, but I don't really want to embarrass myself by giving an explanation in detail, and an intelligent reader should be able to work it out for him/her self.)

This isn't the first time Capital have "got at" me; they were doing so right at the very beginning in summer 1990, when they said, "if he listens to Capital then he can't be all bad"; and Tarrant made remarks about me in his breakfast show in spring 1994, when he said, "you know this bloke? he says we're trying to kill him. We should be done for attempted manslaughter."

Unfortunately I didn't record those previous, much more conclusive instances of harassment by Capital DJs, and Capital Radio tells me they only keep recordings for three months. But lately I've been recording everything, and here is one product of that recording.

Neil Fox was introducing some petite Swedish songstress, sounded like Amelia, when he said something about her petite-ness ;

```
"she's a big big girl, actually she's really about tiny, she's this big,
would you say what less than....."
```

```
then one of his studio staff shouted, "six inches"
```

```
then Fox laughed and said, "less than a meter tall, definitely"
```

What I think the "six inches" referred to should be obvious. I think it's sexual abuse directed at me.

Also there were a lot of words like "crazy", "mad" etc on this programme, which reinforced my belief that this was on purpose directed at myself.

I think Fox may be something of an unwilling participant in this abuse, he doesn't want to be an abuser but the persecutors are using his show and his staff to get at me. This is not the first time this sort of thing has happened from his show; and my guess is that it won't be the last

Virgin Radio-Johnny Boy (21/August/1998)

Certainty level: 60%

On Saturday 15 August 1998 I attended a gathering of contributors to newsgroup uk.misc at London's Victoria railway station. Also present was Simon G, who had previously given this description of what he would be wearing;

```
At 06:36 AM 13/8/98 GMT, Simon wrote:
>further clarification to aid recognition, i'll be wearing
>a t shirt, a brown suede waistcoat, a brown suede miniskirt,
>& a pair of patchwork leggings (& may have a widebrimmed straw
>hat, too).
```

It is my belief that my persecutors, who monitor my home telephone line (and consequently read all modem communications including email), were aware of this meeting, and may even have observed the "meat" taking place.

Following the "meat" it seemed to me that one or two attempts were made by my persecutors to portray me as "gay", on the basis of Simon's suede miniskirt, which in their inventiveness my persecutors attributed to me, not Simon. (Just for the record, Simon is hetero, and has agreed to the above email extract being published.) The following item from Johnny Boy's Wheels of Steel (between 7pm-11pm, Friday 21/8/98) is one such attempt.

```
(conversation) (J=Johnny-Boy, H=Hipster)

J: Texas of course part of V98 this weekend enjoy it if you're going. Keep
your eyes out on Sunday in Chelmsford for Hipster, because he's going to
be there. What are you going to be wearing?

H: I'll be wearing my, er, my suede shorts.
(sycophantic laughter)

J: and believe me he ain't joking, he ain't joking. OK coming next at
Virgin on the Wheels of Steel...
```

Why do I think Hipster's "suede shorts" refers to Simon's mini-skirt? Because "suede" in both cases (obvious!); because "suede shorts" indicates "gay" which they were trying to pin on me; because "shorts" = something short, such as a "mini"-skirt; and because the two DJs both laughed as soon as Hipster said "suede shorts", they knew what the joke was, they knew that they were meant (and probably paid) to find it funny.

Virgin Radio-Johnny Boy (19/June/1999)

Certainty level: 30%

I'm not quite sure about this one, so I've given it a one in three chance of being about me. First the background.... from mid-March 1999 for some three or four months, every weekend, I bombarded Westminster MPs with faxes about the terrible, all-encompassing MI5 Persecution. (Jesting aside, it really is terrible and all-encompassing, in the UK anyway.) Of course each week some MPs replied; but in June 1999, after I'd been at it some three months, I started getting "covert" feedback from Virgin Radio.

The first feedback I got was from Danny Baker, on Sunday 13th June. That weekend I was sending an article which contained biting criticism of the police inaction in this case. Danny Baker on his Virgin radio show started an angry rant that "he knows it's rubbish", ie. he was rubbishing what I'd said in that weekend's faxed article. Unfortunately I wasn't recording this programme.

The next possible Virgin-Radio feedback was a week later on 19th June 1999. This is contained in the audio file above, in which Johnny Boy on his "Wheels of Steel" programme says;

"and if you would like to put a triple play together, ahhh.... because quite frankly Hipster and me are running out of ideas...."

He goes on to counter Hipster's "how dare you" with a protestation that he is "only joking".

What I reckon is that my article faxed to MPs that weekend was forwarded by one of the recipients to Virgin Radio. My article had included the words;

"I am beginning to run out of both new topics and energy to write these articles."

So what I reckon is that Johnny Boy read the article.... and rephrased the above line "run out of ... new topics" to "running out of ideas". I recognise that this is a pretty tenuous inference to make.... but do listen to the audio file, from the "ahhh...." pause in JB's speech you can guess he is about to say something "risky" and at someone's expense. Anyway, I listen to the Wheels of Steel regularly and will continue to do so, recording it as I always do - so any future funny remarks will get immortalised on these pages!

POSK Cafe - 2/Feb/1998
Here are two independent segments, both of which occurred in London on the same day, the first at a Polish cafe, the second on the Tube.

Segment 07:14

Certainty level: 100%

POSK is the Polish Social-Cultural Centre in Hammersmith, London. It has quite a nice cafe which does pierogi, golabki etc. I went there with my mother early in 1998. Seated at the window table were three Polish men talking amongst themselves. One of them let rip with a sexual obscenity which was clearly directed at me (it's the same one that's been heard again and again since about November 1995), and which was recorded on my minidisc walkman. I have not included it in the above excerpt, which shows the reaction of another of the trio to the first man's swearing - namely, "jestes swinia jednak" which in English is "nevertheless you're a swine".

Segment 57:27

Certainty level: 20%

Somewhere on the London Underground. "Psycho" (I think - a little unclear).

BA984 LHR->TXL 13/June/1998

Certainty level: 100%

In June 1998 I travelled on the above British Airways flight to Berlin with my mother, to visit her family. There were two women in seats 30D/E, about 4/5 rows behind us. It was quite obvious from the torrent of abuse during these flight that these women had been instructed to harass me and attempt to obtain a reaction.

I did manage to record much of the flight, but unfortunately much of the recording is unclear because of high background noise on the aircraft. The following three excerpts from the recording are the best I can do.

The segment at position 11:34 minutes on my recording contains a fairly quiet word "paranoid", followed immediately by a much louder "yeah, he's paranoid, yeah". During the flight the abuse was not sexual, as it so often is elsewhere, but attacking my mental health.

"Nutter", between the 2 and 3 second marks of the recording.

A male voice saying "nutter", between the 0.5-1.5 second marks.

One of the women in seats 30D/E said "paranoid" very clearly towards the end of the flight, but unfortunately I had run out of minidisc space and stopped recording by then. There is absolutely no doubt in my mind that these women were directed to harass me. This harassment happens without fail on British Airways flights; I've been on something like three or four BA flights in the last 5 years and it's happened each time. Presumably this is because of international law which says incidents on aircraft during flight are actionable in the airline's country of origin - so my persecutors want a reaction from me, and they want to see me "done" in the UK where they can influence the justice system.

These incidents never happen on foreign-domiciled carriers.

Battersea Library 29/3/99

Certainty level: 60%

This one is quite dull. During the month of March 1999, MI5 made another determined attempt to "get" me, substantially through radio programmes, through Jon Snow on Channel Four News, and through abuse in public, of which this is one example.

Recorded on my minidisc-walkman on Monday 29 March 1999, this audio file consists of two girls talking. One says to the other, "he's got something wrong with him." The usual words. How many millions a year do the Security Service waste on this? But they've denied it - how silly of me to forget. And they're not liars either, are they?

Royal Festival Hall 15/4/99

Certainty level: 100%

Another "day in the life of", this one. January and February were quiet; in March it all started again; by the middle of April the resurgence of abuse had been going on for over a month. And this, with 100% certainty, is one manifestation of the abuse.

On Thursday 15 April 1999, 1pm lunchtime, I was at the booking office at the Royal Festival Hall near Waterloo Station in London, buying a ticket for a friend. A woman was at the counter next to me. She said;

```
"it would kill it, you know, it would just be overkill...
... they can't stop can they"
```

It was obvious to everyone, the ticket agents included, that her comments were directed at me, and that "they" (ie. MI5) were "killing" me.

I've heard similar things said at various other times, but rarely have their intentions been expressed as clearly as this. The woman also expressed the obsessive nature of MI5's preoccupation with me, by saying, "they can't stop can they".

Balham - LT bus (8/July/1999)

Certainty level: 90%

I am very sure about this one. I got back from holidays on Wednesday. There were two incidents, both on the tube, on the way back from the airport. There was a further incident the following day, Thursday, on the bus (the 155 I think) in Balham, where two girls started spouting abuse about "crazy", etc. Naturally I had my minidisc with me and was able to record their words.

The cynical reader might think my demeanour or behaviour had given rise to the taunts of "crazy" recorded above. But I assure you my behaviour on the bus would not have made anyone think I was ill; and the taunts the previous day were the same sexual words as previously; so I'm quite sure that these incidents are either deliberately staged, or indicative of an overall high level of awareness among the London public, particularly in the part of London where I live.

Clapham South (17/Feb/2000)

Certainty level: 100%

In February 2000, MI5's hate campaign against me was in full swing. They sent people into the road where I live in south London, to swear at me and abuse me as I was leaving or returning home. One such instance is recorded on the above audio file.

On Thursday 17 February 2000, I had just left my home, en route for Croydon, when two youths approached, going in the other direction. One of them said with a smile on his face something which I didn't recognize, and still don't understand despite it being on this audio clip. His demeanour made it clear his statement was directed at me. I coughed, and in response to that, he continued his insult, calling me a "wanker", which is very clearly recorded on this audio clip.

Two days later, in the very early morning of Sunday 20 February 2000, MI5 inflicted another insult against me just outside my house, when, returning from Croydon, two youths approached (MI5 agents always go in packs of at least two - they're too cowardly to go anywhere on their own) and one of them said quietly and bitterly to the other that "he's shitty, very shitty".

It is still comparatively rare for MI5 to send people to my house, or to my road, to harass me. Usually they know where I'm going to, since they have bugs on my phone and in each room of my house; and they send people to that location, or on the train or tube getting there.

Clapham Junction (6/May/2000)

Certainty level: 60%

On Saturday 6 May 2000, I was in Clapham Junction, shopping and visiting the library. At precisely 12:29pm, the above audio clip was recorded, in front of Arding and Hobbs department store. One girl was saying to her friend,

```
"He's a homosexual, they can say whatever they want."
```

There are several reasons why I think this comment might be about me. Firstly, temporal proximity to other such incidents. The persecution had restarted about two to three days before this clip was recorded. Cause of restart unknown. Personally I think it's because I was going on holiday to France the following Monday - MI5 do like to take holidays abroad at the taxpayer's expense, and inventing reasons to resurrect their hate campaign just before I go on holiday is something they've done before.

Secondly, although I am not gay, they have used such references against me before. At Oxford Computer Group in 1994, manager Steve Mitchell simultaneously abused me and another employee but saying we were "of a similar bent". Such insults show latent or quite overt homosexuality on the part of the abuser.

Thirdly, the sort of people who abuse on the basis of mental illness are the same people who abuse others on the basis of sexuality, race, religion, etc. If they can abuse a disabled man, then they will surely do so based on the other criteria mentioned.

There is still some room for doubt, though, which is why I have assigned this recording a certainty level of only slightly above evens. But "they can say whatever they want" is what gives the game away; they just choose a differentiating feature on which to base their abuse; and if one such feature gets too boring ("we've called him a nutter for the last ten years so now we'll call him something else") then they invent a different lie to throw at me.

Balham High Road (3/Nov/2000)

Certainty level: 60%

On 3 November 2000, I had just got off the bus in Balham High Road, when I heard a group of schoolgirls shouting and laughing. One of them yelled;

```
"He's an idiot you know."
```

You can hear this on the above clip; it is followed by laughter. I am not quite sure this is about me, which is why I have only given it a two in three probability. I have been attacked many times with the word "idiot", which seems to be a favourite with intellectual lightweights who want to bring down bigger game. (Back in 1992 I was so worried by the attacks on my intelligence that I took the test and joined Mensa...... does that make me a *clever* idiot? Never mind.)

Crescent Grove, Clapham Common (2/Dec/2000)

Certainty level: 100%

This is one of those clips where I am absolutely, 100% certain it's inflicted by MI5 on me, because of background, context. On Saturday 2 December 2000, I was walking from my home to a pub on Clapham Common, and on the way was in proximity to a group of three English youths who were walking the other way. They turned from the main road into a private estate called Crescent Grove. Here is what they said;

```
(first youth) "He masturbates!"
(his mate responds) "Yeah, he masturbates!"
(and again) "Thief!"
```

There is a lot of context associated with this incident, which I will now relate.

Firstly, the verbal sexual abuse is a popular one with MI5, and as a statement about me is currently mostly in their imaginations. The accusation has to be seen relative to MI5's persecutory actions in late November and early December 2000, and in fact for some months leading up to this. Their relevant activities in June 2000 are documented in a message in this evidence item; following from that, they sent someone to simulate an act in front of my window, which was captured on film.

It is the publication of the video of their agent performing the act on himself which caused MI5 to restart this thread of harassment in the first few days of December 2000. But there are some subtleties; I uploaded the digitised video to this website on 26/November/2000; but I did not announce its existence on the newsgroups until Sunday 3/December/2000. These youths' slur was made the previous day, on Saturday 2/Dec. That tells us quite a lot. According to my website logs, there were no accesses to the video file before Sunday 3/Dec. So why did MI5 restart this particular thread of abuse, before their agent's activities were published on the newsgroup? The conclusion we reach is that they were watching my internet connection, either decoding the telephone line, or at the ISP; and/or they may be able to physically see what is on my notebook computer's screen, from RF transmissions from its VGA circuitry. I do not know whether the latter is technically feasible, but the former certainly is, and I have known for years that MI5 bugs my internet activities and phone calls. It is from their observation of my internet connection that they were able to tell, without accessing the video file over the net, that it was of their agent in a compromising position; and it was from that observation that their shouted slur on 2/Dec emanates.

The second accusation, "Thief!", is even more interesting. It relates to occurrences from June of 2000, some six months before these youths threw the word at me. It shows just how wide in reach geographically and temporally the MI5 persecution is; they react to something which happened half a year previously.

In the first half of 2000, MI5 made a determined assault on my friendships. In one particular case, that of Andrzej C. whom I had known for virtually all my life, they partly succeeded. This person made pointed references to me which made it clear he knew what was happening; at one point he started asking "do you know anything about the FBI and the CIA". In June 2000, we went to see a film in the West End. I paid for both of us, and then asked him to return what I had paid for his ticket, some £7.50. He was reluctant to do so. Eventually he returned £5, settling for the lesser gain of £2.50. He and most of his family are on social security benefits, so Andrzej's habit of enriching himself for a few pounds at his friends' expense should perhaps be seen in that context.

I did not call him a thief to his face, but I may have spoken the word while I was at home, either conscious or in my sleep. MI5 have very tight control over everything I do and say in my home through their bugs; if I say anything against someone in "their" camp, they turn round the accusation against me. So, from the fact that A. tried to garner a few pounds at my expense, MI5 create the accusation, six months later..... "thief!".

MI5 Deathsquad in Florida (17/Nov/2001)

Certainty level: 100%

MI5 conspired to kill me in Florida on 17/November/2001, the actual attempt being carried out by a group of men who shouted outside the apartment building where I was living. Unusually their attempt was captured on an audio recording, which is listed on this page as "Entire Track" of approximately 18 minutes, and five clips from that track as shown on this webpage. Equally unusually they first made a threat of what they would do, in the form of an anonymous message on a newsgroup, which is still on the Google archive and is also reproduced on this webpage.

The "entire track" takes several minutes to download to the webpage, and from it are obtained clips 1-5, the start / end times of each clip are shown.

While I was in Florida in Autumn/2001 I was harassed by MI5, more so than usual. They threatened me; on Sunday 9/Sept/2001 Pete and Geoff on their Virgin Radio show started joking about "rohypnol" which is a date rape drug, and a few days previously in Lee's Tavern at the Post Parkside building had a man saying "I was raped, I was raped" .I tried to defend myself and put them off; the result was that they made a tangible threat as stated on 11/November/2001, viz.

```
> They say that when a man with a 45 meets a man with a rifle,
> the man with the pistol is a dead man.
>
> Let's see if that's true.
```

It turned out their threat was for real. On the night of 17/November around 11pm they placed seven or eight people in the park in front of my apartment building, shouting abuse, as shown by the transcript which follows. Their purpose was for me to go outside and confront them, at which point they would shoot me with a rifle. Thus MI5's troublesome victim would be extinguished. Unfortunately for them I did not go out to confront them; instead I stayed inside and recorded the incident on minidisc. Their shouting was so loud that there was nowhere in the apartment to escape from the noise.

Entire Track

I brought the recorded track to an expert in forensic audio, who could hear most of the words on this recording, highlighted and underlined in the following images.

Enclosed you will find the original two source CD's submitted for digital enhancement, as well as two CD's containing enhanced wav files corresponding to all of the files on the source CD's.

After considerable experimentation to optimize intelligibility of each of the files, I produced enhanced versions of each of the files. Two CD's were produced in WAV file format. The files can be played on any personal computer using a Windows Media Player.

As always, for maximum intelligibility, I recommend using a high quality set of headphones. Note that the enhancement process neither adds nor removes any spoken words, nor does it alter the voice-identification properties of the voices.

Following production of the enhanced CD's I reviewed each enhanced file repeatedly with attention to your guide transcript. The words, phrases, and sentences that I was able to hear and recognize consistently, I highlighted, and typed them in BOLD and UNDERLINED on the enclosed transcript guide.

Please email if there are any questions, or if there is additional work to be done in connection with this matter. Your money order in the amount of $2,600. is received. Thank you.

Sincerely,

Paul Ginsberg, President
Professional Audio Laboratories, Inc.

The annotated transcript follows.

m10-t06   (entire track)

```
00:39 [slightly clear]    "kurwa"
00:44 [clear]             "he's watching"
00:50 [clear]             "kurwa"
01:12 [clear]             "I don't wanna shoot people...I want to take pictures"
05:09 [unclear]           "something wrong with the guy"
05:49 [clear]             "you're crazy"
```

```
07:07 [unclear]           "wanker, tadpole"
07:12 [quite clear]       "crazy"
07:26 [slightly clear]    "prostitute"
09:59 [slightly clear]    "wanker"
15:04 [clear]             "yes! wasn't funny"
15:23 [clear]             "I am not a whore"
15:26 [slightly clear]    "schizophrenic"
```

To briefly explain the recording and transcript; there are words of abuse against mental illness, there is verbal sexual abuse of the type they usually shout, and there is one shout about "I don't wanna shoot people... take pictures", which correlates to the written threat MI5 made on 11/November/2001. The phrase is ambiguous, but you don't take photos at 11pm, so it's clearly intended to signal their purpose outside my apartment building that evening.

Clip #1

```
"kurwa" ... "he's watching" ... "kurwa" ... "I don't wanna shoot people...
take pictures"
```

Clip from 00.37 to 01.17.

Clip #2

```
"you're crazy"
```

Clip from 05.46 to 05.53.

Clip #3

```
"crazy" ... "prostitute"
```

Clip from 07.11 to 07.29.

Clip #4

"wanker"

Clip from 09.58 to 10.01.

Clip #5

"yes! wasn't funny" ... "I am not a whore" ... "schizophrenic"

Clip from 15.04 to 15.30.

Why hasn't this been revealed yet?

The reader may be wondering why this and other of security service's behaviour has not yet been examined by the English legal system. The short answer is that the relevant tribunal is the Investigatory Powers Tribunal, which in 15 years of its (and its predecessors') existence has always found against plaintiffs. I complained to the former Security Service Tribunal in 1997 and of course they found against me.

The other reason is the deeply corrupting influence which MI5 inflicts on not just the media but the legal system as well. I brought a case to the Information Tribunal in 2003, which was conducted by lawyers Simanowitz of BWB and Tim Pitt-Payne of 11 King's Bench Walk. There were two hearings, at which I followed lawyers' advice that the grounds of complaint must not be brought into the open, and only technical points of law were to be discussed. Simanowitz told me the priority was to "save you money"; his advice on the November hearing was;

"One thing is crucial, that there should only be one matter discussed at that hearing, which is whether your appeal can be suspended or should be dropped and revived after you have instituted court proceedings. If you start discussing any other issues, given that you have not prepared to discuss them, you will almost certainly lose and the risk is then that they cannot be raised again subsequently."

However the tribunal did want to hear the complaint grounds at that hearing. Pitt-Payne deliberately tried to prevent the hearing even happening but for some reason was unable to stop the hearing. He and MI5's counsel Tam mutually arranged for the complaint to be dispatched with no order as to costs "by mutual agreement between the parties".

At the November hearing MI5's counsel Robin Tam tacitly admitted MI5 were making some action against me and implied a serious crime exemption; which was propaganda, out of sync with their activities towards me since 1990, particularly the media campaign and "newscaster watching".

Essentially my understanding of the legal system was insufficient to realise that I should have told the Tribunal the complaint material. The real culprit is corrupt barrister Tim Pitt-Payne because he made every effort to close down my appeal to the Information Tribunal; in August/2003 he abandoned the case at minimal notice; he arranged the November/2003 hearing with his close friend Robin Tam, so that only technical points were discussed; indeed it was obvious at that hearing that MI5 were controlling both barristers so the Tribunal could not hear the complaint.

Virgin Radio-Jon Holmes (4-5/Jan/2002)

Here are two segments from Virgin FM, one on Friday, the other on Saturday, both from the Jon Holmes evening show.

Segment 1

Certainty level: 80%

In early January 2002 I listened for the first time in some months to Virgin Radio, specifically to the Jon Holmes evening show on Friday 4 January 2002. They promptly attacked me verbally. Again, context is relevant. There are three instances in the space of two minutes on this extract;

```
00:18 "are you lying?"
00:22 "it's not fair"
01:24 "everyone at the amateur c+ turbo programmers club found it
hilarious"
```

The first phrase is a straight slander. MI5 were trying to portray me as a liar at around this time; I have other audio with the same accusation. "are you lying?"; unsophisticated.

It's closely followed by the words "it's not fair". Note carefully the way he says it, quickly, as if to deny what he says. The phrase "not fair" was first created by OCTS MD H S.-W. in Nov/1992, and picked up on my first visit to hospital soon after ("they should have paid your fare"). Again, unsophisticated parrotting of a key phrase.

The third phrase is explicable through contemporaneous context. That morning I had phoned about a C++ course. "c+ turbo programmers club"... again, somewhat brazen we're-listening-to-what-he-says-on-the-phone, and he-can't-prove-it. Something got lost in translation from MI5's watchers to Virgin, because "c+ turbo" means nothing.... there is no C+ turbo language, only C++, of which Turbo C++ is one implementation.

Segment 2

Certainty level: 80%

I wasn't entirely convinced from Friday's programme, but the following evening's show confirmed it. It contained a number of references to my condition, of which the following excerpt is one such;

```
00:09 "I'm not well, and no-one cares"
00:24 "my voice sounds all funny"
01:01 "do you mean people that aren't mad"
01:05 "medical problem is it"
```

"I'm not well" doesn't mean he has a cold; it means he is being sarcastic about my mental illness. "my voice sounds all funny" refers to the change in nature of my voice when acute illness hits. "do you mean people that aren't mad" is obvious. "medical problem is it"..... rubbing salt into the wound.

Balham Hill Post Office (14/Nov/2002)

Certainty level: 80%

By mid-November 2002 the persecution had again dwindled, as happens sometimes, when along came this item. I spent most of my time at home, going occasionally to the shops in Clapham South, or into town to meet people. On this particular Thursday I only left the house once, for less than fifteen minutes to post a letter (special delivery, because my ordinary and recorded delivery letters had been disappearing en route for some time - not that anyone would accuse MI5 of such petty harassment). At the post office counter there was an Asian guy talking into his mobile phone and grinning away. There is a probability that his comments were directed at me, as I will explain further. The second segment of audio closely follows the first segment.

First Segment

```
"you'll do it today? let's meet about 3 o'clock and have some lunch. I got
stuff to do and I'll go to the bank, get this sh.. fucking moving yeah.
Even just a little bit do something. He doesn't understand, you know what
it is, I don't want to tell him again cause then he might, he thinks we're
having a go at him, I'm not having a go at him, I'm explain to him"
```

Explanation: The guy is talking about some bloke who is unnamed, however it might be interpreted as being in code about me. "I'll go to the bank"... variously interpretable, either literally, or as sounds-like "wank" which has been a consistent theme in MI5's abuse. "get this shit fucking moving"... abuse... could be interpreted as MI5's criticism of my inertness. The state spends hundreds of thousands of pounds a year - they want to see some result, not just neutrality and ordinariness. "he doesn't understand"... MI5 claim I'm stupid... but the numbers and bits of paper prove otherwise, so perhaps what that is really about is their agents' subconscious perception of themselves.

"having a go at him"... sounds like they're having a go at me, doesn't it? You might take the audio at face value and assume it's about some other guy, but it's normal MI5 procedure to pretend to be talking about someone else, and make the content of the message very relevant to me, or their perception of me.

Second Segment

```
"for some reason it doesn't get into his head, I don't know why... he's
lost it completely, hasn't he"
```

What reason is there for it not getting into his (my) head? Stupidity is implied. Also implied is that it does get into his head; we're intentionally causing him damage. He's lost it completely... for some time I have suffered from OCD... lost it completely is the persecutors' observation of my illness, which they see through the surveillance on my home, which they caused.

Eclipse pub in Balham (20/Dec/2002)

Certainty level: 70%

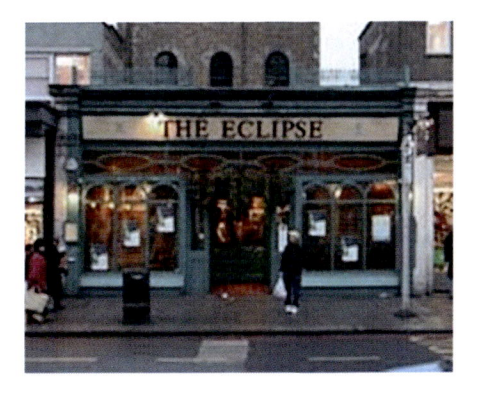

On Friday 20/December/2002 I went to Balham to do some shopping and eating. When I went into the Eclipse pub for a meal there were two girls already at the bar being server, I ordered and sat down near the window. They sat down at the opposite window seat, out of sight. After a few minutes they started screaming repetitively "section, section". They were reading something and were trying to pretend that they were just repeating from what they were reading, but in reality it was quite obvious they were talking about me, specifically to confinement under mental health.

As you can guess the behaviour of these unwise young things shows them to be from the underprivileged category which due to the natural laws of society is seldom seen in the better classes of restaurant - the McDonald's next door is their more usual habitat. My guess is that these two females were deliberately placed in the Eclipse with orders to be offensive to me personally. The alternative would be that no-one had ordered them and they were just being rude on their own account, but that is improbable, for two reasons; first, I was out of sight of them and one does not usually "pick on" a person one cannot see; secondly, there had that afternoon in Balham been other, less distinct incidents immediately preceding this, and it is inferable that MI5 were making quite a serious effort to create a physical incident, as they have done on numerous occasions previously. I give my interpretation a two in three chance of validity.

Barbican Library - 6/Feb/2003

Certainty level: 100%

Here's an item from early February 2003, at which time Security Service were re-igniting hostilities against me, a direct result of my appeal for a legal hearing against their organisation. On Thursday 6/Feb/2003 I went to the Barbican in central London with my mother to visit the library and have a meal. Security Service naturally knew about it because it had been mentioned the previous day in our house which is under constant surveillance on grounds of "National Security", so they may have been able to inform staff there to say something to me, as has been done elsewhere. Two of the people at the Enquiries desk in the library obviously knew of my circumstances, I spoke to one of them who was very polite, and while I was waiting I heard the other speaking with a little less politeness, as recorded on this audio file. He said, "I spy", to start a game of guess what "I spy"; unsubtle, MI5 Spy. Then, at the 34 second mark on this clip he said;

```
"So obvious you couldn't even get that. I shall have to kill you. ha, ha,
ha"
```

The words "I shall have to kill you" are interesting because such overt expression is rarely heard. Security Service wish me extinct. Some years ago they were openly shouting "suicide" at me, so that is established. But there is an element of doublethink in their attitude; they use people's natural prejudice against mentally ill, who are popularly painted by media as being aggressive, to try to tinge the group's view of me and MI5's actions against me. The Security Service religion is that the country's enemies are deadly, and must therefore be extinguished. Hence, we must seize eagerly upon the disabled schizophrenic from Clapham, and throttle him, because who knows what'll happen if we don't.

There may be a subtle agenda of population control in what the Security Service have been doing in this country since 1990. In the current issue of 2600 Magazine (the Hacker quarterly, which I read from time to time) there is a quote from Hermann Goering on page 2; "the people can always be brought to the bidding of the leaders. All you have to do is tell them they are being attacked. It works the same in any country". 2600 printed the quote as a comment on the projected war against Iraq, which does not appear to pose any threat to the territory of those countries which wish to invade it. However the quote is somewhat relevant to my case, which is widely known about within Britain; the security service instructs all right thinking citizens to do MI5's bidding and band together against a common enemy, while at the same time there is a suggestion of "look what'll happen to you if you don't obey us".

Eurostar Waterloo - 18/Apr/2003

Certainty level: 100%

I went to Paris by Eurostar for Easter 2003. During the outbound journey MI5 created an instance of abuse at Waterloo Eurostar station, when a group of men laughed and shouted;

"I'll bet it's of doubtful parentage"

The background is as follows. A schoolfriend from Whitgift, Julian Lewis, who now lives in Bristol and works for ST, confided in me that he had been adopted as a child. In 2003 MI5 discovered this fact and employed it in their abuse, as the audio clip shows. They turned the fact of his having been adopted into the taunt of "doubtful parentage", which is interesting because it is a term of abuse against him rather than me. It also shows that MI5 are somewhat indiscriminate in their targeting; their campaign against me has the support of English people because it is against a "foreigner", but my friend is English, so one wonders what MI5 were trying to achieve with their suggestion that Lewis is a "bastard".

If there is any logic other than the purely abusive nature of security service agents, it may be to drive my friends away from me. During the period 2001-2003 MI5 were very active in turning all my friends against me, against which there is no defence or justice, since no person ever admits it to be happening.

Clapham South (25/Oct/2003)

Certainty level: 100%

On Saturday 25/Oct/2003, returning home from Oddbins, a young black girl was walking the other way along the pavement, at around 7pm. As she passed, she spoke into her cellphone;

`"listen I thought I was committing suicide"`

This is how MI5 stage their incidents of abuse. Typically someone is walking towards me, and as they pass they say something obscene or offensive. In this particular case it was yet another instruction to kill myself.

As the girl passed she made a strange sound, which you can hear on the clip, and I coughed. She then laughed, because there was nothing I could do about what had just happened. If I had objected, they would have had other people there with instructions to beat me up, and on a number of other occasions MI5 have deliberately tried to provoke things so that they would assault me.

Clapham South (27/09/2005)

Certainty level: 100%

Here are two happenings from 27/September/2005.

This web page was written on the night of 27/September, from material captured that day.

I am trying to bring a complaint against MI5, on the grounds of their trying to kill me on 17/November/2001. They have responded for two weeks with a massive volume of verbal abuse. Much of their activity is presumably practiced from other cases because they are adept at making their actions difficult to pin down, as will be evident from the following items. There is also a worrying feature that they are using some sophisticated technology in their activities.

They are facing what is for them an emergency situation because there is a strong probability of some sort of complaint being brought against them soon. Briefly, they have employed the following methods recently;

(1) They have some sort of sound system which repeats a number of phrases over and over again. These are carefully modulated to the current noise level so as to be minimally detectable, but they <u>are</u> detectable, for which I have numerous recordings. MI5 have video surveillance inside my house, so they make the phrases relevant (in their view) to the current activity. For example, I have OCD, and as soon as I repeat an activity a few times, they start with "crazy guy". Their sound system works both in the house - I think they have planted speakers in the neighbours' houses - and also outside in the street, as evidenced by the first recording. I don't know how that works; they have some method of throwing sound, even in the open air, some sort of electronic ventriloquism. They are trying to convince me I hear imaginary voices, but obviously I do not, because a nearby microphone records exactly the same as is registered by my ears.

(2) Usenet readers will have read of the neighbours' annoying kid Mikey Cleveland-Peck who has been shouting abuse through the wall since 1998. Recently things have got much worse; MI5 have made much more trouble; both from the neighbours personally, and from the sound system which appears to be in place on both sides of the house.

(3) MI5 employ their usual methods of following me around and verbal abuse. Some of their comments are blunt repetition of phrases and some are tangential. They employ a lot of resources recently for the public harassment aspect; apparently they have no lack of operatives for these activities. The government agreed to a 50% increase in their staff; and this is what they set their staff to do.

First Segment, Chinese male

```
"masturbates, wanker"
```

They employ several recorded voices which they repeat over and over again. There is an American who keeps saying "something wrong with him" and "crazy guy", and there is a Chinese voice, which whispers loudly as you can hear on this clip, which says "masturbates, wanker" over and over again. There are no English voices - British intelligence prefer to employ other countries to do their dirty work and take the blame, just as happened with the attempted killing of 17/Nov/2001.

The aspect of this recording which worries me particularly is that it was captured in the open air, as I was walking down the street towards my house. They have similarly created speech at other locations, both outside, at Balham Library very recently, and at a cinema. The voices they create are exactly the same; both at my house and at other locations; as is borne out by the recordings.

Second Segment, small child

```
"I won ... I won ... I want it"
```

Returning home this afternoon, a little girl said "I won, I won, I want it"; and soon disappeared into one of the houses on our street. MI5 have previously employed children to speak their phrases, including various obscenities and racist remarks, of which this is such an occurrence. The little girl was told to say those words. What MI5 meant by "I want it" was that they were insisting I "wanted" the abuse they created. Two points; firstly, those words would not have ordinarily registered as being from them, and only because of their intense activities recently. Secondly, when MI5 employ small children, they are covered by the protection afforded to these; you cannot photograph the offending person; on this occasion a man was following, and he would have been instructed to challenge or assault me, had I tried to take any picture. There was a similar happening the previous day, when three mothers with prams near the new Tesco's on our road ran after me and tried to push their prams at me, shrieking "he thinks we're chasing him"; MI5 create incidents which they make it difficult to record, and they are completely unscrupulous in the methods they use.

Clapham South (Sept/2005)

Certainty level: 100%

The eight clips on this page were recorded between 2005-09-22 and 2005-09-26 in the upstairs bedroom of my house in Clapham. As with the related page sept27 these recordings are from a period when MI5 were trying to avoid a complaint of their activities, particularly of November/2001.

In late September the voices were still 'conventional' in the sense that they could be recorded through a microphone onto a minidisc recorder. Soon after the voices apparently began to be inflicted 'voice to skull' which a microphone could not sense, at which point the obscenity level deteriorated. The verbal abuse in the following clips is partly about mental illness, and partly verbal sexual abuse.

The recordings are unclear and you may need to download them and put them on repeat in your media player to identify the words. These are merely a few recordings because such words were being thrown constantly in late September.

Some of these clips may be spoken vocally / conventionally, eg the female voice. The American voice was surely not spoken conventionally but instead 'thrown' using some sort of electronic ventriloquism, because surely there were no Americans in our neighbour's house; so they would have employed some method of modulating the nearby sound environment. That voice sounds similar to the person shouting outside the apartment building on the night of 17/Nov/2001. These recordings were repeated over and over again; and they were calculated to be only slightly louder than ambient noise, so as to make them difficult to record or prove, although I heard those people more clearly than is shown on the recording.

You may ask what the point is of publishing these recordings of MI5's activities. The purpose is because they were preliminary to what may have been an infliction of 'mind control' which began in mid October/2005.

Soon after these recordings there occurred what I believed to be a technological method of directly reading / writing to my mind, and the 'conventional' voices disappeared to be replaced by what I believed to be entirely 'voice to skull' methods which are unprovable. The difficulty with classifying the further occurrences as 'mind control' is that they may have been from my schizophrenia, although I have never previously had hallucinatory voices; and that 'mind control' is unrecordable and unprovable, and I completely disbelieved of any such possibility until the happenings which started in mid October. If the method is technological then its procedure may be formed so as to resemble mental illness, for deniability. I would guess that if it were real then MI5 would have been reluctant to use such technology previously, because I would report it, and they should not use such technology merely to stifle a complaint.

I gave the recordings of the American shouting over the mindcontrol to talented forensic audio specialist Mr Ginsberg, who was able to hear the shout of "kurwa", which is a sexual obscenity. He had the following to say regarding that segment.

> I have reviewed the fourteen segments, using state-of-the-art digital enhancement software. The segments are very brief, some of as little as 2 second duration.
>
> After repeated review, the ones I hear, are as follows:
>
> 2005-09-22 20_47-00.02 "kurwa"

2005-09-22 19_11-02.25.mp3

```
"schizophrenia"
```

American says the word "schizophrenia". The clip is unclear, but the voice is that of an American, and obviously there are no Americans in the vicinity of our house. This segment was recognised by Mr Ginsberg. It seems to be the same person as on the recording of 17/Nov/2001.

| Y | 2005-09-22 19_11-02.25 "schizophrenia" | American voice |

2005-09-22 19_11-20.07.mp3

```
"masturbates"
```

Female voice says "masturbates", which may be a real or 'thrown' voice. MI5's abuse in late 2005 was substantially through sexual obscenities, and while 'conventionally inflicted' it remained moderate; eventually they used 'voice to skull' methods which are unprovable, at which point it got worse.

2005-09-22 19_11-20.32.mp3

```
"masturbates, there is something wrong with him"
```

Female voice says "masturbates, there is something wrong with him" where the latter is their standard phrase.

2005-09-22 19_11-36.07.mp3

`"crazy"`

American voice says "crazy". It seems to be the same person as on the recording of 17/Nov/2001.

2005-09-22 20_47-00.02.mp3

`"kurwa"`

American voice says "kurwa". It seems to be the same person as on the recording of 17/Nov/2001, and the word is again something that same person shouted in 2001. This segment was recognised by Mr Ginsberg. Needless to say, it is unusual to hear an American in Clapham South shouting Polish swear words.

2005-09-23 12_59-00.04.mp3

`"wanker"`

Male voice says "wanker". Again the term is moderate compared to what happened when MI5 began 'voice to skull' methods.

2005-09-26 20_42-03.24.mp3

`"wanking himself"`

Male voice says "wanking himself". This voice may be real or electronically 'thrown'.

2005-09-26 20_42-07.08.mp3

`"he's a wanker"`

Male voice says "he's a wanker" while I was brushing my teeth. This voice may be real or electronically 'thrown'.

2005-09-26 20_42-09.29.mp3

`"wanking"`

Male voice says "wanking", almost inaudibly, again part of the same recording as previous clip, while I was brushing my teeth. The voice may either be real or technologically 'thrown'.

Clapham Junction (4/10/2005)

Certainty level: 100%

Here are two happenings from 4/October/2005.

First Segment, English male

```
"we're all nutters now"
```

On that day I went to Clapham Common and Clapham Junction, with MI5 employing a lot of resources, people following around and abusing me. They had the electronic ventriloquism on Clapham Common again, and they created several incidents of which I kept one recording. At approximately 3pm an old white guy (see picture) talking to another man outside Nando's restaurant on the high street said "we're all nutters now", because I had previously described MI5 agents as mentally ill. When I brought out my camcorder he said something about "filming street signs in San Francisco",and then "let's get out of here" which was an instruction to me to leave London immediately.

Second Segment, Chinese female

```
"one I move out immediately; second I can never go back"
```

Later that day, at Battersea Library in the corridor between the Lending and Reference library, a Chinese girl talking into a phone said the above words. This was one of a number of incidents on that day. It was an instruction from MI5 to leave my home in London immediately and never go back, thus preventing any complaint against them.

Mikey Peck - Bald Wanker (14/Nov/2005)

Certainty level: 100%

`"he's a homosexual"`

This page refers to the neighbours' annoying "kid" Mikey Cleveland-Peck who has been shouting abuse through the wall intermittently since 1998. Some months ago (10/10/2005) I asked his parents for his behaviour to stop, and there seems to have been a reduction, but not a cessation. Its relevance to this site is that the words he shouts are supplied to him by MI5 because they are identical to those from other situations. Sometimes he talks obscenities without shouting, presumably to make it difficult to record on a standard microphone. Mikey also seems to vocalise loudly at his parents occasionally.

Mikey's behaviour gets worse at particular times relevant to MI5's activities, for example in December/2001 when I wrote a data protection request to MI5, he kept shouting obscenities through the wall. It is difficult to catch him doing it, but such a clip appears on this webpage, from 14/Nov/2005, at which time MI5 were apparently using "mindcontrol" technology to read my mind and try to write thoughts into my mind. The behaviour recorded in this clip is relevant to MI5's mind control abuse.

MI5 Crank Call (10/Jan/2008)

Certainty level: 100%

On 10 January 2008 at around 4am in the morning I was in my house in Clapham South, fully awake because I had gone to sleep early the previous day to avoid the mindcontrol. There was a hangup call; someone phoned my number from the UK, with the number marked "withheld" on the caller id, and I phoned up the operator who directed me on to the Nuisance Calls Bureau. They told me they could not trace a call which had already taken place, but if I wished I could place a trace on the line. It was obviously MI5 causing a nuisance at 4am, but I thought they would not call again so I did not ask for a trace to be put on the line. We have two telephones in our house, one near my mother's bed, and one in my room. Ordinarily I would have been asleep in the early hours of the morning, and the call would have reached my mother. However on this day MI5's surveillance of my house would have told them that I was awake and in proximity of the phone. Therefore they made a hangup call at 4am to wind me up.

MI5 phoned again at 4.58am in the morning, and the call was recorded on the automatic call recorded which is linked via USB to my computer, to WAV file. You can hear the call on the above MP3 file. I think the call may have woken up my mother also, but I did not ask her later. The call was obviously intended to wind me up a few days before I left for Canada. MI5 had been increasing the pressure both in real life, where they had been following me around and making comments about me, and over the mindcontrol, which had become more intense.

The caller id indicated "international" but I think the call was from the UK and MI5 were playing around with the phone system. The guy who spoke for two minutes was English and a complete arse, as are most MI5 agents. He claimed his name was Ian Rosenthal and he was calling from the US, but he had an English accent. There is an element of English anti-Semitism because they prefer to encourage other countries' citizens to do the actual abuse, and in this case the caller gave a Jewish name, but clearly had an English accent. I think he may have been one of the MI5 watchers surveilling me in the early hours of the morning. They have a team which I believe does the surveillance 24 hours a day, constantly. He said he was researching ley lines and astrology, and I told him I would report him to the Nuisance Calls Bureau unless he stopped annoying me. This was obviously MI5 because my phone number is ex-directory and does not appear anywhere on my website. It was published by Paul Janik aka Paul Stone aka BigEars about ten years ago; he got it from MI5. Janik is a disgraced ex-councillor from Slough where he had a similar habit of calling council employees late at night and calling people homosexuals until he was struck off for abuse. I believe Paul Janik is unemployed at this time.

Fanatic's Fare for the Common Man

Certainty level: 100%

The article reproduced below was penned by Bernard Levin for the Features section of the Times on 21 September 1991. To my mind, it described the situation at the time and in particular a recent meeting with a friend, during which I for the first time admitted to someone other than my GP that I had been subjected to a conspiracy of harassment over the previous year and a half.

ENTHUSIASMS

Fanatic's fare for the common man

Bernard Levin encounters a missionary who has made it his business to press classic literature on to an unsuspecting public

There is a madman running loose about London, called David Campbell; I have no reason to believe that he is violent, but he should certainly be approached with caution. You may know him by the curious glitter in his eyes and a persistent trembling of his hands; if that does not suffice, you will find him attempting to thrust no fewer than 48 books into your arms, all hardbacks, with a promise that, if you should return to the same meeting-place next year, he will heave another 80 at you.

If, by now, the police have arrived and are keeping a close watch on him, you may feel sufficiently emboldened to examine the books. The jackets are a model of uncluttered typography, elegantly and simply laid out; there is an unobtrusive colophon of a rising sun, probably not picked at random.

Gaining confidence — the lunatic is smiling by now, and the policemen, who know about such things, have significantly removed their helmets — you could do worse than take the jacket off the first book in the pile. The only word possible to describe the binding is *sumptuous*; real cloth in a glorious shade of dark green, with the title and author in black and gold on the spine.

Look at it more closely; your eyes do not deceive you — it truly does have real top-bands and tailbands, in yellow, and, for good measure, a silk marker ribbon in a lighter green. The paper is cream-wove and acid-free, and the book is sewn, not glued.

Throughout the encounter, I should have mentioned, our loony has been chattering away, although what he is trying to say is almost impossible to understand; after a time, however, he becomes sufficiently coherent to make clear that he is trying to sell the books to you. Well, now, such quality in bookmaking today can only be for collectors' limited editions at a fearsome price — £30, £40, £50?

No, no, he says, the glitter more powerful than ever and the trembling of his hands rapidly spreading throughout his entire body; no, no — the books are priced variously at £7, £8 or £9, with the top price £12.

At this, the policeman understandably put their helmets back on; one of them draws his truncheon and the other can be heard summoning reinforcements on his walkie-talkie. The madman bursts into tears, and swears it is all true. And it is.

David Campbell has acquired the entire rights to the whole of the Everyman's Library, which died a lingering and shameful death a decade or so ago, and he proposes to start it all over again — 48 volumes this September and 80 more next year, in editions I have described, at the prices specified. He proposes to launch his amazing venture simultaneously in Britain and the United States, with the massive firepower of Random Century at his back in this country, and the dashing cavalry of Knopf across the water, and no one who loves literature and courage will forbear to cheer.

But I go too fast; much, much too fast.

There can hardly be a book-reading family in this country which does not have a selection of Everyman volumes; I have only to swivel slowly round in my chair to see a couple of score on my shelves, their plain, soldierly spines instantly recognisable. And if my eyes were better, I could call them over without stirring: Tom Jones, Tartarin of Tarascon, Candide, The Brothers Karamazov, Don Quixote, Emerson's Essays (the twelfth book in the first 50 original Everyman volumes), Hazlitt's Spirit of the Age, Wilde complete, Rural Rides, Utopia, Mazzini's The Duty of Man, Areopagitica, Emile, Aristotle's Metaphysics (for which a great honour was reserved), the Iliad, Everyman itself, Juvenal's Satires, Percy's Reliques and the Everyman Encyclopaedia.

Everyman's Library is one of the greatest bibliographical achievements in all the history of reading; founded in 1906, it sold 60 million hardback copies — 15,000 a week for three-quarters of a century — in a range that marked a target that had never been hit before and, I think, has never done so after. (Well, perhaps Allen Lane with Penguin.) The two men who created the monument were J.M. Dent and Ernest Rhys, and their intention was to put out, in a series of standard formats, the whole world's classic literature.

Roll that round your mind for a moment; the *whole* world's classic literature. Editors and translators were summoned up by regiments, printers and binders were shipped wholesale, the sky was blotted out with distributors and booksellers, and the world threatened to fall through a hole in the universe with the weight of readers.

However, that did not happen quickly, and many times it looked as though it would never happen at all; Dent's financing was precarious (he had sworn he would never borrow), and the first years were painful and difficult. Yet he never let himself forget the mighty oath he had sworn: to create "the most complete library for the common man the world had ever seen".

"The common man"; that was to be Dent's customer. When the publisher got down to work, only a quarter of a century had passed since elementary education had been made compulsory in Britain, and general secondary education was only four years old. The nation was barely literate; Dent gambled on the thirst for learning and reading the law had unleashed, as Dickens, a generation earlier, had found a huge well of self-improvement. His trust was not misplaced; the precarious years were forgotten as the volumes — a shilling each — were torn from the shelves.

"A good book is the precious lifeblood of a master-spirit, embalmed and treasured upon purpose to a life beyond life." So said Milton, and his words were adopted by Dent and Rhys for the immense project. But they still needed a name for it. This is how Rhys cried: "Eureka!"

Good titles, like good lyrics (Rhys was a poet as well as a playwright, novelist, essayist and editor) drop from heaven. The finding of one, attractive and explicit, was the puzzle. We discussed a score of likely names for the series, but not one quite convincing. Then, when we had begun to despair of the search, one day on my way through Garrick Street to the publisher's office in Bedford Street, the lines of the old play: "Everyman, I will go with thee and be thy guide, In thy most need to be by thy side" came into my head. Here, unexpectedly, was the waiting word, *Everyman's Library*.

The next problem was what should be the first title in the series: it was solved instantly, for what could it be but Boswell's *Life of Johnson*? The second was less obvious: Lockhart's *Napoleon*. Altogether, in the first 50 volumes, there were Bacon's *Essays*, the *Fairy Tales* of Hans Andersen, Lamb's *Tales from Shakespeare* (ugh, actually), *Ivanhoe*, the *Meditations* of Marcus Aurelius and the six novels of Jane Austen.

It took 50 years for the thousandth Everyman to appear and neither Dent nor Rhys lived to see it. The choice for so grand, so splendid an achievement was not as easy as for the first, but there was no pandering to general popularity, and the honour went to Aristotle's *Metaphysics*.

Finis coronat opus; or so it seemed, not many years ago, when we heard the news that the whole mighty edifice was to be abandoned. No more reprints, no more acquisitions, no more weeding the garden for those plants that had failed to show staying power (all through the years, the wholesome practice of culling and replanting had continued). Everyman volumes would now have to be sought in second-hand bookshops, and there followed a sorry sight: publishers selling the Everyman rights on like a game of pass the parcel.

I don't know where the rights had got to when our wonderful madman took the stage, nor does it much matter. Campbell has not simply rescued the Everyman's Library, nor even revived it; he has recreated it. Every beautiful volume will be accompanied by a substantial newly written introduction, as well as a bibliography and a chronological table of events matched to the author's life and work. Already, Campbell has added new Everyman volumes to the canon; his first 50 include for the first time Lawrence's *Sons and Lovers*, Ford Madox Ford's *The Good Soldier*, Lampedusa's *The Leopard*, Scott Fitzgerald's *The Great Gatsby*, Joyce's *Portrait of the Artist* and Pasternak's *Doctor Zhivago*. (Assuredly, Dent and Rhys would applaud, knowing that such an enterprise can never stand still.)

Campbell points out that many paperbacks are as expensive as, or even more than, some of his fine-edition masterpieces; Proust in paperback, for instance, is £11 per volume. But although such comparisons are significant, and the quality of Campbell's editions outstanding, what is most important by far is the fact that the Everyman Library, that grand monument to learning, pleasure, solace, understanding, wisdom, thought and genius, will continue on its eternal voyage, a voyage which can never end in dropping the anchor, for its cargo may never come to rest. Instead, it must sail forever from port to port, bringing the good news, the great news, the incomparable news, the news that it is still true, and always will be, that In the Beginning was the Word. ●

22 THE TIMES SATURDAY REVIEW SEPTEMBER 21 1991

There is a madman running loose about London, called David Campbell; I have no reason to believe that he is violent, but he should certainly be approached with caution. You may know him by the curious glitter in his eyes and a persistent trembling of his hands; if that does not suffice, you will find him attempting to thrust no fewer than 48 books into your arms, all hardbacks, with a promise that, if you should return to the same meeting-place next year, he will heave another 80 at you.

If, by now, the police have arrived and are keeping a close watch on him, you may feel sufficiently emboldened to examine the books. The jackets are a model of uncluttered typography, elegantly and simply laid out; there is an unobtrusive colophon of a rising sun, probably not picked at random. Gaining confidence - the lunatic is smiling by now, and the policemen, who know about such things, have significantly removed their helmets - you could do worse than take the jacket off the first book in the pile. The only word possible to describe the binding is sumptuous; real cloth in a glorious shade of dark green, with the title and author in black and gold on the spine.

Look at it more closely; your eyes do not deceive you - it truly does have real top-bands and tail-bands, in yellow, and, for good measure, a silk marker ribbon in a lighter green. The paper is cream-wove and acid-free, and the book is sewn, not glued.

Throughout the encounter, I should have mentioned, our loony has been chattering away, although what he is trying to say is almost impossible to understand; after a time, however, he becomes sufficiently coherent to make clear that he is trying to sell the books to you. Well, now, such quality in bookmaking today can only be for collectors' limited editions at a fearsome price - £30, £40, £50?

No, no, he says, the glitter more powerful than ever and the trembling of his hands rapidly spreading throughout his entire body; no, no - the books are priced variously at £7, £8 or £9, with the top price £12.

At this, the policemen understandably put their helmets back on; one of them draws his truncheon and the other can be heard summoning reinforcements on his walkie-talkie. The madman bursts into tears, and swears it is all true.

And it is.

David Campbell has acquired the entire rights to the whole of the Everyman's Library, which died a lingering and shameful death a decade or so ago, and he proposes to start it all over again - 48 volumes this September and 80 more next year, in editions I have described, at the prices specified. He proposes to launch his amazing venture simultaneously in Britain and the United States, with the massive firepower of Random Century at his back in this country, and the dashing cavalry of Knopf across the water, and no one who loves literature and courage will forbear to cheer.

At the time this article was written I had believed for some time that columnists in the Times and other journalists had been making references to my situation. Nothing unusual about this you may think, plenty of people have the same sort of ideas and obviously the papers aren't writing about them, so why should my beliefs not be as false as those of others?

What makes this article so extraordinary is that three or four days immediately preceding its publication, I had a meeting with a friend, during the course of which we discussed the media persecution, and in particular that by Times columnists. It seemed to me, reading the article by Levin in Saturday's paper, that he was describing in some detail his "artist's impression" of that meeting. Most telling are the final sentences, when he writes, "The madman bursts into tears, and swears it is all true. And it is." Although I did not "burst into tears" (he seems to be using a bit of poetic licence and exaggerating) I did try hard to convince my friend that it was all true; and I am able to concur with Mr Levin, because, of course, it is.

At the beginning of the piece Levin reveals a fear of being attacked by the "irrational" subject of his story, saying "I have no reason to believe that he is violent, but he should certainly be approached with caution".

This goes back to the xenophobic propaganda of "defence" against a "threat" which was seen at the very beginning of the harassment. The impression of a "madman running loose" who needs to be controlled through an agency which assigns to itself the mantle of the "police" is also one which had been expressed elsewhere.

In the final paragraph of this extract, his reference to Everyman's Library as having "died a lingering and shameful death a decade or so ago" shows clearly what sort of conclusion they wish to their campaign. They want a permanent solution, and as they are prevented from achieving that solution directly, they waste significant resources on methods which have been repeatedly shown to be ineffective for such a purpose.

Private Eye, 23 Oct 1992

Certainty level: 25%

I'm not really sure whether this cover was intended to get at me, or whether it was re-interpreted after publication to be about me. This issue of Private Eye came out in October 1992, by which time I had been under severe continuous pressure at work and from the general population in Oxford for many months. It had John Major saying to his wife, "Come back, Norma!" under the title "Major's support lowest ever".

There's a story behind this. In late October I was in the local pub (the Rose and Crown, nice traditional name eh) with two people from work, Simon and Phil. Phil had with him a copy of the current Private Eye. These are both "nice people" and on my side, I hasten to add. Simon pointed out the message on the magazine's cover to Phil, and asked "what do you think about that". Phil answered, "Well usually they [Private Eye] get it right". This exchange happened in front of me. Although I was ill at the time (this was before I'd started taking medicines) I hadn't read anything into the Eye cover until these guys pointed it out to me.

Sometime later, again in the same road, a student shouted to one of his friends, "so when are you COMING BACK?", again in front of me.

What I realised Phil thought it meant was a double-entendre, the "coming" referring to the act of ejaculation, the "back" referring to the human back-side. So in a play on words you get a person who is referred to as a back-side ejaculating. Charming.

Of course, Phil could have been wrong. Perhaps there was no such meaning intended by Private Eye. Perhaps he saw meaning which wasn't there. Perhaps the moon is made from green cheese. Who knows?

Articles faxed to, and Faxes received from, British organisations

Between April/1998 and April/2000 I sent some thirty articles (over 24,259 faxes in all) on the subject of the MI5 Persecution to British politicians, media, legal and diplomatic entities in the UK. Towards the end of the transmissions I was starting to send faxes to American Congressmen and media also; that is the point at which a **"policeman from Parliament"** phoned me up and threatened to *"come round and arrest you, do you understand, and put you away for a long time"* unless the articles ceased.

This area of the website lists most of the articles sent by fax during that period, and the majority of the responses from British politicians and media organisations. There are three subsections in this hierarchical part of the site;

- Sent Faxes webpages containing articles transmitted to organisations.
- Received Faxes from Media containing responses from UK media.
- Received Faxes from Parliament with responses from Westminster.

A word on **file formats**. The sent articles were originally composed in Microsoft WinWord, and either faxed directly from my computer using fax-modem, or converted to PostScript and emailed through the TPC email-to-fax gateway. When a recipient responded, their response was received on the JFAX number I provided for that purpose, which sent it to me by email attachment as a multi-page TIFF file. It is that original unedited TIFF file which is supplied on the received faxes webpages in this part of the site.

Prior to sending these faxes, I had sent many many **hundreds of letters during 1995-96**, both from Ottawa where I was then living, and from London during my visits there. These letters were sent to the British media (newspapers) and some American media, Westminster politicians, UK radio and TV stations, and even some European media. You will see some of the fax recipients complaining about the cost of Parliamentary ink in printing out my faxes. Presumably the ink is paid for by the Government and does not come out of individual MPs' pockets. The cost of sending all these letters and faxes ran into the thousands of pounds, at a time when British Telecom was not being generous with the cost of phone calls; and the **entire cost came straight out of my own pocket**. The matter affects my entire life so I judged it right to sacrifice time and resources to this purpose. I also sent numerous text email messages during this period to various email addresses.

The faxes were a central part of my life for two and a half years. Each week I would prepare a new article, and transmit it over the weekend when the cost of phone calls was reduced. At the same time I was involved in an amusing **trial of strength with TPC**, continually finding new methods of circumventing the obstacles they tried to put in my way. They banned my domains, I found new ones; they set time and frequency limits on individual source addresses, so I merely increased the number of source addresses; they disallowed repeated faxing of the same material, so I slightly altered the source material on each iteration. I had written a **Unix networking program** to spit out an email every few minutes, so as not to overload TPC's service; the program was gradually improved, and in April/2000 I made some further changes to increase reliability; it was a useful introduction to Unix sockets programming. Also during that last weekend I started transmitting faxes to the US Congress, using a fax mailing-list I had built up from Congressmen's webpages and other online sources.

During the **weekend of 7/April/2000 (Friday) to 10/April/2000 (Monday)**, I sent a total of 1,276 completed faxes, of which 57 went direct from my computer to UK MPs, 291 by TPC to USA 1-202 mainly Congress (using the TPC cell in Washington DC), and 928 by TPC to UK recipients. Unfortunately this harmless fun was halted by a **police detective** from the station in the Houses of Parliament, who phoned me up on the Monday and shouted at me down the telephone that he would arrest and imprison me "for a long time" if the faxes continued. Suitably browbeaten, I gave my solemn promise that the faxes would cease immediately, and cancelled the fax jobs. He seemed reluctant to give his surname, but eventually admitted what his name was. The detective phoned again twice that week just to make sure I had got the message that the faxes were to stop; if they continued, he said, then he would have to "come round, you see, and your mother wouldn't like that really, would she, it would upset her wouldn't it". The policeman also spoke to my mother on one occasion. Not wishing for the police to harass me in real life as well as on the phone, I repeated my promise of no more faxes.

Perhaps the most remarkable feature of my campaign of communications is the **strict silence** observed by the recipients, the media and politicians. Parliament has absorbed 14,480 (+ a lot more) faxes without anyone daring to anger the Security Service by mentioning out loud what was going on. It is entirely extraordinary that in a so-called "open society" such a thing could happen, and perhaps the observer will gain better understanding of the real "openness" or otherwise of our British society in the light of the rigid silence maintained in this case. It was only when I started actively communicating with the American Congress, who are not all rigidly pro-British, that the firm stamp of suppression fell on my transmissions. As long as it's within Britain, we can contain it; if he complains to other parties then he must be silenced.

Addendum: I sent numerous faxes to US Congress between Sept/20004 to April/2006 and you can see the list of recipients following this link. In 2006 I sent 7,932 faxes to the British Parliament directly from my computer, and you can see an account of those transmissions by following this link. In Feb/March 2007 I sent 1860 faxes to Parliament which attracted the attention of the Police, and you can see an account of those transmissions by following this link.

#

Introduction to the Sent Faxes webpages

Between 1998 and April/2000 I sent some thirty articles on the subject of the MI5 Persecution to British politicians, media, legal and diplomatic entities in the UK. Of those articles 24 are reproduced on this part of the website. They were originally composed as Microsoft Word documents, and saved to HTML form for publication here. A few of them were slightly edited in format for readability.

You will see that these articles cover quite comprehensively what has been going on since 1990, there being quite a lot of material to cover, since it is a rare week that goes by without MI5 making some harassing or threatening action against me. "How could it be True?"... they use the mental illness which they induced in me as a ready explanation for my complaints. Who started it, why did it start, why it continues... these faxed articles provide examination in more depth of the treatment in the [Frequently Asked Questions]() webpages. The sheer meaninglessness of the Secret Police actions is highlighted; their operatives make their livelihoods by cynically exploiting the taxpayers, when in a more responsible country they would be looking at the inside of prison cells.

The validity of this observation is proven by their reaction to my several suggestions in the articles that I would cease sending faxes if MI5's agents (and it's always the same people doing the persecution) desisted from continually harassing me. A number of times, you will see in the faxed articles, I have suggested that we come to a "peace of mind agreement" where I cease complaining and they cease harassing. On one occasion, I wrote to Hugh S.-W., the director of OCTS where I was employed in 1992-94 and who is aware of the circumstances, asking that he intercede to bring this matter to a close, by initiating a meeting between myself and the persecutors to mutually settle our differences; he didn't reply, but MI5 _did_ soon after - they said "This is what you wanted, wasn't it?, some sort of confrontation?". The reality is the people stalking me are not interested in any settlement; for them crime pays, and pays handsomely; moreover it is State-approved crime; the Police will never investigate or take action; it is corruption on an incredible level and scale, and it has gone on for over a decade.

You will see that the articles contain three elements; firstly, there are original written articles, many in the first half of 1999 when I was writing new articles every week and sending them by email and fax during the weekend; then there are "MI5 Persecution Update" articles, which list happenings recent to a particular transmission; and finally there is the "old faithful" Frequently Asked Questions article which was sent on a few occasions during the three year period. These articles generated a number of interesting responses from politicians and other recipients, many of which are documented in the "received faxes" area of these webpages.

I hope you enjoy reading these articles. I'm not as angry as these articles necessarily make out, only sometimes, usually soon after the persecutors have said something unpleasant at me; the purpose of putting lots of fire and ire into the mix is to try to chuck it into the public domain which might lead to MI5 being forced to curb their actions. Unfortunately that aim was not achieved, despite many, many thousands of faxes being sent. Also, if any policemen are reading this, then I'm (a bit) sorry about the rude things I said about "the Bill" in one or two of the articles; the police have never done me any harm (yet) by commission, only by omission of doing anything to investigate my complaints or treat them seriously.

Faxes Sent to British Diplomatic/Legal logs

During the 1998-2000 period my records indicate that I sent at least 3,642 faxes to diplomatic and legal offices located in the British isles, of which 3,345 went via TPC's email-to-fax service and 297 were sent via fax-modem direct from my computer. The actual figure is somewhat higher since, for most of this period, whenever a recipient asked to be deleted from my mailing list, I totally wiped all entries including that from the logfile.

In the records "Y" indicates successful transmission from fax-modem, "N" indicates failed transmission from fax-modem. "E" indicates an error occurred while transmitting via fax-modem and a fax may have been only partly transmitted. "y" and "n" indicate success or failure via TPC.

In April 2000 I changed the method of operation by recording "R" when a recipient requested removal, rather than wiping their details from my mailing list and records; and keeping "B" records for when TPC actioned a ban on a recipient's fax-number, but the recipient did not write to ask me to cease faxing. The purpose of these changes was to keep more accurate and complete records, but the intention was thwarted by the police complaint.

```
441712011004         yyyyYyynyyyyyny
441712210448         yyynYnynyyyyy
441712212818         yyyyYyyyyyyyy
441712215685         yyyyYyyyyyyyy
441712250947         nynnYyynyyyyy
441712252130         nnnnYynnyyyyn
441712253024         ynyyYyyyyyyyy
441712253862         yyyyEyyyyyyny
441712275503         yyyyYyyyyyyyy
441712293215         yyyyYyyyyyyyy
441712330174         nynyYnnnnnnnn
441712331612         yyyyYyyyyyyyy
441712343222         yyynYyyyyyyyy
441712351286         nyyyYnyyyyyyy
441712352263         yyyyYyynyyyyy
441712353680         yynnYyynyyyyy
441712354463         yyyyYyyyyyyyy
441712354557         yynnYnynyyyyy
441712354621         yyyyYyynyyyyy
441712355161         ynnnYyyyyyyyy
441712355684         yyyyEyyyyyyyy
441712359048         yynyYnyynnnnn
441712359717         nyyyYyyyyyyyn
441712359734         nnyyNnynynyny
441712359905         nyyyYyyyyyyyn
441712405333         yyyyYyyyyyyyy
441712407722         yyyyYyyyyyyyy
441712421447         yyyyYyyyyyyyy
441712422511         yyyyYyyyyyyyy
441712424221         yyyyYyyyyynny
441712424282         yyyyYyyyyyyyy
441712425434         yyyyYynnyyyyy
441712427803         yyyyYyyyyyyyy
441712428502         yynyYyynynnny
441712431699         yyyyYyyyynyyy
441712451287         yyyyEyyyyyyyn
441712456583         yyyyYyyyyyyyy
441712456961         nyyyYnynyyyyy
441712456993         ynnnYynnynnnn
441712459552         yyyyYyyyyyyyy
441712485735         yyyyYyyynyyyy
441712553760         yyyyYyyyynyyy
441712569992         yyyyYyyynnnnn
441712586333         yyyyYyyyyyyyy
441712595392         yyyyYynynyyyy
```

441712596213	yyyyYyynyyyy
441712596487	ynnnYyynnnyn
441712627970	yynnYnnnynnnn
441713060095	yyyyYyyyyyyy
441713181301	yyyyYynyyyyny
441713181349	yyyyYyyyyyyy
441713236717	nnnnYnnnyyyy
441713321493	nnnnYyynyyyny
441713330270	yyyyYyyyyyyy
441713338831	yynnYyynnnnn
441713340242	yyynYnyyyyyy
441713440292	yyyyYyyyyyyy
441713530075	yyyyYyyyyyyy
441713530329	yyyyYyyyyyyy
441713530339	yynnYyynynnn
441713530425	yyyyYyyyynyy
441713530464	yyyyYyynnynny
441713530652	yyyyYyyyyyyy
441713530659	yyyyYyyyyyyy
441713530667	yyyyYyyyyyyy
441713530937	yyyyYyyynnnnn
441713530998	yyyyYyyyyyyy
441713531261	yyyyYyyynyyyy
441713531344	yynnYyyyyyyy
441713531488	yyyyYyyyyyyy
441713531699	yyyyYyyynyyyy
441713531724	yyyyYyyyyyyy
441713531726	yynyYyyyyyyy
441713531794	yynnNnnnnnnn
441713532144	yyyyYyynyyyyn
441713532221	yyyyYyyyyyyy
441713532647	yyyyYynnnnnn
441713532911	yyyyEyyyyyyyy
441713533319	yyyyYyynynnnn
441713533383	yynnNyynynnnn
441713533929	yyyyYyyynnnnn
441713533978	yyyyYyyyyyyy
441713534170	yyyyNyyyyyyy
441713534410	yynYyynynnnn
441713534637	yyyyYyyyynyyy
441713534979	yyyyYyyyynnyy
441713535319	yyyyYyyyyyyy
441713535422	ynyYyyyyyyy
441713535778	yyyYyyyyyyy
441713536271	yyyyYyyyyyyy
441713537622	nynyYyyyyyyy
441713537741	yyyyYnyynnnnn
441713537772	yynnYyynynnn
441713537943	yyyyYyyyyyyy
441713538188	yyyyYyyyyyyy
441713538339	yyyyYyyyyyyy
441713538791	yyyyYyyyyyyy
441713538815	nyyyNnnnnnnnn
441713539292	yyyyYyyyyyyy
441713539439	yyyyYyyyyyyy
441713539924	yyyyYyyyyyyy
441713539949	yyyyYyyyyyyy
441713541166	yyyyYyyynnnyy
441713553568	yyyyYyyyyynn
441713610005	yyyyYnnnyyyyy
441713703838	yyyyYyyyyyny
441713707773	yyyyYyyyyynyy
441713711222	nnnnNnnnnnnnn
441713738743	yyyyYyyyyyyyy
441713780712	nynyYyynnnnnn
441713795634	nnnyNynnnnnnn
441713870310	yyyyNyyyyynnyn
441713873289	yyyyYyyyyynyyy
441714040445	yyyyYyyyyyyy
441714041405	yyyyYyyyyyny

```
441714042283    yyyyYyyyyyyyyyy
441714043139    yyyyYnyyyyyyyy
441714043900    yyynYyyyynyyyy
441714044812    yyyyYyyyyyynyy
441714045032    yyyyYyyyyyyyyy
441714046659    yyyyYyyynnnnnnnn
441714048089    yyyyNyyynnnnnnnn
441714050001    yyyyYyyyyyyyyyy
441714050798    yynnYyynynnnnnn
441714051166    yyyyYyyyyyyyyny
441714051360    yyyyYyyyyyyyyyy
441714051387    yyyyYyyyyyyyyyy
441714052084    ynnnYyyyyyyyyyyy
441714053082    ynnnYyynyyynnn
441714053896    yyyyYyyyyyyyyyn
441714054078    yyyyYyyyyyyyyy
441714054267    yyyyYyyyyyynyy
441714054934    yyyyYyyyyyyyB
441714056680    yyyyYyyyyyyyyyy
441714057028    yyyyEyyyyyyyyy
441714057456    yyyyYyyynyyyyyy
441714059955    yyyyYyyyyyyyyyy
441714130374    yyyyYnyyyyyyyyy
441714300502    yyyyYyyynnnnnnn
441714301522    yyyyYyyyyyyyyy
441714301677    yynnYyynynnnnnn
441714309171    yyyyYnnyyyyyynn
441714360319    yynnNnnnnnnnnn
441714364517    ynnnNnnnnnnnnnn
441714365204    yyyyYnyyyyyyyyy
441714368181    yyyyYyyyyyyyyyy
441714517284    yyyyYyyyyyyyyyn
441714531297    yyyyYyyyyyyyyyy
441714821018    yyyyYyyyyyyyy
441714866403    yyyyYynnyyyyyyy
441714869970    yyyyYyyyyyyyyyy
441714905613    yyyyYyyyyyyyynn
441714910691    yyyyYyyyyyynyyy
441714911542    yyyyYyyyyyyyyyy
441714914139    yyyyYyyyyyynyyy
441714914993    yynyYyyyyyyyyyy
441714919347    nynnYyynyyyyyyy
441714919348    yyyyYyyyyyyyyyy
441714934333    yyyyYyyyyyyyyn
441714935105    yyyYyyynnnnnn
441714937456    yyyyYyyyyyyyyn
441714941868    nyynYyynynnnnn
441714951635    yyyyYyyyyyyyyy
441714954035    yyyyYyyyynyynn
441714954441    nyyyYyyynnnnnn
441714957776    yynyYyynynynn
441714958595    yyyyYyyyyyyyyn
441714992283    yynnYyynynnnnn
441714997948    yyyyYynnyyyynn
441714999937    yyyyYyyyyyyyyy
441715227300    nyyyYnnnnyyyyy
441715810053    yyyyYyynyyyyyy
441715811829    yyyyYyyyynyyyy
441715813452    yyyyYyyyyyyyy
441715819585    yyyyYyyyyyyyyy
441715830090    yynyYyyyyyyyyy
441715830118    yynnYyynynnnnn
441715830579    yyyyYyyyyyyyyy
441715830950    yyyyYyyyyyyyyy
441715831341    yyyyYyyyyyyyyy
441715831491    yyyyYyyynnnnnn
441715831606    yyyyYyyyyyyyy
441715831672    nnyyYnnyyyyyyy
441715831723    yyyyYyyyyyyyyy
441715831786    yyyyYyyyyyyyyy
```

441715831926	yyyyYyyyyyyynn
441715832030	yyyyYyyyyyyynn
441715832033	yynnYyynynnnnn
441715832036	yyyyYyyyyyyyyy
441715832044	yyyyYyyyyyyyyn
441715832051	yynnYyynynnnnn
441715832094	yyyYyynnyyyyy
441715832254	yyyyYyyynnnnnn
441715832257	yyyyYyyyyyyyyy
441715832686	yynyYyynynyyyy
441715832823	yyyyYyyyyyynyy
441715833423	yyyyYyyyyyyyyy
441715834928	yyyyYyyyyyyyyn
441715835106	yyyyYyyyynyynn
441715835885	yyyyYyyyyyyyyy
441715837228	yyyyYyyyyyyyyy
441715839123	yyyyYyyyyynyyy
441715839127	yyyyYyyyyyyyyy
441715839144	yynnEyyyyyyyyy
441715839178	yyyyYnyynyyynn
441715839269	yynnYynnnnnnnn
441715844948	yyyyYyyyyyyyyy
441715846354	yyyyYyyynyynnn
441715847716	yyyyYyynyyyyyy
441715892505	nyyyYyyyyyyyyy
441715893430	yyyyYyyynyynyn
441715894440	yyyyYyyyyyyyyy
441715895154	yyyyNyyynyyyyy
441715897725	nyyyEynynyynyy
441716000289	yyyyYyyyyyyyyy
441716001455	yyyyYyyyyyyyyy
441716021820	ynnnYyyyyyyyyy
441716075158	yyyyYyyynnnnnn
441716083746	yyyyYyyynnnnnn
441716294169	yyyyYynyyynyyy
441716647714	yyyyYyynyyyyyyy
441716969911	ynyyYyyyyyyyyy
441717083318	yyyyYyyynnnnnn
441717244174	yyyyYynyyyyyyy
441717247001	yyyyYynyyyynyy
441717249884	yynyYyyyyyyyyy
441717273693	yyyyYnyyyynB
441717275824	yyyyEynyyyyyyy
441717278625	yyyyYynnyyyyyy
441717278960	yyyyYyyyyyyyyy
441717279654	yyyyYyyyyyyyyy
441717279934	yyyyYyyyyyyyyn
441717301683	yyyyYyyyyyyyyy
441717305747	yyyyYyyynnnnnn
441717358147	yyyyYyyynnyynn
441717921708	nyyyYyyyyyyyyy
441717977100	yyyyYyyynnnnnn
441717977435	yyyyYyyynyyyyy
441717977550	yynnYyyyyyyyyy
441717977700	yyyyYyyyyyyyyy
441717977929	yynnYyynyyyyyy
441717978001	ynnnYyynyyyyyy
441717978101	yyyyYyyyyyyynn
441717978308	yyyyYyyyyynyyy
441717978401	yynnYnynynnnnn
441717978699	yyyyEyyyyyyyyy
441717978801	yyyyYyyyyyyyyy
441717978929	yyyyYyyyyyyyy
441718138080	yyyyYyyyyyyyy
441718231348	yyyyYynyyyyyyy
441718231712	yyyyYyyyyynyyy
441718237926	yyynYyyyyyyyyy
441718239695	yyynYyyynyyynn
441718239701	yyyyYyyyyyynyy
441718241435	yyyyYyyyyyyyyy

441718241566	yyyyYyyyyyyyyy
441718310125	ynnnYyynyyyyyy
441718310626	yyyyYnyyyyyyyy
441718312239	yyyyYyyyyyyyyy
441718312430	yyyyYyyyyyyyy
441718312469	yyyyYyyyyyyyyy
441718312575	yyyyYyyyyyyyy
441718314885	yyyyYyyyyyyyy
441718316016	yynyNyyyyyyyy
441718316109	yyyyYyyyyyyR
441718316112	yyyyYyyyyyyynn
441718316968	yynnYyynynnnnn
441718317107	yyyyEyyyyyyyyy
441718317907	yyyyYyyyyyyyyy
441718318102	ynyyYyyynyyynn
441718318129	yyyyYyyyyyyyyy
441718318237	yyyyYyyyyyyyy
441718318479	yyyyNyyyyyyyyy
441718319188	yyyyYyyyyyyyyy
441718362602	yyyyYyyyyyyyy
441718364331	yynyYyyyyyyyyy
441718374526	nyynNynnyyyyn
441718382001	yynnYyyyyyyyy
441718382046	yyynYyyyyyyyy
441718394580	yyyyYyyyyyyyy
441718398746	yyyyYyyyyyyyy
441718398958	yyyyYyyyyyyyy
441719175014	nynnYyyyyyyyy
441719175026	nyyyYyyyyyyy
441719225815	yyyyYyyyyyyyy
441719242704	yyyYyyynnnnn
441719308401	yyyYnnynyyyy
441719350034	yyyyYyyyynyyy
441719366709	yyyyYnyyyyyyy
441719366802	yynyYyyyyyyny
441719366810	yyyYyyyyyyyn
441719367230	yyyYnyyyyyyy
441719367428	yyyYyyyyyyyy
441719371783	yyyYyyyyyyyn
441719372925	yyyYyyyyyyy
441719375402	yyyYyyyyyyyy
441719375687	yyyyYynyyyyyn
441719376108	yyyyYyyyyyyyy
441719376741	nyyyYynnnyyyy
441719377505	yyyyYyyyyyyy
441719377918	yyyyEyyyynnnnn
441719378069	yyyyYyyynyyyy
441719378795	yyyyYnyyyyyyy
441719381615	yyyyYynyyyyyy
441719382595	yyyyYynnnnny
441719579555	yyyyYyyyyyyy
441813127078	yyyyYyyyyyy
441813139624	yyyyYnyynnnn
441813164842	yyyyYnyyyyyy
441813165190	yyynNnnnnnnn
441813431324	yyyyYnynyyny
441814242209	yyyyYyynyyyy
441814530946	nyyyYnyynnyy
441815031152	yyynNnyyyyyn
441815532824	yyyyYyyyyyy
441815682401	yynyYyyyyyny
441815685368	yyyyYnynyyy
441816809801	yyyyYyyyyyyy
441816923910	yyyyYyyynnnn
441817600432	yyyyYyyyyyyn
441817811007	yyyyYyyyyy
441818030564	yyyyYyyyyyyy
441810779854	yyyyYyyynyyn
441818814802	yyyyYyyyyyy
441819800670	yyyyYyyynnnn

441819891371   yyyyEyyyyyyy

No faxes were sent after April 2000.

Faxes Sent to British Media logs

During the 1998-2000 period my records indicate that I sent at least 6,137 faxes to the British media, of which 5,775 went via TPC's email-to-fax service and 362 were sent via fax-modem direct from my computer. The actual figure is obviously higher since, for most of this period, whenever a recipient asked to be deleted from my mailing list, I totally wiped all entries including that from the logfile.

In the records "Y" indicates successful transmission from fax-modem, "N" indicates failed transmission from fax-modem. "E" indicates an error occurred while transmitting via fax-modem and a fax may have been only partly transmitted. "y" and "n" indicate success or failure via TPC.

In April 2000 I changed the method of operation by recording "R" when a recipient requested removal, rather than wiping their details from my mailing list and records; and keeping "B" records for when TPC actioned a ban on a recipient's fax-number, but the recipient did not write to ask me to cease faxing. The purpose of these changes was to keep more accurate and complete records, but the intention was thwarted by the police complaint. Also in April 2000, I added some further fax numbers to my media mailing list and records, which is why some of the faxnumbers below have only a single entry, and some indeed have none.

```
441132420652          yyyyyYyyyyyyyyyyyy
441132439387          yyyyyYyyynyyyyyyy
441132445107          yyyyyYyyyyyynyyyyyy
441132455139          n
441132460037          yyyyyYyyyyyyyyyyyy
441132461105          yyyyyYyyynyyynnnnnn
441132836586          yyyyyYynyyyyyyyyyyy
441142664375          nnyyyyYyyyyyyyyyyyy
441142769089          yyyyyyYyyyynnnyyyyyy
441142853159          yyyyyYyyynyynyyyy
441159012850          y
441159363497          n
441159420433          ynnnnYyynnyyyyyyyyy
441159455243          n
441159527001          ynyyyYynnyyynnyynny
441159550552          yyyyyYyyyyyyynnnnn
441159822568          n
441162311123          y
441162511463          yyyyyYyyyyyyyyyyyy
441162512151          yyyyyYyyyyyyyyyyyy
441162512979          n
441162561303          yyyyyYyyyyyyyyynB
441162640948          yyyyyYyyyyyyyyyyyn
441162667776          yyyyyyyYyyyyyyyyyyyy
441179226744          n
441179238323          yyyyyNynyyyyyyyyy
441179279568          n
441179298612          yyyynYyyyyyynnnnnn
441179317463          y
441179722400          yyyyyyyYyyyyyyyyyyyyy
441179732549          yyyyyyyYyyyyynyyyyyy
441179741537          yyyyyyyYnnynyyyyyyyyy
441179744114          yyyyyyyYyyyyynyyyyy
441179843202          yyyyynYynynyyyynyyy
441202297904          n
441203407129          n
441203551744          yyyyyyYyyyynyyyyyyy
441203695110          y
441203696867          n
441203868202          nyyyyYyyyyyyyyyyyy
441203868205          yyyyyYynyyynyyyyyy
441206561199          yyyyyYynyyyyyyyyyn
441209314345          yyyyyYyvyyyyyyyyy
441212330173          n
```

441212331465	y
441212367220	y
441212434536	y
441213591117	yyynyNyynyyyyyynnyn
441214141120	y
441214148181	yyyyyYnnnnnnnnnnnnn
441214148241	yyyyyEnnnnnnnnnnnnn
441214148634	yyyyyYnnnnnnnnnnnnn
441214148847	yyyyyNnnnnnnnnnnnn
441214148900	nyyyyYnnnnnnnnnnnn
441214155026	n
441214547622	n
441214723174	yyyyyYyyyyyyyyyyyy
441216161011	yyyyyYynyyyyynnnnnn
441216251346	y
441216262041	yyyyyYyyyyyyyyyyyy
441216344766	yyyyyYyyyyyyyyyyyy
441216437239	y
441216666370	yyyyyYyyyyyynnnnnn
441216932753	yyyyyYyyyynyynnnnnn
441216961007	yyyyyYyyynyyyyyyyy
441217066210	yyyyyYyyyyyynnnnB
441217090205	y
441217115824	y
441217533111	nyynnYnyyyynyyyyyyy
441222223157	yyyyyYyyyyyyyyyyyy
441222224947	y
441222229326	y
441222384014	yyyyyYyyyynyyyyyy
441222498151	n
441222552973	yyyyyNyyyyyyyyyyyy
441222555286	yyyyyYyyyyyyyyyyyy
441222555960	yyyyyYyyyyyyyyyyyn
441222597183	ynyyyYyyyyyyyynyyy
441222615966	y
441222665650	n
441222798555	n
441223235161	yyyyyNyyyyyyyyyyyy
441223315052	nnnnnYnnnnnnnynyyyy
441223361508	yyyyyYyyyyyyyyyyyy
441223460832	yyyyyYyyyyyyyyyyY
441223467106	yyyyyYyyyyyyyynyy
441224212163	y
441224633282	nyyyyYyynyyyyyyyyy
441224637289	yyyynYynynnyyyyynyy
441224846800	yyyyyYyyyyyyyyyyyy
441225448688	n
441225460709	y
441225775198	y
441227771558	nyyyyYyyyyyyynnnnnn
441228511195	nyynnYyyynyyyyyyyyy
441228810453	yyyyyYyynyyyyyyyyy
441228818444	yyyyyYyyyyyyyynyyyy
441228819444	yyyyyYyyyyyyyyyyyy
441229870008	ynnyyEyyyyyyyyyyyy
441232246695	yyyyyYyyyyyyynyyyny
441232311740	y
441232338800	yyyyyYyyyynyyyyyyyy
441232338801	yyyyyYyyyyyyyynyyy
441232381915	yyyyyYyyyyynynnnnyn
441232454406	n
441232541550	n
441232682111	y
441232682757	y
441232700029	y
441233641816	y
441233812707	n
441234218580	nyyynEyynyynnyyyyyn
441234270580	y
441235436899	y

441235524024	yyyyyYyyyyynyyyyy
441235822746	y
441235835163	n
441237423333	yyyyyYyyyyyyyyyyyy
441242255671	n
441242584270	y
441242621343	y
441242699666	yyynyYyyyyyyyyyyyy
441243576456	yyyyyYyyyyynnnnnB
441243775878	y
441243786464	yyyyyyyyYyyyyyyyyyyy
441244341677	n
441244678749	y
441245267228	yynnyynnYynyyyyyyynyy
441245492983	nyyyyynEyyyyyyynnyyyy
441246582227	n
441247814974	yyyyyyyYnyyyyyyyyyny
441247818913	yyyyyyyYyyyyyyyyyyyy
441248351443	yyynyyynYynyyyyyyynyyy
441252725007	n
441253301965	yyynyynyYyyynyyynyyyy
441254680821	nyyyEyyyyyyyyyyy
441256492599	y
441257450036	n
441273404280	yyyyyYyyyyyynyyynyy
441273430098	yyynyYyyyyyynyyyyy
441273440229	y
441273486852	y
441274720375	n
441274728534	yynnnYnnnnnnnnnnnyn
441274771680	yyyyyYnyynynnynynB
441274828555	y
441279430009	n
441279431059	y
441279445289	yynnyYynnnnnyyyyy
441285647247	y
441292283665	nyynyYyyyyyyyynyyyy
441293560927	ynyyyYynnnnyyyyyyyy
441293565663	yyyyyYnyyyyyyyynny
441293820517	n
441295270659	n
441296398988	yyyyyEyyyyyyyyyyyyy
441303272292	yyyyyNyyyyyyyyyyyy
441303283874	yyyyyNyynyyyyyyyyy
441305250052	yyyyyYyynyyyyyyyyy
441305250910	yyyyyYyyyyyyyynyyy
441312202443	yynyyyNyyyyyyyyyyynn
441312204344	yyyyyyYyyyyyyyyyyy
441312204819	y
441312254580	y
441312267420	yynyyyYyyynyyyyyyyy
441312283220	n
441312284293	y
441312284333	n
441312285462	n
441312442674	n
441312444785	n
441313152906	y
441313177202	y
441313344473	y
441314462279	y
441315552869	n
441315575881	y
441315579699	y
441315583277	yyyyyYyyyynyyyyyyy
441316621323	y
441316648001	n
441316688741	y
441322550553	nyyyyYyyyynyyyyyyy
441322667633	y

441324630515	y
441325368824	n
441327361514	y
441332290794	yyyyyYyyyyyyyyyyy
441332292229	yyyyyYyynynnnnnnnnn
441332386036	y
441334762661	n
441342850244	y
441343540142	nnnnnYynyyyyyyyyyy
441344770990	y
441352759009	y
441352759821	yyyyyYnnnnnnnnnnnnn
441355262626	y
441372377526	y
441372465041	n
441373452888	y
441376521222	y
441382202188	yyyyyYynyyyynyyyyyn
441382454590	y
441382480230	yyyynNnnnnnnnnnnnnn
441382593252	yyyyyYyyyyyynnnnnn
441387251121	y
441387265629	yyynyYnyyyyyynnynyn
441392425570	nyyyYyyyyyyyyyyyy
441392428048	y
441392444433	yyyyyYyyyyyyyyyyyny
441392444644	yyyyyYyyyyyyyyyyy
441397701007	yyyyEyyyyyyyyyyy
441403234714	y
441412210283	yyyyyNyyyyyynyyyny
441412213595	n
441412264541	n
441412272090	n
441412481099	y
441412482362	yyyyyYyyynnnnnnnB
441412482470	n
441413003030	yyyyyYyyyyyyyynyyy
441413062265	yyyyyYyyyyyyyyyyy
441413062266	nynnnYynnnnnynnnnn
441413062322	yyyyyYyyyyynyynnn
441413312126	yyyyyYyyyynyyyyyyy
441413325448	yyyyyNynnyyyyyyyny
441413327990	y
441413340614	ynnnnYyyyynyynyyyy
441413373031	y
441413382937	yyyyyYnyyynnnnnB
441413382955	yyyyyYyyyyyyyyyyny
441413533292	yyyyyYyyyyyynnnnnn
441415322562	yyyyyYnyyynyyyyyyn
441415521344	yyyyyNyyyyyyyyyyyy
441418870963	nynyyYnyyyyyyyyyy
441420475831	y
441420544044	yyyyyYyynyyyyyyyyy
441423522922	yyyyyYyyyynyyyyyy
441423526294	n
441424870877	nnnyyYnnnnnnnnnB
441428658971	yyyyyYyyyyyyyyyyyn
441428751057	y
441442877407	nnnynYyyyyyyyyyyy
441442877409	nyyyyEyyyyyyyyyyy
441443226500	n
441452300581	y
441452309491	yynyyYyyyyyyyyynyyy
441452423008	yyyyyYyyyyyynnnnnn
441452529446	yyyyyYnyyynnnnnnnnn
441452652750	y
441453759311	n
441453890827	y
441454281094	y
441463243224	yyyyyYyyynyyyyyyyy

441463715384	yyyyyYyynynyyynyyyy
441467632969	yyyyyYyyyyyyyyyyyy
441472341967	yyyyyYyyyyyynynyyn
441473210887	yyyyyYyyyyyyyyyyyy
441473218447	n
441473233279	yyynyYyyyyyyyyyyny
441473741200	yyyyyYynyyyyyyyyyy
441477535756	y
44148149676	yyyyyYyyyyynnnnnnB
441481496768	yyyyyYyynyyyyyyyyy
441481713557	yyynnEynyyyyyyyyyy
441482226409	nyyyyEyyynyyyyyyyy
441482586028	yyyyyYnyyyyyyyyyyn
441482587067	yynyyEyyyynyyynyyy
441482848833	n
441483203378	n
441483304952	yyyyyYyyyyyyyyyyyy
441483454443	yyyynYyyyyyyynynyn
441483506331	y
441483573686	y
441483764895	nyynyNnnnnnnnnnnnB
441484530604	n
441485600672	y
441488686900	n
441489589453	yyyyyYnnnyyyyyyyyn
441491571635	y
441492535248	yyyyyYyynyyyyyyynnn
441492543226	y
441494445400	yyyyyNyyyyyyyyyyyy
441504260067	yyyyyYyyyyyyyynnnn
441504269048	nyynyYyyynnnnnnnnB
441504311177	yyyyyEyyyyyyyyyyyy
441505702333	yyyyyYyyyyyyyyyyyy
441512362180	y
441514710330	yyyynNnnyyynnnynyyy
441514710333	yyyyyYyyyyyyynyyyy
441516321698	y
441516325484	n
441517093389	yyyyyYyyyyyyyynnny
441522511058	yyyyyYnyynyyyyyyyy
441522511616	n
441522514162	yyyyyEyyyyynyyyynyn
441522549911	yyyyyYyyyyyyyyyyyy
441524848787	yyyyyYyyyyyyyyyyyy
441532443430	
44153432569	yyynyYyynyyyyyyyny
441534816817	yyyyyYyyyyynyyyyyy
441534887799	yyyyyYyyyyyyyyyyyy
441536517390	yyyyYyyynyyyyyyny
441539445128	y
441543417154	y
441552560589	
441553617137	n
441553766453	yyyyyYyyyyyyyyyyny
441553767200	nyyyyYnyyyyynynnnyy
441582401214	yyynyYnnnnyyyyyyyn
441582401467	nyyyyYyyyyyyyyyyyy
441582493486	y
441582746978	y
441584875900	yyyyyYnyynynnynyyyy
441590612624	y
441595695696	yyyyyYyyyynnnnnnnB
441603222602	y
441603415781	n
441603507723	y
441603612930	y
441603613483	nyyyyYnyyyyyynnnnn
441603615494	yyyyyYyyyyyyyyyyyy
441603630892	yyyyyYynyyyyyyyyny
441603631032	yyyynYyyyyyyyyyyyy

441603633631	yyynnYyyyyyyyyyyyy
441603633692	yyyyyYyyyyyyyyyyyy
441603666252	yyyyyYynyynyyyynynn
441603666353	yyyyyYyyyyyyyyyyyy
441603667865	yyyyyYyyyyyyyyyyyy
441603761245	yyyyyEyyyyyyyyyyyy
441604230709	yyyyyYyyyyyyyyyyyy
441604670635	y
441604795601	ynnnyYyyyyynynyyyny
441612281020	yyyyyYyyyyyyyyyyyy
441612362427	n
441612364535	nyyyyYyyyyyyynyyynn
441612365804	yyyyyYyynyyyyyyyny
441612369443	yyyyyYyyyyyynyyyyny
441612375353	y
441612889000	yyyyyNnynnnnnnyynny
441616836065	yyyyyYyyyyyyyyyyyy
441618272029	yyyyyYyyyyyyyyyyyy
441618320788	yyyyyYynynyyyyyyyyy
441618325351	y
441618328809	yyyyYyyyyyyyyyyny
441618392066	n
441618398048	n
441618487824	yyyyyYyyyynyyyyyy
441618720206	yyyyYyyyynyyyyyyyn
441618771005	yyyyYnnnnyyyynyyyy
441619692709	n
441622714000	yyyyyYyyyyyyyyyyyy
441623427316	y
441624661411	yyyyyYyynyyyyyyyyy
441625524510	y
441625583537	n
441625584344	yynnyYnnnnnnnnnnnn
441631570057	yyyyyYyyyyyyyynnyn
441634264701	n
441634830573	yyyyyYyyyyyyyyyyyy
441634830930	n
441638665789	n
441642211356	yyyyyYyyyyyyyyyyny
441642244595	n
441642566560	yyyyyYyyyyynyyyyyy
441648763828	nyyyyYnnyyyyynnnnnn
441686623666	yyyyyYnyyyyyynnyny
441702345224	yyyyyYyyyyyyyyyyy
441702556248	n
441703223388	yyyyyYyyyyynnnnB
441703232983	n
441703329404	y
441703335050	nyyyyYyyyyynyyyyyy
441703339648	yyyyyYyyyyyyyyyy
441703339931	nyyyyYnnnnyyyyyyyy
441703630289	n
441705291709	y
441705358863	yyyyyYyynyyyynyyyy
441708727305	n
441708865870	n
441712097484	yyyyyYyynyyynyyyyy
441712110507	nyyyyYyyyynnyyyyyy
441712116270	y
441712174907	n
441712185857	yyyyyYyyyyyyyyyy
441712186460	y
441712216341	nynnnYynnnnnnynnnn
441712220792	y
441712220832	yyyyyEyyyyyynnnnnn
441712221555	n
441712223172	nyyynYyyyyyyyyy
441712225889	yyyyyYyynyyynnnB
441712235631	nyyyyYnnnnnnnnnB
441712241868	y

441712244452	y
441712272005	y
441712290352	yyyyyYyyyyyyyyyyn
441712293395	yR
441712302691	n
441712302818	y
441712322302	ynyyyYyyynnnnnnnB
441712330335	n
441712330397	yyyyyYyyyyyyyyyyy
441712332065	yyyyyYyyyyyyynnnnn
441712333161	n
441712333534	yyyyyYyyyyyyyyyyy
441712333686	y
441712336706	yyyyyYynyyynyyyyy
441712337899	y
441712343300	n
441712368136	nnnnnYnnnnnnnnnnB
441712388446	y
441712401153	y
441712402254	n
441712404171	yyyyyYnnnnnnnyyyyy
441712404399	n
441712405518	y
441712407517	y
441712428961	n
441712430542	n
441712447875	yyyyyYyyyyyyyyyyy
441712478979	y
441712480133	y
441712492751	n
441712500212	y
441712500966	y
441712501204	n
441712512725	y
441712537406	n
441712545950	yynyyEyynnnyyyynnn
441712565326	yyyyyYyyyyyyynnnnn
441712611290	yyyyyYyyyyyyyyyyy
441712613250	yyyyyNyyyyyyynyyyy
441712616023	y
441712626199	y
441712662563	y
441712671396	y
441712700618	y
441712706079	n
441712726653	n
441712734660	y
441712736421	y
441712748994	y
441712749630	y
441712765179	n
441712768633	n
441712780345	y
441712780504	n
441712784425	ynyyyYyyyyyyyyyyn
441712786232	y
441712786941	yyyyyYyyyyyyyyyyy
441712788480	ynnnnYynnynnnnnnB
441712822040	y
441712837037	n
441712842835	yynyYyyyyyyynnnnn
441712843374	yyyyyYnnnnnnnnnnB
441712843641	n
441712844494	n
441712847788	yyyyyEynnnnnnyynyy
441712896392	n
441712932435	yyyyyYyynnyyyyyynn
441712933098	y
441712933405	yyyyyYyynyyyyyyy
441712933517	y

441712933587	y
441713066011	
441713067737	y
441713067800	yyyyyYynyyyyyyyyyy
441713068116	yyyyyYyyyyyyyynyyyy
441713068357	yyyyyYnyyyyyyyyyny
441713122601	n
441713128470	nnyyyYyyyynnnynyyy
441713169003	n
441713231582	y
441713241407	n
441713298377	n
441713313108	n
441713317382	y
441713331690	n
441713347411	n
441713386690	y
441713402019	n
441713446400	n
441713510220	y
441713518290	y
441713532310	nynynNnnnnnnnnnynn
441713536867	n
441713537526	n
441713538118	yyynyYnnyyyyyyyyyy
441713538355	yyyyyYyyyyyyyyyyy
441713538359	yyyyyYynyyyyyyyyyy
441713543728	n
441713548264	y
441713577458	y
441713592228	n
441713735768	y
441713740645	n
441713748741	yyyyyYyyyyyyyyyyyy
441713776103	yyyyyYyyyyynyyyyyy
441713790543	y
441713793866	n
441713794204	n
441713797707	y
441713816903	n
441713825905	n
441713830044	y
441713830273	y
441713830448	n
441713834855	n
441713841781	n
441713853708	n
441713865002	yyyyyYyynyyyyyyyny
441713872764	n
441713883737	yyyyyYyyyyyyynnnnn
441713888172	nnnnnEnnnnnnnnnnnn
441713889958	yyyyyYyyyyyyyyyyyy
441713919111	y
441713932099	y
441713937461	y
441713966466	y
441714001428	y
441714012537	n
441714030668	n
441714044167	y
441714052332	y
441714057062	yyyyyYnnnnyyyyyyyy
441714057064	y
441714057163	yyyyyYyyynyyynnnnn
441714057784	y
441714075700	yyyyyYyyyyynyyyyyy
441714100906	y
441714100966	yyyyyYyyyyyyynyyyy
441714127379	y
441714127771	y

441714130340	n
441714138302	nyyyyYyyyyyynyyyy
441714138303	yyyyyYyyyyyynnnn
441714140262	n
441714165379	y
441714216006	yyyyyYyyyyyyyyyyy
441714216522	y
441714300924	ynnnnYyyyyyyyyyyy
441714301384	y
441714301779	n
441714341197	yyyyyYyyyyyynyyyny
441714361425	n
441714362665	y
441714363562	n
441714363986	n
441714365290	n
441714367218	y
441714376886	y
441714384512	n
441714397318	n
441714700062	yyyyyYyynyyynyynny
441714701062	yyyyyYyyyyyyyyyyy
441714807662	y
441714822293	y
441714822441	n
441714861132	ynyyyYyyyyyynyyyy
441714866565	n
441714872908	yyyyYyyyyyyyyyy
441714900436	y
441714901255	yyyyyYyyyyyyyyyy
441714904706	
441714918212	
441714946652	
441714999377	
441714999751	
441715058220	
441715229623	
441715372661	
441715376004	
441715376721	
441715381330	ynnyNnnnnnnnnnnn
441715386242	yyynYyyyyyyyyyy
441715387872	
441715388625	
441715427921	yyyyyYyyyyyyyyyy
441715802338	
441715805455	nnnnnYyyyyyyynnnn
441715805547	yyyyyEyyynyyyynyy
441715807725	nyyyyNnnnnnnnnnnn
441715814431	yyynyYyyyyyyyyyyy
441715817000	yynynYnnnnnnnnnnn
441715828240	
441715830519	yyyyyYyyyyyyyyyy
441715830701	
441715831519	
441715833441	
441715833563	
441715833769	ynyyyYyynyyyynyyn
441715835901	
441715836608	yyyyyYynynyyyyyy
441715836868	yyyyyYyyyyyynyyyy
441715837073	
441715838353	
441715839504	yyyyYyyyyyyyyyn
441715844381	
441715867187	
441715946700	
441716001058	
441716030095	
441716080020	

441716080114
441716083757
441716118577
441716201594
441716305509
441716309934
441716311070
441716313214
441716315084   yyyyyYyyyyyyynnnn
441716315119   yyyyyYyyyyyyyyyny
441716330244   yyyyyYyyynnynynyy
441716348842
441716360632
441716361053   nyyyyYnnnnnnnnnnn
441716362628   yyyyyYnyyyyyynnnn
441716365375
441716365668
441716371439
441716371630   yyyyyYyynynnnnnnn
441716372127
441716372748   nyyyyYyyyyyyynnn
441716373925   yyyyyYnyynyyyyyyy
441716376868   yyyyyNyynyyyyyyyn
441716539393   yyyyyYyyyynynyyy
441716643349
441716968996
441717003752   yyyynYyyyyyynnnnn
441717003979   nnyyyYynnnnnnyyn
441717040313
441717053030   yyyyyYyyyyyyyyyny
441717131840   yyyyyYyyyyyyynnn
441717136161
441717228512
441717238585   yynyyYynnnnnnnnnn
441717239742   yyyyyYyyyyyyyyyy
441717240404   yyyyyYyyyyyyynnnn
441717276268
441717295098
441717305851
441717340561
441717341792   yyyyyNyyyyyyyyyy
441717345030
441717385509
441717386619   yyyyyYnnynyynnnnn
441717471414
441717650612   yyyyyYyyyyyyyyyy
441717653774   yyyyyNyyyyyyynnnn
441717654409   yyyyyYyyyyyyyyyy
441717655838   yynyyYyynyyynyyyy
441717666100   nyyynYnnnynyyyyyy
441717673959
441717823252
441717825658   yyyynNyynyyyyynyy
441717829902   ynnnnYyyyyynyyyyy
441717920259
441717946584
441717987710
441718136001
441718149899
441718151177   yyyyyYyyyyyynyyyy
441718215387
441718219352   yyyyyYyyyyyyyyy
441718231621
441718277001   ynnnnYynynnnnyyyy
441718277002   yyyyyYyyynyyyyyyy
441718277710   yyynyNnnnnynyyyyy
441718277721   yyynyYnyyyyynyyyy
441718287269   yyyyyYyynnnnnnnnB
441718288692
441718306220

441718311746	yyyyyYyyyyyyyyyny
441718312035	
441718312483	
441718314468	
441718317477	
441718317991	
441718330381	
441718331383	
441718339136	
441718370211	
441718371173	
441718371192	yyyyyyYyyyyyyyyyyy
441718374812	
441718374942	
441718375118	yyyynyYyyyyyyyyyyy
441718377171	
441718378143	yyyyyYyyyyyyyyyyy
441718395805	
441718738200	yyyyyNnnnnnnyyyyy
441718959020	yyyyyYyyyyyyyyyyy
441718969007	yyyyyYyyyyyynnnnB
441719161509	
441719170523	
441719226545	
441719227288	
441719227966	yyyyyYyyyyynyyyny
441719250469	yyyyyYyyyyyyyyyyy
441719250795	
441719282067	yyyyYyyyyyyyyyyy
441719282728	
441719285037	yyyyyYyyynyyyyyyy
441719285440	
441719286974	
441719288144	
441719288405	yyyyyYyyynyyyyyyy
441719288476	yyyyyYyyyyyyynnnn
441719303092	
441719308499	yynyyYyyyyyyyyyn
441719310429	
441719351546	
441719356510	
441719362229	yyyyyYyyyyyyyyy
441719362689	yyyyyNynyyynyny
441719371479	
441719371767	
441719372849	
441719373745	yyyyyYnnyyyyyyy
441719375287	
441719377896	yyyyYynyynyyyyy
441719383165	yyyyyYyyyyyyynnB
441719389066	
441719389751	
441719550110	
441719561435	
441719561469	
441719637192	yyyyyEyyyyyyyyyy
441719733252	
441719736380	yyyyyYyyyynyyyyn
441719737355	
441719766478	
441722415102	yyyynYyyyynyyyyyy
441723500117	
441723500254	
441727834456	yyyyyYyyyynyyyyy
441732350570	
441732362541	
441732369201	yyyyyYyyyyyyyyyyn
441732463918	
441732763285	
441732770049	

```
441732771160
441733269424      yyyyyYyyyyyyyyyyn
441733281445      yyyynYnyyyynnyyny
441733464222
441733897629
441734351232
441734504340
441734568211
441737373848
441743247701
441743271702      yyyyyYyyyyyyyyyy
441745815903
441745855534
441747855722      ynnnnYnyyyyyyyyny
441752222778
441752234595      yyyyyYyyyyyyyyyy
441752255962      yyyyyYyyyyyyyyyy
441752333444      ynnnnNyyyyyyyyynn
441752670730      yyyyyYyyyyyyyyyy
441753512277      yyyyyYyyyyyyyyyy
441753571617
441762391896      ynnnnYyyyynyynnnn
441766762734
441767692365
441772201917      yyyynNyyyyyyyyyy
441772618356      yyyyyNyyyyyyyyyy
441782289115      yyyyyNyyyyyyyyyy
441782641121      yynnnYynnnnnnnynn
441782744110      yyyyYyynyyyynyny
441782747777      nnnnYnnnnnnyyyy
441782812428
441789263102      yyyyyYyyyyyyyyny
441792468194      yyynYnnnnnyyynnn
441792475264
441792511171      yyyyYnyyyyynyyy
441792511965      nnnnYnynyyyynnnn
441793411510
441793414606
441793513650      yyyyyYyyyyyynyyy
441793524318
441793886182
441796474007      yyyyyYyynyyyyyyy
441812001751
441812034067
441812245769
441812450845
441813121930      ynnnnYnnnnynnnyyy
441813126632
441813320495      nynnnYynnnnnnyyyy
441814134503
441814403159
441814442313      yyyyyYyyyyyynnnB
441814467695
441814794040      yyyyyYnynyyyynyyy
441815093190
441815633029
441815670605
441815762782      yyyyyYyyynnyynnnn
441815764284      yyyyyYynyyynynynn
441815767624      yyyyyYyyyyyynnyy
441815990984      yyyyyEyyyyyyynyyy
441815990989
441816006119      yyynyNnnnnnnnnnnn
441816524005
441816528932
441816592409      yyyynYynyyyyyyyy
441816711722
441816813937      nnnnnEnnnnnnnynnn
441816874309
441817401741
```

441817404622   yyyyyYyyyyyyyyyyy
441817413819   yyyyyYyyynyynnnnB
441817491647   nnnnnEnnnnnnnnnnn
441817492831   yyyyyYynnnnnnnnnB
441817496734   yynyyYnnnnyynyyyy
441817496972   ynnnnYyynnyyyyyyy
441817497520   nnyyyYnyyyyyynnnn
441817497554   yyyyyYyyyyyyyyyyy
441817497872   nyynYyyyyyyynyyy
441817498622   yyyyNnnnnnnnnnnn
441817499016   yyyyNnnnnnnnnnnn
441817499259   yyyyYyyyyyyyyny
441817524398   yyyyYyyyyyynyyyy
441817525915   yyyyYyynnnyyyyy
441817597739
441817600588
441817600973
441817611502
441817819794
441818008005   yyyyYyyyyyynyyyn
441818139700   nnnyYnyyyyynyyyn
441818339215
441818527211
441818547476
441818582049
441818788905
441818815151   yyyyYyyyyyyyyny
441818839215
441819000705
441819059729
441819070073
441819431198
441819802041
441819813779   yyyyNynnnnnnnnnB
441819833846
441822614405   nyyyYnnnynnynnnB
441823321044   yyyyYyyynyyyyyyn
441823332539   yyyyYyyyyynyyyny
441823332862
441851704270
441865716418
441865791347   yyyyYyyynyynyyyn
441865843971
441889590588
441892518028
441896759494   yyyyYyyyyyyyyyyy
441902755163   yyyyYyyyyyyynnnn
441902772415
441902838266   yyyyYyyyyyyynnnn
441904488878   yynyYyynyynynyy
441904523698
441904610067   nyyyYnnnnnnnnnn
441904610937   nyyyYyyyyyyyyyyy
441904611112
441904651642
441905748006   ynyyYyynyyyyyyyy
441905766293
441908564893   yyyyYyyyyyyyyyy
441908694008   yyyyYyyyyyyynnnn
441912210112   yyyyYyyyyyyyyyY
441912220013
441912321710
441912325082   yyyyYyyyyyynyyyy
441912612302   yyyyYyyyyyyyyyyy
441912618571   yyyyYynyyyyyyyyn
441914775660   yyyyYyyyyyynyyny
441914880933   yyyyYyyyyyyynnn
441914888611   nyyyYyyyyyyyyyyy
441914889222   yyyyYyyyyyyyyyy
441915670888   nnnnNnnnnnnnnnn

```
441920487056
441923425457
441923664606
441924466522
441926403958
441926424760        yyyyYyyyyyyyyyy
441926831532
441932832532
441932854750
441932859661        yyyyYyyyyyyyyyy
441942884397        yyyyNyyyyyyyyyyy
441946724889
441949836583
441952291035
441962713134
441962861186
441962861646
441970627206        ynnnYnnyynyynnnB
441978758565        yyyyYyyyyyyyyyyy
441978759701        yyyYyyyyyyyyyn
441983821690        yyyYyyyyyyyyyyn
441984623901        yynYyyyynyynnnn
441992555647
```

No faxes were sent after April 2000.

Faxes Sent to British Parliament logs

During the 1998-2000 period my records indicate that I sent at least 14,480 faxes to the British Parliament in Westminster, of which 9,138 went via TPC's email-to-fax service and 5,342 were sent via fax-modem direct from my computer. The actual figure is obviously much higher since, for most of this period, whenever a recipient asked to be deleted from my mailing list, I totally wiped all entries including that from the logfile.

In the records "Y" indicates successful transmission from fax-modem, "N" indicates failed transmission from fax-modem. "E" indicates an error occurred while transmitting via fax-modem and a fax may have been only partly transmitted. "y" and "n" indicate success or failure via TPC.

In April 2000 I changed the method of operation by recording "R" when a recipient requested removal, rather than wiping their details from my mailing list and records; and keeping "B" records for when TPC actioned a ban on a recipient's fax-number, but the recipient did not write to ask me to cease faxing. The purpose of these changes was to keep more accurate and complete records, but the intention was thwarted by the police complaint.

```
441712190076        nnnnnynnEnnnnnnYYNNYYYNENNNNNynynnnnnnnnnnNnnnnnnnn
441712190179        yyyynnyyyYnyyyyynYYYNYYYYYEYEEEyyyyyyynyyyynyyyyy
441712190189        yyynyyyyyYyyyyyyyyYYEYYYYYYYYYYYyyyyyyyyyyyyyyyyyy
441712190243        yyyyyyyyyYnnnnnnnYYYYYYYYYYYYYnynnnnnnnnnnNnnnnnnnn
441712190246        ynnnyyyyyYnyyynyyYYYYYYYYYYYYYYYynyyyynyyyyyyyyyyy
441712190253        yynnnnnnnNnnnnnnnNNNNNNNENNYNNNnnnnnnnnnnnnNnnynnnnn
441712190254        yyyyyyyyYnynynyyYYEEEYYEEYYEYEYyyyynyyynyynyyyyyyn
441712190266        yyyyyyyyYyyyyyyYYYYEYYYYYNYYyyyynyyyynyyyyyyyyy
441712190300        yyyyyyyynYyyyynnYYYYYYYYYYYYYYYnnyyyyyyyyyyyyyyyyy
441712190301        yyyyyyyyyYnnyyyyYYYYYYYENNYYYnyyyynynyynyyynnnB
441712190305        yyynnynyYynnyynYYEYYYEEYYYYEYynyynyyyynyNnyyynyyy
441712190309        ynyyyyyyYynynnYYYYYYYYYYYYYYYYyyyyyyyyyyyyYYyyy
441712190317        yyyyyyyyYyyyyyyYYYNNYYYYYYYEyyyynnyyyyynynnnynn
441712190319        nyyyynnnNnnnnnnNNNNNNNNNNNNNNNnnnnnnnnnnnnNnnnnnnnn
441712190323        nyyyyyyYyyyyyyNNNNNNNNNNNNNNnnnnnnnnnnnnnnnnnnnn
441712190329        yyyyyyyyYyyyyyyYYYYEYYYYYYYYyyyyyynyyyyyyyyyyy
441712190331        ynyynnnnYyynnnnYYNYYYYYNNYYYynynnnnnnnnNnnnnnnn
441712190332        nnynnynyYyyynyyYNYYYYYYYYYYYYynynynnnnnnNnnnnnnn
441712190337        ynyyyyyyYyyyyyyYYYYEYEYYYYYyyyyyyyynyyyyyyyyy
441712190350        yyyyyyyyYyyyyyyNNNNNNNNNNNYYYYynyyyyyyyyyyyyyyyyy
441712190371        yyynnnnnNnynyyyYNNNNNYNNNNNNnnnnnnnnnnnnnnnnnnn
441712190390        yyyyynyynYynynyYYYYYYYYYYYYYYyyyyyyyynnynyyyyyy
441712190409        nnyyyyyyYyyyyyyYYYYYYYYYENYYyyyyyyyyyyyyyyynnyyy
441712190438        yyynnnnnNyyynyyYYYYYYEYYYEYYYyyyynynyyyyyyyyyyyy
441712190446        yynnnnnnYyynynyYYYYYEYYYEYYYyyyyyyyyynyyyyyyyn
441712190448        yyyyyyyyYyyyyyyYYYYYYYEYEYYyyyyyynnynnyyyyyyyy
441712190461        nynnnnyyYnnnnnYYYYYYYYEYYEEYyyyyyynynynnyyyyy
441712190475        yynnnnnnNnnnnnNNNNNNNNNNNNNnnnnnnnnnnNnnnnnnnn
441712190492        yyyyyyyyYyyyyyyEYYYYYYYYYYEYyyyyyyyyyyyyyyyyyyy
441712190495        ynnnnnnNyyyyyyYYEYYYEYYYYYEyyyyyyyyyyyyyyyyy
441712190511        yyynnyynYynnnnnNNNNNNNNNNNNNNnnnnnnnnnnnnnnnnnn
441712190514        yyyyyyyYnyynyyYYYNYYNYNEYYYYyyyyynynnnynyynnnyy
441712190536        yyyyyyyyYyyyyyyYYEYYEYYYYEEyyyyyynynnnYnnnnnnB
441712190559        yyyyyyyyYyyyyyyYYEYYYYYYYYYyyyyyyyyyyyyyyyyyy
441712190573        nyyyyyyyYynnnnYYYYYYYYYYYYYNnnyyyyyyyyynnnnnyy
441712190598        nyyyyyyYynynyyYYYYYEYYYNNNyyyynyyyyyyyyyyynyy
441712190612        ynnnnyyyYnynnyyYYYYYYYYYYEYYyyyyynnynyyyyyyyyy
441712190620        yyyyyyyyYyyyyyyEYEYYYYYYYYYYEyyyyyyyyyyyyyyyyyny
441712190622        yyyyyyyyYyyyyyyYYYYNYNYYYYYyyyyyyyyyyyyyyyyyyyy
441712190628        yyyyyyyyYynyyyYYYYYEYYYYEYYEyyyyynyynnNnnnnnnnnn
441712190638        yynnyyyyYnyyyyyYYYYYYYYYYYYyyyyyyyyyyyyyyyyyyyy
441712190643        ynyyyyyYnynyyyYYYYYYNYYYYYYyynyyynyyyynnnnB
441712190645        yyyyyyyyYyyyyyyYYYYYYYYYYYYyyyyyyyyyyyyyyyyyy
441712190662        nynnnnnnYnnynnnNYNNNYNNNNNYNNnnnnnnnnnnNnnnnnnn
441712190663        nnnnnnnnYnnynyyNNNNNENNNNNNNnnnnnnnnnnNnnnnnnn
441712190664        nnnnnnnnYnnynnNYNNYNYNYYNNYNYnnnyynnyynNnynnnnny
441712190682        yyyyyyyyYyyyyyyYYYYYYYYYYYNYYnyyyyyyynynyyynyyy
```

441712190685	ynyyyyyyYyyyynyYYYYYEYYYYNYEYYyyyyynyyyNnyyyynyyy
441712190696	yynnnyyEnnyyyYEYEYYYEEEYYYyyyyyyyyyyyyyyyyy
441712190698	yyyyyyyyYyyyyyEYYYNNNNNNNNNnyynnyynyyynyyynnnnn
441712190770	yyyyyyyyYynnyyyYYYYYEYYYYYYyyyyyyynyyyyynyynyy
441712190783	yyyyyyyyYyynnnYYYYYYYYNEYYyyyyynyyyyyNnyyyyyyy
441712190789	nnyyyynyYnnnnyyEYNYYYEYENYYEEyyyyyyyynyyyynyyyyn
441712190790	yyyyyyyyYyyyyyyYYYYYYYYYYYYYnnnyyyyyyyyyyyyyyyy
441712190904	yyyyyyyyYyyyyyyYYEEYYYEYYEYYyyyyyyyyyyyyyyyy
441712190912	yyyyyyyyYyyyyyYYYYYYYYYYYYEYynyynyyyyyyyyyyyy
441712190913	yynyyyyyYyyyyyyYYYEENYYEYYYYYyyyyynnyyyyyyynyyy
441712190919	yynnnnnnYynnnnnNYYYEYNYYEYYNEyyynnyyynyynnyyyny
441712190923	yyyyyyyyYyyyyyyYYYEYYYEYYYYYyyyyyyynnyyyyyyyyy
441712190926	yyyyyyyYynyyyyYYEENYEYYEYYYYynyyyyyyyyyyyyyyyy
441712190928	yynyyyyyYnnnnnnNNNNNNNNNNNNNnnnnnnnnnnnnnnnnn
441712190931	yynynyyyYyyyyyyYYYYYYYYYYYYYNnnyyyyyyyyNnnyyyyyy
441712190938	yyyyyyyyYyyyyyyNYYYENYYNYNEEYYyyyynnnnnynNnnnnnnnn
441712190943	yyyyyyyyYynnnnYYYEYYYYENNYEEnnyyynnynyyyyyyyyyn
441712190946	ynyyyyyyYyynyyYYYYYYYYYYYYEyynnnnnnnynnnnnyn
441712190949	yyyyyyyyYynnyyYYEEEYYYNEYNYYYnyynnyyyyyyyynnnB
441712190952	yyyyyyyYyyyyyYYYEYYYYYYEYYyyyyyyynyyyyyyyyyy
441712190957	yyyyyyyyYynnyyYYYYYYYYYYYYyyyyyyyyyyynyyyn
441712190961	nyynnyyYynynyYEEYYYEYYYYYYYyyyyyyynyyyyyyynyn
441712190965	nnyynnnnYnnnnnYYYYYYNYYYYYYnynnnnnnyyNnyyyyyyy
441712190971	yyyyynyYynyyyYYYYYYYYYYYNYyyyyyyyyyyyyyyyynyy
441712190972	yyyyyyyyYyyyyyyYYYYYYYYYYYYyyyyyyyyyyyyyyyyyy
441712190976	nyynnynyYyynnnYYEYYYYYYEYYYyynnyyyyyyynnnnynyn
441712190978	yyyyyyyyYyyyyyYYYYYYYYYYEYEYyyyyyyyyyyyyyyyyB
441712190979	yyyyyyyyYyyyyyYYYYYYYYYYYYyyyyyyyyyyyyyyyyyy
441712190981	ynyyyyyyYyyyyyYYEYYYYEYYYEYyyyyyyyyyyyyyyyyy
441712190986	yyyyyyyyYyyyyyYYYYYYYYEYYYYyyyyyyyyyyyyyyynyyy
441712190987	yyyynyyyYyyynyYYYYYNYNNNNEYYynnnyyyyyyyyyyyyy
441712190994	yyyyyyyyEyyyyyYYYYEEEYNNNNNNNNnnnnnnnnnnNnnnnnnnn
441712191131	yyyyynyyyEynnyyEYYEEEEYEEENEYYyyyyyyyyyNnyyynyyy
441712191137	yyyyyyyyYyyyyyyYYYYYYYYYYYYYNYnyynyyyyyyyyyyyy
441712191145	nnynnyyyNnynnnnYYYYNNNNNYENNyyyynnnyyyNnnynnynn
441712191154	yyyyyyyyYyyyyyyYYYYYYYYYYYYYyynynyyynyynyyyyy
441712191158	ynnnnnnnYyynnnnYYYYYYYYYYYYYynnnnnnnnnnnnnnnnn
441712191161	yyyyyynyYyyyyyyYYYYYYYYYYYYYyyyyyyyyyyyyyyyyy
441712191162	yyyynyyyYnnnnnnYYYYYYYYYYYYyyyyyyyyynyyyyyyy
441712191163	yyyyyyyyYynyynyYYYEYYYYYYYYEyyyyyyyyynyynyyyynR
441712191174	ynnnnnynYyyynynYEYYYYYYYYYNNNyyyyyyyyyyyyyyynyyyy
441712191177	yyyyyyyyYyyyyyyYYYYYYYYYYYYyyyyyyyyyyyyynyyyyyy
441712191179	nyyyyyyyYynyyyyYYYYYYYYYYYYyyynyynnnynyyynynnn
441712191184	ynyyyyyyYynyyyyNNNNNYNYYYYYNNyyynynynnyyyyyyyn
441712191185	nyyyyyyyYnnnyyyYYYEYYYYYYEYYyynnnnnnyyynnnyyyny
441712191198	yyyyyyyyYnnyyyyEYYYYEEYYYYYYynyyyyyyyyynyyyyy
441712191227	yyyyyyyyYyyyyyyYYYYYYYYYYYYYyyynyyyyyyNnnnyyyyny
441712191236	nnnnynynYnnnnnnNNNNNNNNNNNNNnnnnnnnnnnnnnnnnn
441712191263	yyyyyyyyYyyyyyyYYYNYYYYNNNNYNyyynynynyyynnynynn
441712191268	yynyyyyyYnyyyyyYYYYYYYYYYYYYnyyynnyyyyyNnyyynyy
441712191279	yyyyyyyyYyyyyyyYYYYEYYYYYYEYyyyyyyyyynEnnnnnB
441712191280	nnnnnnnnYnnnnnnNNNNNNNNNNNNNnnnnnnnnnnnnnnnnny
441712191395	yyyyyyyyYyyyyyyYYYEYYYYYYYYyyynnyyyyyyyyyyyyn
441712192008	yyyyyyyyYyyynnnYYNNENNNNNNNNNnnyyyyyyyyyyyyyyy
441712192031	yynyyyyyYyyyyyyYYYYYYYYYYYYyyyyyyynyynyyyyyyy
441712192051	yyyyyyyyYynnnnnYYYYYYYNYYYYYyyyyyyyyyyyyyyyynyn
441712192054	yyyyynyyYyyyyyyYEYEYYYYYYYYYyyyyyyynyyyyEnyyyyyyny
441712192064	ynyyyyyyYyyynnnYYYYYYYYYYYYyyyyyyyynyyyyyyyyynn
441712192075	yyyyyyyyYyyyyyyYYEYYYEYYYYNYyyyyyyyyyyyyyyyyy
441712192082	yyyyyyyyYynyyyyyYYYYYEEYYYYNyyyyyyynyyyyyyynyy
441712192112	yyyyyyyyNyyyyyyYYYYYYYYNNEYYyyyyyyyyyyyyyyyyy
441712192117	ynyyyyyyNnynyyyYNYYYYYYNYYyyyyyyyyyyyyyyyyy
441712192130	ynnnnnnnYyynnnYYYYYYYYYYYYYynnnnnnnnnnnnnnnn
441712192148	ynyyyyyyYyyyyyyYYYYYYYYYYYYyyyynyyyynyyyyyyynyy
441712192170	yyyyyyyyYynnnnnNYYYYYNYYYYYyyyyyyyyyyyyyyyyyyn
441712192212	yyyyyyyyYynnnnnNNNNNNNNNNNNNnnnnnnnnnNnnynnnnn
441712192220	yyyyyyyyYynyyyyYYYYYYEYYNYYyyyyyyyyyyyyyyyyyy
441712192221	ynyyynyyYyynnnnYYYYEEEYYNYYYyyyynyyynynyyyyyyny
441712192233	yyynnyyyYyyyyyyYYYYYEEYEEYYYYnnnyyyynyyynyynynyn
441712192252	yyyyyyyyYyyyyyyNYYYYYYYYYNYEYyyynyyyyyyyyyyyyny

441712192262	yynnnyyyYynnyyyNNNNNNNNNNNNNNnnnnnnnnnnnnnnnnnn
441712192269	yyyyyyyyYyyyyyyYYYYYYYYEYYYYyyyyyyyyyyyyyyyyyy
441712192288	yyyynnnnEnnnnnnYEYYYENNNNNNYEyyyyyyyyyyyyyyyyyy
441712192289	yyyyyyyyYyyyyyyYYYYYYYNYYYYYyyyyyyyyyyynyyynny
441712192302	yyynnyyyEnnyyyyEYYYYYNYYYYYYYyyyynynynnnyyynynnyn
441712192328	yyyyyyyyYyynyyyYNYYYYEYYEYYYYyyynyyyyyynyyyyyny
441712192329	yyyyyyyyYyyyyyyYYYYYYYYYEYYEnyyyyyyyyyyyyyyyyy
441712192331	yynyyynyYnnnnnnYYEEYEEYEENNYNNynnnnnnnynnNnynyynny
441712192334	ynyyyyynNyyyyyyYYEEYYEEYYYYEEYyyyynyyynnynnyyynyy
441712192338	ynnnnnnnYyynnnnYYEYYYEYEYYYYynnnnnynnnnnnnnnnn
441712192357	yyynyyyyYyyyyynYEYYNYYYYYYYYyyyyyyyynyyyynynyB
441712192359	yyyynyyyYyyyyyyYYYYYYYYEYYYyyyynyyyyyyyynyyyy
441712192364	nnnnnnnyEynnnnYNYYYYEYENNNNnyyyyyyyynnNnnnnnnn
441712192377	yyyyyyyyYyyyyyyYYYYYYEYYYYYyyyyyyyyyyyyyyyyy
441712192404	yyyyyyyyYyyyyyyNYYYEYYYYYYYYyynynynyyyyyyyyyyy
441712192412	yyynyyyyYyyyyyyYEEYEYNEYNYYYYnyynynnynnnynyyynyn
441712192413	yyyyyyyyEyynyyyYYYYYYEYYYEYYyyyyyyyyynyyyyyyyy
441712192417	yyyyyynyYyynynnNYNYYYYYYYYYYyyyynyyynnNnnyyyyyy
441712192418	ynyynnyYyynnnnNNNNNNNNNNNNNnnnnnnnnnnNnnnnnnn
441712192423	yynnnynyYyyyyyyYYYYYYEYYYEYYyyyyyynnnyynyynyn
441712192425	nnyyyyyyNnnnnnnNYYYYYEYYEYYNyyyynnynnnynnyynnnn
441712192428	yyynnyyyYnnynnyYYNYNYEEEYYYYYynnnynynynyyynnyy
441712192433	yyyynyyyYyynyyyYYYYYYYYYYYYynyyyyyyyynyyyyyyyny
441712192450	nnynyyyYynnnnnYNYYYYYNYYYEYYnyyynnyynnyNnnnnnyB
441712192451	yyynyyyYyyynyyYYYYYYNEYNYYYYyyyyyynyyyNnnnyynny
441712192455	yyyyyyyyYnyyyyyNYYYYYYYYYYYYyyyyyyyyynyyyyyyyyy
441712192461	yyyyynyyYyyyyyYEYYYYYYYYYYYynyyynyyyyyyyyyyyy
441712192476	yyyyyyyyYyyyyyyYYYYYYYYYYYYYyyyyyyyyyyyyyyyyy
441712192477	yyyyyyyyYynnnnnEYYYYYYYYYYYYyyyyyyyyyyyyyyyyy
441712192479	yynyyyyyYyyyyyyYYYYYYYYEYYYEyyynyynyyyyyyyyyny
441712192485	yyyynynnNnnnnnnNYYYYYYYENNYYnnnnnnnnnnnnnnnnnn
441712192494	yyynyynyYnnnnnnNNNNNNNNNNNNNnnnnnnnnnnnnnnnnn
441712192495	yynyyyyYyyyyyYYYYYYYYYYYYyyyyyyyyynnyynnnB
441712192496	ynyyyyyyYyyyyyyYYYEYYYYYYYYYyyyyyyyyyyyyynyynyy
441712192500	yyyyyyyyYyyyyyyYYYYYEYYYYYYYyyyyyyyyyynynyyyn
441712192503	yyynyyyyYnnynyYYNNNNNNNNNNNNnnnnnnnnnnnnnnnn
441712192516	ynnnnnnnNyyyyyNNNNNNNNNNNNNnnnnnnnnnnnnnnnnnn
441712192518	yyyyyyyyYyyyyyyYYYYYYEYYYYYyyyyyyyyyyyyyyyyyy
441712192521	nyyyyyyyYynnyyyYEYYYYYYEYNYYYyyyyyyyyyynyNnnnyyyyy
441712192529	yyyyyyyYynnyyYYYEEEEYEYYENEYynyyyynyyyyyyyyyyy
441712192536	nyyyyyyyYnyyyyyYYYYYYYEYNYYYYynyynyyyynyyynyyyy
441712192539	yyyyyyyyYnyyyyyEEYYYYYYYYYYYYyyyyyyyyyyyyyyy
441712192541	yyyyyyynYynnnnnYYNYYNNEYYYYYYNnnnnyyyyyyyNnnyynnny
441712192545	yyyyyyyyYyyyyyyYYYYYYYYYYYYYyyyyyyyyyyyyyyynyy
441712192557	nyyyyyyyYynnnnnYEYYEYYYYEYYYNYyyyyynnnynynNnnnnnn
441712192564	yyyyyyyyYnyyyyyYYEYYYYYYNYYYyyyynyyyynyyyyyyyyy
441712192567	nynyyyynYynyyyyYYNYYNEYEYYYYYyyyyyyyyyyyyyynn
441712192570	yyyyynyyYyyyyyYYYYYYYYYYYYYYyyyyyynyyyyyynyyyy
441712192571	yyyyyyyyYyyyyynYYYYYYYYYYYYYyyyyyyyynynyyyyyy
441712192573	yyyyyyyyYyyyyyyYYYYYYYYYYYYYyyyyyyyyyyyyyyyyy
441712192586	yyyyyyyyYnyynyyYYYYYYYYYYYYYyyyynyyyyyyyyyynyyy
441712192608	yyyyyyyyYyynyyyYYYYEEYYEYEYEYyyynyynyyyyyyyyyyy
441712192619	yyyynynyYnynyyyYYYYYYNYYEYYYEnnyyynynynnYnnnnnB
441712192621	ynnnnnnnYynnnnnNYNYNNYYYEENNnnnnnnnnnnnNnnnnnnn
441712192622	yyyyyyynYyyyyyyYYEYYYYYYYYYYyyyyyyyyyyyyyyyyy
441712192629	nnnnnnnnEnnnnnnEEEEEEEEEEEEEEnnnnnnnnnnnnnnnnnnn
441712192630	nnnnnnnnYnnnnnnEYYYNYEYEYNYYYnyyynynnynynNnyyyyyy
441712192643	ynyyyyyyYyyyyyyYYYYYYYYYYYYYyyyyyyyyyyNnynyyyyy
441712192651	yyyyyyynYyynyyyYYYYYYYYNNYYyyyyynyyyyynnnyyn
441712192665	yyyyyyyyNynyyyyYYYYYYYYYYYYnnynnnnnnnnyyyyny
441712192671	yyynyyyyYnyyyyyYYYNNNYYYYYYYnnyyyyyyyynyyyyyy
441712192684	yyyyyyyyYnnynyyYYENYYYNEEYYYYynyynnyynyynyyyyyy
441712192690	yyyyyyyYnnyyyyyYYYYNNYYYYYYYyyyyyyyyyyyyyyyyy
441712192694	nnyyyyyyYyyynyyEENYYYYYYYYYEEnnyyyyyyyyyyyyyyy
441712192697	yyynynnnNnnnnnnNNYNYYYNNYNYYYyyynnnyyyyyNnyynyyy
441712192698	yynnnnnYnnnnnnNNEYYYEYYYNNNYYnyyyyyyyyyyynynnn
441712192706	nynnnnnYyyyyyyYYYYYYYYYYYEYyyyynyyyyyyyynyyy
441712192707	nnyyyyyyYyyyyyYYYYYYEYYYYENYnnyyyyynnnyyyyyynB
441712192708	ynyyyyyYnnynyyYYYYYYYYEYEYYYYnnynnnynnnnynnynnnn
441712192710	yyyyyyyyYyyyyyyYYYYYYYYYYYNYYyyyyyyyyyyyyyyynyn

441712192711	ynnnnnnYynyyyyYYYYYYYYYYYYEYnnnnnnnnyyyyyyyny
441712192731	nnyyyynYyyyyyyYYYNYYYYYNYEYYyyyyyyyyyyyyyyyyy
441712192738	yyyyyyyEynyyyyYYYYYYYYYYYYYyyyyyyyyyyyyyyyyyy
441712192747	ynyyyyyYnnnnnnNNNNNNNNNNNNNNnnnnnnnnnnnnnnnnnn
441712192749	yyyyyyyNyyyyyyYYYYYYYYYYYYYyyyyyyyyyyyyyyyyyy
441712192763	yyyyyyyYnnnnyyYEEEEEEEEEEYNYyyyyyyyyyynnyyyyyy
441712192771	yyyyyyyYnnnnnnNNNNNNNNNNNNNnnnnnnnnnnnnnnnnnn
441712192772	yyyyyyyYyyyyyyYYYYEYYYEYYYEYyyyyyyyyyynyynynyynn
441712192782	yyyyyynYyyyyynyYNNYEYYYEYYYYynynnyyyyynyyynyyy
441712192795	yyyyyyYyyyyyyYYYNYYYYYYYYyyyyyyyyyyyyyyyyyy
441712192797	yyyyyyYnnnnnnYYYYYYEYYYYYEyyyyyyyynyyyyyyyyy
441712192798	yyyyyyYyyynnnYYYYYYYYNYYYYnynyynnnynynyyyynyy
441712192799	yyyyyyYyyyynyEYEYYYYYYYYYYynnnyyyyyyyyyyyyyyy
441712192804	yyyynyYyynyyYYYYYYYYYYYNYynyyynyyynnynynyn
441712192810	yyyyyyYynnyyyYEYYYYYYYYYYyyyyyyyyyyyyyy
441712192814	yyyyyyYyyyyyyYYYYYYYYNNYYYnnnnnnnnnnnnnnnnnn
441712192820	yynnnnYnyyyyyYYYYYYYYYYNNYYnyyyyyynynnNnynynynn
441712192834	nynnnnNynnnnnEEYYENYYNNEYYYyynnyyynnnnnnnnnny
441712192849	yyyyyyYyyyyyyYYYYYYYYYYYyyyyyyyyyyyyyyyny
441712192872	nyyyyyyYnnnnnYYEYYYYYYYYYYnyyynyynnynyynyyyyy
441712192873	yyyyyyYyyyyyyNNNNNNNNNNNNNnnnnnnnnnnNnnnnnnnn
441712192879	yyyyyyYnyyyyyYYYYEYYYYYYYyyyyyyyyyyyyyynyny
441712192905	yyyyyyYyyyynnYYYNNNNNYYNYEYynyyynyyyyyyynyyyy
441712192912	yyyyyyYyyyyyyYYEYYEEYYYYYEYyyyyyynyyyyyyynyyy
441712192921	nyyyyyYyynyynEYYYYYYYYYEEYNynnnnnynnynynyyyyy
441712192949	yyyyyyYyyynynYYYYYYYYYYYYYyyyyyyyyyyyyyyynn
441712192957	yyyyyyYyyyyynYYYEYYYYYYYEYyyyyyyyyyyyyyyyyy
441712192965	ynyyyyYyyyyyyYYYYYYYYYYYYYyynynyyyynyyyyyyyy
441712192969	ynnnnnYnnyyyyYNEEYYNYNEYEYNYnnnynyyyynNnyynnyny
441712192991	ynnyyyYyynyyyYYEEYYYYYYEYYYnyyyyynynnnEnnnnnnB
441712193000	nnynynNynnnnnNNNNYNNNNNNNNNnnnnnnnnnnNnnnnnnnn
441712193010	yyyyyyYyynynyNYYEYEYYYYEYYNYyyynnnnyynNnynnnyny
441712193047	yyyyyyYynyyyyYYYYYEYYYYYYEyyyynyyyyyyyyyyyy
441712193085	yyyyyyNyyyyyyYYYYYYYYYYYYYyyyyyyyyyyyyyyyy
441712193373	yyyyyyEyyyyyyYYYYYYYYYYYEYyyyyyynyyynYnnnnnnB
441712193382	yyyyyyYyyyynyYYEYYYYYYYEYEYnnnyynnyyyyynnnyy
441712193398	yyyyyyYyyyyyyYYYYYEYYEYYYyyyyyyynyyyyyyynyyy
441712193434	nyyyyyYyynyyyYYYYEYNYYYYYYYynyyyynnnnyyyyyyyy
441712193496	ynyyyyYnnnynnNYEYNYEYYYYYEyyyynnnnnnyynnyyyyy
441712193541	nyyyynNyyyynyYYNYYYYYYEYYYYnnnnnnnnnnNnnnnnn
441712193552	nyyyyyYynnnynNNNNNNNNNNNNNnnnnnnnnnnnnnnnnnn
441712193637	yyyyyyYnyyyyyYYYYEYYYYYYYnnnnnnnnnnnnnnnnnn
441712193640	yyyyyyYnyyynyYYNYYYYYYYENEYnnnnnnnnnnEnnnnnnnn
441712193665	nyynyyEyyyyyyYYEENYYYYNYYEYyyyyyyyyynyyyyyyyy
441712193690	yyyyyYyyyyyyYEYYYYYYEYYYYyyyyyyyyyyyyyyyyyy
441712193709	nnnnnnYnnnnnyYYYYYYYYYYEYYnyyyyyyyyynyynnyy
441712193727	yyyynYyyyyynnYYYEEYNYYYNYNNyyyynyynnnNnnyynnyn
441712193801	yyyyyyYyyyyyyYYYYYYYYYYYYYyyyyyyyyyyyyyyyyy
441712193806	yyyyyyYyyyyyyEYYEYYYYYYYEEyyyyyyyyyyyyyyy
441712193816	yyyyyyYyyyyyyYYYYYEEYYYYYyyyyyyynyyyynyyyynnn
441712193819	ynnnnnYyyyyynYYYYYYYNNNNNNnnnnnnnnnnnnnnnnnn
441712193823	nnnnnnNnynyyyNYYYNYEYEEYYEYYyyynnyyynnyyynyyynyR
441712193824	yyyynyYyynyyyYYYYYYYYYYYYyyyyyynyynyynnnyyn
441712193827	ynnnnnYyyyyyyYYEYYYYYYYYYEnnyyynnnynyyyyyyny
441712193829	yyyyyyYnnnnnnYNYYYYYYYYYYnnnnnnnnnnnnnnnnn
441712193847	yyyyyYnyyyyyYYYYYYYYYYYYyyyyyyyyyyyyyyyyyy
441712193849	yyyyyyYyyynyyYYYYYYYYYYYYyyyyyyyyyyyyyyyyyy
441712193866	yyyyyyYyyyyyyYNYYYYYYYYYYYyyyyyyyyyyyyyyyyy
441712193870	yyyyyyNnyyynyEYYYEEEYYYYEYYnnyynyyyyyyyyyyny
441712193889	yyyyynYNynnnnnNNYNNNNNNNYNNnnnnnnnnnnNnnnnnnyn
441712193895	yynyyyYyyyyyyYYYEYYYYYYEYNyyyyyyynyyynyyyyn
441712193899	yyyyyyYyyyyynYYYYEYEEENYYYYynnynyyyyyyynynny
441712193921	yyyyyyYyyyyyyYEYYYYYYYYYyyyyyyyyyyyyyyyyy
441712193931	yynnnnYyynnnnEYYYEYYYYYYYYynnnnnnnnnnnnnyyy
441712193935	ynnyynYyynyyyYYYYYYYYEYEYYEyyynnnnyyyyyyynyyyy
441712193952	yyyyyyEnyyynyYYYYYYEYYYYEYyynnnnnnnnnnnnnnnnn
441712193957	yyynyyYyyyyyyYYYYYEYYNNNYEEnnyyyynyyynyyyyyyy
441712193967	yyyyyyNynnnnnYYYYYYYYYYYEYyyyyyyyyyyyNnyyyyyyy
441712193980	nyyyyyYynynyyYYYYYYYYYYYYYyyynnyynnnnnnnnnnnn
441712193983	ynnyyyYnnnnnnYYEEYYYYYYYYYEnynnnnnnnnNnnnnnnnn

441712193987	nynyyyYnnnnnnNYYYYYYYYENYNYnnynnnynnnnNnnnnnnnn
441712193998	ynnyyyYyyynyyYYYEEYYEYEYYYYynyyyyyyynyNnyyynnyn
441712193999	yyyyyyYnyyyyyYYEEYYEYEYYYYYyyyyyyyyyyyynyynnn
441712194013	nnnnnnNynnnnnNNNNNNNNNNNNNNnnnnnnnnnnnnnnnnnnn
441712194042	nnnnnnNynnnnnNNNNNNNNNNNNNNnnnnnnynnnnNnnnnnnn
441712194064	nnnnnnNnynnnnNNNNNNNNNNNNNNynnnnnnnnynnnnnnnnn
441712194166	yyyyyyNyynynyYYYYYYYYYEYYNYyyynyynnyyNnyyyyyyy
441712194262	yyyyyyYyyyyyyYYYYYYYEYYYYYyynyynnnnnNnnnnnnnn
441712194279	nyyyyyYnnyyyyYYYYYYYYYYYYYyyyyyyyyyyyyyyyyyny
441712194285	yyyyyyYyyyyyyYYYYYYYYYYYYYyyyyyyyyyyyyyyyyyyy
441712194293	nyyyyyYnnnnnnYYYYYYYYYYYYNnnnnnnnnnnnnnnnnnn
441712194303	yyyyyyYynyyyYYYYYYYYYYYYyyyyyyyyyyyyyyyyy
441712194308	yyyyyyYynnnnnYYYYYYEYYYYYYyyyyyyyyyyyyyyyyyy
441712194352	yyyyynYnnnnnnYYNNYNNYNNNNNNnynnynnynyyyyyyyny
441712194357	yyyyynYynyyyyYYYYYEEYYYEEENyyyyyyyyyyynynynyy
441712194358	yyyyyyYynnnnnYNYYYNYYYYYYYYyyynyyynnyyyyyyyyy
441712194397	yyynyYyyyyyyYYYYYYYEYYYYYYyyyyyyyynyyynyyyyy
441712194403	yyyyyyYyyyyyyYYYNYNYYYYYYYYynynyyyyyyNnnynyn
441712194466	yyyyyyYyyyyyyYYYYYYYYYYYYYyyyyyyynyyyyyyyyyy
441712194479	yyyyyyYyyyyyyYYYYYYYEYNNYYnnnnnnnnnnnnnnnn
441712194499	yyyyyyYyyyyyyYYYYYYYEYYYyyyyyyyyyyyyyyyyy
441712194518	yyyyynYnyyynyYYNYYYEYYYYYYnnnnnnnnnnnnnnnnnn
441712194525	yyyyyyYyyyyyyYEYYYEEEYYYEYYYyyyynyynyyNnynynyy
441712194536	yyyyynNnnnyyyYYYEENYYYEYYYYEnnyyyyynyyynnnnnnn
441712194711	yyyyyyYyyyyyyYYYYYYYYYYYYYyyyyyyyyyyyyyyyyyy
441712194727	yyyyyyYnnnnnnNNNNNNNNNNNNNNnnnnnnnnnnnnnnnnn
441712194759	yyyyyyYyyyyynYYNYYYYYYYYYYyyyyyyyyyyyyyyyyy
441712194780	yyyyyyYyynyyyYYYEYYYEYYYYYynyyyyyyyyyyNnyyynyy
441712194800	yyyyyyYyyyyyyYYYYYYYYYYYYYYnyyyyyyyyyyyyyyyy
441712194801	yyyyyyYynyyyyYYYYYYEYYYYYYYnyyyyynyyyyyyyyyyy
441712194803	ynyyynYynnnnnYYYYEYEYYNYEYYyyyyyyyyyyyyyyyyy
441712194815	yynyyyYyyyyyyYYYYYYYYYYYYyyyyynyyyyyyyyyyyn
441712194828	yyyyyyYyynyyyYEYYYYYYNYYYNynyynnynnnyyNnyyyyyy
441712194830	nyyyynEnnnnnnEEEEEEEEEEEEEEnnnnnnnnnnnnnnnnnnn
441712194831	nyyyyyYnnnnnnYYEYYYYNNNNNNNynnnnnnnnnnNnnyyyyy
441712194836	yyyyyyYyyyyyYYYNYYYYYYYYYYyyyyyyyyyyyyyyyyy
441712194837	ynyyyyNyyyyyYYYEYYEYYYYYYYEYynyyyyyyyyyyyyyyy
441712194841	yyyyyyYyyyyyEYYYYYYNYYYYYYyyyyyyyyyyyyyyyyy
441712194843	ynyyyyYyyynyEYYYYYYYYYNYYYyyyyyyyynyyyyynnyy
441712194844	yyyyyyYyyyyyyYYYYEYEYYYYNEYYEynyyyyynynnyYnnnnnB
441712194846	yyyyyyYyyyyyyYYYYNNNYYYYYYYyyyyyyynyyyyyyyynn
441712194855	yyyyyyYyyyyyyYEYYYEEYYYNNNNynnnnynnnynNnyyynnn
441712194864	yyyyyyYyyyyyyYYYYYYYYYYYYYyyyyyyyyyyyyyyyyy
441712194867	yyyyyEyyyyyyyYYYYYYYYYYYYYYyyynyyyyyyyyyyyyy
441712194868	yyyyyyYyyyyyyYYYYYYYEEYYYYnyyyyynyyyyynnyyn
441712194873	yyyyyyYnyyyyyYNYYYYYYEYYNYYyyynynyyyyyyyyyyB
441712194877	yyyyyyYyynyyyYYYYYYYYYNYNNYYyyynynyyyyNnyynyyn
441712194878	nyyyyyYnnnnnYYYYYYYYYYYNYYyyyyyyyyyyyyyyyyy
441712194880	yyyyyyYyyyyyyYYYYEENYYEYYYYEnynynnnynynyynnB
441712194881	yyyyyyNnyyyyyYYYYYYYYEYYYYyyyyyyyyyyyyyyyyy
441712194884	yyyyyyYyyyyyyYYYYNYYYEYYYYYyyyyyyyyyyyyynyyy
441712194894	ynnnnnYyynnnnNYEYEYEYYYYYEEYEyyynnnynyynnNnynyyy
441712194899	yyyyyyYyynyyyYYYYYNYYYYYYYEYyyyyyyyyyynynynyy
441712194901	yyyyyyYyyyyyyYEYYYYYYYYYYYEYyyynyyyyyyyNnynyyyy
441712194903	yyyyyyYyyyyyyYYYYEYYYYYYYYYyyyyyyyyyyynyyyy
441712194924	nyyynyYyynnnnNYYYEEYYYEYYYEyynnnynyyyyyyyyyy
441712194931	ynyyyyYyyyynyYYYYYEYYYYYNYyyyyyyynyyyyyyyyyy
441712194939	yyyyyyYyyyyyyYNYYYYYEEYYYYEyyyyyyynyyyyyyyyy
441712194964	yyyyyyYnyyyyyYYYYYYYYYYYYNYynyyyyynynnynnyn
441712194970	yyyyyyYyyyyyyYYYYYYYYYYYYYyyyyyyyyyyyyyyyyy
441712194979	yyyyyyYnyyyyyYYYYYYYYYEYYYYyyyyyyyyynNnynnyn
441712194983	yyyyyyYnnnnnnEEYYYYYEYYEEEYEYnynynnnnnnnyyyyy
441712194992	yyyyyyYyynyyyYYYYYYYYEYEYEYyyyynnyyyyyyyyyy
441712194996	yyyyyyEyyyyyyYYEYYEYYYYYYENNnnnnnnnnnNnnnnn
441712195106	yynyyyNnnnnnnNNNNNNNNNNNNNNnnnnnnnnnnnnnnnnn
441712195127	yyyyyyYnyyyyyYEYYYYYYYYYYYyyyyyyynyyyyyyyyy
441712195136	yyyyyyYynnnnnNYEEYEYYYYYYEYYYynynnnnynyynnnnn
441712195165	nnynnyNnnynnnYYNNNNNNNNNNYNYnynnnnnnnynNnynnnn
441712195233	nyyynnNnnnnnnNNNNNNNNNNNNNNnnnnnnnnnnnnNnnnnnn
441712195241	nnynyNnnnnnnNNNNNNNNNNNNYNYnynnnnnnnynnynynnn

441712195275	yyyyyyYyyyyyYYYYYYYYYYYYYYYyyyyyyyyyyyyyyyyyn
441712195322	nyyyyyYnyyyyYEYEYYYYYYYYYYyyyyyyyyyyyynyyyny
441712195333	yyyyyyYyyyyyYYYYEYEYYEYYYYyyyyyyyyynyyyynyyny
441712195371	yyyyyyYynyyynYYENYEYYYYYYYYyyynyyynnyyynynnynn
441712195381	yyyyyyYynyyyyYYEYYYYYYYYYYYyyyyynnyyynyyyyynyy
441712195418	nnynnyNnnnnnnNNYNNNNNNNNNNNNnnnnnnnnnynnnnnnnn
441712195452	nnnnnyNnnnnnNNNNNNNNNNNNNNYnynnnnnnnynnnnynnn
441712195461	yyyyyyYyyyyyyYYYYYEYYEYYEYYyyyyyyynynyyyyyyyy
441712195482	nyyynnNnnnnnnNNNNNNNNNNNNNNNnnnnnnnnynnnnynnnn
441712195502	yyyyyYynnnnnNNNEYYYYYYYYYYyyyyyynyyyynnyy
441712195568	yyyyyyYyyyyyYYYYYYYEYYYYYyyyyyyyyyyyyyyyy
441712195581	yyyyyyYyyynyyYEYNYYYNYYYNYYyynyyynyynynyyyny
441712195604	yyyyyyYynyyyyYYYYYYYYYYYYENnnnnnnnnnnyyyyyyn
441712195650	yyynnnYyyyyyYYYEYYYYYNNYEYNynnnnnnnnnnnnnnn
441712195687	ynnnnnNnynnnNYYNYNENYYYYYNYyyyyyyynyyyyyyyyyy
441712195713	yynnnnYyynnnYNNNNNNNNNNNNNYYynnnnnnnnnnyyyyyy
441712195725	yyyyyyYynyyyyYYYEYYYYYYYYYyyyyyyyyyyyyyyyyyy
441712195728	yyyyyyYnyyyynYYYYYYNYYYYYYYyyyyyyyyyyyyyyyyyyn
441712195734	yyyyyyYyyyynyEYYYYYYYYYYYYyyyyyyyyyyyyyynyy
441712195743	yyyyynYyyyyyyYYYYYYYYYYEYYyyyyyyyyyyyyyyyyy
441712195814	yyyyyyYnyyyyyEYYYYYYEYYYYYyyyyyyyyyyyyyyyyy
441712195820	yyyyyyYyyyyyYYYYYYYYYYYYYyyyyyyyyyyyyyyyy
441712195826	yyyyyyYynyyyyYYYYEEYYEEEYYYYyyyyyyyyyyyyyyyy
441712195834	nyyyyyYynnnnnYNNNNNNNNNNNNNNnnnnnnnnnnnnnnnn
441712195839	yyyyyyYyyyyyyYNYYYYYYYYYyyyyyyyyyyyyyyyy
441712195847	yyyyyyYynnnnnYYYYYYYYYYYYYYYnyyyyyyyyyynyyny
441712195853	yyyynyYyyyyyyYNEYNEYYYYYYYyynnyyyyyyyyyyyyy
441712195854	yyyynyYyyyyynYYYYYYYYNYYYYYnyyyyyyyyyyyyyyyy
441712195856	yyynyyYynyynyNYYYYYYYYEYYYEYyynnnnnnyynnynnn
441712195890	yyyyyyYyyyyyyYYYYNYYYEYYEYYyyyyyyyyynyyyyy
441712195892	yynynnYnyyyyYYYYYNYNEYYEYNNNnnnnnnnnnnnnnnn
441712195894	nyyyyyYyynynyYYYYYYYYNYEYYYyyyyynyynyyyynnnB
441712195897	yyyyyyYyyyyyYYYYYYYYYYYYYYEyyyyyyyyyyyyyyyy
441712195898	ynnnnnYnyyyyYYYYYYEYYYNYYyyyyyyyyyynyyy
441712195903	yyyyyyYyyyyyYYYYEYYYYYYYyyyyyyyyyyyyyyyy
441712195906	yyyyynYyynynEYNEYNEEYEYYEYYEnynyyyyynnnynyynyy
441712195910	yyyyyyYynyyyyEYYYYYEYYEYYYEYYyyyyyyyyyyyyyyyy
441712195919	yyyyyyYynyyyEYYYYYYEYEYYYYynyyyyyyyyyyyyyy
441712195930	ynnnnnYyyyyyyyYYYYYYYYYYYYYYYynnnnnnnnnnnnnnnn
441712195933	yyyyyyYynnnyyYYEYYYYYYYYEYYyyyyyyyyyyyyyyyyy
441712195939	ynnnyyYyynyynYYYYYEYYYYEYYyyyynyyyynyynynnyny
441712195942	yyyyyyYynnnnnNNNNNYYNYNNNNNYYnyynnnnnnnynnynyyyy
441712195944	yynnnnYynnnnnYYYYYYYYYYYYYNYYyynynnyyyyyyyyy
441712195945	yyyyyyYnyyyyyYYEYYYYYYYYYEYyyyyyyyyyyyyyyyny
441712195951	yynynnYyynnnnYYYYYEYYYYYYYYYynnnnnnynnnnnnnnn
441712195959	yyyyyyYnnnnnnNNNNNNNNNNNNNNnnnnnnnnnnnnnnnnn
441712195962	nyyyyyYyyyyynYYEYYYYYEYYYYYyyynyyynynnyyyyyyy
441712195969	yyyyyyYnyynyYYYYYYYYYYYYYyyyyyyyyyyyynyyyny
441712195982	yyyyyyYynyyyyYYYEYYEYYYYYEYyyyynyyyyyyyyynyny
441712195997	yyyyyyYyyyyyYYYYYYYYYYYYYYyyyyyyyyyyynnnnnnn
441712195999	nyyyyyYyyynnNNYNNNNNNYYYYYYynnnnnnnnnnnnnnnn
441712196045	yyyyynYyyyyyYYYYYYYYYEYYEYyyyyyyyyynyyyyyyy
441712196050	yyyyyyYnyyyyYYYYYYYEEYYYNEYynynynnyyyyyyyyy
441712196052	yynnnnnYynnnnYYEYYYYYYYYYYYynnnnnnnnnnnnnnn
441712196059	nyyyyyYyyyyyEEYYYEEENYYYYEYyyyyyyyyyyynyyynyn
441712196126	nyyynyYyyyyyyYYYYYYYYYEYNNNNnnnnnnnnnnnnnnnn
441712196156	nyyyyyYyyynnYYEEYYYEEYEYEEYYyyyyyynnyyyyynyyynn
441712196201	nyyyyyYynnnnYYYYYYYYYYYYYYYyyyyyyyynyyyyyyy
441712196261	yyynyyYyyyyyYYYYYYYYYYYYYYyyyyyyynynyyyyynyy
441712196279	nnyyyyYyyyyyYYYYYYYYYYYYYYYyyyyyyyyyyyynyyyyyny
441712196290	yynyyyYynnnnNYYYYYYYEYYYYYnyyyyyynyyyyyynnyy
441712196362	yyyyyyYyyyyyEYYYEYYYYEYYYEYyyyynyyyyyyyyyyyyy
441712196386	ynnynnYnyyyyYYYYYYYYYNEYYYYYyyyyyyyyyyyyyyyyy
441712196396	yyyyyyEyyyyyYYYYYYYYEYYYEYYyyyyyyyyynyyyyyyny
441712196398	yyyyyyYynnnnEYNYENYYYYYNNYYNnnyynnnnnnnnnnnnn
441712196409	yyyyyyYynyyyYEYYYYYYYYYYYNYyyyyyyyyyyyyyyyyy
441712196488	nnynnnnYnnynnNNNNNNNNNNNNNNNNnnnnnnnnnnnynnnnn
441712196498	nnnnnnEnnynnNNNNNNNNNNNNNNNNnnnynnnnnnnnnnnn
441712196567	yyyyyYyynnYYYYYYYYYYEENYYYyynyyynynynnynnnB
441712196586	yyyyyyYyyyyyYYYYYYYYYYYYYYYyyynyyyynyyyyynyy

441712196606   yyyyyYynyyYYYYYYYYYYYNYYYEyyyyyyyyyyyyyyyy
441712196607   nyyyyYyyyyYYYYYYYYYYYYYYYyynyyyyyyyyyyyyyy
441712196618   yyyyyYyyyyyYYYYYYYYYYEYYYYyyyyyyyyyyyyyyyy
441712196623   yyyyyYyynyyYYYYYYYYYYYYYYYyyynynynnnnynnynn
441712196660   yyyyyYyyynyYEYYEYYYYYYYEYEYynynyyyyyyynyyyyy
441712196716   ynnnnYynynyEYYYYNNYYYEYEYYYYnyyyyynnynyynynnyy
441712196726   yyyyyYnyyyyYYYYYYYYYYEEYYYYyyynyyyyyyyyyyyy
441712196732   yyyyyYyyynyNNYYNENNYYYNENYEYyyyyyyyyyyyyyynny
441712196760   yyyyyYyyynyYYYYYYYYYYYYYYYyynyyyyyyyyyyyyyy
441712196791   yyyyyYyyyyyYYYYEYENYYYYYYYYynnyyyyyyyyyyyyyy
441712196793   yyyyyYyyyyyYYYYEYYYYEYYYYEYyyyyyyyyyyyyyyynnyy
441712196818   yyyyyYynnnnYYYYYYEYYYEYYENNnnnnnnnnnnyyynnnyy
441712196820   yyyyyYyyyyyYEYYYNYYEYYYYYEYyynyyyyynynnnnnnnn
441712196825   yyyyyYyyyyyYYYYYYYYYYYYYYYyyyyyyyyynyyyyyyyy
441712196826   ynnnnYyyyyyYYYYYEYYYYYYYYEyyyyyyyyyyyyyyyyy
441712196828   yyyyyNyynnnYYNYNYYNNNNNNYEYNnnnnnynnyynyyy
441712196835   yyyyyYyynnnENYYEYYYYYYYYYEYynyyyyyynnnyyynyyn
441712196837   yyyyyYyyyyyYYYYYEEYYYYYYYEynnnnynnnnnnnnnyn
441712196838   yyyyyYnnnnnYYYYYYYYYNYYYYNnnnnnnnnnnnnnnnnn
441712196839   yyyyyYyynnyYYYYYYYYYYYYYYYyyynyyyyyyynnyyy
441712196848   yyyyyYyyyyyYYYYYYYYYEYYYYYyyyyyyyynyyyyyyyyyy
441712196864   yyyyyYyyyyyYYYYEYYEYEEEYYYyynyyyyyyyyyyyyy
441712196867   yyyyyYyyyyyNYYYYYYYYYYYYYNYynynyyyyyyyynnyyy
441712196877   nyyyyYyyyyyYEYYYYEEYYYYYEEyyyynynyyyyyyyyyy
441712196884   yyyyyYyyyyyYYYYYYYEYYYYYYYyyyyyynyyyyyyyyn
441712196886   yyyyyYyyyyyYYYYYYYYYYYYYYYyyynnyyyyyyyyyyyR
441712196898   ynnnnYynyyyYYYYNYYYEYENNYYYyyyyyyynyynyyynnny
441712196938   yyyyyYynnnnEEYYYYYYYYYYYYYynyyyyynnnnnnnnnn
441712196943   yyyyyYyyyyyEYYYYYYYEYEYYYEYyyyyyyyynyyyyyynn
441712196956   nyyyyYyyyyyYYYYEYYYYYYYYEYyyyyyyynyyyyyyyy
441712196974   yyyyyYyynynENYYNYYYYYYEYYyyyyyyyyyyynyyyn
441712196977   yyyyyYyyyyyYYYNNNNYYYNNEYnyyynynnyynynnnnnn
441712196979   nynynYnnyyyYYYYYYYYYYYYYYYnnnnyynnnnnnnnynnn

No faxes were sent after April 2000.

MI5 Persecution: How Could It Be True?

If you have the patience to read these articles you will be struck by how apparently fantastic the claims being put forward are. You may ask yourself why such seemingly nonsensical assertions are made. This matter has been discussed on the Internet's UK-local newsgroups for three years now, and the denizens of the uk.misc newsgroup (the so-called "miscreants") have come up with a number of theories to explain these posts; it has been variously suggested that they are a troll (an artificial creation for the amusement of its author), that they are made by MI5 themselves with the purpose of discrediting other conspiracy theories, and that the poster is mentally ill and the articles are symptomatic of the illness (the view held by most miscreants).

You may see the newsgroup posts for yourself at website;

http://www.pair.com/spook/

Should you wish to reply you can do so;

    by **fax** to 0171-681-1190   by **email** to bu765@torfree.net

Are these claims the product of mental illness, or is that just a cover?

The most obvious explanation, that the claims made result from the admitted mental illness of the author, is the one which the persecutors intend be the one accepted without consideration being given to the possibility of the claims being true. The persecutors have actually been very clever about this, both in selecting as their target someone who was known from school or university as being borderline schizophrenic, and in ensuring the nature of their persecution corresponds to what often features in the delusions of a schizophrenic.

The very first incident of the persecution occurred in June 1990, when I was still a student at university in London. It consisted of a reaction (giggling) from the newsreader, Sue Carpenter of ITN, to what she saw happening in my living-room at my parents' home where I was living. Before your imagination gets the better of you I should make clear that what the newsreader was reacting to was not too embarrassing in nature; my mother had brought an apple for me into the the room, and Sue Carpenter found this amusing.

I recognized that Carpenter had reacted to what she had seen in my living-room, yet this idea still seemed completely fantastic to me. My reaction was to continue watching television, particularly the news, to see if this incident would be repeated. It was, many times, both on BBC and ITV. An intelligent person would have thought to obtain a video recorder and capture some of these incidents in order to try to explain to an observer what he saw in these broadcasts. Unfortunately, I failed this test of intelligence, since I did not record these programmes. I have recently attempted to obtain from ITN tapes of their news programmes dating back to summer 1990, but, unhappily, they have advised me that they do not have complete programmes including newsreaders' comments dating back to that period.

From the outset, the persecutors structured their actions to ensure that any complaint would be met with disbelief, and dismissed as delusional. This is why they chose as their target someone who was known at school and university to be borderline mentally ill; and it is why they fired the first shots of their campaign through the broadcast media. Schizophrenics commonly believe the media harass them; it would be exceptional for "full-duplex television" to exist in reality. Those with schizophrenia also commonly believe people are talking about them; again, the persecutors have shown themselves very rarely, but act through intermediaries, both in the workplace, and in public and during travel.

Mental illness is not the cause of these claims, but the simulation of its symptoms is a cover used by the persecutors to deny their victim the ability to have his compaints believed.

What evidence exists to support these claims of "interactive television/radio"?

Quite frankly, I have very little evidence to support my claims. You may examine the "Evidence" area of my website to see such evidence as I have been able to gather. None of it is remotely conclusive. The "smoking guns" all date back to 1990/91, and it is really rather late now to start trying to look for material dating back seven or eight years. In 1997 I started tape-recording every programme I watched or listened to. I also started carrying with me a high-fidelity minidisc-recorder with good quality microphone to catch incidents of public harassment, but this also has not been as successful or conclusive as I had hoped.

Perhaps the best item in the "Evidence" section is the audio file "Life is so hard" (it is labelled with Garfield the cartoon character on the site), which I have given a certainty level of 100%. This item relates to harassment at my workplace in Canada in 1996. A co-worker called Mark was coming up with phrases and expressions which were repeating things being said at my Canadian residence, consequently leading me to believe that my apartment and home phone were bugged, and that the persecutors were passing their gathered information on to Mark. On one particular evening I said in my apartment, "life is so hard, and then you die". The following day I was able to record Mark saying exactly the same phrase at work.

Unfortunately when "they" know you are recording them, they simply don't say things which would unambiguously show harassment. When Mark the co-worker knew he was being recorded, he only made his remarks out of range of the recorder, for example outside the building. When the TV newscasters or radio disc jockeys know they are being taped, they limit themselves to saying things which are ambiguous, which even in my mind may or may not be personally directed against me.

Who knows about this persecution?

Surprisingly many people know. People in the media, such as BBC and ITN newscasters including Martyn Lewis and Michael Buerk, and radio disc jockeys such as Chris Tarrant of Capital Radio, know what is going on, and take part in it. Some co-workers at my former workplaces in England and Canada have known about the harassment. Quite a few people in the general public are also included. I believe the police are aware of the persecution, but, unfortunately, have chosen not to take any action to stop it. I have complained at my local police station in London several years ago, and I have stated on the internet newsgroups that I have done so, hence the police will be well aware of my wish to see the matter resolved. I believe their inaction denotes a dereliction of duty, but without good evidence, I am powerless to compel them to take steps to prevent further harassment, or deal with what has already taken place.

What is the purpose of sending these faxes?

These faxes are being sent to three distinct groups of people, namely Members of Parliament, the media, and diplomats & legal people. As you will have observed I am making use of the email-to-fax gateway at Demon Internet to send these faxes. I am forced to use this gateway since I currently live in North America, and cannot afford the high cost of direct phone calls to the UK.

My purpose in publicising my claims is firstly to discourage the persecutors from continuing their campaign, and also to attempt to bring their campaign out into the open, and thus perhaps identify the persecutors. Neither aim has been achieved yet, but I hope that with sufficient stimulation these aims may yet be accomplished.

The problem with the second aim is that those who read this article will fall into two groups, those who don't know anything about the persecution and consequently will disbelieve my claims as delusional, and those who **do** know about the harassment and may have some idea of who is behind it, but realise that if the harassers are exposed and the truth brought out into the open, then powerful British institutions will substantially lose prestige, and be exposed to ridicule.

It would give me hope to believe that these faxes will create a third group of people, those who find out that I am telling the truth, and who follow their consciences in standing up and seeing justice done. Only time will tell if this hope will be realized.

MI5 Persecution: "Why do you think MI5 are responsible?"

The question of who is ultimately responsible for this eight-year harassment is one which is very difficult to answer, as the persecutors have never clearly made their identities known to the persecutee. However, I believe I am correct in attributing the continuing victimisation to elements of the British Security Service MI5, and in this article, I will try to explain the reasons for this belief.

You are (once again!!) encouraged to read the full story on the World Wide Web at address;

http://www.pair.com/spook/

The British internet magazine ".net" featured my website on page 17 of their March 1998 issue (number 42). Their review kindly describes it as an "excellent site" and gives some details of what the net surfer will find there. Should you wish to reply to this article you can do so;

      by **fax** to   0171-681-1190   by **email** to   bu765@torfree.net

"When did you first suspect MI5 were responsible?"

Over Easter 1995 I went to see a local solicitor in London with a view to talking to the police about the harassment. Soon afterwards I did go to my local police station in Clapham and spoke to an officer there. The solicitor made a comment which suggested to me that the persecution I had been experiencing may have been organised by an intelligence service.

Up to this point, I did not have any clear idea as to who was behind the harassment. Only their agents were visible, in the media, on television news programmes, and on the radio; in the workplace, where things said at my home were repeated verbatim; and in some cases abuse in public and during travel, for example on the trip to Poland in June 1992 which I have already described.

Both from the fact that widely disparate individuals and organisations were employed as agents in the campaign against me, and from the fact that an entity would be required to marshal their resources in the areas of spying on my home and giving gathered information to their agents, it was clear to me that a single entity was responsible for carrying out the campaign. Yet from June 1990 until Easter 1995 I did not have a clear idea of who might be responsible. I guessed that perhaps some private individual or group of persons who saw themselves as my enemies had perhaps paid private detectives to organise the harassment. Alternatively, since the campaign had started in the media, I made a far-fetched supposition that perhaps it was an ad-hoc group of media people who had set themselves up in opposition to me. After Easter 1995 I saw that these guesses were wrong, and I made an I believe much more accurate estimate as to who my enemies really are.

"Why couldn't a private group be behind the persecution?"

There are several reasons why a private individual or group would not be behind this campaign.

Quantity of resources / Money. Here is what one Usenet (internet newsgroup) participant had to say (several years ago) on the topic of how much money it would cost just to keep the surveillance going.

```
PM: >But why? And why you? Do you realize how much it would cost to keep
PM: >one person under continuous surveillance for five years? Think about
PM: >all the man/hours. Say they _just_ allocated a two man team and a
PM: >supervisor. OK., Supervisor's salary, say, £30,000 a year. Two men,
PM: >£20,000 a year each. But they'd need to work in shifts -- so it would
PM: >be six men at £20,000 (which with on-costs would work out at more like
PM: >£30,000 to the employer.)
PM: >
PM: >So, we're talking £30,000 x 6. £180,000. plus say, £40,000 for the
PM: >supervisor. £220,000. Then you've got the hardware involved. And
PM: >any transcription that needs doing. You don't think the 'Big Boss'
PM: >would listen to hours and hours of tapes, do you.
```

```
PM: >
PM: >So, all in all, you couldn't actually do the job for much less than
PM: >a quarter million a year. Over five years. What are you doing that makes
PM: >it worth the while of the state to spend over one and a quarter million
PM: >on you?
```

A private individual or group would not spend over a million pounds to verbally torture a victim without some financial motive or gain. Private industry is driven by the profit motive, and there is no financial profit to be had from carrying out a campaign in this way. If a private enterprise were behind it then they would have taken direct physical action a long time ago.

State enterprises, on the other hand, can afford to be wasteful, since they are funded by the taxpayer. They do not have to show a money profit. The employees or contractors employed by a state organisation such as MI5 are driven by their own personal profit motives, to make the most money out of their employers for the longest period of time. MI5 is funded to the tune of £150M p.a.; even a few hundred thousand a year would to them be affordable if their managers could convince themselves of the necessity of what they were doing.

Quality of resources / Technical resources - electronic and other surveillance. In summer 1994 a reputable and competent private detective agency was employed to conduct a counter-surveillance sweep of my home in London. They charged us over £400 for this, conducted a thorough search for radio transmitting devices, hard-wired "probe" microphones and also tested the telephone line. They found nothing. This was not altogether surprising, since it had been made very clear to me that there **were** bugs in my home; the "buggers" would not have made this clear unless they had felt their bugs were of sufficient sophistication as to be safe from detection.

But there is another lesson to be gained from the failure of the private detectives to find anything. The agency employed was one of the most reputable in London. They were employed on the principle of "setting a thief to catch a thief", for if the harassment were being carried out by private detectives, as I then believed, then surely another set of private detectives would be able to find the bugs that they had planted. That these "private eyes" were unable to find anything, and that the harassers were confident that they would not be able to find any bugs, points to the harassers being an order of sophistication above a private agency, and leads me again to believe that a state intelligence service is responsible for the surveillance and harassment.

Quality of resources / Technical resources - Interception of Postal service. In summer 1994 when I emigrated to Canada to try to escape the harassment, I wrote letters home to my family and friends in London. Quite soon after my arrival in Canada, the harassers were able to find precisely where I was staying. The only way I can see of "their" being able to find out my new address was by interception of my letters to the UK.

Later in 1994, I conducted an experiment to see if my letters home were indeed being read. In a letter home I wrote of being depressed and talked in vague terms of suicide. I deliberately chose this topic, since I believed it was the outcome my harassers were trying to achieve, and that if they read the letter, they would "echo" its contents. Sure enough, soon afterwards there were two incidents of people shouting "suicide" at me in public places in Canada.

It is inconceivable for a private agency to have the ability to intercept postal mail. The state security service on the other hand is well known to engage in these activities.

Quality of resources / Access to Media. One of the strangest aspects of this case is the access "they" have to the broadcast and print media. I still do not understand what could persuade newscasters such as Martyn Lewis and Michael Buerk, who consider themselves "gentlemen", to behave in an almost voyeuristic way by "peeking" into the living room of one of their viewers. A year ago I wrote to the BBC asking if these newscasters would confirm or deny the accusations made against them. The BBC replied that their newscasters had denied the accusations, but refused to do so in writing.

It is well known that MI5 have the ability to plant stories in certain newspapers, but convincing television newscasters to "watch" a viewer while they read the news would surely be very difficult for them to accomplish, unless they presented themselves to these journalists as being, for example, a group in the media who were seeing to it that I got my "deserved" treatment. MI5 has a history of manipulating the media, so it might not be too difficult for them to accomplish such a trick, whereas a private group would not have this ability.

"Have they ever denied that they are the Security Service?"
No. Never. This is in fact the main reason why I believe "they" are MI5 and not a privately funded group. If my guess had been wrong then I am sure that "they" would have crowed over my mistake, but they have never admitted nor denied that they are employees of MI5.

In early January 1996 I flew on a British Airways jet from London to Montreal; also present on the plane, about three or four rows behind me, were two young men, one of them fat and voluble, the other silent. It was quite clear that these two had been planted on the aircraft to "wind me up". The fat youth described the town in Poland where I had spent Christmas, and made some unpleasant personal slurs against me. Most interestingly, he said the words, "he doesn't know who we are".

Now I find this particular form of words very interesting, because while it is not a clear admission, it is only a half-hearted attempt at denial of my guess that "they" = "MI5". Had my guess been wrong, the fat youth would surely have said so more clearly.

"If MI5 were behind it, why would they wish to mask their involvement?"
I have heard a number of times a belief from people in the media that it is they, the media people, who are behind the abuse. In spring 1994 Chris Tarrant the Capital Radio D.J. said sarcastically on his breakfast show, "You know this bloke? he says we're trying to kill him. We should be done for attempted manslaughter". We, we, we. Tarrant thought it was a media conspiracy.

Returning to the question of "interactive watching" by television newscasters, it would again be much easier for them to take part in that sort of activity if they convinced themselves that the surveillance and abuse were organised by "their own", by media people. It must be second nature to MI5 to mask their involvement in the matters they deal with; in this case, they pretend the campaign is organised by a group in the media, and any journalists who suspect otherwise keep their silence.

Conclusion
Over the last three years I have stated with some force my belief that MI5 are responsible for my misfortunes. I have done so on Internet newsgroups, in letters and faxes to people in politics and the media in the UK, and in 1997 I made a formal complaint to MI5 regarding their activities; the Security Service Tribunal replied in June 1997 that "no determination in your favour has been made on your complaint". (I believe the statement by the Security Service Tribunal can be disregarded, as they have never, ever made a ruling in favour of a complainant.) In three years of naming MI5 as my oppressor "they" have never denied the charge. To me, their silence on this point indicates that my guess was accurate. I believe my persecutors stand identified. The question of why they should carry out this campaign is one I will try to answer in a future article.

> **MI5 Persecution Update: Friday 15 May, 1998**
>
> The persecution has been quite severe for the last week. It appears that my enemies are reacting to the steady stream of faxes making their way over the Atlantic to the fax machines of Westminster politicians and the media. Here is what's happened in the last few days;
>
> The week started off with an incident in the cafeteria at a local shopping centre where I habitually drink my morning coffee. My enemies have concentrated since winter 1995/96 on throwing a particularly horrible sexual slander against me. They "put people up" to repeat this slander against me, and this is what happened again here.
>
> On Thursday morning (yesterday), instead of going to the usual cafeteria I went to a nearby convenience store for coffee. The same horrible sexual slander was shouted at me very loudly by a member of staff as I walked into the store. This was the first time I had ever bought morning coffee in that shop. The other staff obviously knew what was going on, one of them said, "they screwed up my life".
>
> The fax gateway I use to send these faxes to the UK has been working hard these last few days to shut down my access by barring the accounts I use to send these faxes.
>
> I have received an anonymous threat from fax number 0171-219-6101 (the machine gave its name as "ETRA-HoC") which said, "Stop sending to this fax no 0171-219-6101 or else" (the consequences of continued transmission were unspecified). I invited the sender to apologise for his threat, but received no response.
>
> This all adds up to quite a severe reaction to my faxes of the last few weeks. I actually find this quite heartening since it shows that my faxes are finding the mark and there may yet be a breakthrough in my efforts to expose the Security Service conpiracy of abuse against me which has now been going on for eight years.

MI5 Persecution: "Why would they be doing this to you, sir?"

This article will concentrate on the difficult question of "Why". The question which forms the title of this piece was asked of me by the police officer I spoke to in Easter 1995, when I went to make my complaint.

There are really two sides to this question. Firstly, why should MI5 be harassing anybody in this fashion? Secondly, if they choose to behave in this way, why should they have selected me in particular, and not somebody else? Alternatively, why did the persecution start, and why is it continuing?

I do not have definite answers to either side of this question, since my persecutors have usually kept themselves hidden and only acted through other parties. To know "why", one would have to know who the persecutors are, and something of their personalities, since their abuse is almost certainly symptomatic of a personality disorder of the abusers. Certain things however can be deduced about the abusers from the nature of their behaviour, and I will talk about this later in the article.

You are reminded that the full story is on the World Wide Web at address;

`http://www.pair.com/spook/`

Reply   by **fax** to   0171-681-1190   by **email** to   bu765@torfree.net

Why did it start?

It is clear that the persecution must have been initiated by someone who knew me personally, either at school, or at university, or socially, and knew that I was borderline mentally ill, since this is what makes me a target for the persecutors. Unfortunately, the originators have never been identified, and there are several possible candidates. Neither has the link from the originators of the persecution, to the persecutors themselves, ever been made clear. So who are the originators?

University Staff
The identity of the originators may lie in the timing of the persecution. It started in June 1990, while I was finishing a course at Imperial College in London, and a year after I graduated from Cambridge, where I received a degree in computer science. At Cambridge I had achieved some notoriety in the computer lab from various nefarious exploits. Roger Needham attacked me by saying that "there were great hopes for it, but it failed terribly". When I started at Imperial I found that my reputation had preceded me; Cambridge computer lab had spoken to I.C. lecturers about me. I.C. lecturer Frank McCabe summed up commenting about "setting up a straw man so you can tear him down". (Despite being "torn down" by the Cambridge computer lab's lecturers, I still achieved a good first degree and a Master's degree at Imperial.)

Other students at university
So, the originators may have been university staff who knew me from my student days. But there are other possibilities. I had other enemies at university, including some fellow students. At my Cambridge college it was common knowledge that my mental health was dubious, and it was known that I talked to myself in my sleep - the floor and walls were quite permeable to noise, so other students heard. I was given the nickname "gibber" because of this habit. Sometime later, I managed to catch myself talking in my sleep when I woke up in the middle of the night.

Here is a quote from a participant in the internet newsgroup where I have been posting for the last three years;

```
>One thing which has been missing from this discussion is this simple
>prognosis: that maybe he is right and that, despite his admitted
>mental condition, there really is a campaign against him organised by
>now-influential ex-students of his university.
```

People I knew socially
I had yet other enemies in 1990 (I am a man of many enemies!). In January 1990 I broke up with some people I had been going out with socially. One of them, by the name of Andy Turner, wrote a letter to Alan Freeman, who at the time was a Radio 1 DJ. Freeman read part of the letter out on his Rock Show, about the "one who wore out his welcome with random precision", saying "that's a hell of a letter you wrote there Andy", and "with a schizophrenic you're never alone".

It is my belief that Andy Turner and his friends were trying to make trouble for me, and Turner wrote to Freeman with this in mind. Freeman may have discussed the letter with others, and things may have snowballed from there. This is, of course, pure supposition. The fact is that I do not know who the originators are, and can only guess.

Once it started, why is it continuing?
The answer to this question is obvious. It is unacceptable to the "powers that be" in the UK to have somebody running around who knows he has been targeted by the Security Service and media organizations, and who is in a position to embarrass British institutions. This has become particularly evident in the last week; as I send more faxes to UK politicians and media, so the pressure on me grows, and the volume of abuse increases.

Part of the reason the persecution continues is in the personalities of the abusers, and it is this subject to which I will turn to next, since the key to understanding the persecution lies in understanding those who carry it out, as much as we can.

The Security Service operatives, the persecutors, are they psychopaths?
Let us first examine the definition of the term "psychopath". DSM-IV defines "anti-social personality disorder" as a "pattern of disregard for and violation of the rights of others ... deceitfulness, irritability and

aggressiveness ... consistent irresponsibility and lack of remorse". The Harvard Mental Health Letter of Sept 1995 describes these people as using "charm, manipulation, intimidation and violence to control others and satisfy their own needs. Lacking in conscience and in feelings for others, they cold-bloodedly take what they want and do as they please", having "no guilt or regret".

I must say, reading this description of the condition, that it fits the persecutors perfectly. The persecutors have never shown the slightest remorse or guilt. Even when I was severely ill, they continued to abuse me. They have repeatedly blamed their actions on me, which is another trait common amongst psychopaths. They have no respect for my legal or personal rights, and they use intimidation and verbal violence.

If the MI5 operatives are psychopaths then it would explain both why the persecution started, and the degree of verbal violence. Psychopaths by definition damage other people; here, the MI5 operatives find an outlet for their personality disorder, through "cripple-kicking".

Xenophobia on the basis of mental illness, and race

My enemies have made clear many times that one of the reasons they are persecuting me is because of my admitted mental illness. However, it is my belief that they are also persecuting me because I am not of ethnic English origin, and the fact that there have been several incidents of an overtly racist nature reinforces this view.

In one case, two youths on a tube train in London made openly racist references to me as a "soft toy, not up to British Standards". Another person near my home made remarks about "Polish people". In yet another incident in Croydon, a youth made comments about "foreigners".

But the main thrust of their xenophobia is because of my mental illness. I should make clear that I do not look ill; if you met me, you would not know that I had the illness. I take a relatively low dose of medication, and feel quite well. But the persecutors have repeatedly harped on about my supposed serious mental illness; they have called me a "nutter", a "schizophrenic", etc. They have also persuaded other people to use these terms of abuse. They are able to get away with this because abusing the mentally ill is still something which is mostly acceptable in Britain; the media do it, "nutter" is not taboo in the way that "nigger" is.

Conclusion

There are several groups of people who might have wished to cause me trouble, and I still do not know who originated the persecution. Nor do I know how the originators came to be in contact with the (presumed) Security Service operatives who have been carrying out the campaign. To know conclusively why it started, we would have to know who started it, and this information is not available.

However, we can infer some things about the personalities of the persecutors from their methods, and from the degree of verbal violence they employ. It is clear that a main reason for the continuing harassment is the psychopathic disorder of the MI5 agents who carry it out. That they have never been "brought to book" for their misdeeds reinforces their belief that they do no wrong; and, unhappily, until they are brought to book, their persecution campaign looks set to continue.

MI5 Persecution: .net Magazine Applauds my Website

The March 1998 issue (number 42) of .net Magazine reviews the "MI5 Persecution" website

```
http://www.pair.com/spook/
```

describing it as an "excellent site". The webpages describe in detail the nature of my persecution since 1990 by what are believed to be elements of the UK security service. You may reply;

       by fax to   `0171-681-1190`   by email to   `bu765@torfree.net`

(snip image)

You are encouraged to read the web pages which include
a FAQ section outlining the nature of the persecutors, their methods of harassment through the media, people at work and among the general public
an evidence section, which carries audio and video clips of media and workplace harassment, rated according to how directly I think they refer to me
factual descriptions of the state security agencies involved
scanned texts of the complaints I have made to media and state security agencies involved
posts which have been made to netnews over the last three years on this topic

MI5 Persecution Update: Friday 13 November, 1998

If You Intend To Reply, Please Read This
If you have any questions or observations you would like to share with me, then you are very welcome to reply to my fax number 0171-681-1190. But please.... keep your response to one page if you can! I have had several people faxing my article back to me, including one MP faxing back twenty pages. I do not know if he had anything intelligent to say in his 20-page fax because I applied judicious use of the "Delete" key on my computer. Faxes over a page or two will be deleted without being read.

MI5 Resume Hostilities in Response to these Faxes
When I wrote last week's "MI5 Persecution Update" I remarked how quiet my life had become. No longer! MI5 have restarted hostilities with a vengeance the past week, in response I believe to the faxes I have been sending to members of the House of Commons.

On Saturday 7 November I went to Clapham Picture House cinema to see the film "Antz" (a very enjoyable film). At the cinema, I was verbally assaulted by a group of teenagers with the words "still crazy", repeated about ten times. There was a film with that name showing at the cinema, but it was clear their abuse was directed at me. I do not look ill, so why would they pick on me? answer, the incident was set-up by the persecutors. One of the teenagers also said to another, "I don't know what we're laughing at".

The following day, Sunday 8/11/98, I was on my way to play squash when I was verbally assaulted by a youth who said "it was so funny", without the slightest trace of humour. What he meant by this phrase was that I was funny, and they were trying to humiliate me. I have heard this phrase "it was so funny" used at me before many, many times over the last eight and half years.

You are reminded that the full story is on the World Wide Web at address;

`http://www.pair.com/spook/`

Reply   by fax to   0171-681-1190   by email to   bu765@torfree.net

Please Encourage Keith Hill MP to Help Me
I live in a bugged house, bugged both for audio and video. My movements are monitored by MI5. The Security Service have followed me to Canada, to Poland and the Continent, to the States. I cannot work anywhere, not in England, not in Canada, because MI5 will destroy whatever employment I am able to obtain. I have asked Keith Hill MP to help me, and he has refused.

The situation is intolerable. It is Mr Hill's job to help me out of this mess. So, please, as I said in the last fax a week ago: Do not waste your time returning multiple copies of my faxes to my fax mailbox, as some of you have done. Instead;

Please encourage Keith Hill M.P. to help me.

His phone number is 0171-219-6980   FAX number is 0171-219-2565

I am sorry to be using this device to encourage Mr Hill to help, but I think eight and half years are quite enough and it is time something was done to bring this matter to a close.

MI5 Persecution : BBC Newscasters Spying on my Home

This week's topic is the quite extraordinary claim that BBC newscasters such as Martyn Lewis and Michael Buerk have spied on my living room while they read the news. I currently have an advert running for the next six months in Private Eye's "Eye Say" column (at a cost of over £200) which says,"MI5 Persecution - BBC Newscasters Spying on my Home"; the story of my campaign in the Eye is on my Website at;

> http://www.pair.com/spook/evidence/plaint/priveye.htm

BBC's staff magazine Ariel also ran my advert "BBC Newsreaders Spying on my home" for one issue in the Personal category on 8/July/1997 before it was spotted and axed by editor Robin Reynolds; please see webpage; http://www.pair.com/spook/evidence/plaint/ariel.htm

Beginnings

The very first incident in the "MI5/BBC Persecution" occurred in June of 1990, when a newsreader reacted to what she saw in my living room at home as she read the news. My mother had brought an apple for me into the room, whereupon the newsreader smirked and giggled, apparently finding this funny. I couldn't believe what I was seeing. I carried on watching news and other television programmes to see if presenters would show signs of "interactive watching"; to my surprise, this happened again and again. Unfortunately, I did not have my wits sufficiently about me to videotape these programmes, and it is now almost impossible to obtain recordings dating back to 1990.

Most of the "TV watching" has occurred on the news, and most of it in summer 1990, although some as late as autumn 1993. My website has a few extracts of what might be politicians "getting at" me, in particular John Major and interviewer Dimbleby sharing a joke about the "Knutsford Guardian" which is almost certainly about me.

I sold my portable TV in autumn 1990 and stopped watching television regularly. I realise now that this may have been a mistake. What I should have done was to watch TV and listen to the radio, but tape-record everything and make a note of what each excerpt meant to me. I would then be in a much stronger position as regards to evidence that I am now. That is what I am trying to do now, but unsurprisingly the TV/radio presenters have stopped getting at me, now they know they are being recorded.

Examples of Media Harassment

Here are a few examples which I can still remember of media harassment;

In early 1992 I was watching the BBC news with Martyn Lewis on a small black-and-white portable television at my then home in Oxford. I threw a term of abuse at Lewis; he flinched, then gave a grin and made a comment from which I understood that he had been on my side, but might have changed his mind as a result of what I'd just said to him.

Victor Lewis Smith in his TV (BBC2?) program at the end of 1993, had a taxi-driver saying, "they're all out to get me", to which VLS replied, "but you're quite intelligent aren't you?" (what a nice chap VLS is, compliments no less!)

Paul Daniels the TV magician, sometime in 1990-92 (sorry I can't be more precise but it was so long ago), made a "crying face" and put his face in his hands, which was his way of expressing that I was frequently crying in 1990-92, and that he and other media people found my crying funny.

Kenny Everett (deceased) on some talk show, compared me to a "huge ape" who "scratches himself"; he made some other remarks about what the "ape" got up to which unfortunately I can't remember. (I remember that Everett's comments were quite sympathetic and human, but were obviously about me.)

Stephen Fry on another talkshow (Wogan I think) talking about "masturbatory fantasies", he then referred to me with the words "you prat"; I wonder if the studio audience knew what he was talking about and to whom his comments were directed?

Griff Rhys Jones on Clive James' TV show, made a "lunatic face" (wide fixed grin) to which I said to the TV that he had a "face like a horse's arse", to which Clive James said to GRJ "did you hear that?"

Crimestoppers summer 1990, remarks by a Midlands police officer on the programme, while Nick Ross was presenter (as far as I can remember). The officer talked about "in car entertainment". Nick Ross said to officer, "why don't you stop doing it?" to which he replied, "we can't while he's like this".

BBC2 Newsnight in autumn 1993 had a piece on football hooliganism. A black interviewee said apparently of the hooligans, but in fact of me; "they're just idiots, carry on with the surveillance".

There was an incident with Jonathan Ross which I remember clearly; he was on both BBC and ITV television at the same time, one (ITV I think) was recorded, the other channel was live. Ross has a speech impediment which causes him to pronounce his "r"s as "w". I sarcastically said something about "Mr Woss" to the recorded channel, then turned over to where he was live, and he repeated "Woss" with heavy emphasis and sarcasm.

On the radio, in spring 1994, Chris Tarrant made a sarcastic remark in his morning show, saying "he says we're trying to kill him, we should be done for attempted manslaughter", to which another of the studio staff said, "oh no, don't say that". His comment was in reply to a comparison I'd made the previous evening between my persecutors and the Polish secret police who murdered dissidents.

Martyn Lewis Denies & Lies, But Won't in Writing
In February 1997 I wrote to BBC Viewer & Listener Correspondence and asked them to investigate the claim that their newscasters had engaged in "interactive watching". They replied that they had asked Martyn Lewis and Michael Buerk whether they had engaged in such practices, and that they had both made verbal denials to VLC, but were refusing to put their denials in writing.

I can understand that they might think that if they were to make written denials to me, then many other people with my condition might write to them with similar questions. But I've asked a couple of journalists if they've been writing about me, they've made written denials, I've believed them, and I have not put their denials on my website because, since I believe their denials, it would not be relevant to publish them.

To me it looks as if Lewis and Buerk are happy to lie verbally but not in writing, because written falsehoods would place them unambiguously in the wrong, whereas they can try to talk their way out of verbal lies if they are ever caught, or perhaps even deny the verbal lies completely? If they lie without shame, then why would they have any shame about future lies about lying?

One of the strangest aspects of "TV watching" is that Buerk and Lewis have convinced themselves that their "interactive spying" is reasonable behaviour. Martyn Lewis thinks of himself as a "gentleman". He expressed in 1992 that he was "on my side". If this matter ever comes out into the open, I wonder what these newscasters will have to say for themselves, and what the British public will make of their behaviour?

Media Persecution Evidence on my Website
You may directly access the Evidence section on my website at URL;

```
http://www.pair.com/spook/evidence/evidence.htm
```

The category currently contains four video segments, a number of audio files and three published articles. The first video of ITN's John Suchet is unfortunately a mistake - after looking at it again it is obviously not about me. The two Ken Clarke excerpts may or may not be about me; it is funny that he should keep on harping about "paranoia" and "madness", but I have given these ratings of only 30% certainty, as it is more likely that they are not about me in particular, and Clarke is simply displaying the normal prejudices against the mentally ill found in much of society.

The piece I find most interesting is the Dimbleby/John Major interview from April 1997. I have assigned this a 90% rating. Dimbleby starts by emphasising a report from the "Knutsford Guardian". Major recognizes what's going on and joins in with a falsely apologetic "heaven forfend". The emphasis is on the first syllable pronounced "nuts" in "Knutsford", which is repeated three times. Of course this is hardly anywhere near convincing evidence; the really clear items were all in 1990-92, and they are basically unobtainable now.

If you're reading the website, have a look at the two files from David Hepworth's programme on GLR radio. The first one from 21/Feb/1997 has him talking about an "embarassment" of prizes and "absolute obscene", in reference I believe to the verbal sexual abuse that was being used against me at the time (and which unfortunately is still current). In the second file dated 9/May/1997 he again talks about "absolute embarrassment" of prizes, followed by laughter. To my mind he knows I am listening to his programme, and deliberately makes these remarks for my benefit, with very little attempt to disguise their purpose.

Bernard Levin - "Fanatic's Fare for the Common Man"

On 21 September 1991 this article by Bernard Levin appeared in The Times. It is reproduced in the Evidence section of the website, or may be accessed directly at URL;

http://www.pair.com/spook/evidence/evfiles/levfan.htm

To my mind, Levin's article described the situation at the time and in particular a recent meeting with a friend, during which I for the first time admitted to someone other than my GP that I had been subjected to a conspiracy of harassment over the previous year and a half.

Levin writes about a "madman running loose about London" who "bursts into tears, and swears it is all true. And it is." I am pleased to agree with his assertion that "it is all true" because the truth is what I presented to my friend in September 1991 and it is what is being presented to the readership of these articles now.

Conclusion

The harassment, in particular media persecution, was at its strongest in 1990-92. Today, I am recording everything I watch, read and listen, and the media have pretty much given up. It is now incidents "in public" which make up what there is of MI5's persecution. But much of the material from 1990-92 still exists in archives, although the organisations which have those archives generally won't make the material available to the public, for copyright and other reasons.

MI5 can no longer employ the media to persecute me, partly because journalists now know who is behind the persecution, and also because I would publish any instances. My mistake during 1990-92 was to not record instances as they happened; I've learned from that mistake, and know better now.

> **MI5 Persecution Update: Friday 19 March, 1999**
>
> *If You Intend To Reply, Please Read This*
> Please.... keep your response to one page if you can! I have had several people faxing my article back to me, including one MP faxing back twenty pages. Faxes over a page or two will be deleted without being read.
>
> *They've started again. Why? I have no idea.*
> Unhappily, the persecutors, whoever they might be, have started their activities again over the last two weeks. Usually they try to blame their activities on their victim, but this time they have stopped even pretending that the persecution is my fault. Their verbal abuse appears as gratuitous as it is vicious.
>
> Last Sunday 14 March, I went for a meal in London's Chinatown with some friends. As we were walking down Gerrard St, a man shouted loudly, twice, the obscenity which has been directed at me for some three years now. This followed previous incidents where the same words had been used. It is very upsetting to be verbally abused in this way and to know that the cowardly abusers are guaranteed to "get away with it" because if you report it then it will be assumed to be part of your illness.
>
> You are reminded that the full story is on the World Wide Web at address;
>
> www.five.org.uk
>
> Reply   by fax to   0171-681-1190   by email to   bu765@torfree.net
>
> Keith Hill MP (Labour - Streatham), my elected representative, as ever refuses to help.

MI5 Persecution : How to Identify the Persecutors

Usually delusional thinking does not allow the perpetrators to be identified, or the alleged persecution to be proved. My so-called "delusions" are different, because I have several times over a period of some nine years seen the same people, in widely varying places. Most importantly, their names have been recorded, on aircraft passenger lists and hospital register; and if only the police would do their job conscientiously then the persecutors could be identified and this unhappy story brought to a final conclusion.

BA93 Heathrow->Toronto, 10 June 1993

In 1993 I flew to Toronto for a holiday. On disembarking from the aircraft, a group of four men who travelled together looked in my direction, and one of them said, laughing, "If he tries to run away we'll find him".

I was absolutely stunned when I heard this. I wasn't surprised that they had followed me to Canada, but it shocked me that they had been on the same flight, and that one of them had foolishly given their group away. Unfortunately I was so stunned that I made no attempt to stop them as they got off the flight and proceeded into the terminal. I did not see these people again during my visit to Toronto. I do not know whether they followed me, or whether they were only part of a larger group, some of whom may have already been on the ground and awaiting my arrival.

Over the next few years I made a number of attempts, all unsuccessful, to obtain the passenger list for this flight. British Airways keeps passenger flight coupons for each flight; so if only the police would do the job that is being asked if them, then these four persecutors could be identified, and thus their employing organisation, which is very likely to be the Security Service, determined.

These four men were, apart from the joker who looked the odd man out in the pack, very serious individuals. They appeared to be in their forties or fifties, and my impression on seeing them was that they might have been former soldiers. Their campaign against me concentrates on how "funny" their abuse is; but in this they are plainly lying, because they realise how awful will be the damage to the establishment of which they form part, if the truth about the persecution ever sees the light of day.

The riddle of "Alan Holdsworth"

During Oct/Nov 1996 I saw a doctor several times about an infection, and on 2 Nov 1996 I went to Emergency at the Ottawa Civic Hospital and saw Dr Worthington, who was then Chief of Emergency Medicine. I had to wait several hours before being seen, and several people jumped ahead of me in the queue. One of these was a grey-haired man in his forties or fifties. This may have been one of the men on the BA flight in 1993; I cannot be sure. When Dr Worthington asked his name, he loudly said, "Tad", which is the common abbreviation of _my_ name. Dr Worthington looked puzzled, glanced at the sheet in front of him, and said, "but your name is Alan Holdsworth isn't it?". (I am pretty sure his Christian name was Alan; I cannot be sure of the surname). The man looked put out, and said quietly, "yes".

Unfortunately, I did not follow up this incident immediately. Some time later, I wrote to Dr Worthington to ask the name of this patient, but he refused to give the name out.

I saw this person again two and a half years later, at Ottawa Airport, just as I was about to leave for England. In the warm weather, he was wearing a coat and woolly cap, and pacing up and down in a menacing and aggressive manner. Presumably he thought he was pretending to be a "nutter" and in this way was getting at me; my impression is that he doesn't need to pretend, Holdsworth or whatever his name is is clearly a psychopath and in a healthy society such a person would be locked up, instead of being paid public money to exercise his psychopathic instincts. But today's Britain, a country where the MI5 secret police are given free rein and nobody dares raise a voice in protest, is not a healthy society.

"He doesn't know who we are"

For some reason, whenever I take a British Airways flight, I get hassled by the "persecutors who won't admit they're MI5". Since this business started, I have travelled BA three times; once in June 1993 BA93 (see above), once to/from Europe during Dec 95/Jan 96, and once in June 1998 with my mother to visit her family. The last journey, I was abused by two "plants" who kept repeating, loudly, "paranoid" (I have this recorded on minidisc). Presumably British Airways gives MI5 the seating plans for their flights, which allows MI5 to position their agents of abuse three rows behind me, so I can't face them, and they are throwing abuse at the back of my head. I have travelled BA as infrequently as possible; to Canada, I usually travel Air Canada.

Anyway, let's return to the second of the three BA trips, and in particular to the flight on 2 January 1996 from Berlin Tegel, to Heathrow, and onwards to Montreal Mirabel. I'd waited all night at Tegel for the flight, and was very tired on reaching Heathrow. On the plane to Montreal, two youths sat about three/four rows behind me and to the right, in the window seats. One of them, a rather fat "asshole" to use the Americanism (it fits), kept on going on about "this bloke", saying among many other things, "he doesn't know who we are".

Now that form of words is particularly interesting, because from May 1995, some 8 months previously, I had been vigorously denouncing the "MI5 Persecution" on Usenet. So if I'd guessed wrong, then you might expect the harassers to crow about it; which they have not done. If I had guessed right, and the persecutors have been silent before and since this flight, then they could either admit they were MI5, which would be a very serious thing for them to own up to, or they could brazenly lie, in which case I would report their lie, and since many people must surely know who they are, they would lose all credibility. So they have remained silent; apart from this one phrase on the BA flight, where one of their agents said, "he doesn't know who we are". Note carefully that this phrase is NOT a denial, it only appears to be a denial; since it does not say that my guess was wrong; it only states the objective fact that I do not know the identity of the persecutors, without giving any information as to the validity of my guess. Which leads me to posit that my guess was correct.

> **MI5 Persecution Update: Friday 25 March, 1999**
>
> If You Intend To Reply, Please Read This
> Please.... keep your response to one page if you can!. Faxes over a page or two will be deleted without being read.
>
> *The Usual Words*
> The persecutors-who-won't-admit-they're-MI5 have been active again this week. On Saturday 20/3/99 I visited Ravenscourt Park in west London, and was verbally assaulted with the usual words, "something wrong with him". This audio file is on the web at URL;
>
> > www.five.org.uk/evidence/evfiles/rvpk2003.htm
>
> This afternoon (Friday 26/March) I was again verbally assaulted while travelling by bus. The same sexual obscenity was thrown at me, and the incident was recorded on my minidisc-walkman. Because of the deeply offensive nature of the slander, I will not be posting this on the website.
>
> You are reminded that the full story is on the World Wide Web at address;
>
> www.five.org.uk
>
> Reply   by fax to   0171-681-1190   by email to   bu765@torfree.net
>
> Keith Hill MP (Labour - Streatham), my elected representative, as ever refuses to help.

MI5 Persecution : Browse Website www.five.org.uk

The March 1998 issue (number 42) of .net Magazine reviews the website describing it as an "excellent site". Since August 11, 1996 over 50,000 people have browsed this website.

You are encouraged to read the web pages which include
a FAQ (frequently asked questions) section outlining the nature of the persecutors, their methods of harassment through the media, people at work and among the general public
an evidence section, which carries audio and video clips of media and workplace harassment, rated according to how directly I think they refer to me
objective descriptions of the state security agencies involved
scanned texts of the complaints I have made to media and state security agencies involved
posts which have been made to netnews over the last four years on this topic

This article outlines what is to be found on the webpages, which you are encouraged to browse for the complete story.

Frequently Asked Questions

Your excursion through the website starts with the "FAQ - Frequently Asked Questions" portion. MI5's campaign of harassment against me has been going on for almost 9 years, and its longevity and breadth is reflected in the FAQ. Many thousands of people in Britain and abroad, including some recipients of this fax, have known for many years of MI5's activities against me. The FAQ describes the mass "Omerta suppressing its publication"; we pretend Britain is part of the "Free World", yet the British Secret Police, which is what MI5 are, carry on for many years a campaign which politicians and the media know about, and rely on the silent complicity of so many thousands of people.

The FAQ's introductory article names those who are "in the know"; media figures like Martyn Lewis, Michael Buerk, entertainment figures like Chris Tarrant, politicians and many in the general public, "all united in a conspiracy which breaks the laws which the UK does have regarding harassment, and all completely uncaring for any semblance of decency or elementary respect for individual rights."

Broadcast media play a key role in the harassment. The very first incident in June 1990 was when a television newsreader reacted to what she saw happen in my living room at home; such incidents of "interactive television" are still happening in 1999. The same goes for radio stations such as Capital FM. In spring 1994, Chris Tarrant on his Capital morning show made an aside to someone else in the studio, about a person he didn't identify. He said, "You know this bloke? He says we're trying to kill him. We should be done for attempted manslaughter". Tarrant and Capital have made strenuous efforts to avoid answering this charge.

Perhaps worst of all, MI5 have deliberately set-up many incidents in public places such as tube stations, shops, cinemas, where they have paid people to throw abuse at me. Since MI5 obtains funds to the tune of £160 million a year to fund its criminal activities, it has funds both to pay its operatives and to "buy" media figures and members of the public to take part in its campaign of persecution.

The Security Service are professional liars. They throw slanderous abuse, yet they refuse to admit out loud that they are doing so. When challenged about their activities through the Security Service Tribunal they lie and deny their activities. They induce other workers and managers at places of employment to take part in their campaign of abuse, presumably by buying them in the same way they buy media figures.

Complaints, and Press Coverage (BBC Lies, MI5 Lies)

As you might expect I have challenged both the Security Service, through the Security Service Tribunal, and offending broadcasters, to own up to what they have been doing. And as you might also expect, all of these people have lied through their teeth. Still worse, they have refused to commit unambiguous lies on paper; they have couched their lies in bureaucratic language, and allowed others to make false assurances and tell lies on their behalf. So when their lies are exposed, they will then tell further Clintonesque lies about how they weren't really telling lies in the first place!

On 6/Feb/1997 the BBC told me they would "never engage in any form of surveillance activity such as you describe". The BBC told me Buerk and Lewis had refused to put their lies in writing, but had stated verbal falsehoods denying my accusations of "interactive watching" during news broadcasts. Clearly Buerk and Lewis fear being caught and exposed, so they hide behind their Viewer Correspondence department.

In March 1997 I issued a summons against the BBC to try to "smoke them out". This summons was struck out as "disclosing no reasonable cause of action", because I had acted as a Litigant-in-Person and most LiP summons are treated thus. My case was arguable in law, so the striking out was unjust.

In June 1997 the Security Service Tribunal wrote to me regarding the complaint I had brought against MI5 in February. They say, "The Security Service Tribunal have now investigated your complaint and have asked me to inform you that no determination in your favour has been made on your complaint." I think you can guess the contempt which I feel for the Security Service Tribunal, who have never made a determination against MI5, and act as merely a whitewashing body for the Security Service. Unsurprisingly in May 1997 the Interception of Communications Tribunal gave the same result.

The last few items of "Press Coverage" give details of mentions of the MI5 Persecution in various magazines and newspapers such as BBC's Ariel, the Observer and .net magazine.

Evidence

Some audio and video clips of evidence have been recorded. My weakness in this area is because most of the really unambiguous evidence would have been obtainable in 1990-92, but I wasn't taping anything at the time, and it's very difficult to now obtain recordings from that period.

The audio clip "Life is so Hard" relates to harassment at my workplace in Canada. In the latter half of 1996, I was sitting near to co-worker Mark Lee, who kept coming out with words and phrases which showed MI5 were supplying him with data from my home life. For example, I would say something on the telephone at home, and the following day he would repeat verbatim what I had said. When Mark Lee saw I was recording what he was saying, he started to make his remarks more ambiguous, or make the obvious ones out of earshot of the recorder.

However, during the evening of 12 November 1996, at home in my apartment (flat to you UK-ers), I said "life is so hard, and then you die". A nihilistic, negative thing to say, but quite distinctive. The following day, 13 November, Mark said loudly, "life is so hard eh, and then you die" followed by loud laughter. I captured this on my tape-walkman and the computer-audio file is posted on the website.

There are a number of other audio files in the website's "Evidence" area demonstrating the abuse to which MI5 subject me to through their paid agents.

Also in this section is a very interesting article by journalist Bernard Levin, which followed a meeting I had with a friend in 1991, and to my mind describes in some details Levin's "artist's impression" of the meeting. He talks about a "madman" who "bursts into tears, and swears it is all true. And it is."

Internet Newsgroup (Usenet) archive

From May 1995 until the present day, this matter has been discussed exhaustively on internet newsgroups. The most interesting articles from the first two years of posts are documented here. This area is worth reading since most of the questions which the reader would ask, have been asked at some time or another by someone on usenet. Perhaps the very first article posted sums it all up so succinctly;

```
Date: Thu May  4 18:27:24 1995
Newsgroups: alt.conspiracy
Subject: BBC's Hidden Shame

Remember the two-way televisions in George Orwell's 1984? The ones which
watched you back? Which you could never get rid of, only the sound could
be turned down?

Well the country which brought Orwell into the world has made his
nightmare follow into the world after him. Since 1990 the British have
been waging war against one of their own citizens using surveillance to
invade privacy and a campaign of abuse in the transmitted media in their
efforts to humiliate their victim.

And the most remarkable thing about it is that what they do is not even
illegal - the UK has no laws to protect the privacy of its citizens, nor
does it proscribe harassment or abuse except in the case of racial abuse.

A lot of people in England know this to be going on, yet so far they have
maintained perfect "omerta"; not a sound, not a squeak has escaped into
the English press, and for all the covert harassment absolutely nothing
has come out into the public domain.

Have the British gone mad? I think we should be told.
```

So how much deeper will the persecutors-who-won't-admit-they're-MI5 sink in their campaign of lies and intimidation? Each time I thought they could sink no lower, they have managed to surprise me. You thought it could never happen here? When the MI5 British Secret Police make their smears against me, it is the corruption of the Establishment, which they are part of, that is demonstrated.

MI5 Persecution Update: Friday 16 April, 1999

If You Intend To Reply, Please Read This
Please.... keep your response to one page!. Faxes over a page or two will be deleted without being read.

BBC newscaster Nicholas Witchell can't stop himself laughing
During 1990-91 there were very many instances of "interactive television" where newscasters and other TV presenters saw on a screen before them what was happening in my home, and reacted, frequently by laughing at me. During this period I unfortunately did not record these programmes. For the last year or two, I have been recording everything I watch, and there has been a drastic decrease in such incidents.

However, on occasion, television presenters do still engage in "interactive watching" and react to what they see. This has been evident with Jon Snow of Channel Four News recently - a particularly interesting case, since it has been established that he cannot be corrupted by money (it is well-documented that MI5 offered him a tax-free salary and he turned them down). I wonder what device MI5 are using to encourage him to do the "interactive watching"?

On Saturday 10 April 1999 at 7pm, Nicholas Witchell on BBC2 News reacted when he saw that I was watching the programme, and I have his reactions stored safely on videotape. I have watched this tape several times and I am entirely confident that my evaluation of his reactions is correct. For several minutes his upper lip quivered in mirth as he attempted to keep a straight face. Then finally his self-control evaporated through the excuse of a weak joke and his face collapsed into a grin.

The strange thing is that I don't know *why* he was laughing at me, what I had done recently to "deserve" to be laughed at. The MI5 persecutors usually manage to invent some justification as to why people should laugh at and/or abuse me ("he's an X", "it was so funny" etc), so Mr Witchell could have been laughing for any number of reasons. Perhaps he found the views I have been expressing in these articles amusing? I suppose if you're paid enough money and ordered to laugh then even the most innocuous thing becomes funny.

Jon Snow of Channel Four News can't stop himself smirking, either.
On 12 February 1999 I was watching Channel Four News presented by Jon Snow. As usual, I was recording the programme, so that if anything out of the ordinary happened, I'd be able to go back and watch it again.

Now, Jon Snow, by his own claim, is uncorruptible. He says he turned down an offer of a substantial tax-free salary from MI5 - they wanted to make him their mouthpiece, and he told them where to get off.

So you will be most surprised to learn that Jon Snow "interactively watched" me that evening, and on many other evenings. Approximately fifteen minutes into the programme, he announced that the US President would be making a live appearance at about 7.30pm; I looked at the clock on the mantelpiece; and Snow saw me looking at the clock, and visibly tried to suppress a smirk.

Uncorruptible, are you, Mister Snow? If not money, then why are you watching me, Mister Snow? Are they forcing you to watch me? Can't you turn the monitor off, Mister Snow?

You are reminded that the full story is on the World Wide Web at address;
www.five.org.uk
Reply   by fax to   0171-681-1190   by email to   bu765@torfree.net

Keith Hill MP (Labour - Streatham), my elected representative, as ever refuses to help.

Comparing the MI5 Persecution with German "Final Solution"

It might seem offensive to compare the mass murder of millions of civilians in wartime with the peacetime persecution of merely one person. Yet the comparison has been coursing through my mind for several years now, because the brutality of German intent to "sub-humans" is very much comparable to the brutality of British intent to someone they vituperate and term "not up to British standards". The methods may differ, but the persecutors' mindset is the same.

The Germans first targeted the mentally disabled, too

During WW2 millions of ethnic Russians, Poles, Jews, mentally ill, gypsies and other minorities were rounded up and murdered in purpose-built camps by the German regime, in the name of "racial superiority". Fifty years on, the British Secret Police, MI5, instituted a campaign of mass hysteria; but in their cowardice, limited their activities to one single victim.

It is instructive to note that the early German "cleansing" effort was directed primarily not at Jews, but at the mentally ill. The Nazis set up the T4 project in the thirties to "cleanse" away 70,000 mentally disabled people, including schizophrenics and epileptics. After WW2 the Jews with their media influence used the reaction from the holocaust to roll back anti-semitism in the Western countries; however, the mentally ill are today still a persecuted group in the modern Western world as they were under the Nazis (the current Jewish home secretary in the UK intends to bring in laws for incarceration without any criminal charge for some mentally ill people - he protects his own minority, but does nothing for the other minorities in today's society), and this continuing bias forms a central cause for the current acts of persecution in the UK.

Widespread knowledge of what is happening to the "un-British" minority

In both the German persecution of the thirties and early forties, and the current British persecution, many, many people are well aware of what's happening. There is widespread complicity through inaction of populace; and in a substantial proportion of the mainstream population, the persecution had/has widespread enthusiastic support; yet in both the German case in the 1940s and the British today, the existence of persecution is a mass secret which must be never admitted out loud. In the recent Lawrence case this "secret bigotry" has been termed "institutionalised racism", and that is a very good word for what the British are doing today The persecutory attitudes and omerta regarding them are so deeply ingrained in the national psyche that they define the national mood

During WW2 many Germans knew minorities were disappearing, and through inaction quietly condoned their government's mass murder of "un-German" minorities and inferior "foreigners"; and in the 1990s, similarly, many English people know what the MI5 British Secret Police have been doing, and not only condone it, but actively take part, because of xenophobia against the "un-British" unit minority that is the target of "British" actions. This attitude by the British persecutors has been made explicit through the words "he's not up to British standards"; the British seem to have found their very own "untermenschen" to victimise.

Why these obsessive "holy wars" happen

This type of aggression occurs when the majority is threatened or humiliated in some way, economically, militarily or culturally. In pre-WW2 Germany the threat was primarily economic and military, following Germany's humiliating defeat in the first world war and the reparations it was forced to pay. In modern Britain, one might guess that the majority English who are behind the persecution feel pressured by the swiftly diminishing status of Britain in the world, and the rapidly increasing coloured colonisation of their country, which in time will see the ethnic English a minority in their own land, and their more antisocial elements, unable to reply to the obvious threat, instead project their aggression onto another, weaker, unit minority

In both cases there is a whiff of "holy war" or irrational obsession with the persecution. Certainly the German behaviour fifty years ago bordered on the not-quite-sane, and the current British behaviour towards their chosen victim is strongly tinged with a leave-taking of reason. And the choices open to the victims are the same, since MI5 will never allow me to escape them, "if he tries to run away we'll find him", just like the commandant of Auschwitz telling the new arrivals, "the only escape is through the chimney".

The Victim Will Destroy Us if We Don't Destroy Him First
The persecutors' propaganda is the same. Fifty years ago the Germans said, "if we don't do it to the Jews then the Jews will do it to us"; and MI5's propaganda in the early nineties concentrated on their victim as a "monster" and a "terrible threat we must all defend against". Defence, of course, is through remorselessly attacking the victim, which in the British case is what happened continuously from 1990-92, and is still happening today.

And there is a similarity in the perception by rational people of the victims. The Jews were a harmless, "polite" minority who did almost nothing to defend themselves when the crunch came; likewise, I have never harmed anyone, nor hit back despite the countless provocations of the abusers. And the persecutors have the same mindset; they are authoritarian, devious and brutal. I have to admit that there is a similar lack of "fight against might" in both cases as well; I have never defended myself physically, because that would be a signal for the MI5 persecutors to start physical assaults against me, with the blame attached to myself; likewise, the Jews were well-known for co-operating in their own mass extinction, making no attempt to defend themselves.

Eviction becomes Extinction
The first element of German oppression was forced emigration to other countries; and the MI5 persecution also had the effect of forcing me out of Britain, attempting to settle in a distant country. namely Canada. But the British persecution is worse in this respect than what the Nazis did, because MI5 followed me to Canada and continued to harass me there, with the aim of snuffing out my life; and I am quite sure that if I were to try to make a life for myself again in Canada, then the MI5 persecutors would follow and make life unbearable for me again. Eviction from homeland turns into something worse, namely overt extinction of victim.

"You were used as an experiment in some form."
Even in surprisingly minor details, the similarities between the Nazi effort against "un-Germanic" minorities fifty years ago, and the current MI5 effort against an "un-British" unit minority, are to be found. For example, the Germans excused to themselves their brutality by inflicting some "medical experiments" on their prisoners as a rationale for their actions; and something I have heard several times over the years from MI5 is that their persecution of me is excusable because it they are "experimenting" on me; in particular, a newsgroup contributor who is known to have MI5 connections said in February 1997;

```
the only way an average person like you could have become a target is:
     (1)    You were considered "important" [....], or
     (2)    You were used as an experiment in some form.
```

If my case is an experiment then what was it a trial run for? The possibilities make you shudder. If their experiment succeeds and they do extinguish my life, which group will be next for the treatment?

Humiliation of "Untermenschen"
There are similar techniques of increasing persecution and humiliation of the minority. The Germans first did the Jews out of work (as MI5 has repeatedly attacked my employment and forced me out of work), then stripped them of assets and differentiated them from the rest by forcing them to wear star-of-David; as I have been differentiated from the rest and tagged by having my face known to many thousands.

The techniques of humiliation and sexual humiliation are again similar. The Nazi SS guards forced women to strip and endure taunts, while MI5 inflict violation of privacy using their "spy-cams" and throw violent and depraved sexual taunts at their victim.

The Nazi logic for choosing Slavs, jews and gypsies to populate their concentration and extermination camps was that these were sub-human "untermenschen" who had no right to live on the same level as "civilised" Germans. By ancestry I am Slavic and while in Germany I have seen their contempt for my people continuing today. Yet during the MI5 persecution, British people too have expressed their contempt for my race, too, and marked me out as a "foreigner". A different time, a different country, yet so many of the themes are the same.

The Nazi maltreatment was brought to a halt by military defeat, with criminal trials of the worst offenders at Nuremberg forcing the Germans to face up to their war crimes. Since the MI5 persecution is carried out by the "permanent goverment" establishment in the UK, a change of political administration makes no difference to the course of the persecution, and the Security Service continues its campaign against a troublesome "untermenschen" minority.

"We are decent fellows" say the Brutal Persecutors

During the course of researching this article I read part of the very interesting book, "Hitler - A Study in Tyranny", by Alan Bullock. This volume contains a quote from Himmler on the "Final Solution";

```
"Most of you know what it means when a hundred corpses are lying side by
side, or five hundred or one thousand. To have stuck it out, and at the
same time .... to have remained decent fellows, that is what has made us
hard. This is a page of glory in our history which has never been written
and is never to be written."
```

In the MI5 persecution, too, there is a thread of deliberate brutality to the sick and vulnerable, while the persecutors maintain that "we are decent fellows". There is almost a conscious schizophrenia in the self-attitudes of the Security Service operatives and those in the public who they employ against me, which reflects the contradiction evident in the German attitude above. On the one hand, they stoop to the lowest and most base behaviour; yet at the same time, the MI5 operatives tell themselves that since they are civilised British people, then surely they must by definition be "decent fellows". Any indecency is made the fault of the victim; "he's making us persecute him, so we need feel no guilt".

Yet the conduct is atypical of the way these peoples see their normal modes of behaviour. Before WW2 Germany was not a country particularly noted for its anti-semitism, and the organised slaughter was not typical of normal German behaviour up to that point. Similarly, the current MI5 abuse goes against the grain of British self-image as being "reserved" and "decent", since they are using terms of abuse which are common among blacks and other supposedly less-developed races, but not among the English.

Conclusion

The ultimate aim of both persecutions is the humiliation and physical extinction of the persecuted group. The Germans did this in a very direct way; the British Secret Police MI5 are acting indirectly and relying on self-extinction of their target, because in peacetime and in the current somewhat false climate of "political correctness" more direct methods are impossible. If MI5 undertook more direct action the mass "omerta" would be broken.

I have written this article with sincerity to show how a historically recent persecution in another country parallels what is being done in this country today. In both cases, the evil-doers are of their countries' establishments, and rely on widespread tacit support to maintain the persecution and omerta around it. While the holocaust was undoubtedly the greater evil, it is important to be aware of the fact that had the Germans not been defeated fifty years ago, their plans would have gone through to total completion. In Britain today no force threatens the "permanent government" of which the Security Service forms a part; and it looks very unlikely that the wrongs perpetrated by the MI5 secret police will ever be revealed to public view, and the British secret state brought to justice for its evil actions.

MI5 Persecution Update: Friday 30 April, 1999

If You Intend To Reply, Please Read This
Please.... keep your response to one page!. Faxes over a page or two will be deleted without being read.

Somewhere between 0 and 100%
The last few days there have been no clear recordable instances of abuse. However, while travelling on the Underground, while walking around near my home and going to friends' homes, I am constantly troubled by thoughts that those people over there might be about to get at me; that the couple sitting in the opposite seats laughing are in fact laughing at me; et cetera, et cetera.

A comment by a scientist to the BSE inquiry sticks in my mind. He described the possible scale of the epidemic as "between 0% and 100%". It might not be happening, it might not happen at all, to any discernable degree.... or it might be total. Without clear recording, which seems to have become impossible the last couple of weeks, there is no way of knowing whether the harassment really is continuing, whether we have entered a temporary hiatus, or whether perhaps it has perhaps stopped for now.

But for the time being I think there aren't any reasons to dicontinue these faxes. I only re-started them six weeks ago in response to a resumption of MI5 harassment; and I think I will need to be more convinced of absence of persecution before I discontinue my complaints.

The Newscasters are still watching
In the last few weeks there have been at least a couple of fairly overt instances of "interactive watching" by newscasters. I reported this in a previous "MI5 Persecution Update".

These instances are really very rare compared to 1990-91, when there were many dozens of such occurrences. Undoubtedly the reduction is due to my practice of videotaping everything I see. Recently I had the opportunity of showing this year's "happenings" (Jon Snow/Nicholas Witchell) to my psychiatrist, and he agreed that in both cases the newscasters were expressing merriment without visible cause, and that objectively it might be possible for my claims to be true - although of course other people reported similar thoughts to him, and this thinking is usually a symptom of illness.

Read About the MI5 Persecution on the World Wide Web
The March 1998 issue (number 42) of `.net Magazine` reviews the website describing it as an "excellent site". Since August 11, 1996 over 50,000 people have browsed this website.

You are encouraged to read the web pages which include
a FAQ (frequently asked questions) section outlining the nature of the persecutors, their methods of harassment through the media, people at work and among the general public
an evidence section, which carries audio and video clips of media and workplace harassment, rated according to how directly I think they refer to me
objective descriptions of the state security agencies involved
scanned texts of the complaints I have made to media and state security agencies involved
posts which have been made to netnews over the last four years on this topic

You are reminded that the full story is on the World Wide Web at address;
                       www.five.org.uk
Reply   by fax to   0171-681-1190   by email to   bu765@torfree.net

Keith Hill MP (Labour - Streatham), my elected representative, as ever refuses to help.

MI5 Waste Taxpayer Millions on Pointless Hate-Campaign

Recently I was talking to an independent observer about the nature and purpose of the perceived campaign of persecution against me. The person I spoke to, a highly intelligent man, said he was struck by the utter pointlessness of the perceived campaign against me. He also said that, if my theories were in fact true, many people would have to be involved, in the surveillance itself, and in the technical side of the delivery of information from my home to TV studios for example, if the "interactive watching" were happening as described. He voiced these thoughts without any prompting from me; but both I and other observers had arrived at pretty much the same conclusions, some years ago.

I saw a team of four men at Toronto Airport in 1993

To carry out the surveillance alone, full-time, would employ four or five men, or their equivalent in terms of man-hours. Each man would "work" an eight-hour shift, so you would need at least three men doing the surveillance, plus a connecting link / manager. An indicator that this estimate is correct arrived in 1993, when I was accosted by one of a group of four men at Toronto Airport; he said, laughing, "if he tries to run away we'll find him". Plainly these were the men who had been involved in the intrusive surveillance of me for the preceding three years.

On other occasions, I have seen the same man on two or three occasions. On one such occasion, at Ottawa's Civic Hospital in November 1996; he gave his name to the doctor as "Alan Holdsworth" or some such; my hearing is not very good sometimes and I am not sure of the surname, although I am sure "Alan" was his first name. I saw exactly the same man again in Ottawa, at the airport, in July 1998. Obviously, other people must be "working" with this person; he would not be the sole agent employed in this case.

Usenet readers' views on the Cost to MI5 of Running the Campaign

Here's what a couple of other people on internet newsgroups / Usenet (uk.misc) had to say regarding the cost of running such an operation...

```
PO: >Have some sense, grow up and smell reality. What you are talking about
PO: >would take loads of planning, tens of thousands of pounds and lots of
PO: >people involved in the planning, execution and maintenance of it. You
PO: >must have a very high opinion of yourself to think you are worth it.
```

and......

```
PM: >But why? And why you? Do you realize how much it would cost to keep
PM: >one person under continuous surveillance for five years? Think about
PM: >all the man/hours. Say they _just_ allocated a two man team and a
PM: >supervisor. OK., Supervisor's salary, say, £30,000 a year. Two men,
PM: >£20,000 a year each. But they'd need to work in shifts -- so it would
PM: >be six men at £20,000 (which with on-costs would work out at more like
PM: >£30,000 to the employer.)
PM: >
PM: >So, we're talking £30,000 x 6. £180,000. plus say, £40,000 for the
PM: >supervisor. £220,000. Then you've got the hardware involved. And
PM: >any transcription that needs doing. You don't think the 'Big Boss'
PM: >would listen to hours and hours of tapes, do you.
PM: >
PM: >So, all in all, you couldn't actually do the job for much less than
PM: >a quarter million a year. Over five years. What are you doing that makes
PM: >it worth the while of the state to spend over one and a quarter million
PM: >on you?
```

Those are pretty much the sort of calculations that went through my head once I stopped to consider what it must be costing them to run this operation. At the very least, a quarter million a year - and probably much more, given the intrusive and human-resource-intensive methods employed. Times nine years. Equals well over two million pounds - and probably much, much more.

It's wasteful for someone with my skills to be unemployed
The wastefulness of the MI5 campaign against me is not just that of futile expenditure on their side. It is also extremely wasteful for someone with my talents to be unemployed and on a disability pension. I am highly qualified in numerate disciplines, yet am unable to work, specifically because of the MI5 hate-campaign against me. It is a terrible waste of resources for a supposedly efficient economy like that of the UK to be squandering the talents of a skilled and capable worker.

I made every effort to remain in employment for as long as I could, but ultimately I was defeated by MI5's employment of massive resources specifically targeted on my workplaces with the sole aim of seeing me evicted from those workplaces. You might expect this sort of behaviour from the Stasi or some other secret police force in a communist country where labour is cheap, and the government's aim on seeing its citizens confined; but for a supposedly free and efficient economy like Britain's, the wastefulness resulting both directly and indirectly from the Security Service's activities is simply criminal, and should never be allowed.

The international dimension means the costs are multiplied many times over
For much of the last nine years I have lived abroad, and I have also visited other countries on a temporary basis at various times. Almost throughout the period of my being abroad, the British Secret Services have followed me, and attempted to institute the same conditions of harrassment as inflicted in the UK. In fact, they have expressed their intentions towards me quite explicitly; the man on the Toronto flight, saying "if he tries to run away we'll find him".

If the costs to MI5 of operating round-the-clock in the UK are high, their costs overseas must be astronomical. On a couple of occasions I have been abroad for only a few days, yet MI5 have gone all-out to institute regimes of harassment against me where I've been. For example, in 1992 I went abroad for the first time since the harassment started (apart from a couple of day-trips to Calais), to visit southern Poland. I thought MI5 would leave me alone since I was only going abroad for about ten days, and surely it would be pointless and economic insanity for them to spend money creating a presence in a distant country for a period of only a few days. Yet the harassment started on the coach from London to Dover, continued in Poland, and continued still on the coach back to England.

Quite clearly, many, many people must have been involved in the harassment on this trip to Poland in 1992. I am at a loss to understand why MI5 bothered to harass me on this trip. Did they think I might have wanted to live in Poland to escape the harassment in England? Did they want to cut off that route of escape? I have never had any intention of living there. It is clear that their harassment of me in June 1992 in Poland had nothing to do with sanity or logic. The Secret Services are sometimes laughingly called the "intelligence" services - yet the so-called "services" they provide are nothing to do with intelligent behaviour, and more to do with wasting taxpayer millions on feeding their peculiar obsessions with a "nobody from south London".

Then they did exactly the same thing on my next trip to north-west Poland over Christmas 1995, again without reason, either reason in the sense of cause, or reason in the sense of sanity. If I were to visit Europe again, as I will this summer, they will doubtless seek to mess up my holidays yet again - and yet again, without cause, and in a manner which suggests very strongly that if the Security Services ever had any sense, then they have surely taken leave of them over the last nine years.

Four years of persecution in Canada
The persecution re-started within less than five minutes of my arrival in Canada, as documented above, and in the "frequently asked questions" article on the website. The words, "if he tries to run away we'll find him" spoken by one of the harassers at Toronto Airport are now imprinted on my mind.

A year later I emigrated to Canada, intending to find a job and settle there, hoping that MI5's interest in me might dim with time. I did manage to find work there, but my hopes of avoiding Security Service interest were ground into dust. As detailed above, I saw the same man in November 1996 and July 1998, both times in Ottawa. Apart from these encounters, there were numerous incidents between 1994 and 1998 of harassment, of an identical nature and in most cases using identical words to what had occurred in the UK. It became quite clear to me that the permanent surveillance and harassment operation which MI5 had subjected me to in England was being continued.

For a team of four or five men to be employed overseas must cost a lot more than if they operate in their home country. And for MI5 to continue the operation for a period of over four years, continuously, must cost many hundreds of thousands of pounds. This confirms my belief that the state is funding the campaign against me, since only a state-sponsored agency would be so wasteful of resources, over such a period of time.

Cost of MI5 "Watchers"

It is a matter of fact that the Security Service receives current annual funding of £160M. Divided by 1850 staff, works out at £86,000. But the unit annual cost of each "watcher" must be much higher than this, especially given the frequently mobile and overseas nature of their actions of the last few years. A very conservative figure might be a little over £100,000 pa for each of a team of five people, or half a million pounds per year. For nine years, so far. So the most conservative estimate of the surveillance element alone is perhaps four or five million pounds since 1990.

This guesstimate is of course theoretical - I am not privy to inside details of how MI5 split their funding. But to take some other examples, the cost of a US counter-surveillance specialist per day is USD 5,000. Even if the agents permanently assigned to me are not of this calibre - even if they employ specialists when difficult work planting bugs etc is encountered - their salary and support costs must still be very high. The individual agents are doing well for themselves as they are well-paid to exercise psychopathic instincts which in any sane society would see them in prison; but the taxpayers who must fund this terribly wasteful exercise are being "done" out of hundreds of thousands of pounds each year.

It must be emphasised that the above estimates are highly conservative. Besides the surveillance operation, it must carry a high cost in man-hours to propagate covert slanders through the population; to setup and maintain the "interactive watching" links to TV and radio stations, which these organisations continue desparately to "lie and deny"; and to induce antipathy in co-workers which would not otherwise exist.

Why they are wasting Millions of Pounds on a "Nobody from South London"

As remarked in the prologue to this article, it is really most extraordinary that the Security Service spends a chunk of its budget, every year for nine years so far, on a meaningless campaign against a "nobody from South London". That they are spending such a large amount of money has been confirmed to me on several occasions, usually by oblique references to "it's costing this country millions". The supposed "logic" behind the persecution is that MI5 wish to avoid their harassment of me, and the involvement of the UK media, to be made public; yet as the reader will appreciate that is a circular argument, "they're doing it because they want to keep it secret and avoid humiliation for themselves and their country" begs the question, "why did they start doing it in the first place?", to which in truth I myself do not know the answer.

Plainly MI5 with its rich budget can afford half a million pounds a year to waste on a "nobody from South London". Some time ago I was talking to a British surveillance professional on Compuserve who told me "this work costs a lot of money and is usually because the person I am following has done something (usually criminal) to warrant all this money and time being spent." Yet in this particular case it is plainly not the "victim's fault" that the harassment is taking place. The hate-campaign against me is completely the creation of the obsessive psychologies of the MI5 agents who have made themselves my persecutors; it is obviously a "personal" campaign for them, and for years they misuse taxpayer funding to feed their insane, unnatural and fixated fantasies.

Four Years of "MI5 Persecution" Posts on Internet Newsgroups

For approximately the first three years of the MI5 persecution, from June 1990 until late 1992, I kept as quiet as possible, in the hope that by not reacting, MI5's interest in me would decrease and they would simply go away of their own accord. This is the sort of behaviour some people employ against bullies; if the bullies aren't getting a reaction, then they might simply go away and victimize someone else.

Unfortunately, this tactic didn't work. The quieter I became, the more shrill and hysterical the noise from the Security Service operatives. For about two years I didn't watch TV news at all. Yet this only heightened their obsessed fixation; they continued to follow me wherever I went, they continued to induce harassment at work by managers and fellow workers, and they continued to encourage me to commit suicide. They seemed to regard my refusal to react as a crime which they would have to "put right" by ever more extreme forms of abuse.

Finally, in 1995, I changed tactics radically. Since late 1994 I had had accounts with internet providers in Ontario, Canada. I discovered the cornucopia of internet newsgroups, on every topic from consumer electronics, to politics and legal topics, and I discovered online services such as Compuserve and AOL. In May 1994, I made the first posting to the conspiracy newsgroup, on the subject of "BBC's Hidden Shame".

BBC's Hidden Shame

The internet newsgroup discussion, which has now reached its fourth anniversary, started with an article in alt.conspiracy, which I reproduce here.

```
Date: Thu May  4 18:27:24 1995
Newsgroups: alt.conspiracy
Subject: BBC's Hidden Shame

Remember the two-way televisions in George Orwell's 1984? The ones which watched you back? Which
you could never get rid of, only the sound could be turned down?

Well the country which brought Orwell into the world has made his nightmare follow into the world
after him. Since 1990 the British have been waging war against one of their own citizens using
surveillance to invade privacy and a campaign of abuse in the transmitted media in their efforts to
humiliate their "victim".

And the most remarkable thing about it is that what they do is not even illegal - the UK has no
laws to protect the privacy of its citizens, nor does it proscribe harassment or abuse except in
the case of racial abuse.

A lot of people in England know this to be going on, yet so far they have maintained perfect
"omerta"; not a sound, not a squeak has escaped into the English press, and for all the covert
harassment absolutely nothing has come out into the public domain.

Have the British gone mad? I think we should be told
```

At this point, I did not name MI5 as my persecutors. I was still unsure that they were the ones responsible for the "psychological terrorism". In followup posts however I did name them; and the persecutors have never denied the claim; so I think my guess is valid. (The Security Service Tribunal in 1997 have said "no determination in your favour was made", but it is a well established fact that MI5 lies routinely to the Tribunal which has never found in favour of a plaintiff, so no conclusions can be drawn from this.)

This first post was made to alt.conspiracy, but further posts were made to the UK-local newsgroups, in particular uk.misc but also uk.legal and uk.politics (which is now called uk.politics.misc). Some time ago I tried to take the battle to the Compuserve forums, UKPOLITICS (which is now called UKCURRENT - current affairs), but my articles were censored by the forum operators. Such censorship is impossible on the internet newsgroups.

Police Refuse to Act

I have complained several times to the Metropolitan Police, who have each time refused to help.

```
From: Green <Green@guidion.demon.co.uk>
Newsgroups: uk.misc,uk.politics,alt.politics.british,soc.culture.british
Subject: Re: MI5 Persecution: Why Aren't the British Police Doing Their Job?
Reply-To: Green@guidion.demon.co.uk
Date: Sun Apr  7 21:13:30 1996

In article <DpIE0r.736.0.bloor@torfree.net>
           bu765@torfree.net "Mike Corley" writes:

> Last Easter (1995) I went into the local police station in London and spoke to
> an officer about the harassment against me. But I couldn't provide tangible
> evidence; what people said, in many cases years ago, is beyond proof, and
> without something to support my statements I cannot expect a police officer to
> take the complaint seriously.

This in itself dos not suggest that the police have it in for you. The old bill
operates on extremely tight spending limits forced on them by that pillock Michael
Howard, and without evidence, they often have higher priorities than chasing something
that cannot go to court.

I doubt that the police are actually being leant on, but they probably realise that if
they looked into this, they would be leant on hard. The met always stays away from
anything that looks like it has Defence, Security or secret service interest already,
because they realise that they are below these government agencies in the general
pecking order.

If I walked into my local nick and complained that MI5 were snooping on me, they would
show me the door without even looking at my evidence, because that bored desk seargant
with only five years to go before he retires doesn't want to start fucking about with
somebody who has incurred the wrath of Stella Rimington. He would rather deal with the
lost dogs and driving licence producers, eat his cheese and pickle sandwiches and piss
off home at the end of his shift than have some high ranking spook having a go at his
boss and getting him a bollocking.

In short, you have earned much sympathy but little surprise.  Just remember that saying
about the enemy of your enemies.
```

Most recently, I wrote in March 1999 to Charing Cross Police Station CID. They did not acknowledge or reply to my letter. When I phoned them up, the detective I'd written to treated me to a sadly not unusual display of police bigotry, with an uneducated rant about "your paranoid rubbish".

It would be nice to think that such uneducated bigotry is something other than wholly typical of police behaviour, but unfortunately that is an illusion that is rapidly dispelled.

Uncorruptible Jon Snow of Channel Four News

From previous articles the reader will know what I think Jon Snow has recently been watching me while he reads Channel Four News in the evening. Recently I digitized a few moments of one such broadcast, where his face twists into a smile, without there being anything in the news broadcast to cause merriment. Here is a usenet post from some time ago on MI5's "bought and paid for" tools in the so-called "free" press.

```
Peter Harding (harding@ermine.ox.ac.uk) wrote:
: I was at speakers' corner on Sunday. There was one chap who was bellowing
: about something or other, I don't know what, but one thing he said to
: someone caught my ear:

: "BBC, MI5, same thing."

Can't disagree with that sentiment.

Wasn't it documented that MI5 sometimes "bought" journalists and broadcasters?
I remember reading a report by some jouralist who had been offered an extra
tax-free income by MI5 to become their covert mouthpiece, and had refused.
.............................................................................
> : >mouthpiece, and had refused.
> :
> : It was Jon Snow of Channel 4.
>
> Was it reported in any of the papers?

It has been reported several times. The most recent was in Private Eye,
a few months back. As I recall they also wanted information from him;
```

```
journalists would be a natural choice for members of the Security Service
and the Secret Intelligence Service for information sources.

> It might be interesting to see what he had to say regarding their
> attempt to recruit him.

He was most concerned that many others would have accepted such an
offer. However, we can probably make an educated guess as to some of
those who accepted: Nigel West (Rupert Allason, MP) and Chapman Pincher
would come near to the top of the list.

--
\/ David Boothroyd. Socialist and election analyst. Omne ignotum pro magnifico.
British Elections and Politics at http://www.qmw.ac.uk/~laws/election/home.html
I wish I was in North Dakota. Next General Election must be before 22nd May '97
The House of Commons now : C 324, Lab 272, L Dem 25, UU 9, PC 4, SDLP 4, SNP 4,
UDUP 3, Ind 1, Ind UU 1, Spkrs 4. Government majority = 1. Telephone Tate 6125.
```

Corrupt Security Service agents steal millions from taxpayers

Money is of course a factor in the grand equation which is the MI5 persecution. It costs money for the Security Service to "buy" people in the media etc. But that is only a small part of their expenditure of taxpayers' resources. Most of the expenditure is directly on the salaries if the agents involved; and in this post I put forward the theory that MI5 are trying to draw out their involvement for as long as possible, very cynically, to maximise their income and line their own pockets.

```
At each stage they have tried to pretend that I am something out of the ordinary. Either I was very
stupid ("he's an idiot") or very clever ("he's like a genius"). Either I was a threat to Western
civilization (Levin once referred to me as the next Hitler) or I was completely defenceless ("a
soft toy").

Now, it should be obvious to any person with common-sense that I am not out of the ordinary in any
way. I have an IQ which is average for the Web, I am racially white European, and there are plenty
of other people with schizophrenia or epilepsy out there who haven't been targeted for MI5
attention, so why me?

I think the answer is that the MI5 agents who harass me have cynically exploited the situation by
painting me as extraordinary in order to assure themselves of well-paid employment funded by the
ordinary British taxpayer. To put it bluntly, they are stealing millions of pounds from the
taxpayer to feed their own pockets.

This assertion is supported by the observation that it's the same agents who are doing the
harassment. Six months ago in a local hospital I was harassed by someone whose face I had seen (he
had stared straight at me aggressively, at the time I just thought it was some nutter but it turns
out he was one of "them") aboard a KLM flight a couple of years ago. It's presumably been the same
people most of the time. I've seen the way contractors act when they don't want their positions
terminated. Would these agents really want to lose their well-paid employment harassing me?
Presumably they are promising their bosses a "breakthrough" (ie my demise) real-soon-now and have
been for the last seven years, while all the while these MI5 agents skim millions off the taxpayer.

I wouldn't mind a job like that. Perhaps if I persecute myself a little bit, like standing in front
of a mirror and shouting mindless obscenities, do you reckon I'd get a slice of the cake? I mean,
I'd be lowering my morale wouldn't I, so wouldn't that qualify for some of that lovely taxpayer's
loot?
```

MI5 Lie and Deny Harassing me

In 1997 I complained to the Security Service Tribunal. This year Nick Brooks, current Tribunal Secretary, confirmed to me that he could not think of a single case where the Tribunal had found in favour of a complainant. Here is my usenet post from two years ago.

```
Subject: MI5: "It wasn't us"
Newsgroups: uk.misc,uk.legal
Organization: Toronto Free-Net

"The Security Service Tribunal have now investigated your complaint and have asked me to inform you
that no determination in your favour has been made on your complaint."

Signed ER Wilson, Tribunal Secretary

Well that's a relief then. All that spamming for nothing eh. Gaw blimey, if they say they're not
doing it then it can't be them, can it?
```

In a recent letter to Mr Brooks I expressed the opinion that the Tribunal were unable to fulfil their responsibilities in the face of MI5 falsehoods. Nevertheless, I do intend to make another complaint to the Tribunal in the near future, despite the Tribunal appearing to be a toothless watchdog.

Discrimination against a Unit Minority

MI5 have been very clear in their instructions as to what I should do. They have openly shouted at me the word "suicide", and also from the other abuse it is clear that they want my existence terminated.

This point is covered in more detail in a previous article. The following post describes the xenophobic nature of MI5's campaign against me. They have refined their bigotry down to a unit minority, yet they make use of the discrimination against the mentally ill which is a feature of current British society.

```
Subject: Re: MI5 says "Kill Yourself"
Newsgroups: uk.misc,uk.legal,uk.politics.misc,uk.media
References: <zlsiida.4248.3258FE24@fs1.mcc.ac.uk> <53eeev$cmg@axalotl.demon.co.uk> <5$
Organization: Toronto Free-Net
Distribution:

iain@hotch.demon.co.uk (Iain L M Hotchkies) wrote:
>Indeed. If you've ever had a 'conversation' with someone suffering
>from florid schizophrenia, you'll know how difficult it can be to
>'argue' with them.

I don't have florid symptoms. But I'm in a difficult situation, because those people who don't
know, aren't going to believe, and those who do, they just go along with the crowd. It's never a
good idea to go against the grain, and the grain here is defined by interests in the establishment
and the media. Even people who could say out loud what was happening won't, because then there's a
risk that they'll be seen as traitors and ostracised.

Usually this type of 'hidden abuse' is racial and targetted at a racial
minority within a country. You keep the minorities out of the good jobs, but you don't admit
discrimination exists. It happens everywhere, not just in Britain. The persecution that is going on
now is in reality a refined form of racism. Instead of "nigger" it's "nutter", and abusing the
mentally ill is still socially acceptable today. In 50 years it might not be, but today there isn't
any social or legal sanction against it.

So really they've refined racial harassment down to a minority of one. The
words may be different, but the methods are the same.
```

#

MI5 Persecution: BBC Newscasters Lie & Deny They're Watching Me

Central to the persecution campaign waged against me for some nine years now by the Security Service is their use of the media, and in particular the broadcast media, to make clear to me that I am under surveillance and being watched within my own home, even by BBC newscasters while they read the news. This is really an act of arrogance; MI5 and their tools in the television and radio are so sure that they can never be caught, that they have many times made explicity clear on broadcast programmes that they are as capable of seeing me as I am of seeing the broadcast pictures. Even when they have known I am taping the programmes they still carry on this practice; for examples of TV and radio presenters caught "in action", see the Evidence area of my website.

If you wish to reply to this article......
then please include your name and fax number! I provide the means for recipients to send me their thoughts on the topics discussed, but ask that you provide me with your fax number or email address if you require a response. Also would you please send not more than one or two pages, if by fax. Thank-you!

    Read about the MI5 Persecution on the Web at   www.five.org.uk

Reply to this artice by **fax** to 0171-681-1190   by **email** to bu765@torfree.net

It started with a Newscaster, and it continues with Newscasters today

The very first incident in the story started with a reaction by an ITN newscaster, Sue Carpenter, in June of 1990, almost nine years ago now. She reacted to what she saw in my living room at home as she read the news. My mother had brought an apple for me into the room, whereupon the newsreader smirked and giggled, apparently finding this funny. I couldn't believe what I was seeing. I carried on watching news and other television programmes to see if presenters would show signs of "interactive watching"; to my surprise, this happened again and again. Unfortunately, I did not have my wits sufficiently about me to videotape these programmes, and it is now almost impossible to obtain recordings dating back to 1990.

However, I have been busy recording everything I've watched the last couple of years, and the taping has yielded some nuggets, which you will find if you point your Web browser at the "evidence" area of my website, whose URL address is given above. Strangely it is not particularly the BBC who are "after me" at the moment (with the exception of occasional fire from Nicholas Witchell), but that supposed paragon of virtue and decency Jon Snow of Channel Four TV News (he actually works for ITN), who once claimed he'd turned down MI5's offer of a tax-free salary. I will cover Snow's recent actions in a future article.

BBC's Hidden Shame

The first ever Usenet post (internet newsgroup article) on the subject of the MI5 bugging / BBC watching occurred, as stated in a previous article, in early May 1995. It is reproduced here;

```
Date: Thu May 4 18:27:24 1995
Newsgroups: alt.conspiracy
Subject: BBC's Hidden Shame

Remember the two-way televisions in George Orwell's 1984? The ones which watched you back? Which
you could never get rid of, only the sound could be turned down?
Well the country which brought Orwell into the world has made his nightmare follow into the world
after him. Since 1990 the British have been waging war against one of their own citizens using
surveillance to invade privacy and a campaign of abuse in the transmitted media in their efforts to
humiliate their "victim".
```

I suppose "BBC's Hidden Shame" is more of a wish than a fact. It may be hidden, but the BBC and other media and security organisations seem to have no shame whatever in their anti-social, not to say criminal, actions. Nor do the general public, who seem quite happy to parrot the vilest obscenities without much hesitation or apparently thought.

Martyn Lewis, Nicholas Witchell and the rest

Most of the harassment occurred in 1990-92, when I wasn't making any recordings, and the BBC won't release copies of current affairs programmes from that period.... so although I can remember there were many incidents in that time, even many specifics, I can't dig up the actual programmes to flesh out the bones.
This year, there has been at least one incident with Nicholas Witchell as newsreader, which I have successfully recorded and digitized, i.e. converted into a computer Quicktime movie file. This has not yet found its way onto my website (I'm a busy man, dont'cha know) but you can be sure I will let the readership of these articles know when that clip makes it onto the web. The Witchell clip was recorded on Saturday 10 April 1999 at 7pm, and shows Witchell trying to restrain his features from collapsing into a smirk. First his upper lip quivers for several minutes, then with the non-excuse of a non-joke his entire face twists into a grin. It looks as if he finds me so funny, that he allows himself to submerge any pretence at professionalism in a sea of MI5-inspired sarcasm and harassment.

The two BBC newscasters whose reactions to me I can remember most vividly over the years are Martyn Lewis and Nicholas Witchell. I can remember thinking years ago that Michael Buerk was also seeing me at home; and if the other two are watching then there would be no reason why he wouldn't be doing the same; but in all honesty I cannot remember a single clear instance of his reacting through facial or verbal expression to me.
I can remember several instances of Martyn Lewis reacting to what he saw of me, however. In early 1992 I was watching the BBC news with Lewis on a small black-and-white portable TV at my then home in Oxford. I threw a term of abuse at Lewis; he flinched, then gave a grin and made a comment from which I understood that he had been on my side, but might have changed his mind as a result of what I'd just said to him.
And in spring 1991 I remember Martyn Lewis clearly reacting to what he saw of me at my then accommodation in Woking, Surrey, by continuing to stare at some fixed point near the camera after the news had finished - presumably this is where the monitor interactively showing pictures of my room was located.

Why would BBC and other Newscasters Watch and Harass Me, Watching Them?

This is a very difficult question, and I don't actually know the answer. It is a matter of record that the Secret Services are very much part of the Establishment. The recent exposure of the "MI6 Agent List" on the internet, and its coverage in the newspapers, reveals how much MI5 and MI6 are recruited from the ranks of the Establishment. Obviously the relationship is bi-directional; the Establishment influences MI5/MI6, but the secret services (well, perhaps not so secret now we know who works for MI6!!!) also influence the machinery of power and information dissemination i.e. media in this country. So they must have a lot of covert leverage with the BBC and ITN.

Some of this leverage is obviously through bribery. It is a matter of record that MI5 tried some years ago to "buy" Jon Snow of Channel Four TV. He turned them down - obviously they must have approached other media people as well, and from the lack of other reports of people turning them down, it may be presumed that some other journalists will have accepted the sugared carrots put before them. Ironically, Jon Snow has been taking part in the recent "watching" actions against me - but why he has allowed himself to be used by the secret services is something which I do not know.

Perhaps the Security Service uses blackmail to twist arms of journalists into co-operating with them? I have always thought there was something slightly odd about Martyn Lewis's demeanour. At the time of the Ron Davies "rough trade" scandal it was reported that MI5 had known all about Davies' predilections and the sham of his pretence to be a happily married man. Perhaps MI5 have been able to dig something up from Martyn Lewis's private life to blackmail him into acting on their behalf? And if there wasn't anything before the "newscaster watching" started then there most certainly is something now.... once they've started watching, the newscasters will surely wish their activities to remain covered-up, and co-operate with the security service.

"Newscaster Watching" Deliberately Constructed to Mimic Schizophrenia

Presumably this is the first case in history of television journalists actually taking part in acts of real-time, live spying and reacting against one of their viewers. What you have to understand, though, is that I was quite mentally healthy in June 1990, certainly relative to November 1992, when after two and a half years of harassment I was finally admitted to hospital as an out-patient. MI5 decided from the outset that they would make me mad; they constructed the media harassment to resemble what would be reported by a person with mental illness; and then they carried on years of abuse to inflict on me the condition which they wished to use as an excuse to cover up their abuses.

I sold my portable TV in autumn 1990 and stopped watching television regularly. I realise now that this may have been a mistake. What I should have done was to watch TV and listen to the radio, but tape-record everything and make a note of what each excerpt meant to me. I would then be in a much stronger position as regards to evidence that I am now. That is what I am trying to do now, but unsurprisingly the TV/radio presenters have stopped getting at me, now they know they are being recorded.

When I started publicising my case on internet newsgroups in 1995, I was met with the disbelief one might expect to be accorded to a mentally ill person who talks about "newscaster watching" and media persecution. Some newsgroup participants thought I had started a "troll", an invention made to obtain a reaction; one bright spark even suggested a group of psychology students were behind the articles. But most people thought the articles were symptomatic of derangement - and that is *exactly* what MI5 want people to think. MI5 chose me as a target because I was mildly mentally ill at the outset in 1990, although I stress my illness then was very mild in comparison with November 1992, and because they knew that enough abuse would (a) make me much more seriously ill, and (b) once I was more ill, they would "get away" with a harassment deliberately constructed to look like the symptoms of paranoid schizophrenia.

Martyn Lewis Denies & Lies, But Won't in Writing

In February 1997 I wrote to BBC Viewer & Listener Correspondence and asked them to investigate the claim that their newscasters had engaged in "real-time spying" on me. They replied that they had asked Martyn Lewis and Michael Buerk whether they had engaged in such practices, and that they had both made verbal denials to VLC, but were refusing to put their denials in writing.

To me it looks as if Lewis and Buerk are happy to lie verbally but not in writing, because written falsehoods would place them unambiguously in the wrong, whereas they can try to talk their way out of verbal lies if they are ever caught, or perhaps even deny the verbal lies completely? If they lie without shame, then why would they have any shame about future lies about lying?

BBC-VLC also said that the BBC "would never engage in any form of surveillance activity" such as that described. Clearly Martyn Lewis and the rest have lied to their own organisation's personnel about their criminal actions. So much for the "objective", "truthful" BBC, a nest of shabby liars.

Summons against the BBC, for Nuisance caused by Newscaster Spying

In March 1997 I issued a civil summons against the BBC, seeking injunction against further "newscaster spying", and token damages for what the BBC had done to me until that date. The purpose of the summons was to try to "smoke out" the BBC, since obviously I did not have good evidence which would be necessary for either a civil or criminal case to be made against them. My summons was worded as follows;

```
1. The plaintiff is and was at all material times residing at [home address]. At some time prior to
or during June 1990, persons of unknown identity entered Plaintiff's premises and installed
concealed television equipment in said premises.
2. A campaign of harassment was launched against the Plaintiff by the persons of unknown identity,
which in part took the form of instigating harassment by BBC TV newscasters (including specifically
Michael Buerk and Martyn Lewis) as they read news bulletins, by making direct and personal comments
to Plaintiff.
3. The campaign's purpose was to subject Plaintiff to great mental stress and induce mental
breakdown. As a result of it Plaintiff did indeed suffer from severe mental strain in 1990-97.
4. In order to avoid the mental strain being caused to him the Plaintiff has been compelled to stop
watching BBC TV news. Defendant therefore committed the tort of private nuisance, since normal use
of home was interfered with.
5. Plaintiff claims a permanent injunction prohibiting further nuisance, and damages for nuisance
suffered limited to £5,000.
```

Naturally, my attempt to smoke-out the BBC and its lying newscasters failed. The BBC's litigation department sought to have my summons struck out; and they succeeded in doing so, on the grounds of my action "disclosing no reasonable cause of action". I was also prevented from issuing further civil claims against the

BBC without leave of the Court. Apparently litigants-in-person frequently / usually have their claims struck out with this wording, regardless of the merit of their claims.

BBC Suppresses my Claims of "Watching by Newscasters"

BBC's staff magazine Ariel ran my advert "BBC Newsreaders Spying on my home" for one issue in the Personal category on 8/July/1997 before it was spotted and axed by editor Robin Reynolds; please see webpage;

>   http://www.pair.com/spook/evidence/plaint/ariel.htm

Clearly the BBC will not allow claims of its wrongdoing to be made public in the media channels it controls. On several occasions people said to my face that harassment from the TV was happening. On the first day I worked in Oxford, I spent the evening in the local pub the Rose and Crown with the company's technical director Ian, and Phil, another employee. Ian made a few references to me and said to Phil, as if in an aside, "Is he the bloke who's been on TV?" to which Phil replied, "Yes, I think so".

The reader might think that mere "watching" by newscasters etc might be a relatively benign happening. But it is not; it is part of MI5's framework of harassment and lies. On many occasions the reactions of the BBC's newscasters to me has been in the nature of sarcasm, implicit contempt and abuse. This is visible in Witchell's news programme mentioned above, where he engages in abuse by laughing at me during his newsreading. It was particularly visible in the early period of 1990-92, and as late as Autumn 1993, when during a Newsnight broadcast Jeremy Paxman interviewed a football person about soccer hooliganism, and the interviewee gave vent to an unsubtle rant about "they're idiots, they're just idiots, keep up the surveillance". Paxman started grinning, showing he understood and was taking part in the abuse being perpetrated on that programme.

Conclusion

The MI5 Persecution started with harassment by television newscasters, and today harassment by TV and radio presenters still forms a key part of MI5's activities against me. When this business started in June 1990 I was in relatively good health of mind. Years of persecution by the secret police and their mouthpieces in the state-run BBC and other media eroded my health until MI5 achieved their aim of seeing me rendered mentally ill in November 1992. The diagnosis which was forced on me unfortunately and ironically meant that my reports of the harassment are disregarded, because the mentally ill are second-class citizens in today's Britain. Yet TV and radio harassment continues, albeit in a reduced form, despite my taping all the programmes I watch, resulting in my being able to obtain and demonstrate objectively on the website instances of media presenters attacking me. Unfortunately these recorded instances are quite tenuous; I might understand them, the presenters understand what it is they're doing, but despite many thousands of people knowing the truth of the "newscaster watching", the omerta continues and they continue to refuse to admit the truth of the matter. It is a terrible indictment of British society that there is not even one decent person willing to speak out. I look forward to the day when the truth does finally emerge, and the mass corruption which has allowed the MI5 persecution to take place is finally purged and the Establishment criminals caught and appropriately punished.

MI5 Persecution: Molestation during Travel

MI5's persecution of me varies in intensity. Since 1990 it has been steady for perhaps 80% of the time; there was a notable quiet period in 1993, and another quiet period in Jan-Feb 1995, as well as a hiatus in the first two months of 1999. It puzzles me that they cease and restart, seemingly without any logic or reason. But one aspect of MI5's activities against me which is relatively predictable is this week's article's topic, which is Molestation during Travel. Almost every time I cross the Atlantic, go to the Continent or even try to enjoy a holiday in this country, you can bet that MI5 will be there doing their utmost to wreck it all.

This aspect of the harassment is particularly relevant as I will be travelling to Europe again in a month's time, with naturally the Minidisc recorder in tow; so it will be interesting to see if I can record the abuse which will almost certainly take place, either on the Tube going to the airport, at the airport, on the flight, in the terminal building - MI5 have previously instituted instances of abuse at each of these locations, so we'll see how much taxpayers money they waste this time, and whether it will prove possible to capture their abuse on minidisc.

If you wish to reply to this article......

then please include your fax number! I provide the means for recipients to send me their thoughts on the topics discussed, but ask that you provide me with your fax number or email address if you require a response. Also would you please send not more than one or two pages, if by fax. Thank-you!

Read about the MI5 Persecution on the Web at   www.five.org.uk

Reply to this artice by **fax** to   0171-681-1190   by **email** to   bu765@torfree.net

June 1992 in Poland's mountain resort of Zakopane

The persecution started in June 1990, and for the first two years I stayed in the UK apart from a couple of brief day trips to Calais. By the summer of 1992 I'd had enough of being cooped up in England with abusive fellow employees egged on by an abusive secret police service, and decided to spend 10 days in southern Poland, on what was intended to be a holiday at the mountain resort town of Zakopane.

Unfortunately the psychopaths of the Security Service were not willing to allow me to enjoy a holiday in peace and quiet. The journey to Zakopane was by coach from the meeting point at London's Victoria coach station (National Express) followed by ferry followed by another coach across Europe. As we left Victoria a youth and his girlfriend started a loud tirade of abuse directed at "this bloke", where the "bloke" was never named, but it was very clear that the "bloke" was myself. The youth said "they" had "found somebody from his school, and he was always really stressed at school, a real psycho". Again, the label "they" was not elaborated on, but it was clear that "they" = the persecutors from MI5. The boy also said, "he was in a bed and breakfast for only one night and they got him". By a not unexpected coincidence I had been in a B&B in Oxford a week previously, which had been booked from work; other things lead me to the conclusion that the company's offices were bugged for most of the 2 1/2 years that I was there, so "they" would have known a room in the B&B had been booked. After a few minutes of this I went back to where they were sitting and asked where they were travelling. The boy named a village in France, and the girl's giggling suddenly ceased; presumably it permeated to her brain cell what the purpose of the boy's abuse was.

It is now very clear to me that MI5 were trying to have me incarcerated, assaulted or killed on this trip across Europe. The degree of verbal violence inescapably leads to this conclusion. When we arrived at our destination, it became clear that many people, both in our tour group and its guide, and among the ordinary residents of the town, knew there was a movement under way to "get" me. MI5 employed many people and significant resources for an action which they knew would only take a maximum of ten days. A commercial operation would never have felt able to waste such resources on such an unproductive and temporary action; only a state-sponsored, taxpayer-funded entity like the Security Service would be able to be so wasteful.

To give some examples of what happened in those ten days; I was walking in some woods outside the town, when a Polish woman, looking at me, said the English "shit" in a strongly Polish-accented voice. For the first three years 1990-92 MI5 had been trying to force this word on me. Another example; I was walking near my "hotel" when a mother said laughing to her child, "a wiesz ze to prawdziwy wariat" which means "you know he's a real madman". And the "TV reacting" happened there too; on Polish TV, a bemused looking journalist said to another, "to jest sprawa Anglikow", which means "it's the concern of the English", in other words, none of our business, despite what the English are trying to force down our throats.

Just before we left for home, I went with some others from our group to a nearby bar. There a man shouted at me the same sexual obscenity which MI5 have constantly thrown at me these last three years. I think MI5 try to justify their various terms of abuse by repeating them at me until I say them, either while conscious or while talking in my sleep; and then they seize on my saying those words to "prove" that the obscenities are "my fault", et cetera. This rather stupid reasoning of theirs can actually be seen as indicative of the psychopathic condition attributed to them in a previous article; blaming the victim for the crime you inflict on him is how psychopaths think.

Nor did the persecutors let up during the return trip. Returning on the ferry over the channel, a rather insalubrious-looking guy talked to his mates about "and you know this bloke, he's really mad you know, he's really mad". On the National Express return coach to London, a group of five or six young people started shouting at me. I slumped in my seat and tried to avoid presenting a target, so they got ever more strident - "what's the matter with you, can't you hear us?" One of the other people who had been on the trip to Poland asked them why they were shouting at me, and they said, "he's been to Cambridge", to which the co-holidayer asked them, "have *you* been to Cambridge?" presumably thinking they were aggrieved fellow students, but they answered "no". Even after I left the coach at Elephant and Castle abuse continued; in the tube station, two kids started throwing abuse at me; one of them said to the other, "and you know he works?" to which the other answered "yes".

Immediate Aftermath of November 1992

As you will know from previous articles, my manager at OCG - ARIS/Oxford, Mr Mitchell, induced a mental breakdown in me in the months leading up to Nov/92. The diagnosis was regarded by the persecutors as a victory for them, because few if any people give credence to allegations of harassment when they are made by somebody suffering from schizophrenia. There is also a bias against the mentally ill, an "institutionalised bigotry" in society comparable to the institutionalised racism against blacks.

However, MI5 did not let up on persecuting me following Nov/92. In December 1992 I flew by charter jet to Alicante in Spain for two weeks recuperation. MI5 planted one of their people on the flight, a youth who tried to start some noises that "he's a nutter". One of the other passengers replied, "oh he's a nutter is he? oh well!" and the youth shut up and said nothing for the rest of the flight. I think it would be fair to say that the youth on the flight was embarrassed by what he had been asked to do in making the flight "uncomfortable" for me; he sounded defensive rather than aggressive.

My first trip to Canada in June 1993

I've already covered this in a previous article so I'll just give a brief summary here. On 10 June 1993 I flew British Airways from Heathrow to Toronto's Pearson Airport. On de-planing from the aircraft, one of a group of four fellow passengers looked at me and said, laughing, "if he tries to run away we'll find him". It was quite obvious that these four men were the ones who had been harassing me since 1990.

I did nothing to apprehend them or bring this incident to the attention of the airport authorities, mostly because this was my very first visit to Canada, and the last thing I wanted was to get into a dispute before I had even finished disembarking. In retrospect, I can see this was a terrible mistake; I should have made every effort to detain and identify these people.

Subsequently I have made numerous attempts to obtain the names of these people from British Airways passenger lists, by talking to BA, through a lawyer in Ontario, through a solicitor in England, through the UK police, and also through private detectives in the UK. But all my efforts have come to nothing. BA have told me they keep passenger lists for a period of seven years, so they will still have the list for this 1993 flight. I did not see or hear anything during the rest of my visit to Ontario in 1993 which would have lead me to believe that I was being watched or followed.

Journey across Canada in summer 1994

As I think I've already said in previous articles I emigrated to Canada in late May 1994. For six weeks between late May 1994 and early July 1994 I travelled across Canada from coast to coast, starting in Toronto, visiting various cities and ending up in British Columbia. I saw this both as something of a holiday, and the chance to get to know a little better my adopted country.

As you can guess, MI5 followed me everywhere I went during these six weeks. In Toronto, where I started this trip in late May, I was spoken about by one youth to another with the words "he's an idiot", to which the other replied, laughing sympathetically, "good luck to him".

A couple of days later I went to Montreal and stayed at the YMCA downtown. As you can guess (this is all so predictable, isn't it?) MI5 followed me there and bugged my room at the YMCA. Not only that, but they managed to set-up an instance of "newscaster reaction" from a local television station; while I was watching a Vermont TV news programme on the set in my room, the woman reporter said, "well they're just tired and they want to go home", which sounds like a pretty unprofessional thing to say until you realise she was trying to say of me that I was the one that was supposed to be tired, and they (ie MI5) wanted me to go home to the UK.

On the bus journey across the North American continent, it was quite clear that MI5 were following me every step on the way. For the first part of the journey they actually put someone on the bus with me, a youth who said at me "that guy's paranoid" and tried to incite other passengers to attack me. I stopped for a couple of days in Winnipeg in central Canada, and on leaving the town heard on the radio a female presenter ranting about "insanity! insanity!". It is very tiring travelling such a long distance by bus; I took the journey in two steps, each of about 36 hours; and it is especially tiring when you know MI5 are watching you and harassing you every step of the way.

When I finally got to Vancouver, MI5 instituted the usual harassment, in very short order. I was surprised how quickly they were able to induce hatred towards me in elements of the general populace; the Security Service must have employed a number of agents and serious resources in a very short period of time; and for no real gain, because I haven't been back to BC for almost five years, so all their "work" appears to be for nothing. In downtown Vancouver a street person said in front of me, "they're all talking about him". For a few days I was staying at Paul's Guest House (345 W.14th Ave); on the day I left, the owner Paul shouted at no-one in particular, "he's going to Victoria" - which was quite accurate, I was indeed going to the provincial capital Victoria on Vancouver Island. But I had not told anyone at the guest house where I was going; I had only mentioned to my parents back in England on the phone that I was going away from Vancouver for a few days. Which leads me to suppose that MI5's bugging of the phone in my parents' house yielded the "intelligence" that I intended to visit Victoria, and they had passed the information on to Paul.

When I got to Victoria it was again obvious that the persecutors were "doing their stuff" there as well. On the street I was identified as being English, although I had not said anything so my accent hadn't given me away; and returning by ferry to the mainland, I was abused by a Canadian woman who said, "he's a nutter! you can run but you can't hide". During my years in Canada I have never heard the word "nutter" on any other occasion; I do not think it is part of Canadians' vocabulary; so the Canadian woman on the ferry, who was obviously talking about me, must have been supplied with this word by the English persecutors. And once I got back to Vancouver, staying at the Austin Hotel on Granville St, I listened to a conversation in the apartment block directly opposite, and a man saying, "he's paranoid, so that's as bad as it can be, so why are they doing this to him?".

Holiday in the States, August 1995

By 1995 I was living in Canada, and in August I went down the eastern seaboard to Florida and as far as Key West by car. As you can guess (this is all so boring and predictable, isn't it?) MI5 followed me every step of the way. I can see in retrospect that this must have been quite easy for them as they had my car bugged, both on the inside to listen to anything that was said and what radio station I was listening to, as well as what must have been a tracker device installed to track it across long distances.

The first city I visited was Philadelphia. In the old Congress Hall where the first US Congress assembled, the woman guide started referring to my situation, saying that "all these people in Europe were watching it", and they were "a little paranoid" at this 18th-century experiment in democracy. Also I had recently written a newsgroup post where I'd described a (female) poster as "wet-nosed" (implying "canine"), and a young girl in Philadelphia remarked, "so he thinks we're dogs?" There were two or three more incidents during this holiday in the eastern States, including a radio station down near Miami, showing "they" had tracked me all the way there, and were bugging the inside of my car; but I didn't record the details and I've forgotten some of it now. Also down in Miami Beach a French tourist in a lift expressed support for me with the words, "c'est incroyable" ie. it's incredible, meaning that MI5's well-known actions against me were beyond belief.

To go back a bit, in about May/June 1995 I'd visited New York, again by car, and was insulted several times by people using the same words that had been used against me in England. In Central Park, and elderly Englishman (not a real gentleman - but then the Engish view of themselves as "gentlemen" etc is quite laughable) looked at me and said "idiot". And while I was eating in a streetside restaurant a New York youth started laughing and said something like, "I can't believe it, he's actually here" - I think that was because I had had an expressed wish to visit New York for some years before this, although after this visit I won't be going there again for a very long time.

Visit to Poland December 1995/January 1996

In December 1995 I flew (BA again, unfortunately - every time I've flown BA one of these incidents has happened, presumably MI5 is happier setting up harassment on British-domiciled carrier) from Montreal to Berlin and travelled on to Poland to visit family. MI5 naturally harassed me in Poland during my brief stay. They followed me around and got Polish people to take part in the harassment. In one case two Polish youths talked in front of me saying in English (with marked Polish accents), "fucked up men, fuck you". There were also other incidents which I don't remember too clearly since it was some time ago.

The return flight connected through Heathrow, and in the transit lounge MI5 again set-up harassment against me. In Poland they were talking their abuse in English, and in London they set Polish people after me to speak in Polish; they heard me on the phone to my father, and said "a wiesz ze to Polski wariat", in an almost sympathetic, inclusive fashion (translation. "you know he's a Polish nutter"). Once on the flight to Montreal I was again set upon by two English youths, one of whom spoke and the other listened. The aggressive "fat bastard" youth said, "if he wants to be a wanker" (it's my fault they're harassing me, you see), self-justification that "he's a nutter" (so we have to keep on abusing him, because he's ill), as well as talking about the town in Poland where I had been staying. He also said, "he doesn't know who we are", but as already remarked in a previous article, that was at best a half-denial of my guess expressed in internet newsgroups that the people after me were MI5 - if anything it's a half-confirmation rather than a half-denial.

Conclusion

These incidents are still going on. You can hear digitised audio files of abuse on a BA flight to Berlin in 1998 on the Web at address   `http://www.five.org.uk/evidence/evfiles/txl1306.htm`

On this flight they were again attacking my mental health; "paranoid, he's paranoid" and "nutter" are discernable. The last "during travel" contact was at Ottawa Airport on 21 July 1998, when "Alan Holdsworth" the psychopath MI5 agent, dressed as a vagrant, was pacing aggressively in the departure area. In three weeks I will again be travelling to Europe; we will see what fresh acts of molestation MI5 perpetrate during this trip.

MI5 are Afraid to Admit They're Behind the Persecution

MI5 have issued a formal denial of any involvement in my life to the Security Service Tribunal, as you might expect them to; but, more importantly, the persecutors have never denied that they're from the Security Service, despite several years of accusations from my corner on usenet and in faxed articles. I am not surprised that the Security Service Tribunal found "no determination in your favour". I am however a little surprised that the persecutors have refused to confirm my identification of them; by doing so, they implicitly admit that my guess was right.

If you wish to reply to this article......

then please include your name and fax number! I provide the means for recipients to send me their thoughts on the topics discussed, but ask that you provide me with your fax number or email address if you require a response. Also would you please send not more than one or two pages, if by fax. Thank-you!

    Read about the MI5 Persecution on the Web at   www.five.org.uk

Reply to this artice by **fax** to   0171-681-1190   by **email** to   bu765@torfree.net

"No determination in your favour" says the Security Service Tribunal

In 1997, I made a complaint to the Security Service Tribunal, giving only the bare outlines of my case. I do not think it would have made very much difference if I'd made a much more detailed complaint, since the Tribunal has no ability to perform investigatory functions. It can only ask MI5 if they have an interest in a subject, to which MI5 are of course free to be "economical with the truth". A couple of months after my complaint the Tribunal replied that;

```
The Security Service Tribunal have now investigated your complaint and
have asked me to inform you that no determination in your favour has been
made on your complaint.
```

Needless to say this reply didn't surprise me in the slightest. It is a well established fact that the secret service are a den of liars and the Tribunal a toothless watchdog, so to see them conforming to these stereotypes might be disappointing but unsurprising.

It is noteworthy that the Tribunal never gives the plaintiff information on whether the "no determination in your favour" is because MI5 claims to have no interest in him, or whether they claim their interest is "justified". In the 1997 report of the Security Service Commissioner he writes that "The ambiguity of the terms in which the notification of the Tribunal's decision is expressed is intentional", since a less ambiguous answer would indicate to the plaintiff whether he were indeed under MI5 surveillance. But I note that the ambiguity also allows MI5 to get away with lying to the question of their interest in me; they can claim to the Tribunal that they have no interest, but at a future date, when it becomes clear that they did indeed place me under surveillance and harassment, they can claim their interest was "justified" - and the Tribunal will presumably not admit that in their previous reply MI5 claimed to have no interest.

"He doesn't know who we are"

In early January 1996 I flew on a British Airways jet from London to Montreal; also present on the plane, about three or four rows behind me, were two young men, one of them fat and voluble, the other silent. It was quite clear that these two had been planted on the aircraft to "wind me up". The fat youth described the town in Poland where I had spent Christmas, and made some unpleasant personal slurs against me. Most interestingly, he said the words, "he doesn't know who we are".

Now I find this particular form of words very interesting, because while it is not a clear admission, it is only a half-hearted attempt at denial of my guess that "they" = "MI5". Had my guess been wrong, the fat youth would surely have said so more clearly. What he was trying to do was to half-deny something he knew to be true, and he was limited to making statements which he knew to be not false; so he made a lukewarm denial which on the face of it means nothing, but in fact acts as a confirmation of my guess of who "they" are.

On one of the other occasions when I saw the persecutors in person, on the BA flight to Toronto in June 1993, one of the group of four men said, "if he tries to run away we'll find him". But the other three stayed totally quiet and avoided eye contact. They did so to avoid being apprehended and identified - since if they were identified, their employers would have been revealed, and it would become known that it was the secret services who were behind the persecution.

Why are MI5 So Afraid to admit their involvement?

If you think about it, what has been going on in Britain for the last nine years is simply beyond belief. The British declare themselves to be "decent" by definition, so when they engage in indecent activities such as the persecution of a mentally ill person, their decency "because we're British" is still in the forefront of their minds, and a process of mental doublethink kicks in, where their antisocial and indecent activities are blamed on the victim "because it's his fault we're persecuting him", and their self-regard and self-image of decency remains untarnished. As remarked in another article some time ago, this process is basically the same as a large number of Germans employed fifty years ago against Slavic "untermenschen" and the Jewish "threat" - the Germans declared, "Germans are known to be decent and the minorities are at fault for what we do to them" - so they were able to retain the view of themselves as being "decent".

Now suppose this entire episode had happened in some other country. The British have a poor view of the French, so let's say it had all happened in France. Suppose there was a Frenchman, of non-French extraction, who was targeted by the French internal security apparatus, for the dubious amusement of French television newscasters, and tortured for 9 years with various sexual and other verbal abuse and taunts of "suicide". Suppose this all came out into the open. Naturally, the French authorities would try hard to place the blame on their victim - and in their own country, through the same state-controlled media which the authorities employ as instruments of torture, their view might prevail - but what on earth would people overseas make of their actions? Where would their "decency" be then?

This is why MI5 are so afraid to admit they're behind the persecution. Because if they did admit responsibility, then they would be admitting that there was an action against me - and if the truth came out, then the walls would come tumbling down. And if the persecutors were to admit they were from MI5, then you can be sure I would report the fact; and the persecutors' support would fall away, among the mass media as well as among the general public. When I started identifying MI5 as the persecutors in 1995 and 1996 there was a sharp reduction in media harassment, since people read my internet newsgroup posts and knew I was telling the truth. The persecutors cannot deny my claim that they're MI5, because then I would report their denial and they would be seen as liars - but they cannot admit it either, as that would puncture their campaign against me. So they are forced to maintain a ridiculous silence on the issue of their identity, in the face of vociferous accusations on internet newsgroups and faxed articles.

Have MI5 lied to the Home Secretary?

In order for the Security Services to bug my home, they would either have needed a warrant from the Home Secretary, or they might have instituted the bugging without a warrant. Personally I think it is more likely that they didn't apply for a warrant - I cannot see any Home Secretary giving MI5 authority to bug a residence to allow television newscasters to satisfy their rather voyeuristic needs vis-a-vis one of their audience. But it is possible that the Security Service presented a warrant in some form before a home secretary at some point in the last nine years, for telephone tapping or surveillance of my residence, or interception of postal service.

So the possibility presents itself that a Home Secretary might have signed a warrant presented to him based on MI5 lies. Just as MI5 lie to the Security Service Tribunal, so they might have lied to a Home Secretray himself. MI5 and MI6 are naturally secretive services former home secretary Roy Jenkins said, they have a "secretive atmosphere .... secretive vis-a-vis the government as well as [enemies]". Jenkins also said he "did not form a very high regard for how they discharged their duties".

It was only a few years ago that MI5 was brought into any sort of legal framework through the "Security Service Act 1989" which defined their role as protecting national security against "threats from espionage, terrorism and sabotage, from activities of agents of foreign powers, and from actions intended to overthrow or undermine parliamentary democracy by political, industrial or violent means". Allowing newscasters to spy on their audience is not included in the 1989 Act - and such an activity would surely be denied by any Home Secretary, if MI5 made clear the purpose of a requested warrant. Either MI5 have asked for a warrant and lied about its purpose, or they've been carrying on their harassment of me without any legal basis whatsoever.

Conversations with Anthony and his MI5 contact

For two or three years I was in regular contact on the intenet newsgroups with a person who was known to all by the pen name Anthony. He was friendly with police types and claimed to personally know a man who "has access to people inside MI5". In 1996, he sent me the following email;

```
My man said earlier this week words to the effect that there is always a
bit of truth in everything. His remark confused me. If you have any idea
why MI5 or any other organisation should be interested in you then publish
those facts loudly and publicly on the Internet.  Then they would have no
further purpose in targeting you because your information was out in the
public domain.
```

I have published the facts of newscasters "watching" me loudly and publicly - yet MI5 continue to harass me.

"Always a bit of truth in everything"? Well, the MI5 man said it! Truth, in Everything I have said! An unusual moment of veracity for an MI5 operative - they're not usually given to very much veracity.

Home Office representative is "delighted"

My former employers at what used to be Oxford Computer Group, and is now ARIS/Oxford, knew all about the persecution, and indeed some of them took part in the harassment against me. The following email was posted by technical directory Ian C. to all employees in February 1992.

```
Date: February 11, 1992
From: IAN
Subject: Police 5

Said Pc Hayle "we were delighted to take advantage of the excellent
training
[...snip...]
said to be "delighted". A delighted home office representative was
unavailable for comment but said "unofficially we are delighted".
```

My interpretation of the final line of this email is that the Home Office "representative" was "delighted" because the security service were very happy that I was "incarcerated" in a job where they knew I was being abused by other employees, at the instigation of MI5. And the MI5/Home Office representative's delight was well founded, because as covered in previous articles, I was indeed abused by co-workers and OCG managers for almost a year until I was forced to take time off sick. Obviously these OCG managers and fellow workers knew who was behing the persecution - hence Ian C.'s description of the "home office" source of the harassment campaign.

A year later I tried to challenge OCG managing director Hugh S.-W. over what had happened in 1992. He, maintaining eye contact and his usual expression of sincerity, told total and utter lies about OCG managers' abuse of me in 1992. Plainly OCG-ARIS/Oxford fear their activities against me in 1992 being made public; they fear the truth, and they fear their cooperation with the instigators being identified.

Could this harassment be by Private Detectives or other MI5 proxies?

It is a matter of record that the Security Service frequently uses for its "work" semi-independent agencies such as private detective agencies staffed by former police officers or former MI5 operatives. Gary Murray in his 1993 book "Enemies of the State" describes in detail his many years working for the secret state. The main purpose of employing freelancers is to be able to disclaim them if they are caught.

Could this sub-contracting be how the current harassment campaign against me is conducted? On balance, I don't think so. Certainly MI5 are employing members of the public and presumably paying them to take part in the victimisation, but I do not believe the management of the campaign is done at any level other than from within MI5 themselves. The technical resources, the "bugging and burgling" is clearly done at a level higher than even good private detectives could achieve. And the access to the media and broadcast journalists is something that could only be done by people with a plethora of media contacts, ie. only by MI5 themselves.

And the BBC and media deny they're being used by MI5.....

You might expect the secret services to lie when challenged with the truth of what they are doing. After all, spies by their nature lie about their doings, and British spies are just as shabby and dirty liars as spies from any country. And you might expect British spies to systematically harass their own citizens - it happens in many other countries, British people aren't special in any way although some of them seem to think they are, and suppression of domestic dissidents goes on in the United Kingdom just the same as everywhere else.

But the extraordinary thing is that British media organisations like the state- and taxpayer-funded BBC take such an active part in the MI5-inspired campaign of harassment. We have after all heard of MI5 trying to bribe broadcast journalists; but surely there must be a substantial number who are not bought or blackmailed by the Security Services, and who take part in the "abuse by newscasters" of their own volition? The BBC is supposed to be independent of the government of the day as well as the Establishment in general. While perhaps it is childish to think that the BBC is anything other than effectively state-controlled, the degree of collusion between the BBC and the British Secret Police MI5 is something you would not find in many countries. Individual tele-journalists in other countries would have enough self-esteem not to allow themselves to be controlled by their secret police - seemingly, BBC broadcasters like Martyn Lewis and Nicholas Witchell have such a low opinion of their employing organisation that they see no wrong in dragging the BBC's no-longer-good name through yet more mud, at the mere request (whether supported by financial or other inducements) of the British secret Police, MI5.

And when challenged, these broadcasters LIE about their involvement, with just as little shame as MI5 themselves. The BBC's Information dept have said that;

```
"I can assure you that the BBC would never engage in any form of
surveillance activity such as you describe"
```

which is an out-and-out lie. Buerk and Lewis have themselves lied to their colleagues in the BBC's Information department over the "newscaster watching", but unsurprisingly they refuse to put these denials in writing. Doubtless if the "newscaster watching" ever comes to light, Buerk and Lewis will then continue to lie by lying about these denials. So much for the "impartial" BBC, a nest of liars bought and paid for by the Security Services!

Conclusion

It is obvious that the persecution is at the instigation of MI5 themselves - they have read my post, and only they have the surveillance technology and media/political access. Yet they have lied outright to the Security Service Tribunal. Similarly, BBC newscasters Michael Buerk and Martyn Lewis have lied to members of their own organisation. The continuing harassment indicates they are all petrified of this business coming out into the open. I will continue to do everything possible to ensure that their wrongdoing is exposed.

MI5 Persecution Update: Friday 11 June, 1999

If You Intend To Reply, Please Read This
Please.... **keep your response to one page** if you can! I have had several people faxing my article back to me, including one MP faxing back twenty pages. **Faxes over a page or two will be deleted without being read.** Also, please include your email address fax number if you want a reply - thanks.

Harassment in a pub in Clapham, Tuesday lunchtime
Once a month, or once every other month, I meet a Polish friends of mine who lives in Clapham North, and sometimes we go to a particular pub near where he lives. The last time was some two months ago; I did not have my minidisc-walkman with me, and consequently was seriously harassed by people MI5 had instructed to harass me, in the pub.

This Tuesday, 8 June 1999, we again went to the same pub for a pre-meal drink. This time I did have my minidisc-walkman with me. As you can guess, we were followed into the pub by a couple of young people (I'm getting older and older - isn't it funny how the MI5 agents all look young these days?). They started talking about my situation, in particular some travel I had booked the previous day. Unfortunately, they were talking fairly quietly, and my minidisc didn't pick up their speech.

MI5's schizophrenic reasoning is that simultaneously I am very important and worthy of their acts of persecution, and I am also totally unimportant and their abuse of me "doesn't matter". Perhaps they should test their agents and managers for obsessive personalities or psychotic features in the same way as employees are drug-tested. MI5 might lose their "worst cases" employees if some psychological testing were applied to their recruitment procedure.

Toothless Watchdogs. What a Surprise.
Recently I have been engaging in communications with two watchdogs, the Security Service Tribunal which deals with complaints against the security service (and always clears MI5 of any wrongdoing), and the Data Protection Registrar, which is mandated to investigate misuse of personal data held on computer.

In a letter to Nick Brooks, Security Service Tribunal secretary, dated 20 April, I asked him if the Tribunal, as an allegedly independent body, had the means to investigate complaints against MI5 other than asking MI5 to themselves investigate complaints. To my disappointment, his reply two weeks later answered the question only indirectly, in the negative. Whatever the reader might think of the merits of the case I have been putting before you in faxed articles this last year and half, you will surely recognise that it is a significant anomaly for the Tribunal to have no independent means of investigating complaints, particularly given the view expressed even by previous home secretaries that the security services are untrustworthy.

You are reminded that the full story is on the World Wide Web at address;

www.five.org.uk

Reply   by **fax** to 0171-681-1190   by **email** to bu765@torfree.net

MI5 Persecution: No Justice for the Victims of MI5

In a previous article I detailed the similarities between the current MI5 Persecution in England, and other historical instances of similar persecution, notably that by the Nazi Germans in the thirties and forties. The Germans persecuted first the mentally ill, the epileptics and those suffering from schizophrenia, then moved on to racial groups; in today's Britain the persecution is again directed at those with mental illness, which the British in their cowardice find easier than taking on racial groups as the Germans did. But just as in Thirties Germany there was no recourse against a malign and omnipotent state, so the MI5 Secret Police in the modern British Fascist State allow no justice for their victims.

No Recourse Against the Security Service's Illegal Harassment
It has become apparent to me over the last nine years just how loaded the dice are in today's Britain, a fundamentally fascist country which masquerades as a democracy. Britain is a democracy in name only; the Establishment, the defence and MI5 secret police are always there, regardless of which party has been voted into power most recently - and from "New Labour's" conduct in office one finds it difficult to tell them apart from Old Tories, in their crackdowns on the sick and vulnerable in society.

In thirties Germany the victims of the Nazi regime had no legal recourse against their State oppressors; and in today's Fascist British state, the victims of the Establishment and its MI5 Secret Police similarly have no recourse against the illegal state-funded and organised oppression. There is supposed to be a mechanism for dealing with MI5 crimes, in the shape of the Security Service Tribunal and Commissioner; yet these have never found favour of a plaintiff. One might as well ask the Nazi SS to investigate crimes against epileptics or Jews as ask the Security Service Tribunal to investigate MI5 crimes against British citizens; it is quite obvious what the answer is going to be, regardless of what you say to them, and what evidence you provide. The Tribunal and Commissioner are a mere formality, a whitewashing body to give the Secret Services a veneer beneath which they hide their shabby criminality.

"Institutional Racism" and Bigotry in the Metropolitan Police
The recent inquiry into the racist murder of Stephen Lawrence found clear evidence of systematic and deliberate racism in the Metropolitan Police, which cannot have surprised anyone. Commissioner Sir Paul Condon accepted a somewhat lukewarm definition of institutional racism as being "unconscious". In truth, and this truth must surely be obvious to anyone who has any familiarity or encountered the great British police, the Met has not just "unconscious" racism, but very clearly "conscious" and deliberate racism, of the kind that would have done Thirties Germans proud. And it is a bastion of such open racism - when many other parts of society are learning to live in a multicultural environment, the Met is still living in the past in its attitude to the minorities.

But in addition to the systematic racism confirmed by the Lawrence inquiry, there is also something much more relevant to this case, which is systematic police bigotry against the physically and mentally disabled, which I personally have experienced in my dealings with the police over the years. You cannot expect equal treatment if you are mentally disabled. I tried to make a complaint to the police in 1995 about the harassment I had been subjected to for several years. As soon as they found out I had mental illness, they refused to even talk to me. I tried again in March 1999; the police made various threats to me, while ranting about "your paranoid rubbish" in reference to the complaints expressed to them.

The police refusal to do the job they are employed and paid to do is extremely serious, particularly as this case is highly important, indeed key to the whole issue of British self-perception at the end of the 20th century and the beginning of the 21st century. Britain has lost much in the last fifty years - it has lost an empire, it has lost its self-respect and its identity as a people. If the MI5 persecution finally makes it into the light and the Security Services are seen for the rather cheap bullies their behaviour indicates, it will have a massive and harmful effect on British self-perception in the new century.

Security Service Tribunal - Blatant Whitewashing
A few weeks ago I spoke on the phone to Nick Brooks, the Secretary of the Security Service Tribunal, which is supposed to deal with cases of MI5 transgression. I asked him if the Tribunal had ever found in favour of a plaintiff and against the Security Service. He answered that as far as he knew, it had not.

I also asked Mr Brooks if the Tribunal had any means of investigating allegations of criminal activity by MI5, other than asking MI5 themselves if they had engaged in such activity. His rather circuitous written reply states that the 1989 Security Service Act provides that "it shall be the duty of every member of the Service to disclose or give to the Tribunal such documents or information as they may require for the purpose of enabling them to carry out their functions under this Act". Which is a very round-about way of saying - "No" - the Tribunal has no way of investigating MI5 crimes - None At All.

Setting up the S.S. Tribunal, and creating a Security Service Commissioner, was really an act of falsehood by the government. It is generally recognised that MI5 are out of reach of the normal criminal justice system - the police, as we have seen, have no interest in pursuing any investigations which might lead to them uncovering illegal acts by the Security Service - and the Tribunal and Commissioner are plainly a whitewash and nothing more. The government has perpetrated a cruel joke by creating legislation which purports to "govern" the actions of MI5 and MI6 but which in fact does no such thing, and by setting up the Tribunal and Commissioner, who have no real-world function and are only there to give the semblance of justice when in reality no checks at all exist on the Security Services, as even previous Home Secretaries have admitted.

Nobody elects the MI5 Secret Police
We are told by the media what a wonderful thing it is that we have, this "democratic" system of government. We must export this wonderful invention, by mass bombing and genocide if need be, to other less fortunate countries. Yet when you look at the implementation of "democracy" in Britain, it is quite substantially a lie. Labour in power is if anything more reactionary than the previous Tory regime. And nobody elects the unaccountable secret services. MI5 and MI6 in practice do not answer to the government; in a previous article I quoted Roy Jenkins speaking of "a secretive atmosphere.... secretive vis-a-vis the government as well as [enemies]", and a "lack of frankness" from MI5.

If the government wanted to, it could reform the secret services and ensure they acted in conformance with the laws which have been enacted for them in the last ten years. But apparently the present government does not see any need to ensure security service compliance with the law. As noted above, the regulatory machinery for MI5 is deliberately weak; the Tribunal has no independent means of investigation, and it is simply a waste of time complaining to the Tribunal or Commissioner.

Every so often, fresh revelations come to light of secret service transgressions. We have heard from Shayler that MI5 bugged Jack Straw and Peter Mandelson; we have heard from Peter Wright that MI5 plotted to see Wilson ejected from office; yet so closed is the system of government that the law is never enforced against MI5 when they "bug and burgle" everyone from politicians to ordinary citizens.

No Justice from the Legal System, either
Britain has a civil and criminal justice system which effectively limits many complaints from being heard. For a civil complaint to be brought before a court, you need a solicitor willing to act on your behalf. Supposedly it is possible to represent yourself as a Litigant-in-Person, but in practice it is well known that LiPs almost invariably have their cases struck out before trial on the basis of being "frivolous and vexatious" or "disclosing no cause for action in law". This is exactly what happened to me in 1997 when I twice tried to take the BBC to court for spying on me in my living room at home; my case was twice struck out, and on the second occasion an order was made against me that I could not bring further civil litigation against the BBC without leave of the court.

As the reader can guess it is quite impossible for a person with schizophrenia, who complains about the secret services and media interfering in his life, to find a solicitor willing to represent him in legal action against the persecutors. I have quite a lot of evidence of the continuing persecution which I have posted on the website, even if the evidence is quite tentative and perhaps open to varying interpretations. But I have tried several firms of solicitors; some of them have acted unprofessionally and abused me; all of them have refused to represent me. My psychiatrist gave me the name of the firm of Bindman and Partners in central London, and I have approached them twice. On each occasion they refused to accept my instructions. Plainly the problem with Bindmans, which they have admitted, is their bigotry against mentally disabled people; yet this is not just something that is wrong with Bindmans, it is something that is wrong with the legal system as a whole, since the legal system necessitates finding a solicitor willing to represent you in order to bring a case to court, but it does not have a mechanism for providing a lawyer in the case where no solicitor is willing to take on your case. So the British legal system is such as to prevent cases such as mine from ever receiving an airing in a court.

So much for the civil courts. But the criminal justice system is no better. Two years ago the Protection from Harassment Act came into force. But again, while the Act is all very well on paper, in practice it is unenforceable in my case, since it would require Police action to see the law implemented, and if the police cannot even be trusted to conduct a murder investigation competently (in the Lawrence case), then what chance is there of their investigating complaints against the Security Service? Of course, it would be possible for me to personally issue proceedings through a private prosecution either against MI5 themselves, or against one or more of their media tools; but here we see the same problems as with the civil courts, because first of all I would have to find a lawyer willing to act on my behalf. Litigants-in-person do exist in the criminal courts, but the Attorney General can bring such a prosecution to an end by taking it over and entering a plea of "nolle prossequi"; and I suspect that if I were to bring a private prosecution against either MI5 or one of their media tools, then this is exactly what would happen.

So much for British justice. But if anything the wrongs that have been perpetrated on me by the British justice system are quite mild to what others have suffered. Others have been wrongly convicted based on police evasions and lies, and spent many years in jail based on false charges. I should count myself lucky that despite the best efforts of the MI5 secret police, I have not acquired any criminal charges or convictions; which shows that for all their resources and influence, and the clear imperfections in the British legal system, there are still limits on how much subversion MI5 can achieve.

The latest in a long line of injustices
A comment I heard during the recent scandal of the police mishandling of the Lawrence murder investigation is that "it's not as if the police themselves murdered him". This is not a particularly wise statement to make about the case, since it could be argued that the four alleged murderers were aided in their crime by the expectation that the police would deliberately botch the investigation - which of course is exactly what the police did.

But in my case, this would be a completely inaccurate thing to say - since the MI5 secret-police have expressly been trying to nine years now to see an end put to my life, either by having me incarcerated and my liberty ended, or by forcing self-termination on me. It is **exactly** as if the secret police "themselves murdered [me]", since that is what their aim is in their campaign against me.

The public has heard of instances of police mishandling of cases, of police manufacturing evidence, lying in court, extracting false confessions to clear up crimes, et cetera. Various instances of extra-legal activity by the secret services have also come to light in the last few years. The unhappy truth is that what MI5 have been doing to me for the last nine years is really nothing out of the ordinary for them. To me it seems unbelievable that this sort of systematic campaign of harassment, which thousands and thousands of people in this country and abroad are well aware of, could exist for such a long period of time with the media maintaining "omerta". But my case is not the first such instance of persecution by the "British secret police", and judging by the lack of any real controls on MI5, I very much doubt it will be the last.

MI5 Have Systematically Destroyed My Life

This is getting depressing. From the feedback I've received, the recipients of these faxes are tired of hearing my complaints, and in truth I am tired of sending them. The reason I haven't yet ceased sending faxes is because I cannot think of any other effective means of replying to MI5's actions against me, and I feel I have to do something to try to defend myself. Three/four years ago I got the MI5 harassment out of my system by posting about it on Internet newsgroups, and for a few months this tactic was quite effective - I received (and indeed still do today) support from newsgroup regulars, and felt I could make my voice heard and break the MI5 monopoly on access to the British media. But that was years ago, and today nobody gives a tinker's cuss about my internet posts - so I have sought to escalate matters by communicating directly with the politicians who allegedly say how this country is supposed to be run.

Of course, it's quite expensive to keep up a campaign of fax messages for many weeks. Each set of faxes takes approx 50 hours to send over the weekend, and costs perhaps £35. My phone bill for the last quarter was £350. These figures are naturally insignificant compared to what MI5 have been spending against me over a similar period. It also takes a lot of time and energy to create a new article every week, and try and find new and fresh aspects and viewpoints on MI5's persecution of me. I am beginning to run out of both new topics and energy to write these articles.

So I have a suggestion to put before the MI5 persecutors who have been wrecking my life since 1990. In a few days' time I will be going on holiday to Poland and Germany, for a couple of weeks. Previously, almost every time I have travelled by plane, or gone anywhere on holiday, the MI5 "wreckers" have been most assiduous in destroying these trips. My suggestion is; **if MI5 leave me alone on this next trip, I will cease transmitting these articles**. If, however, there are any clear instances of harassment (and I am very capable of recognising MI5 harassment when I see it), then I will make public these instances and publish any recordings I may make of them, and, unwillingly and unhappily, continue the articles.

If you wish to reply to this article......
then please include your fax number! I provide the means for recipients to send me their thoughts on the topics discussed, but ask that you provide me with your fax number or email address if you require a response. Also would you please send not more than one or two pages, if by fax. Thank-you!

Read about the MI5 Persecution on the Web at   www.five.org.uk

Reply to this artice by **fax** to   0171-681-1190   by **email** to   bu765@torfree.net

Keith Hill MP (Labour - Streatham), my elected representative, as ever refuses to help.

MI5 Refuse to Allow me to have a Normal Life
It's kind of difficult to contemplate having a normal existence when you know your entire house is bugged from top to bottom, for audio and, very unpleasantly, video; when your employment is systematically destroyed, over and over again; when every time you leave the country your travel is disrupted by MI5 plants on the plane yelling abuse at you..... you get the idea. I would like to have some semblance of a normal life, like my Polish and English friends do. But MI5 have made this impossible, and they have leached massive resources from the taxpayer to institute a life not worthy of the name on me.

A few years ago MI5 were very open about their aims in persecuting me. They were shouting "suicide" at me, both in Canada where I lived at the time, and during my occasional visits to London. You can't get much clearer than that. There have been instances as recently as a few weeks ago of this intention being voiced by their side; on 15 April 1999, a woman at the next ticket counter at the Royal Festival Hall said;

"it would kill it, you know, it would just be overkill... they can't stop can they"

meaning that "they" were trying to "kill it" i.e. me and they "can't stop". The audio file is at;

www.five.org.uk/evidence/evfiles/rfh1504.htm

I wonder why they "can't stop". Nobody (who doesn't know already) believes my claims - so what difference would it make, if they were to "stop" persecuting me? Perhaps what this person's remarks indicates, is the depth of the obsession MI5 have with this case. They have chosen at random a person from the general population, and done their worst to ruin my life. What is wrong with these people, that they persecute a national of the country whose citizens they are supposed to protect?

No Chance of a Harassment-Free Job

Since the harassment started in 1990 I have had three jobs, the first near Guildford, the second in Oxford, and the third overseas in Canada. All three jobs have been systematically destroyed by MI5. It is so ironic that MI5 employs a team of agents, each well compensated for their efforts, to persecute just one person paid a mere fraction of what they get for their "work". In fact, it is a joke that MI5 is allocated resources for this sort of effort. If this area of government were run along commercial lines then MI5 would be very rapidly closed down, they produce nothing of any value, instead spending their time obsessed with the bugging and surveillance of their former employees like Shayler, dangerous subversives like Straw and Mandelson, and "threats to national security" like yours truly.

Applying for my first post university job

When I was applying for my first post-university job in the closing months of 1990, I found at two or three job interviews that MI5 had got there ahead of me. Interviewers knew what words to repeat from what had been said at my home recently; MI5 had supplied them with words to hurt me, and the "British secret police" were trying to wreck my job search and discourage me from joining the world of work. This and the continuing harassment in the media and by the public meant that the search for a job took very much longer than it would ordinarily be expected to take for a person with my qualifications.

With my first job near Guildford came the knowledge that MI5 were doing everything possible to make me lose the job. Despite their efforts I managed to stay in work for ten unhappy months, during which they made very clear to me that they were bugging my workplace, my accomodation in Woking, my car, my home..... and they also made clear that they had "got to" my employer in Guildford.

Employment with Oxford

I was able to find a new job, with Oxford Computer Training Services (now ARIS/Oxford), quite quickly. But it became very clear, very quickly, that MI5 were treating this job the same as the first; they tried to get the other employees and in particular the managers to attack me. It was plainly MI5's intention that I be sacked fro this job. But I was not sacked; instead, after almost a year of abuse from OCTS managers, I was forced to seek medical help, and had to take two months off for medical leave. OCTS MD Hugh Simpson-Wells was motivated in keeping me on by the fear that if he sacked me, then I would take him to court for the treatment OCTS managers had meted out to me during 1992.

Emigration to Canada

When I emigrated to Canada in 1994, I did think that perhaps MI5 would leave me alone, given that I had made the effort to leave the UK and try to find a new life overseas. I could not see any reason why they would continue to harass me over in Canada. But clearly the MI5 agents had their salaries to think about, since continue to harass me they most certainly did, at my home in Ottawa, and by getting fellow employees to speak against me, as had happened with previous jobs in the UK.

MI5 are denying me a future in work

Former Chief Constable of Devon and Cornwall John Alderson had this to say regarding MI5's activities;

```
"MI5 is not under the same restraints as the police. They infiltrate
organisations, people's jobs and lives. They operate almost like a
cancer."
```

Currently I am on disability, and I can see that MI5 are denying me a future in work. It would be an insult to logic for me to return to work and find a job, in the knowledge that an entire team of MI5 agents, paid in total many times what I would be earning, would have the objective of seeing me "done down" in the employment, and ejected from the place of work. This situation is completely wrong and nonsensical - I would very much like to have a job, but MI5 are preventing me from even thinking about returning to work. The culture of secrecy in MI5/MI6 means there is no objective oversight of their expenditure, when external oversight and greater transparency might lead to wasteful and illogical operations such as that against me being shelved.

Watched and Harassed at my Home and Accommodation

As you will know if you have been reading these articles, MI5 have watched and harassed me at my home, and at every accommodation I've had since 1990. They've also watched me at neighbours' houses in London, and at short-term accommodation such as hotels and bed-and-breakfasts. They have used the "words" gained from these watching activities against me, by passing these words on to other people such as OCTS managers for them to make clear that I am being watched where I live.

Harassed at rented rooms in Oxford in 1992

This was at its worst in 1992 in Oxford, where during the week I lived at rented accommodation in Oxford, and at weekends returned to my parents' home in London. I was being severely harassed by managers at my place of work, OCTS; and it was clear from the things they said that they were being supplied by MI5 with details of my home life, that they were being supplied with words to repeat at me.

In 1992 I moved house in Oxford many times, living at a total of five rented accommodations in ten months. In January I started off living in a rented room at Headington near the ring road / A40 intersection; then when it became clear that house was being bugged, moved to a rented room in Botley, some miles away. It was at the house in Botley that I had an "interactive watching" experience with Martyn Lewis while he was reading the news; I threw a term of abuse at him; he first flinched, then gave a grin, and said something which let me understand that he had been "on my side" until then, but as a result of what I had just said, he was no longer "on my side".

So I moved house again. This time to a place in Cowley, near the Rover car works, where I stayed for a few weeks. Because of continuing harassment at work, I soon moved from this accommodation, to yet another rented room on Iffley Road. By this time I was very ill and being abused continuously at work. Again, MI5 followed me to the rented room on Iffley Road, and created new instances of "newscaster watching". There was a television in the room which I watched, and as you can guess the newscasters got at me when I was watching the television. Also once I was assaulted, if that's the word for what happened, on leaving the house; a youth grabbed me by the coat lapels, roughed me up a bit with various terms of abuse. I did not report this assault to the police, because what was happening to me at work was very much worse, and nobody seemed to think that that was worthy of being reported to the police. Later that day at work, Alex G, a fellow employee, said "I heard he was assaulted".... I had not told anyone at work about the incident that morning..... so once again it was made very clear that MI5 were watching my rented accommodation and giving information about what was going on there to managers at work.

So I moved house yet again in late autumn 1992, this time to a rented room in a large house on Woodstock Road. I stayed there for several weeks as the situation at work deteriorated due to OCTS managers' abuse, until I was forced to take sick leave from work for two months and attend hospital as an outpatient; at which point I gave notice on the room, and returned to London.

MI5 continued to harass me after the diagnosis of serious illness was made. As reported previously, they harassed me on a flight to Spain in December 1992; and in 1993, when I returned to live and work in Oxford, they again bugged my rooms, as well as my workplace, although the intensity of the harassment was very much less than in 1992.

Watched, followed and harassed in Canada

It dismayed me to find that MI5 would not leave me alone after I had settled in Canada. In January 1995 I rented an apartment at the Bayshore complex in Ottawa's west end. For some weeks there was no sign of the "buggers". But then it started all over again. They first bugged my car, which had a car alarm installed - the alarm went off two or three times in a single evening, and the following day gave a signal that the car had been broken into. Then they bugged my apartment, and in particular they installed bugs on the phone line in my apartment.

In September 1995 I moved to a new apartment in Ottawa's Bytown Market area, the restaurant and entertainment heart of Canada's capital. This proved a serious mistake. In the west end I had been fairly distant from the centre of town where MI5 concentrated their efforts at turning people against me. In the Market area it was much easier for the persecutors to motivate people to harass me, and over the next couple of years there were frequent instances of harassment by the general public.

From 1995 I had some Polish friends in Ottawa, and as the reader can guess, MI5 have spent much effort trying to break up this friendship. They supplied various things about my home life to these friends, for example where I was living in the Market, directly over the road were the studios of a music radio station, which you had to "look up" to see; and MI5 told these friends that I was "looking up" to see the radio station; so the friends then replayed these words back to me, that I was "looking up". MI5 have also made various sexual slanders against me, and these friends also unwittingly replayed some of the words they had been imprinted with by the MI5 persecutors.

MI5 Will Never Allow Me to have a Normal Life
I have heard many excuses as to why MI5 continuously prevent me from having a normal life. We are told that MI5 are defending the country against a terrible evil - at the start of their persecution campaign their slanders were false to the point of ridicule - I was the "next Hitler", no less. We are told MI5 work "long term". Lies, lies, lies. It is MI5 themselves who are the terrible evil - it is against MI5 that the country needs to be defended. I am a perfectly ordinary British citizen - I have never done anything wrong in my life, for the last nine years the MI5 British Secret Police have been breaking the law, and such is the deference towards them, even from the politicians who receive these faxes every week, that the chances of the MI5 criminals being caught and punished are vanishingly close to zero.

When I have travelled abroad, they always put their people on the flights, on the journeys I undertake, to continue the harassment, so that I am put off further overseas travel, and chained to my home in London. Yet even this is illogical, because when I lived in Canada, they would still put people on flights back to the UK.... and what possible reason would they have for doing that? Perhaps the truest words to describe the MI5 persecution is that reason has nothing to do with their activities - sane people do not behave in the way the MI5 British Secret Police have been doing.

Summer 1999 - more MI5 harassment?
In only a few days time I will be going to Europe again. This time I have deliberately chosen to travel by a non-UK airline; so we will see if they put their paid agents on this foreign carrier, we will see if they try to harass me on this non-British flight.

If they do harass me on this trip to Europe, or if they resume the harassment in London after I return home, then I will continue to report their activities in these faxes. As I said at the beginning of this article, I would very much like to not have to send these articles any more, but that is not my decision to make - it is entirely up to MI5 to cease their pointless persecution of me, once and for all.

MI5 Persecution Update: Friday 9 July, 1999

If you wish to reply to this article......

then please include your fax number! I provide the means for recipients to send me their thoughts on the topics discussed, but ask that you provide me with your fax number or email address if you require a response. Also would you please send not more than one or two pages, if by fax, unless you have something to say that needs more than a couple of pages. Thank-you!

Harassment in Poland, July 1999

And still it continues.... in my last fax I said that provided MI5 made no attempts at harassment during my two-week holiday this summer, or after I returned to England, then I would discontinue these faxes. Unfortunately MI5 have continued to harass me, both during the holiday and after my return to London. I really don't want to continue these articles, since they take up so much time and effort, not to mention expense; but the Security Service won't even let me have a holiday in peace and quiet, so I have to make further efforts to bring their activities out into the open.

In early July I visited my aunt and her family in Poland. On Saturday 3 July 1999, I went to a family barbecue at an allotment outside the city. One of my aunt's family has previously shown himself to be in the "enemy" camp, by saying the Polish equivalent of "something wrong with him", and various other unprovoked insults. It is disappointing that one of my family could forsake the usual ties of blood and take part in the actions against me, but that's the way it is. This guy turned up at the barbecue, and started making insults against me. In particular, he started to say something about the video camera which I had brought along on the trip, and the relevance of the video-camera to my fight against the persecution. It seemed pretty obvious to me that my enemies had told him to turn up to this occasion, and most likely schooled him in precisely what words to say; since he's an unintelligent person and would not be able to think for himself what insults to make against me.

Harassment in London, week ending Friday 9 July 1999

Got back to London Wednesay afternoon. Two incidents on the Underground returning from the airport. Unfortunately I wasn't recording because I wasn't expecting trouble, so these slipped through the net. One of these was verbal sexual abuse, of the type I've heard many, many times before these last three-and-a half years.

Yesterday, Thursday 8/July/1999, I switched on Heart FM which had never "got at" me before.... and the presenter started making jokes about "mad, crazy" etc. Again, wasn't recording this because I'd never had any trouble from this radio station and wasn't expecting any.

Also yesterday, on a bus (155?) from Balham to Clapham, a couple of girls started harassing me with taunts of "crazy". By now I was expecting trouble and recorded an audio file of this instance of abuse, at web URL;

       www.five.org.uk/evidence/evfiles/bus0425.htm

The cynical reader might think my demeanour or behaviour had given rise to the taunts of "crazy" recorded above. But I assure you my behaviour on the bus would not have made anyone think I was ill; and the taunts the previous day were the same sexual words as previously; so I'm quite sure that these incidents are either deliberately staged, or indicative of an overall high level of awareness among the London public, particularly in the part of London where I live.

You are reminded that the full story is on the World Wide Web at address;

       www.five.org.uk

Reply   by fax to 0171-681-1190   by email to bu765@torfree.net

MI5 Persecution: Harassment through the Radio

One of the aspects of the MI5 persecution has been harassment through the broadcast and print media; and one of the aspects of harassment through the broadcast media is being "got at" by radio presenters. This being "got at" from the radio takes various forms, the most obvious form being through overt or hidden words and insults. But there are other, subtler forms. In Canada a couple of years ago, I used to listen to the local radio stations every morning driving to work, and listened to the music only, switching between radio station presets rapidly as soon as a presenter's voice came on, so that I would not be subjected to any verbal harassment by the D.J.s. But they found a way around this; they kept on playing the same song, every bl**dy morning at the same time, which had the words "all coming back to me"; the perceptive reader will remember that the words "coming back" have special meaning (see the Private Eye cover at web URL;

>   www.five.org.uk/evidence/evfiles/norma.htm

for the hidden meaning).

```
And that's not the only time they've allowed the songs themselves to be
used as abuse against me; many years ago Radio-1 in the UK did exactly the
same, and the DJ even made it explicitly clear by saying, "don't you
sometimes feel as if the songs were made just for you".
```

"We should be done for attempted manslaughter" says Chris Tarrant

Capital Radio DJs have been "in on it" from the start. One of the first things I heard in the summer of 1990 was from a Capital DJ who said, "If he listens to Capital then he can't be all bad" (supportive, you see. We're not bastards). Much of what came over the radio in 1990 is now so far away the precise details have been obliterated by time. No diary was kept of the details, and although archives if they exist may give pointers, the ambiguity of what broadcasters said would leave that open to re-interpretation.

In spring 1994, Chris Tarrant on his Capital morning show made an aside to someone else in the studio, about a person he didn't identify. He said, "You know this bloke? He says we're trying to kill him. We should be done for attempted manslaughter".

That mirrored something I had said a day or two before. What Tarrant said was understood by the staff member in the studio he was saying it to; they said, "Oh no, don't say that" to Tarrant. If any archives exist of the morning show (probably unlikely) then it could be found there; what he said was so out of context that he would be very hard put to find an explanation. A couple of days later, someone at the site where I was working repeated the remark although in a different way; they said there had been people in a computer room when automatic fire extinguishers went off and those people were "thinking of suing for attempted manslaughter".

Pirate Radio "gets at" me

In another incident in 1990/91, I'd been listening to a pirate radio station in South London for half an hour, when there was an audible phone call in the background, then total silence for a few moments, followed by shrieks of laughter. "So what are we supposed to say now? Deadly torture? He's going to talk to us now, isn't he?" which meant that they could hear what I would say in my room. Note the word "deadly" - they give away their purpose.

It constantly surprised me that MI5 are so easily able to subvert broadcasters, and, in this case of the pirate station, to do so, so quickly. I think the answer to this question is that they must have very wide contacts in the broadcast media; presumably some or in fact many of those contacts are literally "bought". In the same way as they tried to buy Jon Snow of Channel Four news, they must have bought many broadcasters and use them both directly to make insults against me, and promulgate their points of view; but also, they must use these "bought" broadcasters to influence other television and radio presenters, who might not even be aware that it was on MI5's behalf that they were being influenced to "get at" me.

BBC-Radio-1 D.J.s celebrate my job termination in November 1991

This is another one from the "early years". At the beginning of November 1991 my employment in Woking, Surrey was terminated. Chris Tarrant of Capital-FM had already made nasty remarks about both my work for the company, and the managers of the company themselves - "so they're not really a serious company, well they'd have to be to employ you wouldn't they".

So when I was terminated, as you can expect, BBC Radio 1 D.J.s celebrated. On the Saturday afternoon (either 9/Nov/1991 or 16/Nov/1991 - I cannot remember precisely) I briefly listened to Radio-1 and heard the disc jockeys loudly proclaiming "you're useless, you should be sacked". On the same day, I went down to the Kwik-Fit in Tooting to get my car's tyres replaced, and in the office ran into a couple of their staff, one of them with an Australian accent, who said "what do you think about it then? It's getting killed on the radio."

Plainly, if a random car-repair shop in Tooting knew about the persecution, then many thousands of other people across the capital and all over the country must have known. And the phrase "getting killed" shows very clear awareness of what the MI5 Persecutors' intentions towards me were in 1991, and judging by the continuing harassment, still remain today.

Recent Feedback from Virgin-Radio

As readers will know, from mid-March 1999 for some four months, every weekend, I have bombarded Westminster MPs with faxes about the terrible, all-encompassing MI5 Persecution. (Jesting aside, it really is terrible and all-encompassing, in the UK anyway.) In June 1999, after I'd been at it some three months, I started getting "covert" feedback from Virgin Radio.

The first feedback I got was from Danny Baker, on Sunday 13th June. That weekend I was sending an article which contained biting criticism of the police inaction in this case. Danny Baker on his Virgin radio show started an angry rant that "he knows it's rubbish", ie. he was rubbishing what I'd said in that weekend's faxed article. Unfortunately I wasn't recording this programme.

The next possible Virgin-Radio feedback was a week later on 19th June 1999. This is contained in the audio file above, in which Johnny Boy on his "Wheels of Steel" programme says;

"and if you would like to put a triple play together, ahhh.... because quite frankly Hipster and me are running out of ideas...."

He goes on to counter Hipster's "how dare you" with a protestation that he is "only joking". You can listen to this incident on my website at URL;

    www.five.org.uk/evidence/evfiles/virgin2.htm

What I reckon is that my article faxed to MPs that weekend was forwarded by one of the recipients to Virgin Radio. My article had included the words;

```
"I am beginning to run out of both new topics and energy to write these
articles.
```

So what I reckon is that Johnny Boy read the article.... and rephrased the above line "run out of ... new topics" to "running out of ideas". I recognise that this is a pretty tenuous inference to make.... but do listen to the audio file, from the "ahhh...." pause in JB's speech you can guess he is about to say something "risky" and at someone's expense. Anyway, I listen to the Wheels of Steel regularly and will continue to do so, recording it as I always do - so any future funny remarks will get immortalised on my website! (There was a previous incident from August 1998 which is preserved at web URL;

    www.five.org.uk/evidence/evfiles/virgin1.htm

but I am sufficiently uncertain about it that I have not included it in this article.)

First Ever Radio Reference - Alan Freeman of BBC-Radio-1

The first time I was ever referred to on the radio was sometime in May or June of 1990, by Alan Freeman of BBC-Radio-1. Note that this isn't an "interactive listening" episode, it's different, this was Freeman reading out a letter from one of my "real life" enemies.

I'd acrimoniously broken up with some former friends in January of 1990, and I think they were still trying to cause me trouble in June of that year. Freeman on his rock show read out a letter from an "Andrew Turner"; one of my acquaintances from January 1990 had been called Andy Turner, so I think it's the same guy. Freeman quoted Turner as saying various things about me, in particular Freeman said "that's a hell of a letter you wrote there Andy", "with a schizophrenic you're never alone", and something about the "one who wore out his welcome with random precision" (from the words of the Pink Floyd song).

When I was looking for primary causes of the MI5 persecution, this letter which Freeman had read out on his programme struck me as being potentially one of the sources of the persecution. I know Turner and various others in that group were very bitter at what they saw as their failure and my undeserved success, and they were quite determined to upset the applecart. Of course several other primary causes are possible; I do not know why MI5 chose me as opposed to someone else, and MI5 are hardly likely to tell me.

"Absolute Obscene" David Hepworth of GLR

This one I've assigned a 100% rating on the website. There are actually two separate incidents, which are linked through the D.J.'s choice of words. The first incident can be heard in computer audio at web URL;

> www.five.org.uk/evidence/evfiles/glrhep1.htm

On 21/Feb/1997, I was listening to BBC GLR, by stealth. Back in 1990 I used to have Capital blaring out of the speakers all over the garden ("if he listens to Capital then he can't be all bad", thanks ever so much). But now I listen on my walkman on headphones with the volume turned right down. It could not possibly be overheard by any listening device, no matter how sensitive, because sound does not carry from the phones.

Yet somehow they are still able to tell which station I am listening to on the walkman. And last night, I bravely tuned to GLR 94.9FM at around 8.45pm. Everything went well for the first half hour or so. Around 9.10pm, Hepworth said the following after the song "Come Around" by the Muttonbirds.

```
"coming up after this, we got the rock-and-roll A-level, we have, I
assume, Brian do we have an embarrassment of prizes in there, we do, don't
we, absolute obscene amounts of prizes, there will no doubt be a riot at
the back door, and that's, er, A-level coming up after this"
```

The key phrases in what he said are, "EMBARRASSMENT of prizes", and what he himself emphasized verbally, "ABSOLUTE OBSCENE amount of prizes". It is my belief (based on content and tone of voice) that when he spoke these phrases he knew I was listening, and that the phrases refer directly to my situation. The "EMBARRASSMENT" is the embarrassment he and other media people would feel at having their wrongdoing exposed; the "ABSOLUTE OBSCENE" (which he verbally emphasized) described the disgusting sexual abuse which the harassers have been throwing at me.

There was a second incident, on 9/May/1997, which may be found on the web (with computer audio) at URL;

> www.five.org.uk/evidence/evfiles/glrhep2.htm

This incident again contains the words "absolute embarrassment of prizes", with the same emphasis as the first instance, and laughter following the phrase. So they're aware of the complaint I made on Usenet after the first incident; and they are so arrogant that they do exactly the same again. They are so arrogant, they know they are being recorded and that what they say will be published on the web, but they don't care. What corrupt media, and what a corrupt country to have such corruption in its media.

Three Years of "MI5 Persecution" Faxes

If you wish to reply to this article......
then please include your fax number! I provide the means for recipients to send me their thoughts on the topics discussed, but ask that you provide me with your fax number or email address if you require a response. Also would you please send not more than one or two pages, if by fax, unless you have something to say that needs more than a couple of pages. Thank-you!

You are reminded that the full story is on the World Wide Web at address;

www.five.org.uk

Reply   by **fax** to   0171-681-1190   by **email** to   bu765@torfree.net

Keith Hill MP (Labour - Streatham), my elected representative, as ever refuses to help.

Ten Thousand Faxes, and Still No Breakthrough
In the last three years I have sent at least 5,301 faxes directly from my computer, and 4,478 faxes through Demon's extremely useful TPC.INT service, to politicians and the media, in the subject of the "MI5 Persecution". This has obviously cost me quite a lot of money, not to mention time and effort. The aim of all this communication has been to try to put discussion of the "MI5 persecution" into the public arena; unfortunately, this aim has not been achieved, yet.

This fax will be my last transmission for the time being, since the summer recess is almost upon us. Depending on what the persecutors do between now and the autumn, I may or may not resume faxing later this year. In the article dated 18/6/99 I said I'd stop the articles if MI5 left me alone; but they seem to have no fear of these articles, since they kept pursuing me in Poland and after my return to the UK. Again, **if they leave me alone this summer then I won't have to resume the articles in the autumn**; but I think it's fairly obvious that MI5 have nothing better to do with their time than to go after me, and it's almost pointless to make this offer when I know they won't cease harassing me.

TPC.INT 1996, 1997, 1998.....
Three years ago I was living in Canada, and the only economic way of sending faxes to the UK was through the international email-to-fax gateway TPC.INT. This highly useful and totally free service converts emails (which may have Postscript-formatted attachments) into faxes which it delivers to any number within the UK. Using the telephone book, I constructed a computer database of M.P.s' fax numbers, and used this database to deliver copies of the "FAQ - frequently asked questions" article which I'd written some time earlier.

This service is still operational, but given that I have resided in London for the last year, I do not need to use Demon's service when I can send articles directly from my own computer using its fax/modem, which is what I have been doing since 1998. However, instead of just sending the FAQ article, I've been composing articles on various aspects of MI5's treatment of me. Since their activities have been going on for nine years now, and there have been various aspects to their actions; they have harassed me at work, at home, through the media, etc; I have so far not run out of things to say, particularly since their harassment of me is still ongoing, and I have been able to record the actual words used by their paid agents on my minidisc-walkman. Since mid-March 1999 I have been sending these articles pretty much every weekend.

Anyway, as mentioned above, I intend this to be the final transmission before the summer recess, and it would be nice not to have to continue these articles in the autumn. But that's something that depends on them, not me, and their attitude is unfortunately clear.

Why am I sending these articles?
Because I want the harassment to stop. The cynical reader might think from these articles that I "thrive on adversity" and would be lost without the harassment to complain about; but that is not the case. In a perfect world I would like to return to work, in a job unsullied by MI5's attempts to ruin it; I would like to live in a house which wasn't bugged, with my words being repeated at me wherever I go; I would like a normal life. I

do not particularly thrive on adversity; I am beaten down by adversity; the purpose of these faxes is to try to bring the whole matter out into the public arena, where the rights and wrongs would be visible to all, and once that were to happen, the adversity might cease. I have had something approaching a normal life a couple of times in the last nine years, but always, in the end, MI5 turn up and ruin it. I just want these people out of my life, permanently, and the only way of doing that is to kick this business into the public arena, and shame MI5 so that they are incapable of doing me further damage.

Having said that, unfortunately it seems fairly obvious by now that these faxed articles are not going to achieve that aim. Some of the recipients know what I am saying is true; but they choose to stay quiet - wisely, because if they were to admit the truth of these articles, then they would bring the wrath of MI5 down on their heads. Presumably most recipients do not know these articles are true; their reaction to me is the same as my reaction to the other apparently deluded people who have sent me email after reading my webpage to tell me it happened to them too; the reaction being, "leave me alone, I don't want to know". It's sad that many M.P.s have given me this reaction, because my case genuinely is different; I genuinely am telling the truth, and the harassment genuinely is happening to me, and some recipients of this fax know this to be true.

"Write to your own M.P."

My local M.P. is Mr Keith Hill, Labour-Streatham. He refuses to have anything to do with me. He refuses to represent me, he refuses to talk to me, he has told me not to communicate with him. He has done absolutely nothing to help me, and he has told me he will do absolutely nothing to help me.

Other M.P.s, recipients of these faxes, have for quite some time been telling me, "write to your own M.P.". On 23 March 1998, Paul Burstow M.P. wrote to me; "Whilst I take the issues that you raise seriously, there is a strict Parliamentary convention that one Member of Parliament does not take up another's casework. Can I suggest that you write to your own M.P. at the House of Commons?" Hopefully the above paragraph will make clear that I _have_ written to my own M.P. and he has proved unhelpful.

Other M.P.s have told me the same thing. On 21 May 1998, John McFall M.P. told me, "... there is a parliamentary convention that M.P.s do not take up cases of people not in their constituency..... therefore can I suggest that you write to your local M.P. who will be better able to assist you." And on 8 June 1998, Michael Foster M.P. wrote to me that "M.P.s are inundated with unsolicited faxes .... M.P.s have a considerable amount of constituent work to deal with, thus other M.P.s constituents cease to be of concern in so far as they should have a voice and representation".

Simon Hughes M.P. wrote to me on 5 November 1998, "There is a strict parliamentary convention which states that I am not able to represent individuals who are not constituents of mine. My advice is that you find out who your own Member of Parliament is rather than circulating your story to all M.P.s.". To my suggestion that Keith Hill M.P. was doing nothing to help me, George Foulkes M.P. sent the following faxed response; "If Keith Hill your own M.P. cannot help no-one else in the House of Commons can." But it is clearly not a case of "cannot" help, but "will" not" help. I have detailed in letters to Mr Hill specific ways in which he could help me, first of all by finding a lawyer to represent me. It is Mr Hill's job as a Member of Parliament to represent his constituents; if he chooses not to do so, then it reflects badly on him.

Kate Hoey Sympathises, but says, "Write to your own M.P."

Here is part of a letter Ms Hoey sent to me on 15 June 1999.

```
I appreciate that you have concerns about the persecution and harassment
that you feel you are experiencing but I note that your MP is in fact
Keith Hill. There is a very strict Parliamentary code which means that
M.P.s can only take action on matters that relate to their own
constituents. I am aware that you are not happy with the fact that you do
not feel Mr Hill will assist you but I am afraid that I cannot take any
action on your behalf.
```

Ms Hoey plainly belongs in the camp of people who do not know about the reality of the "MI5 Persecution". She doubts its existence; "the harassment you feel you are experiencing". She urges me to see Mr Hill's assistance, as have other M.P.s detailed above.

Really, the fact that I am unable to obtain assistance from any other M.P., if my own alleged "representative" Mr Hill chooses not to represent me, is a very basic weakness in the Parliamentary system. Being forced to rely on your own M.P., when that M.P. is selective as to the constituent cases he undertakes, is simply an error in the system. Either M.P.s should be compelled to undertake all cases placed before them by their constituents; or if they are not so compelled, then it should be possible for their constituents to place their cases before other M.P.s.

With the system as it is now, cases like mine "fall through the cracks". My own M.P. won't even talk to me, and has on several occasions refused to be of any assistance whatsoever. I seem to remember that following the death of Mr Fayed's son in Paris, he wrote to many M.P.s to request that they place questions before the Government over the possible role of the secret services in this alleged killing. If he was able to write to M.P.s who have "no jurisdiction", then why shouldn't I do the same?

A Year in the Life

Prior to April 1998 I had merely been sending by postal service and by fax copies of the "FAQ" article summarising the entirety of the MI5 persecution. But in April 1998 I started sending freshly written pieces on what was being done to me, with "MI5 Persecution Update" pages listing events in the MI5 Persecution which had occurred to me recently. The "persecution update" pages were particularly valuable to me, since although I may not have any way of preventing MI5 making verbal slanders against me, at least I can record them on the minidisc-walkman which I carry around with me much of the time, and once they have been recorded, I can psychologically expel them from my system by posting the computer audio files on my website (in the Evidence section), and informing fax recipients of the nature of recent incidents and the location of computer files describing these incidents. The internet and the fax-machine is a powerful tool in the fight against the evil of the Security Service.

The first such article, as mentioned, was in April 1998 and titled **"MI5 Persecution: How Could It Be True?"**. This article covered the very basic question of whether the claims I make are the product of mental illness, which I do suffer from, or whether MI5 have used my illness as a cover for their activities, and indeed have induced (particularly in 1992) a much worse state of illness than I would otherwise have, for the express purpose not only of damaging me but also of ensuring that my future claims of being persecuted by them would be considered symptomatic of that illness and therefore disregarded.

The second article in April, **"Why do you think MI5 are responsible?"** asks the question, "have they ever denied that they are the Security Service?" to which the answer is a very clear "no they haven't". If I'd been wrong in my guess then "they" would surely have crowed over my mistake, but they have never admitted or denied that they are employees of MI5.

In early January 1996 I flew on a British Airways jet from London to Montreal; also present on the plane, about three or four rows behind me, were two young men, one of them fat and voluble, the other silent. It was quite clear that these two had been planted on the aircraft to "wind me up". The fat youth described the town in Poland where I had spent Christmas, and made some unpleasant personal slurs against me. Most interestingly, he said the words, "he doesn't know who we are".

Now I find this particular form of words very interesting, because while it is not a clear admission, it is only a half-hearted attempt at denial of my guess that "they" = "MI5". Had my guess been wrong, the fat youth would surely have said so more clearly.

In November 1998 I sent two articles on successive weekends, the first about **"Harassment at Work"** and the second on **"BBC Newscasters Spying on my Home"**. The first covered mainly events at my former employers in Oxford during 1992, when I was harassed constantly by manager Steve Mitchell for most of 1992, and was forced to begin attending hospital as an outpatient as a result. This harassment was obviously of Mitchell's own volition, since I observed him harass similarly another new worker two years later; but it was also at MI5's instigation, since they kept providing him with words from my home life which he then proceeded to abuse me with. Yet this is not the only employment that MI5 have destroyed; the MI5 persecution has lasted from the end of my student days until the present time, during which I have had three jobs, all of which have been in various ways destroyed by MI5's deliberate actions.

In **March 1999** I decided to try to force the issue once and for all. Ever weekend for the last four months, apart from two weeks when I was on holiday, I have sent original articles by fax directly from my computer to Westminster politicians. Here is a summary of the articles of the last four months;

9903a	How to Identify the Persecutors
9903b	Browse Website www.five.org.uk
9904a	Their use of Schizophrenia to discredit my claims
9904b	Comparing the MI5 Persecution with German "Final Solution"
9904c	MI5 are Plainly Trying to Kill Me
9904d	MI5 Waste Taxpayer Millions on Pointless Hate-Campaign
9905a	Four Years of "MI5 Persecution" Posts on Internet Newsgroups
9905b	MI5 Agents are Clinical Psychopaths
9905c	BBC Newscasters Lie & Deny They're Watching Me
9905d	Molestation during Travel
9906a	MI5 are Afraid to Admit They're Behind the Persecution
9906b	No Justice for the Victims of MI5
9906c	MI5 Have Systematically Destroyed My Life
9907a	Harassment through the Radio

To my deep worry these fourteen faxed articles have still not achieved the objective of kicking the matter out into the public arena and forcing an admission either from the persecutors, or from those "in the know", which includes some M.P.s.

I don't really know what else to do to try to bring the "MI5 persecution" out into the open. I would have expected that these weekly faxed articles would have had some effect, but the only result has been M.P.s telling me to contact my own representative Mr Hill who refuses to talk to me. I understand the convention that M.P.s deal with their own constituents and not those of other M.P.s, but there seems to be a gap in the process since it allows your own M.P. to refuse to deal with you, and then you are totally denied any representation at all.

Conclusion
The only conclusion I can inform the readership of these articles of, is that there is no conclusion to this matter, yet! Three years of intermittent articles, and four months of faxes every weekend, have been absorbed by some of the most powerful people in the country, to no effect.

Whether these articles continue in the Autumn is entirely up to the "opposition". I offered them a cessation of complaints if they would leave me alone on holiday in June/July, and they went right ahead and harassed me anyway, on holiday and after I returned to London. If MI5 cease their activities now, then I won't have to continue these faxes in the autumn; but I suspect they won't cease, which means you're in for more articles later this year. **"There will be no conclusion."**

MI5 Want Me to Send You these Faxes

If you wish to reply to this article......
then please include your fax number! I provide the means for recipients to send me their thoughts on the topics discussed, but ask that you provide me with your fax number or email address if you require a response. Also would you please send not more than one or two pages, if by fax, unless you have something to say that needs more than a couple of pages. Thank-you!

You are reminded that the full story is on the World Wide Web at address;

www.five.org.uk

Reply   by **fax** to 0171-681-1190   by **email** to bu765@torfree.net

Keith Hill MP (Labour - Streatham), my elected representative, as ever refuses to help.

MI5 seem to Want to Spin this Business out for as Long as Possible

The MI5 persecution has now been going on, starting from June 1990, for well over nine years. If I knew how to put an end to it then I would do so. Of course MI5 have indicated how they wish to finish the matter, by finishing me off; they indicated this very clearly years ago when they were shouting "suicide" at me.

But a deeper truth is that the MI5 agents carrying out the persecution rely on it for their income and their livelihood. They have absolutely no interest in anything other than spinning out the whole business, because that is how they will maximise their earnings from their employer for the "work" they do against me.

A vital part of the fantasy structure MI5 have created about me is that I am somehow a worthwhile target. If you bother to read these faxes, if you browse my website, or perhaps read my posts on the uk.misc newsgroup, you will have by now twigged that I am a totally insignificant person who in a proper dictatorship like East Germany would not merit five minutes of Stasi time. But Britain is improper in the methods of its corruption, and the Security Service seeks to present me as being a an evil fascist, an evil communist, an evil something-else, and even a "national institution".

It occurs to me that to some extent I am playing into their hands, into their scheme of things, by writing these articles and sending these faxes. By doing these things, I elevate my profile, and fuel MI5's paranoid obsession with me. But to stop sending faxes would be to give up the only hope I have of seeing their campaign "outed" and justice done. Certainly there is no point going to the police again; and as remarked in a previous article, the Security Service Tribunal routinely whitewashes every complaint that is placed before it.

So although MI5 seems to want me to continue sending these faxes, doing this is the only real chance of getting this business out into the open. And so I'll continue trying to kick down their house of cards. At least my situation is less serious than that of some other victims of the secret services; unlike Shayler I am not broke and exiled; unlike Fayed I have not lost a son to the posited activities of the secret services. All I have lost is some of my health, some of my life, and some of my possible career.

MI5's Abuse of me is without Cause or Reason

It constantly puzzles me that MI5 refuse to leave me alone, wherever I go and whatever I do, or rather, whatever I don't do, since I'm not a very socially or otherwise active person. When I am in England, they chase me all over the place, and once they've found me, they pay people to shout rude words at me. When I am in Europe, they again chase me all over the place, and as usual pay people to shout obscenities at me. When I am in Canada or visiting the States, they faithfully chase me all over the place, and when they find me, pay people to shout obscenities at me.

It is hard to avoid the conclusion that these MI5 operatives who chase me are total lunatics. You will remember from a previous articles the assessment "MI5 Agents are Clinical Psychopaths". They have tried to blame me for what they do and what they say; yet their lies have been wafer-thin, and are clearly seen to be oiled by the money which they acquire from the Government, and ultimately from the taxpayer.

They have tried various lies to put the blame on me; "we have to abuse him because he's a nutter", as if there weren't many tens of thousands of other people with schizophrenia in the United Kingdom. Their choice of abuse words is telling; subconsciously perhaps they realise that it is they who are the "nutters", and they try to project their own illness onto their target.

MI5 Operatives have Nothing Else to Do With Their Time
I've seen the same "Alan Holdsworth" person three or four times over a period of several years. I saw him at the Civic Hospital in Ottawa in the Emergency Ward, where he falsely declared his name to be "Tad"; at Ottawa airport in summer 1998; and on board another flight in 1995.

So what we see from the above paragraph is, the same people are delegated to watch me for many years. Without me, they wouldn't have a job. They literally have nothing else to do with their time, except indulge their voyeurism against me. With this observation, we come to the core of MI5's campaign against me; these people are not fit for any job other than the exercise of voyeurism against me, and if sanity were to land on MI5 then they would be out of a job. If sanity were truly to land then these people and their employers would be prosecuted for offences under the Protection from Harassment legislation, which they are clearly breaking.

It is one of the ironies of their campaign that MI5 have been trying to make me an object of ridicule for completely trivial things I have done, while MI5 themselves have simply not mentioned how ridiculous is their own behaviour and that of broadcast media journalists, in spying on me while they read the news for example. If the whole truth of this business is ever exposed, and despite all my efforts it still seems there is a block on its exposure in Britain, then the rights and wrongs will be clear to all, and no amount of MI5 lies will be able to change that. MI5 presumably do realise just how damaging such a revelation would be both to themselves, and to broadcast media such as the BBC and ITN, because there has not been even the slightest chink in the armour, despite four and a half years of my complaints on internet newsgroups and by fax to politicians and the media.

MI5's Final Kick in the Teeth to the British State
For someone like myself born in the late sixties it seems peculiar to think that Great Britain once used to have a say in the destiny of foreign peoples in far-off sections of the globe. Modern Britons tacitly accept the lowering of their country to a third-rate power reliant on the United States for what little say it has in the world. A third-rate power, now "reverse-colonised" by third world peoples it once ruled and riven with internal problems so severe the government hardly dares acknowledge them.

To this third-rate power the MI5 secret police are delivering the final kick in the teeth through a campaign of persecution which is guaranteed to hold the state up to ridicule throughout the world when it is finally exposed. As a "thought experiment" suppose the French or the Spanish security service had done to one of their own born citizens what MI5 has done in this country. Suppose say the Spanish had planted hidden cameras in his home, for the perverted pleasure of their state television newscasters, just as hidden cameras have been placed in my home for the perverted pleasure of Martyn Lewis, Nicholas Witchell et al. Suppose the Spanish service had for nine years been trying to force suicide on their target; at times, so blatantly that they shouted the word "suicide".

Now suppose they were caught.

Of course, as long as MI5 aren't caught, they're laughing. The psychopathic security service agents gets their kicks from shouting abuse at me; the newscasters, Lewis, Witchell etc get their jollies, "it was so funny", we were watching this bloke and he couldn't do anything about it.

But once they're caught, the sky falls in. Of course, the "patriotic" MI5-funded media in Britain will try to put the best spin on the MI5/media activities; it was the target's fault, of course. But most of the world bears no allegiance to Britain. If this business is ever exposed then a weakened Britain will become the laughing-stock of the world. And I promise you, the security service's persecution of me will be exposed. MI5 has delivered a final kick in the teeth to the British state, and I will do everything I can to ensure the world hears about what they have done.

Metropolitan Police Refuse to Investigate the MI5 persecution
I have on a couple of occasions tried to motivate the police to investigate MI5's actions against me. On each occasion they have refused to do so. In 1995 I went to my local police station and spoke to an officer there; he refused to accept my complaint, and seemed interested only in seeing me leave the station as quickly as possible.

Earlier this year I had some communications with Det.Sgt.Richards of Charing Cross police. Again I asked him to deal with MI5's actions against me. Unfortunately DS Richards conformed to the negative stereotype of the bigoted, ignorant "copper"; he said, "I have read your various bits on the internet. I'm afraid there is no substance or credence to it. It's an absolute load of rubbish. I don't investigate rubbish. I can't be more blunt or to the point than that."

You have to wonder at the state of law enforcement in Britain. If the victim of a murder is black, as happened in the Lawrence case, the police deliberately botch the investigation. If the victim of a crime is mentally ill, and the perpetrators are the secret services, as in my case, then the police refuse to even begin to investigate the crimes committed. Politically Britain is a third-rate country, but from the point of view of obtaining justice, Britain ranks down there with third-world countries. You almost feel that MI5 and their media buddies would not even have any shame if their activities against me were exposed; after all, why should they? they have the money, they have the control, OK so perhaps they've broken a few dozen laws, but doesn't the fact that the police are too corrupt to investigate these crimes, doesn't that prove that in fact no crimes have been committed?

I should say again what I have said earlier in this article. My losses over the last nine years have not been as great as those of other victims of British Secret Police malefaction. Fayed lost his son to their murderous activities; in my occasional communications with former MI5/MI6 employees I have been informed that a "permanent solution" is not uncommon for opponents of the British secret police. I have lost health and financially, but am obviously well enough to keep fighting my case. Others have lost much more than I. If the joke which is British "law enforcement" refuses to enforce laws against the security services then that is something that is recognised in other countries and Britain's stock correspondingly falls. Not that it has very far to fall; the days when England had any say in the world are long gone.

MI5 Want These Faxes to Continue
Before the holiday, I said that if MI5's harassment of me stopped, then I would cease my complaints. They have known very well that if they continued to harass me then I would resume the fax campaign in the autumn. Yet they have not stopped persecuting me. Recently a woman outside my domicile screamed her head off with abuse in the direction of my window; and on Saturday 2 October, when I was shopping at a nearby supermarket, a man shouted the particularly vile sexual swear word which I have heard many times before over the last few years.

MI5's attitude shows complete arrogance. Yet it also shows that they want the faxes to continue and deliberately try to provoke me into sending further faxes. The reasons for this are given in the first paragraphs of this article; the MI5 operatives who persecute me have nothing else to do with their time; to make their campaign, against an apparently unreacting target, have some value, they have to force me to react in some way against their actions; and by reacting in this way, by bringing their campaign to the attention of British politicians, I play into their hands, by giving their campaign the attention and importance which they feel it deserves.

In the short term, by sending these faxes, perhaps I am doing something they want me to do, but in the longer term it is undoubtedly more in my interest than theirs for their activities to be exposed. If their operatives truly do wish to see these faxes continued then they are committing a serious mistake, because it significantly increases the risk if M.P.s (some of whom already know about MI5's activities against me) are advised of my side of the story.

I will continue to monitor and record the secret service's activities against me over the next few weeks. If they diminish and cease, as I hope they will, then I may be able to call a halt to these faxes; but that it something which is entirely up to them; recently their continued harassment makes clear that they do wish the faxes to continue, and in all sincerity I do think they will continue their activities and make it impossible for me to cease these faxes. It may trouble you to receive these articles, but it troubles me much more to be on the receiving end of a national persecution campaign; and while Britain does not have free speech provisions as does Canada in the Charter of Rights and Freedoms, and the US in the first amendment to the constitution, in practice I do not think anyone is going to try to have me locked up for speaking the truth. I still cherish the hope that the veracity I express will be shown for what it is, and that the truth will prevail and make me free.

Removing the Mask of Anonymity from the MI5 Operatives

Undoubtedly one factor encouraging the MI5 agents' actions against me has been the fact that they can shelter behind a mask of anonymity while they carry out their abuse. This is both a sign of their realisation that their actions are criminal; for crimes are harder to pin down and make a coherent complaint about when their perpetrators are unknown; and it is a sign of their cowardice, since they lack the backbone to say things to my face themselves; instead they almost always rely on third parties to carry out the actual acts of abuse.

On a few occasions I have seen the perpetrators, but on each occasion they have managed to preserve their anonymity. They travelled on the same British Airways flight as me in 1994; but BA have ever since refused to give up the passenger list for the flight, and the police and lawyers have proved useless in obtaining their identities from the list. Also one of them followed me into A&E department of Ottawa's Civic Hospital a couple of years ago, and gave his name as (if I heard correctly) "Alan Holdsworth"; but the doctor refused to give out his identity when I later tried to speak to him.

If only we knew the identities of the individual operatives, then it would be possible to find out the identity of their employing organisation. But I think we know the latter already, since I have been accusing them on internet newsgroups for four and a half years now, and they have never denied my guess. Indeed, when I was travelling in January 1996 back to Ottawa, two youths on the (British Airways again, unfortunately) flight made a lot of noise at me, one of them saying to the other that I "didn't know who we are". That is a wafer-thin denial; I had been saying for a year that they were MI5, so a stronger denial would be necessary if my guess were truly mistaken. I think the lukewarm denial was worse than no denial at all, since it confirmed my guess that the employing agency was indeed MI5.

Conclusion

It has been suggested to me that by sending these faxes I could be making trouble for myself; but I don't think so. My psychiatrist knows what I am doing; indeed I have given him a couple of these articles for him to cast an eye over.

I don't want to have to send faxes for the next year, or the year after that. But that is entirely up to MI5. If they continue to persecute me then I am forced into defending myself. The ball is in their court, and it is entirely up to them what they do. If as I suspect it is their intention that these faxes continue, if that is what they insist will happen then so be it.

Faxes Sent to US Congress logs

During Sept/2004 to April/2006 I sent numerous faxes to the US Congress in Washington D.C. containing the FAQ article about the MI5 persecution. The following records detail a total of 19721 faxes successfully transmitted. My reason for sending to US Congress was that MI5 had tried to kill me on US territory in November/2001. I used the database of congressional contact numbers maintained by congressmerge.com. Remarkably there were only three replies to the numerous faxes sent during this period. Presumably Congressmen receive many faxes and ignore most of them.

In the records is listed the fax number sent to, the count of successful fax transmissions, the count of failed fax transmissions, and the name of the Congressional recipient.

```
12022281265,32,13,Sen Sam Brownback (R- KS)
12022244700,22,20,Sen Max Baucus (D- MT)
12022283398,22,23,Sen Lamar Alexander (R- TN)
12022248858,37,7,Sen Barbara A. Mikulski (D- MD)
12022251988,33,6,Rep William J. Jefferson (D - LA02)
12022261000,37,2,Rep Todd R. Platts (R - PA19)
12022258628,7,24,Rep Lamar S. Smith (R - TX21)
15633275087,0,21,Rep Jim Nussle (R - IA01)
12022246295,31,12,Sen John W. Warner (R- VA)
12022257313,27,12,Rep Richard H. Baker (R - LA06)
12022280360,38,6,Sen Richard G. Lugar (R- IN)
12022253402,37,2,Rep George P. Radanovich (R - CA19)
12022240139,40,3,Sen Joseph R. Biden Jr. (D- DE)
14159566701,20,25,Sen Barbara Boxer (D- CA)
12022250254,37,2,Rep Wayne T. Gilchrest (R - MD01)
12022260791,32,7,Rep Timothy V. Johnson (R - IL15)
12022251891,38,1,Rep Sherwood L. Boehlert (R - NY24)
12022255077,33,6,Rep Michael R. McNulty (D - NY21)
12022252961,37,2,Rep Mary Whitaker Bono (R - CA45)
12022257822,37,2,Rep Louise McIntosh Slaughter (D - NY28)
12022256923,38,1,Rep Jerrold Nadler (D - NY08)
12022250017,36,3,Rep James P. Moran (D - VA08)
12022252695,38,1,Rep Ike Skelton (D - MO04)
12022253529,37,2,Rep Deborah Pryce (R - OH15)
12022252256,38,1,Rep Corrine Brown (D - FL03)
12022255724,37,2,Rep Charles W. Boustany Jr. (R - LA07)
12022249369,31,13,Sen Tom Harkin (D- IA)
12022242693,36,9,Sen Susan Collins (R- ME)
12022240103,37,7,Sen Saxby Chambliss (R- GA)
12022281375,38,4,Sen Mike Crapo (R- ID)
12022242207,39,3,Sen Jon Kyl (R- AZ)
12022282856,25,18,Sen John Cornyn (R- TX)
12022280380,38,4,Sen James M. Inhofe (R- OK)
12022280282,37,7,Sen Hillary Rodham Clinton (D- NY)
12022281382,33,12,Sen George Voinovich (R- OH)
12022245432,38,5,Sen George Allen (R- VA)
12022281377,33,11,Sen Evan Bayh (D- IN)
12022282183,38,4,Sen Bill Nelson (D- FL)
12022281229,30,15,Sen Arlen Specter (R- PA)
12022253336,38,1,Rep Zoe Lofgren (D - CA16)
12022260852,32,7,Rep Wally Herger (R - CA02)
12022261272,37,2,Rep Vito Fossella (R - NY13)
12022255903,37,2,Rep Vic Snyder (D - AR02)
12022256328,38,1,Rep Trent Franks (R - AZ02)
12022260996,35,4,Rep Tim Holden (D - PA17)
12022252356,39,0,Rep Thomas E. Petri (R - WI06)
12022254300,34,5,Rep Steny H. Hoyer (D - MD05)
12022252266,37,2,Rep Sherrod Brown (D - OH13)
12022253119,37,2,Rep Shelley Berkley (D - NV01)
12022259615,28,3,Rep Randy Neugebauer (R - TX19)
12022262279,39,0,Rep Peter T. King (R - NY03)
12022253393,36,3,Rep Paul Ryan (R - WI01)
12022253290,32,7,Rep Patrick J. Kennedy (D - RI01)
12022259511,37,2,Rep Mike Fitzpatrick (R - PA08)
```

```
12022253084,34,5,Rep Michael F. Doyle (D - PA14)
12022251512,37,2,Rep Melvin L. Watt (D - NC12)
12022257830,33,6,Rep Melissa Bean (D - IL08)
12022254886,39,0,Rep Martin Olav Sabo (D - MN05)
12022253004,34,5,Rep Marsha Blackburn (R - TN07)
12022255729,37,2,Rep Mark Green (R - WI08)
12022257711,34,5,Rep Marcy Kaptur (D - OH09)
12022265452,33,6,Rep Lee Terry (R - NE02)
12022250074,26,3,Rep Kenny Marchant (R - TX24)
12022255633,34,5,Rep Julia Carson (D - IN07)
12022259420,39,0,Rep Judy Biggert (R - IL13)
12022252185,39,0,Rep Jon Porter (R - NV03)
12022253284,37,2,Rep John N. Hostettler (R - IN08)
12022260371,39,0,Rep John D. Dingell (D - MI15)
12022254382,38,1,Rep Jo Ann S. Davis (R - VA01)
12022250378,37,2,Rep Jim Kolbe (R - AZ08)
12022255124,38,1,Rep Jerry Moran (R - KS01)
12022256498,34,5,Rep Jerry Lewis (R - CA41)
12022255822,39,0,Rep Jeb Bradley (R - NH01)
12022267290,37,2,Rep Jane Harman (D - CA36)
12022255759,36,3,Rep James P. McGovern (D - MA03)
12022250699,38,1,Rep James L. Oberstar (D - MN08)
12022252313,37,2,Rep James E. Clyburn (D - SC06)
12022261278,35,4,Rep James A. Leach (R - IA02)
12022251166,25,14,Rep Henry J. Hyde (R - IL06)
12022253407,37,2,Rep Henry E. Brown Jr. (R - SC01)
12022255663,39,0,Rep Harold E. Ford Jr. (D - TN09)
12022255774,39,0,Rep Greg Walden (R - OR02)
12022255609,37,2,Rep George Miller (D - CA07)
12022250003,39,0,Rep Geoff Davis (R - KY04)
12022259903,31,0,Rep Gene Green (D - TX29)
12022251589,39,0,Rep Gary L. Ackerman (D - NY05)
12022254986,38,1,Rep Fred Upton (R - MI06)
12022250437,36,3,Rep Frank R. Wolf (R - VA10)
12022259665,37,2,Rep Frank Pallone Jr. (D - NJ06)
12022253318,39,0,Rep Frank A. LoBiondo (R - NJ02)
12022255513,35,4,Rep Eliot L. Engel (D - NY17)
12022253178,39,0,Rep Elijah E. Cummings (D - MD07)
12022253547,33,6,Rep Edward Whitfield (R - KY01)
12022251018,38,1,Rep Edolphus Towns (D - NY10)
12022250235,38,1,Rep Duncan Hunter (R - CA52)
12022255687,39,0,Rep Dennis Rehberg (R - Montana At Large)
12022252014,38,1,Rep David E. Price (D - NC04)
12022250016,19,20,Rep Dan Burton (R - IN05)
12022256393,32,7,Rep Dale E. Kildee (D - MI05)
12022255392,39,0,Rep Chaka Fattah (D - PA02)
12022255758,33,6,Rep Carolyn McCarthy (D - NY04)
12022255730,34,5,Rep Carolyn Kilpatrick (D - MI13)
12022260347,34,5,Rep Brian M. Higgins (D - NY27)
12022260386,18,3,Rep Bobby Jindal (R - LA01)
12022255662,33,6,Rep Bobby Etheridge (D - NC02)
12022255898,38,1,Rep Bennie G. Thompson (D - MS02)
12022250182,28,11,Rep Barney Frank (D - MA04)
12022257564,39,0,Rep Alan B. Mollohan (D - WV01)
12022281264,41,3,Sen William H. Frist (R- TN)
12022246471,40,4,Sen Wayne Allard (R- CO)
12022242262,41,3,Sen Trent Lott (R- MS)
12022246008,31,2,Sen Tom Coburn (R- OK)
12022285765,41,3,Sen Tim Johnson (D- SD)
12022282190,41,3,Sen Thomas R. Carper (D- DE)
12022249450,39,5,Sen Thad Cochran (R- MS)
12022242354,40,4,Sen Ted Stevens (R- AK)
12022242725,35,10,Sen Russell D. Feingold (D- WI)
12022282717,36,8,Sen Ron Wyden (D- OR)
12022281168,40,5,Sen Robert F. Bennett (R- UT)
12022280002,41,4,Sen Robert C. Byrd (D- WV)
12022280604,41,3,Sen Rick Santorum (R- PA)
12022280400,41,3,Sen Richard J. Durbin (D- IL)
12022243416,40,4,Sen Richard C. Shelby (R- AL)
12022282981,21,0,Sen Richard Burr (R- NC)
```

```
12022280900,36,9,Sen Pete V. Domenici (R- NM)
12022241651,38,7,Sen Paul S. Sarbanes (D- MD)
12022240238,40,4,Sen Patty Murray (D- WA)
12022243479,40,4,Sen Patrick J. Leahy (D- VT)
12022243514,37,7,Sen Pat Roberts (R- KS)
12022246331,31,14,Sen Orrin G. Hatch (R- UT)
12022241946,34,10,Sen Olympia Snowe (R- ME)
12022241152,41,4,Sen Norm Coleman (R- MN)
12022242499,38,6,Sen Mitch McConnell (R- KY)
12022246519,35,9,Sen Mike DeWine (R- OH)
12022280359,40,4,Sen Michael Enzi (R- WY)
12022285171,21,0,Sen Mel Martinez (R- FL)
12022249735,39,3,Sen Mary Landrieu (D- LA)
12022280908,41,3,Sen Mark Pryor (D- AR)
12022282186,41,1,Sen Mark Dayton (D- MN)
12022280514,41,1,Sen Maria Cantwell (D- WA)
12022245301,38,4,Sen Lisa Murkowski (R- AK)
12022243808,38,5,Sen Lindsey Graham (R- SC)
12022282853,40,4,Sen Lincoln D. Chafee (R- RI)
12022281067,41,1,Sen Larry E. Craig (R- ID)
12022247776,40,2,Sen Kent Conrad (D- ND)
12022285036,20,0,Sen Ken Salazar (D- CO)
12022240776,39,5,Sen Kay Bailey Hutchison (R- TX)
12022244952,39,4,Sen Judd Gregg (R- NH)
12022249750,41,1,Sen Joseph I. Lieberman (D- CT)
12022282197,39,3,Sen Jon S. Corzine (D- NJ)
12022280724,20,1,Sen Johnny Isakson (R- GA)
12022284131,40,5,Sen John Sununu (R- NH)
12022285429,20,1,Sen John R. Thune (R- SD)
12022282862,33,9,Sen John McCain (R- AZ)
12022248525,38,7,Sen John F. Kerry (D- MA)
12022282193,34,11,Sen John Ensign (R- NV)
12022247665,40,3,Sen John D. Rockefeller IV (D- WV)
12022281518,36,9,Sen Jim Talent (R- MO)
12022281373,33,12,Sen Jim Bunning (R- KY)
12022243149,40,2,Sen Jeff Sessions (R- AL)
12022242852,38,5,Sen Jeff Bingaman (D- NM)
12022280776,41,3,Sen James M. Jeffords (I- VT)
12022285143,20,1,Sen James DeMint (R- SC)
12022244680,41,1,Sen Jack Reed (D- RI)
12022249787,38,4,Sen Herb Kohl (D- WI)
12022247327,39,3,Sen Harry Reid (D- NV)
12022283997,38,6,Sen Gordon Smith (R- OR)
12022284054,41,1,Sen Frank Lautenberg (D- NJ)
12022241100,41,1,Sen Elizabeth Dole (R- NC)
12022242417,40,2,Sen Edward M. Kennedy (D- MA)
12022283954,41,1,Sen Dianne Feinstein (D- CA)
12022280325,41,1,Sen Debbie A. Stabenow (D- MI)
12022285061,21,0,Sen David Vitter (R- LA)
12022246747,39,4,Sen Daniel K. Inouye (D- HI)
12022242126,39,6,Sen Daniel K. Akaka (D- HI)
12022241724,39,3,Sen Craig Thomas (R- WY)
12022248594,41,1,Sen Conrad R. Burns (R- MT)
12022245213,38,4,Sen Chuck Hagel (R- NE)
12022248149,38,4,Sen Christopher S. Bond (R- MO)
12022241083,41,1,Sen Christopher J. Dodd (D- CT)
12022283027,41,1,Sen Charles Schumer (D- NY)
12022246020,38,4,Sen Charles E. Grassley (R- IA)
12022241388,38,4,Sen Carl Levin (D- MI)
12022241193,39,4,Sen Byron L. Dorgan (D- ND)
12022281371,41,1,Sen Blanche Lambert Lincoln (D- AR)
12022280012,39,4,Sen Ben Nelson (D- NE)
12022285417,21,0,Sen Barack Obama (D- IL)
12022253494,37,2,Rep Zach Wamp (R - TN03)
12022252202,37,2,Rep Xavier Becerra (D - CA31)
12022258798,38,1,Rep William M. Thomas (R - CA22)
12022253486,30,1,Rep William M. (Mac) Thornberry (R - TX13)
12022251725,33,6,Rep William Lacy (Bill) Clay Jr. (D - MO01)
12022255714,38,1,Rep William L. Jenkins (R - TN01)
12022255658,37,2,Rep William D. Delahunt (D - MA10)
```

12022253286,37,2,Rep Walter B. Jones Jr. (R - NC03)
12022252995,36,3,Rep Virginia Foxx (R - NC05)
12022255681,37,2,Rep Virgil Goode (R - VA05)
12022255144,37,2,Rep Vernon J. Ehlers (R - MI03)
12022264623,38,1,Rep Tom Tancredo (R - CO06)
12022254656,36,3,Rep Tom Price (R - GA06)
12022253301,37,2,Rep Tom Latham (R - IA04)
12022264183,20,1,Rep Tom Lantos (D - CA12)
12022266299,39,0,Rep Tom Feeney (R - FL24)
12022255241,29,2,Rep Tom DeLay (R - TX22)
12022253512,38,1,Rep Tom Cole (R - OK04)
12022253489,38,1,Rep Todd Tiahrt (R - KS04)
12022252563,38,1,Rep Todd Akin (R - MO02)
12022253143,35,4,Rep Timothy H. Bishop (D - NY01)
12022253719,39,0,Rep Tim Ryan (D - OH17)
12022251844,34,5,Rep Tim Murphy (R - PA18)
12022261385,36,3,Rep Thomas W. Osborne (R - NE03)
12022261331,38,1,Rep Thomas Udall (D - NM03)
12022255910,39,0,Rep Thomas M. Reynolds (R - NY26)
12022253071,38,1,Rep Thomas M. Davis III (R - VA11)
12022255590,38,1,Rep Thomas H. Allen (D - ME01)
12022254218,35,4,Rep Thelma Drake (R - VA02)
12022252667,38,1,Rep Thaddeus McCotter (R - MI11)
12022258913,39,0,Rep Terry Everett (R - AL02)
12022255907,38,1,Rep Ted Strickland (D - OH06)
12022255547,36,3,Rep Ted Poe (R - TX02)
12022256942,37,2,Rep Tammy Baldwin (D - WI02)
12022252948,34,5,Rep Susan A. Davis (D - CA53)
12022253289,38,1,Rep Sue W. Kelly (R - NY19)
12022253389,39,0,Rep Sue Myrick (R - NC09)
12022255851,36,3,Rep Steven R. Rothman (D - NJ09)
12022259599,33,6,Rep Steve Pearce (R - NM02)
12022253193,38,1,Rep Steve King (R - IA05)
12022254669,38,1,Rep Steve J. Israel (D - NY02)
12022253012,39,0,Rep Steve Chabot (R - OH01)
12022253307,37,2,Rep Steve C. LaTourette (R - OH14)
12022253984,38,1,Rep Stephen Lynch (D - MA09)
12022252267,36,3,Rep Stephen E. Buyer (R - IN04)
12022251339,39,0,Rep Stephanie T. Jones (D - OH11)
12022255823,37,2,Rep Stephanie Herseth (D - South Dakota At Large)
12022252082,35,4,Rep Spencer Bachus (R - AL06)
12022261134,29,2,Rep Solomon P. Ortiz (D - TX27)
12022252016,29,2,Rep Silvestre Reyes (D - TX16)
12022257856,38,1,Rep Shelley Moore Capito (R - WV02)
12022253317,31,0,Rep Sheila Jackson-Lee (D - TX18)
12022252203,34,5,Rep Sanford D. Bishop Jr. (D - GA02)
12022261033,37,2,Rep Sander M. Levin (D - MI12)
12022258221,38,1,Rep Samuel B. Graves (R - MO06)
12022251485,28,3,Rep Sam Johnson (R - TX03)
12022256791,38,1,Rep Sam Farr (D - CA17)
12022257452,35,4,Rep Russ Carnahan (D - MO03)
12022256025,38,1,Rep Rush Holt (D - NJ12)
12022255688,29,2,Rep Ruben Hinojosa (D - TX15)
12022261115,37,2,Rep Roy Blunt (R - MO07)
12022252193,37,2,Rep Roscoe G. Bartlett (R - MD06)
12022254890,38,1,Rep Rosa L. DeLauro (D - CT03)
12022266553,21,0,Rep Ron Paul (R - TX14)
12022262019,38,1,Rep Ron Lewis (R - KY02)
12022255739,35,4,Rep Ron Kind (D - WI03)
12022253549,39,0,Rep Roger F. Wicker (R - MS01)
12022253186,37,2,Rep Rodney P. Frelinghuysen (R - NJ11)
12022255639,38,1,Rep Rodney Alexander (R - LA05)
12022255974,38,1,Rep Robert Wexler (D - FL19)
12022254977,38,1,Rep Robert R. Simmons (R - CT02)
12022260792,37,2,Rep Robert Menendez (D - NJ13)
12022256583,39,0,Rep Robert E. Andrews (D - NJ01)
12022254392,36,3,Rep Robert E. (Bud) Cramer Jr. (D - AL05)
12022258354,36,3,Rep Robert C. Scott (D - VA03)
12022255587,39,0,Rep Robert B. Aderholt (R - AL04)
12022250088,39,0,Rep Robert A. Brady (D - PA01)

```
12022254036,39,0,Rep Robert (Robin) Hayes (R - NC08)
12022251992,37,2,Rep Rob Portman (R - OH02)
12022255857,39,0,Rep Rob Bishop (R - UT01)
12022269739,38,1,Rep Rick Renzi (R - AZ01)
12022250442,37,2,Rep Rick Boucher (D - VA09)
12022260861,36,3,Rep Richard W. Pombo (R - CA11)
12022254420,36,3,Rep Richard R. Larsen (D - WA02)
12022258112,39,0,Rep Richard E. Neal (D - MA02)
12022253251,38,1,Rep Richard (Doc) Hastings (R - WA04)
12022250999,38,1,Rep Ric Keller (R - FL08)
12022259249,37,2,Rep Ray LaHood (R - IL18)
12022251541,38,1,Rep Raul Grijalva (D - AZ07)
12022252558,33,6,Rep Randy (Duke) Cunningham (R - CA50)
12022253059,34,5,Rep Ralph Regula (R - OH16)
12022253332,30,1,Rep Ralph M. Hall (R - TX04)
12022255603,33,6,Rep Rahm Emanuel (D - IL05)
12022252944,39,0,Rep Phil Gingrey (R - GA11)
12022253103,34,5,Rep Phil English (R - PA03)
12022252493,36,3,Rep Peter J. Visclosky (D - IN01)
12022260779,39,0,Rep Peter Hoekstra (R - MI02)
12022250032,39,0,Rep Peter A. DeFazio (D - OR04)
12022255878,31,0,Rep Pete Sessions (R - TX32)
12022250764,35,4,Rep Paul E. Kanjorski (D - PA11)
12022251985,38,1,Rep Paul E. Gillmor (R - OH05)
12022250316,35,4,Rep Patrick McHenry (R - NC10)
12022264523,38,1,Rep Patrick J. Tiberi (R - OH12)
12022260327,34,5,Rep Nydia M. Velazquez (D - NY12)
12022261176,38,1,Rep Norman D. Dicks (D - WA06)
12022250546,37,2,Rep Nita M. Lowey (D - NY18)
12022259061,39,0,Rep Nick Joe Rahall II (D - WV03)
12022254580,38,1,Rep Neil Abercrombie (D - HI01)
12022258272,38,1,Rep Nathan Deal (R - GA10)
12022258259,37,2,Rep Nancy Pelosi (D - CA08)
12022254488,29,10,Rep Nancy L. Johnson (R - CT05)
12022256754,39,0,Rep Mike Turner (R - OH03)
12022254335,38,1,Rep Mike Thompson (D - CA01)
12022266866,38,1,Rep Mike Sodrel (R - IN09)
12022258216,37,2,Rep Mike Simpson (R - ID02)
12022268485,37,2,Rep Mike Rogers (R - AL03)
12022253382,38,1,Rep Mike Pence (R - IN06)
12022252943,37,2,Rep Mike Michaud (D - ME02)
12022255773,33,6,Rep Mike McIntyre (D - NC07)
12022252699,38,1,Rep Mike Honda (D - CA15)
12022251783,29,0,Rep Mike Conaway (R - TX11)
12022255955,35,4,Rep Michael T. McCaul (R - TX10)
12022252291,37,2,Rep Michael N. Castle (R - Delaware At Large)
12022255820,38,1,Rep Michael J. Rogers (R - MI08)
12022260577,38,1,Rep Michael G. Oxley (R - OH04)
12022259322,39,0,Rep Michael Capuano (D - MA08)
12022252919,30,1,Rep Michael Burgess (R - TX26)
12022254085,33,6,Rep Michael Bilirakis (R - FL09)
12022251314,35,4,Rep Michael A. Ross (D - AR04)
12022259460,36,3,Rep Michael A. Ferguson (R - NJ07)
12022262274,38,1,Rep Melissa A. Hart (R - PA04)
12022257854,36,3,Rep Maxine Waters (D - CA35)
12022260774,35,4,Rep Maurice D. Hinchey (D - NY22)
12022260771,39,0,Rep Martin T. Meehan (D - MA05)
12022267840,38,1,Rep Mark Udall (D - CO02)
12022250837,35,4,Rep Mark S. Kirk (R - IL10)
12022256475,37,2,Rep Mark Kennedy (R - MN06)
12022253132,29,0,Rep Mark Foley (R - FL16)
12022253479,39,0,Rep Mark Edward Souder (R - IN03)
12022255602,33,6,Rep Marion Berry (D - AR01)
12022260346,37,2,Rep Mario Diaz-Balart (R - FL25)
12022255870,39,0,Rep Marilyn Musgrave (R - CO04)
12022260112,39,0,Rep Major R. Owens (D - NY11)
12022252515,29,2,Rep Lynn Westmoreland (R - GA08)
12022255163,36,3,Rep Lynn C. Woolsey (D - CA06)
12022257810,39,0,Rep Luis V. Gutierrez (D - IL04)
12022260350,37,2,Rep Lucille Roybal-Allard (D - CA34)
```

12022261230,20,1,Rep Louie Gohmert (R - TX01)
12022255859,32,7,Rep Loretta Sanchez (D - CA47)
12022255632,38,1,Rep Lois Capps (D - CA23)
12022253073,31,0,Rep Lloyd Doggett (D - TX25)
12022261012,30,9,Rep Linda T. Sanchez (D - CA39)
12022258576,39,0,Rep Lincoln Diaz-Balart (R - FL21)
12022265172,37,2,Rep Lincoln Davis (D - TN04)
12022255608,37,2,Rep Leonard L. Boswell (D - IA03)
12022255396,21,0,Rep Lane Evans (D - IL17)
12022255524,31,0,Rep Kevin Brady (R - TX08)
12022255712,38,1,Rep Kenny C. Hulshof (R - MO09)
12022260777,37,2,Rep Kendrick B. Meek (D - FL17)
12022252004,35,4,Rep Ken Calvert (R - CA44)
12022255683,26,5,Rep Kay Granger (R - TX12)
12022260828,35,4,Rep Katherine Harris (R - FL13)
12022257926,39,0,Rep Juanita Millender-McDonald (D - CA37)
12022252013,36,3,Rep Joseph R. Pitts (R - PA16)
12022251909,37,2,Rep Joseph Crowley (D - NY07)
12022256001,37,2,Rep Jose E. Serrano (D - NY16)
12022261224,31,8,Rep John W. Olver (D - MA01)
12022255915,37,2,Rep John Tierney (D - MA06)
12022255444,37,2,Rep John T. Doolittle (R - CA04)
12022259187,38,1,Rep John Sullivan (R - OK01)
12022255880,36,3,Rep John Shimkus (R - IL19)
12022269669,21,0,Rep John Salazar (D - CO03)
12022251765,38,1,Rep John S. Tanner (D - TN08)
12022266599,28,1,Rep John R. (Randy) Kuhl Jr. (R - NY29)
12022255709,39,0,Rep John P. Murtha (D - PA12)
12022250464,35,4,Rep John M. Spratt Jr. (D - SC05)
12022260621,39,0,Rep John M. McHugh (R - NY23)
12022254696,37,2,Rep John Linder (R - GA07)
12022250351,38,1,Rep John Lewis (D - GA05)
12022251031,39,0,Rep John Larson (D - CT01)
12022260821,39,0,Rep John L. Mica (R - FL07)
12022252595,38,1,Rep John Kline (R - MN02)
12022256440,39,0,Rep John J. Duncan Jr. (R - TN02)
12022256234,35,4,Rep John E. Sweeney (R - NY20)
12022255796,37,2,Rep John E. Peterson (R - PA05)
12022250072,39,0,Rep John Conyers Jr. (D - MI14)
12022255886,30,1,Rep John Carter (R - TX31)
12022255713,38,1,Rep John Boozman (R - AR03)
12022253377,36,3,Rep John Barrow (D - GA12)
12022253462,35,4,Rep John B. Shadegg (R - AZ03)
12022254381,31,0,Rep John A. Culberson (R - TX07)
12022250704,38,1,Rep John A. Boehner (R - OH08)
12022251942,31,8,Rep Joel Hefley (R - CO05)
12022252455,37,2,Rep Joe Wilson (R - SC02)
12022256281,35,4,Rep Joe Schwarz (R - MI07)
12022262356,39,0,Rep Joe Knollenberg (R - MI09)
12022253052,30,1,Rep Joe Barton (R - TX06)
12022258671,39,0,Rep Joe Baca (D - CA43)
12022250562,33,6,Rep Jo Bonner (R - AL01)
12022260326,38,1,Rep Jo Ann Emerson (R - MO08)
12022250778,35,4,Rep Jim Saxton (R - NJ03)
12022257986,39,0,Rep Jim Ryun (R - KS02)
12022256351,36,3,Rep Jim Ramstad (R - MN03)
12022256197,35,4,Rep Jim McDermott (D - WA07)
12022258039,39,0,Rep Jim McCrery (R - LA04)
12022253013,38,1,Rep Jim Marshall (D - GA03)
12022255679,38,1,Rep Jim Gibbons (R - NV02)
12022258440,37,2,Rep Jim Gerlach (R - PA06)
12022255652,37,2,Rep Jim Davis (D - FL11)
12022259308,35,4,Rep Jim Costa (D - CA20)
12022261035,37,2,Rep Jim Cooper (D - TN05)
12022250899,38,1,Rep Jesse L. Jackson Jr. (D - IL02)
12022250285,38,1,Rep Jerry F. Costello (D - IL12)
12022253414,37,2,Rep Jeff Miller (R - FL01)
12022255686,34,5,Rep Jeff Fortenberry (R - NE01)
12022264386,38,1,Rep Jeff Flake (R - AZ06)
12022264888,30,1,Rep Jeb Hensarling (R - TX05)

```
12022261606,38,1,Rep Jay Inslee (D - WA01)
12022266890,37,2,Rep Janice Schakowsky (D - IL09)
12022254042,38,1,Rep James T. Walsh (R - NY25)
12022255976,38,1,Rep James R. Langevin (D - RI02)
12022255638,39,0,Rep James D. Matheson (D - UT02)
12022262269,36,3,Rep Jack Kingston (R - GA01)
12022261170,30,9,Rep J. Randy Forbes (R - VA04)
12022250697,32,7,Rep J. Dennis Hastert (R - IL14)
12022253263,35,4,Rep J. D. Hayworth (R - AZ05)
12022255620,37,2,Rep Ileana Ros-Lehtinen (R - FL18)
12022260683,36,3,Rep Howard P. (Buck) McKeon (R - CA25)
12022253196,39,0,Rep Howard L. Berman (D - CA28)
12022258611,29,10,Rep Howard Coble (R - NC06)
12022255467,32,7,Rep Hilda A. Solis (D - CA32)
12022251641,31,8,Rep Henry Cuellar (D - TX28)
12022252237,29,2,Rep Henry Bonilla (R - TX23)
12022254099,38,1,Rep Henry A. Waxman (D - CA30)
12022254975,37,2,Rep Heather A. Wilson (R - NM01)
12022250940,39,0,Rep Harold Rogers (R - KY05)
12022258135,37,2,Rep Gwen Moore (D - WI04)
12022253216,38,1,Rep Gresham Barrett (R - SC03)
12022264169,38,1,Rep Gregory W. Meeks (D - NY06)
12022250027,36,3,Rep Grace Napolitano (D - CA38)
12022266559,37,2,Rep Ginny Brown-Waite (R - FL05)
12022253246,39,0,Rep Gil Gutknecht (R - MN01)
12022253521,39,0,Rep Gerald C. (Jerry) Weller (R - IL11)
12022257074,39,0,Rep Gene Taylor (D - MS04)
12022266962,37,2,Rep Gary Miller (R - CA42)
12022253354,37,2,Rep G. K. Butterfield Jr. (D - NC01)
12022258698,37,2,Rep Frank D. Lucas (R - OK03)
12022263805,37,2,Rep Fortney (Pete) Stark (D - CA13)
12022253190,38,1,Rep F. James Sensenbrenner Jr. (R - WI05)
12022261463,37,2,Rep Ernest J. Istook Jr. (R - OK05)
12022250011,34,5,Rep Eric I. Cantor (R - VA07)
12022254403,39,0,Rep Emanuel Cleaver II (D - MO05)
12022251100,37,2,Rep Elton Gallegly (R - CA24)
12022255914,37,2,Rep Ellen O. Tauscher (D - CA10)
12022260335,38,1,Rep Edward R. Royce (R - CA40)
12022260092,37,2,Rep Edward J. Markey (D - MA07)
12022261477,30,1,Rep Eddie Bernice Johnson (D - TX30)
12022251655,36,3,Rep Ed Pastor (D - AZ04)
12022254987,38,1,Rep Ed Case (D - HI02)
12022260893,37,2,Rep Earl Pomeroy (D - North Dakota At Large)
12022258941,36,3,Rep Earl Blumenauer (D - OR03)
12022259048,38,1,Rep E. Scott Garrett (R - NJ05)
12022258398,38,1,Rep E. Clay Shaw Jr. (R - FL22)
12022250566,36,3,Rep Doris Matsui (D - CA05)
12022259594,38,1,Rep Donald Sherwood (R - PA10)
12022254160,39,0,Rep Donald M. Payne (D - NJ10)
12022255284,33,6,Rep Donald A. Manzullo (R - IL16)
12022250425,39,0,Rep Don Young (R - Alaska At Large)
12022252422,33,6,Rep Diane E. Watson (D - CA33)
12022255657,39,0,Rep Diana DeGette (D - CO01)
12022253404,37,2,Rep Devin Nunes (R - CA21)
12022252807,19,1,Rep Dennis Moore (D - KS03)
12022255745,33,6,Rep Dennis J. Kucinich (D - OH10)
12022250819,38,1,Rep Dennis Cardoza (D - CA18)
12022262052,20,1,Rep Debbie Wasserman Schultz (D - FL20)
12022259497,38,1,Rep David Wu (D - OR01)
12022254628,39,0,Rep David Scott (D - GA13)
12022251984,38,1,Rep David L. Hobson (R - OH07)
12022257018,37,2,Rep David Dreier (R - CA26)
12022253516,39,0,Rep Dave Weldon (R - FL15)
12022254282,21,0,Rep Dave Reichert (R - WA08)
12022259679,38,1,Rep Dave Camp (R - MI04)
12022253303,37,2,Rep Darrell Issa (R - CA49)
12022255699,38,1,Rep Darlene Hooley (D - OR05)
12022255641,39,0,Rep Danny Davis (D - IL07)
12022250145,38,1,Rep Dana Rohrabacher (R - CA46)
12022261298,34,5,Rep Dan Lungren (R - CA03)
```

```
12022251012,37,2,Rep Dan Lipinski (D - IL03)
12022253038,38,1,Rep Dan Boren (D - OK02)
12022260691,37,2,Rep Cynthia McKinney (D - GA04)
12022258137,38,1,Rep Curt Weldon (R - PA07)
12022260439,21,0,Rep Connie Mack (R - FL14)
12022251593,38,1,Rep Collin C. Peterson (D - MN07)
12022253973,37,2,Rep Cliff Stearns (R - FL06)
12022250375,38,1,Rep Christopher Van Hollen Jr. (D - MD08)
12022259629,38,1,Rep Christopher Shays (R - CT04)
12022257768,35,4,Rep Christopher H. Smith (R - NJ04)
12022259177,34,5,Rep Christopher Cox (R - CA48)
12022255629,39,0,Rep Christopher Cannon (R - UT03)
12022256798,35,4,Rep Chris Chocola (R - IN02)
12022250350,30,1,Rep Chet Edwards (D - TX17)
12022260776,36,3,Rep Charlie Norwood (R - GA09)
12022263944,27,2,Rep Charlie Melancon (D - LA03)
12022260778,37,2,Rep Charles W. Dent (R - PA15)
12022255797,39,0,Rep Charles W. (Chip) Pickering (R - MS03)
12022266422,38,1,Rep Charles H. Taylor (R - NC11)
12022252946,37,2,Rep Charles F. Bass II (R - NH02)
12022250816,35,4,Rep Charles B. Rangel (D - NY15)
12022251915,31,0,Rep Charles A. Gonzalez (D - TX20)
12022253392,37,2,Rep Cathy McMorris (R - WA05)
12022254709,35,4,Rep Carolyn B. Maloney (D - NY14)
12022261169,39,0,Rep Candice Miller (R - MI10)
12022259764,37,2,Rep C. W. (Bill) Young (R - FL10)
12022253029,39,0,Rep C. L. (Butch) Otter (R - ID01)
12022253094,38,1,Rep C. A. (Dutch) Ruppersberger (D - MD02)
12022253478,39,0,Rep Brian Baird (D - WA03)
12022255879,34,5,Rep Brad Sherman (D - CA27)
12022250181,37,2,Rep Brad Miller (D - NC13)
12022260333,39,0,Rep Bobby L. Rush (D - IL01)
12022253394,39,0,Rep Bob Ney (R - OH18)
12022261177,38,1,Rep Bob Inglis (R - SC04)
12022259681,37,2,Rep Bob Goodlatte (R - VA06)
12022259073,38,1,Rep Bob Filner (D - CA51)
12022255278,39,0,Rep Bob Beauprez (R - CO07)
12022252486,39,0,Rep Bill Shuster (R - PA09)
12022255782,39,0,Rep Bill Pascrell Jr. (D - NJ08)
12022251968,39,0,Rep Betty McCollum (D - MN04)
12022256790,38,1,Rep Bernard Sanders (I - Vermont At Large)
12022259219,38,1,Rep Benjamin L. Cardin (D - MD03)
12022252122,39,0,Rep Ben Chandler (D - KY06)
12022254744,39,0,Rep Bart Stupak (D - MI01)
12022256887,38,1,Rep Bart Gordon (D - TN06)
12022259817,33,6,Rep Barbara Lee (D - CA09)
12022253057,36,3,Rep Barbara Cubin (R - Wyoming At Large)
12022269567,39,0,Rep Artur Davis (D - AL07)
12022267253,36,3,Rep Anthony Weiner (D - NY09)
12022255776,36,3,Rep Anne M. Northup (R - KY03)
12022258890,38,1,Rep Anna G. Eshoo (D - CA14)
12022252504,35,4,Rep Ander Crenshaw (R - FL04)
12022260611,35,4,Rep Allyson Schwartz (D - PA13)
12022255615,36,3,Rep Allen Boyd (D - FL02)
12022251171,33,6,Rep Alcee L. Hastings (D - FL23)
12022258714,36,3,Rep Albert Russell Wynn (D - MD04)
12022252947,32,7,Rep Al Green (D - TX09)
12022255893,37,2,Rep Adam Smith (D - WA09)
12022255828,35,4,Rep Adam Schiff (D - CA29)
12022260585,38,1,Rep Adam Putnam (R - FL12)
12022260341,21,0,Del Madeleine Bordallo (D - Guam At Large)
12022258757,18,3,Del Eni F. H. Faleomavaega (D - American Samoa At Large)
12022253002,20,1,Del Eleanor Holmes Norton (D - District of Columbia At Large)
12022255517,21,0,Del Donna M. Christian-Christensen (D - Virgin Islands At Large)
12022252154,20,1,Com Luis G. Fortuno (R - Puerto Rico At Large)
12022253706,0,8,Rep William M. (Mac) Thornberry (R - TX13)
12022255951,5,3,Rep Tom DeLay (R - TX22)
12022267742,0,8,Rep Solomon P. Ortiz (D - TX27)
12022254831,0,8,Rep Silvestre Reyes (D - TX16)
12022253816,3,5,Rep Sheila Jackson-Lee (D - TX18)
```

```
12022254201,0,8,Rep Sam Johnson (R - TX03)
12022252531,1,7,Rep Ruben Hinojosa (D - TX15)
12022252831,0,8,Rep Ron Paul (R - TX14)
12022254005,1,7,Rep Randy Neugebauer (R - TX19)
12022256673,0,8,Rep Ralph M. Hall (R - TX04)
12022252231,3,5,Rep Pete Sessions (R - TX32)
12022257772,2,6,Rep Michael Burgess (R - TX26)
12022267378,0,8,Rep Lynn Westmoreland (R - GA08)
12022254865,0,8,Rep Lloyd Doggett (D - TX25)
12022254236,0,8,Rep Lamar S. Smith (R - TX21)
12022254901,1,7,Rep Kevin Brady (R - TX08)
12022255071,3,5,Rep Kay Granger (R - TX12)
12022266996,0,8,Rep John Salazar (D - CO03)
12022253864,3,5,Rep John Carter (R - TX31)
12022252571,0,8,Rep John A. Culberson (R - TX07)
12022252002,1,7,Rep Joe Barton (R - TX06)
12022259129,8,10,Rep Jim Nussle (R - IA01)
12022263484,0,8,Rep Jeb Hensarling (R - TX05)
12022254511,1,7,Rep Henry Bonilla (R - TX23)
12022251688,5,3,Rep Gene Green (D - TX29)
12022258885,3,5,Rep Eddie Bernice Johnson (D - TX30)
12022258456,9,9,Rep Debbie Wasserman Schultz (D - FL20)
12022258673,8,10,Rep Dave Reichert (R - WA08)
12022256820,9,9,Rep Connie Mack (R - FL14)
12022256105,1,7,Rep Chet Edwards (D - TX17)
12022253236,2,6,Rep Charles A. Gonzalez (D - TX20)
12022250739,9,9,Rep Bobby Jindal (R - LA01)
12022255866,14,4,Rep Louie Gohmert (R - TX01)
12022260622,9,1,Rep John Salazar (D - CO03)
12022255574,9,1,Rep Amory Houghton (R - NY31)
12022254951,8,2,Rep Martin Frost (D - TX24)
12022253133,5,5,Rep Mark Foley (R - FL16)
12022252234,8,2,Rep Charles W. Stenholm (D - TX17)
12022250563,9,1,Rep Billy Tauzin (R - LA03)
12022284609,11,1,Sen Ben Nighthorse Campbell (R- CO)
12022282577,11,1,Sen John Breaux (D- LA)
12022282090,11,1,Sen Zell Miller (D- GA)
12022281374,11,1,Sen John Edwards (D- NC)
12022281372,11,1,Sen Peter Fitzgerald (R- IL)
12022246603,11,1,Sen Tom Daschle (D- SD)
12022244293,11,1,Sen Ernest Hollings (D- SC)
12022242237,12,0,Sen Bob Graham (D- FL)
```

No faxes were sent after April 2006.

Introduction to Received Faxes from Parliament 2006

In 2006 I had another crack at communicating with our democratically elected representatives in Westminster. My own MP, Keith Hill (Labour - Streatham) was refusing to help me, so I chose to fax the entire House of Commons using a directory of numbers I had purchased from Dod's Parliamentary Communications at a cost of £ 323. I sent the politicians detailed and considered articles in the hope that they might have something useful or interesting to comment on in relation to MI5's massive abuse of human rights for sixteen years, but I was disappointed because all the Parliamentarians did was to scream shrilly about "cost of ink". One or two of the most extreme cases even threatened me if I did not stop the faxes, as you can see from the following responses. Special mention must go to the pillock David Davies MP who repeatedly faxed back 240 pages of my articles, which, since I use a fax to email service, was dealt with by expeditious use of the "delete" key.

The table-of-contents frame lists each fax by filename, date received, and MP making the response. The faxes stopped because I left for Canada in late August 2006 to try to escape the mindcontrol, and that attempt to escape was successful. To read these faxes in Windows you may need a TIFF viewer such as alternatiff or Cartesian Products viewer.

In total I sent 7,932 faxes to Parliament in 2006. A detailed listing of the recipients' counts follows. In the records is listed the fax number sent to, the count of successful fax transmissions, the count of failed fax transmissions, and the name of the Parliamentary recipient.

```
72190983,8,12,Sir Peter Soulsby
72196805,12,8,Sir Patrick Cormack
72192991,12,8,Sir Michael Spicer
72192705,0,20,Rt Hon Patricia Hewitt
72192619,12,8,Rt Hon Nick Raynsford
72193640,0,20,Rt Hon Margaret Hodge
72194880,4,16,Rt Hon Jane Kennedy
79256996,12,8,Rt Hon Jacqui Smith
72192639,9,11,Rt Hon Hilary Benn
72190949,0,20,Rt Hon Hazel Blears
72190495,5,15,Rt Hon George Howarth
72192428,13,7,Rt Hon Geoffrey Hoon
72192276,0,20,Rt Hon Dawn Primarolo
72193890,0,20,Rt Hon Alan Beith
72192347,26,7,Mr Nigel Dodds
72190958,19,1,Ms Siân James
72193047,21,19,Mr Ian Cawsey
72190209,0,20,Ms Natascha Engel
72196107,3,37,Ms Michelle Gildernew
72191513,18,2,Ms Linda Riordan
72193664,4,16,Ms Karen Buck
72192906,13,7,Ms Kali Mountford
72192381,0,20,Ms Julia Goldsworthy
72194397,13,7,Ms Joan Walley
72196045,17,3,Ms Joan Ruddock
72192115,16,4,Ms Helen Southworth
72190977,5,15,Ms Geraldine Smith
72195581,18,2,Ms Bridget Prentice
72190770,4,16,Ms Ann Coffey
72192544,13,7,Mrs Rosemary McKenna
72191797,0,20,Mrs Iris Robinson
72190980,14,6,Mrs Eleanor Laing
72192503,9,11,Mrs Anne McGuire
72191957,8,12,Mrs Angela Watkinson
72190938,22,3,Mr Vernon Coaker
```

```
72192585,11,9,Mr Tony Lloyd
72196491,16,4,Mr Tom Brake
72196496,0,20,Mr Tobias Ellwood
72194919,10,10,Mr Timothy Boswell
72195275,12,8,Mr Terry Rooney
72195169,0,20,Mr Stewart Jackson
72191049,0,20,Mr Stephen Williams
72190922,13,7,Mr Russell Brown
72194358,0,20,Mr Ronnie Campbell
72196828,6,14,Mr Roger Gale
72196187,13,7,Mr Robert Wareing
72194865,16,24,Mr Eric Illsley
72195400,15,5,Mr Robert Flello
72195699,13,7,Mr Piara Khabra
72190667,0,20,Mr Philip Davies
72192356,16,4,Mr Peter Kilfoyle
72191184,10,10,Mr Paul Keetch
72192545,0,20,Mr Paul Clark
72190974,16,4,Mr Paul Burstow
72193987,13,7,Mr Patrick Hall
72194478,6,14,Mr Oliver Heald
72191468,5,15,Mr Neil Turner
72195015,9,11,Mr Michael Clapham
72192389,13,7,Mr Mark Oaten
72191745,18,2,Mr Khalid Mahmood
72192110,2,18,Mr Ken Purchase
72190957,13,7,Mr Kelvin Hopkins
72192133,7,13,Mr Jon Trickett
72192522,33,7,Mr Brooks Newmark
72190939,1,19,Mr John Smith
72196141,13,7,Mr John McFall
72192829,0,20,Mr John Maples
72190442,5,15,Mr John Leech
72192969,12,8,Mr John Heppell
72192340,12,8,Mr John Barrett
72195657,5,15,Mr Jim Murphy
72191976,11,9,Mr Jim Knight
72192696,13,7,Mr Jim Dobbin
72192728,14,6,Mr Jeffrey Ennis
72190696,3,17,Mr Jeffrey Donaldson
72194870,16,4,Mr Jamie Reed
72194993,14,6,Mr James Plaskitt
72193888,12,8,Mr James Duddridge
72196866,22,18,Mr Ivan Lewis
72195492,16,4,Mr Ian Taylor
72190390,12,8,Mr Ian Pearson
72194488,9,11,Mr Ian Austin
72191742,0,20,Mr Gregory Barker
72196948,0,20,Mr Graham Stuart
72192691,0,20,Mr Gordon Prentice
72191227,17,3,Mr Gerry Sutcliffe
72194303,19,1,Mr Frank Cook
72194945,7,13,Mr Fabian Hamilton
72192783,10,10,Mr Eric Pickles
72196898,13,7,Mr Eric Martlew
72192090,16,4,Mr Eric Joyce
72194153,0,20,Mr Eddie McGrady
72194992,3,17,Mr Douglas Carswell
72190901,14,6,Mr Desmond Swayne
72190028,9,11,Mr Dennis Skinner
72191979,8,12,Mr David Wright
```

```
72191738,19,1,Mr David Heyes
72195939,14,6,Mr David Heath
72193606,0,20,Mr David Hamilton
72190910,9,11,Mr David Drew
72193713,14,6,Mr David Crausby
72190328,6,14,Mr David Clelland
72191772,17,3,Mr David Cairns
72194126,6,14,Mr David Borrow
72192804,17,3,Mr Bill Rammell
72195901,4,16,Mr Ben Wallace
72192495,12,8,Mr Barry Gardiner
72194381,8,12,Mr Andy Burnham
72191740,11,9,Mr Alistair Burt
72191951,13,7,Mr Albert Owen
72193006,0,20,Mr Alan Campbell
72193963,0,20,Mr Adrian Sanders
72191264,13,7,Miss Anne Begg
72196839,16,4,Dr Stephen Ladyman
72198018,12,8,Dr Roberta Blackman-Woods
72191967,11,9,Dr Richard Taylor
72191860,0,20,Dr Nick Palmer
72190264,15,5,Dr Des Turner
72194812,9,11,Mr Jim McGovern
72194866,7,13,Rt Hon Richard Caborn
72194519,17,2,Ms Dawn Butler
72192759,10,10,Mrs Betty Williams
72190971,14,6,Mr Phil Willis
72190260,11,9,Mr Nick Clegg
72196379,4,16,Mr Michael John Foster
72195969,13,7,Mr Mark Pritchard
72192564,15,5,Mr David Lidington
72198188,19,1,Mr David Laws
72198319,0,20,Mr Richard Benyon
72190559,18,2,Rt Hon Sir Menzies Campbell
72191506,20,0,Rt Hon David Cameron
72193823,20,0,Rt Hon Bruce George
72195856,39,1,Rt Hon Alan Johnson
72192148,14,6,Ms Janet Anderson
72192233,20,0,Ms Ann Keen
72195722,19,1,Mrs Maria Miller
72190943,17,3,Mrs Christine Russell
72191751,18,2,Mr Wayne David
72192417,18,2,Mr Tony McNulty
72195826,19,1,Mr Tony Baldry
72192433,16,4,Mr Paul Flynn
72191963,9,11,Mr Norman Lamb
72195220,20,0,Mr Mark Hendrick
72196290,18,2,Mr Jim Cousins
72192328,14,6,Mr Jeremy Corbyn
72194952,19,1,Mr Edward O'Hara
72195520,20,0,Mr Derek Wyatt
72193642,19,1,Mr Derek Twigg
72190913,20,0,Mr David Watts
72193998,20,0,Mr David Ruffley
72190936,19,1,Mr David Mundell
72195814,20,0,Mr David Lepper
72190357,19,1,Mr David Lammy
72190919,20,0,Mr David Kidney
72192163,19,1,Mr David Evennett
72191885,20,0,Mr Boris Johnson
72191737,17,3,Mr Alan Reid
```

```
72193705,39,1,Mr Adam Price
72196820,20,0,Dr Howard Stoate
72194873,20,0,Sir Stuart Bell
72194526,20,0,Sir Robert Smith
72190976,20,0,Sir Peter Tapsell
72196886,24,1,Sir Nicholas Winterton
72196094,20,0,Rt Hon Tom Clarke
72191145,20,0,Rt Hon Theresa May
72192702,18,2,Rt Hon Tessa Jowell
72195838,18,2,Rt Hon Stephen Dorrell
72195041,20,0,Rt Hon Stephen Byers
72194213,19,1,Rt Hon Sir Malcolm Rifkind
72196825,18,2,Rt Hon Sir Gerald Kaufman
72192566,19,1,Rt Hon Sir George Young
72195600,18,2,Rt Hon Sir Alan Haselhurst
72192211,19,1,Rt Hon Ruth Kelly
72193840,19,1,Rt Hon Peter Lilley
72193816,20,0,Rt Hon Peter Hain
72194405,20,0,Rt Hon Oliver Letwin
72195941,18,2,Rt Hon Nick Brown
72195945,20,0,Rt Hon Michael Meacher
72194884,17,3,Rt Hon Michael Mates
72196901,19,1,Rt Hon Michael Martin
72190360,20,0,Rt Hon Michael Howard
72192528,20,0,Rt Hon Michael Ancram
72194780,20,0,Rt Hon Margaret Beckett
72195952,15,5,Rt Hon Kevin Barron
72194841,19,1,Rt Hon Kenneth Clarke
72192565,19,1,Rt Hon Keith Hill
72190377,20,0,Rt Hon John Redwood
72195906,18,2,Rt Hon John Gummer
72192771,40,0,Rt Hon Ian McCartney
72194877,19,1,Rt Hon Harriet Harman
72195734,16,4,Rt Hon Gordon Brown
72195815,19,1,Rt Hon Gavin Strang
72190601,17,3,Rt Hon Frank Field
72196956,20,0,Rt Hon Frank Dobson
72192990,20,0,Rt Hon Francis Maude
72192688,19,1,Rt Hon David Maclean
72195860,17,3,Rt Hon David Davis
72195903,20,0,Rt Hon David Blunkett
72192586,19,1,Rt Hon Clare Short
72194881,20,0,Rt Hon Charles Kennedy
72190526,16,4,Rt Hon Charles Clarke
72192889,19,1,Rt Hon Bob Ainsworth
72192413,20,0,Rt Hon Ann Widdecombe
72195943,20,0,Rt Hon Ann Clwyd
72190046,20,0,Rt Hon Andrew Mackay
72195930,13,7,Rt Hon Alun Michael
72196943,20,0,Rt Hon Alan Williams
72195854,32,15,Rev Ian Paisley
72190912,20,0,Ms Yvette Cooper
72191790,19,1,Ms Vera Baird
72194550,20,0,Ms Theresa Villiers
72190986,20,0,Ms Siobhain McDonagh
72190864,20,0,Ms Sarah  McCarthy-Fry
72192642,19,1,Ms Sally Keeble
72194581,8,12,Ms Rosie Winterton
72191793,17,3,Ms Meg Munn
72198768,19,1,Ms Meg Hillier
72191157,18,2,Ms Maria Eagle
```

```
72192898,20,0,Ms Lynda Waltho
72194837,20,0,Ms Liz Blackman
72198105,32,0,Ms Kerry McCarthy
72195000,20,0,Ms Justine Greening
72190991,19,1,Ms Judy Mallaber
72192335,16,4,Ms Joan Ryan
72196196,18,2,Ms Jessica Morden
72192112,20,0,Ms Glenda Jackson
72190489,18,2,Ms Gillian Merron
72195955,14,6,Ms Emily Thornberry
72196876,19,1,Ms Dari Taylor
72190468,19,1,Ms Claire Ward
72192769,20,0,Ms Christine McCafferty
72194298,18,2,Ms Celia Barlow
72191277,19,1,Ms Caroline Flint
72193847,20,0,Ms Barbara Keeley
72191158,20,0,Ms Barbara Follett
72196556,20,0,Ms Anne Snelgrove
72195239,20,0,Ms Anne Milton
72191770,20,0,Ms Ann McKechin
72190926,17,3,Ms Angela E Smith
72198598,20,0,Ms Angela C Smith
72190883,20,0,Ms Alison Seabeck
72190956,20,0,Mrs Sylvia Heal
72192324,19,1,Mrs Sandra Gidley
72192592,20,0,Mrs Louise Ellman
72190987,19,1,Mrs Linda Gilroy
72190473,20,0,Mrs Laura Moffatt
72190960,20,0,Mrs Julie Morgan
72192755,20,0,Mrs Joan Humble
72193010,20,0,Mrs Janet Dean
72192762,19,1,Mrs Cheryl Gillan
72190378,18,2,Mrs Caroline Spelman
72191898,20,0,Mrs Annette Brooke
72191760,20,0,Mrs Anne Moffat
72192557,19,1,Mrs Angela Browning
72193935,16,4,Mr William Cash
72191947,19,1,Mr Tony Cunningham
72191943,38,2,Mr Mark Tami
72191769,20,0,Mr Tom Harris
72194857,20,0,Mr Tim Yeo
72190461,17,3,Mr Tim Loughton
72192810,17,3,Mr Tim Farron
72190367,20,0,Mr Steve McCabe
72192949,20,0,Mr Stephen Timms
72195982,16,4,Mr Stephen Pound
72190584,20,0,Mr Stephen O'Brien
72194953,20,0,Mr Stephen Hesford
72190462,20,0,Mr Stephen Hammond
72196567,19,1,Mr Simon Hughes
72191183,20,0,Mr Shailesh Vara
72196477,20,0,Mr Sadiq Khan
72191747,20,0,Mr Roger Williams
72192608,20,0,Mr Robert Walter
72196867,20,0,Mr Robert Syms
72192933,17,3,Mr Robert Marshall-Andrews
72190083,20,0,Mr Richard Shepherd
72192256,19,1,Mr Richard Ottaway
72192170,20,0,Mr Richard Burden
72195851,20,0,Mr Philip Hammond
72190788,19,1,Mr Philip Dunne
```

```
72190992,18,2,Mr Phil Woolas
72192964,10,10,Mr Phil Hope
72193985,19,1,Mr Peter Viggers
72191212,20,0,Mr Peter Bottomley
72192775,19,1,Mr Peter Atkinson
72192527,20,0,Mr Peter Ainsworth
72192252,19,1,Mr Paul Truswell
72191754,17,3,Mr Paul Holmes
72194614,20,0,Mr Paul Goodman
72191986,20,0,Mr Paul Farrelly
72191961,20,0,Mr Patrick Mercer
72195665,20,0,Mr Pat McFadden
72193641,20,0,Mr Paddy Tipping
72193955,20,0,Mr Owen Paterson
72190445,20,0,Mr Norman Baker
72192561,20,0,Mr Nigel Waterson
72191295,20,0,Mr Nick Herbert
72192683,20,0,Mr Nick Harvey
72192690,20,0,Mr Nick Ainger
72194899,20,0,Mr Neil Gerrard
72195898,18,2,Mr Mohammad Sarwar
72191746,38,2,Mr Mark Simmonds
72194759,40,0,Mr David Gauke
72190978,18,2,Mr Mike Gapes
72190911,19,1,Mr Michael Wills
72190263,19,1,Mr Michael Moore
72191393,16,4,Mr Michael Jabez Foster
72194829,20,0,Mr Michael Gove
72196791,20,0,Mr Michael Fallon
72194903,20,0,Mr Matthew Taylor
72192749,18,2,Mr Martin Salter
72195728,20,0,Mr Martin Linton
72193415,17,3,Mr Martin Horwood
72190965,20,0,Mr Marsha Singh
72194935,20,0,Mr Mark Todd
72193826,20,0,Mr Mark Prisk
72191709,20,0,Mr Mark Hoban
72190937,20,0,Mr Mark Harper
72191858,19,1,Mr Mark Francois
72194894,20,0,Mr Mark Fisher
72191980,19,1,Mr Mark Field
72192795,20,0,Mr Malcolm Wicks
72192334,19,1,Mr Malcolm Bruce
72191431,20,0,Mr Liam Byrne
72190970,18,2,Mr Lee Scott
72192325,16,4,Mr Laurence Robertson
72191753,19,1,Mr Kevin Brennan
72191759,20,0,Mr Kevan Jones
72193922,20,0,Mr Keith Vaz
72190975,17,3,Mr Keith Simpson
72190643,20,0,Mr Julian Brazier
72192590,20,0,Mr John Randall
72195965,19,1,Mr John Mann
72190779,20,0,Mr John MacDougall
72193806,19,1,Mr John Horam
72192273,19,1,Mr John Hayes
72192676,17,3,Mr John Grogan
72196059,18,2,Mr John Greenway
72191743,20,0,Mr John Baron
72192706,19,1,Mr John Austin
72193895,18,2,Mr Joe Benton
```

```
72195872,20,0,Mr Jimmy Hood
72193804,20,0,Mr Jim Paice
72192776,19,1,Mr Jim Fitzpatrick
72192686,7,13,Mr Jim Dowd
72190024,20,0,Mr Jeremy Wright
72191163,18,2,Mr James Gray
72194907,6,14,Mr James Cunningham
72190514,17,3,Mr James Clappison
72190903,17,3,Mr Ian Stewart
72191948,18,2,Mr Ian Lucas
72192238,17,3,Mr Ian Davidson
72190134,20,0,Mr Huw Irranca-Davies
72191895,20,0,Mr Hugo Swire
72191765,20,0,Mr Hugh Robertson
72190346,19,1,Mr Hugh Bayley
72192844,20,0,Mr Henry Bellingham
72190438,19,1,Mr Harry Cohen
72192510,20,0,Mr Gregory Mulholland
72190685,20,0,Mr Greg Pope
72196801,20,0,Mr Greg Hands
72195245,20,0,Mr Greg Clark
72190659,20,0,Mr Grant Shapps
72191649,20,0,Mr Graham Brady
72195859,20,0,Mr Gordon Marsden
72198693,20,0,Mr Gordon Banks
72191198,18,2,Mr Gerald Howarth
72196372,20,0,Mr George Osborne
72192879,19,1,Mr George Galloway
72192414,20,0,Mr Gary Streeter
72191154,20,0,Mr Gareth Thomas
72192536,12,8,Mr Fraser Kemp
72190682,19,1,Mr Frank Doran
72192633,19,1,Mr Elfyn Llwyd
72194883,18,2,Mr Edward Leigh
72192875,20,0,Mr Edward Garnier
72190250,19,1,Mr Edward Davey
72192718,15,5,Mr Ed Vaizey
72192070,15,5,Mr Don Touhig
72192695,20,0,Mr Don Foster
72194803,17,3,Mr Dominic Grieve
72192671,17,3,Mr David Hanson
72190952,15,5,Mr David Chaytor
72192245,20,0,Mr David Amess
72191438,20,0,Mr Danny Alexander
72190904,20,0,Mr Damian Green
72191449,19,1,Mr Dai Havard
72193373,18,2,Mr Crispin Blunt
72195905,20,0,Mr Colin Breed
72192289,20,0,Mr Clive Betts
72196938,18,2,Mr Christopher Chope
72190214,20,0,Mr Chris Huhne
72191763,20,0,Mr Chris Grayling
72190505,20,0,Mr Charles Walker
72191977,19,1,Mr Charles Hendry
72195388,18,2,Mr Brian Donohoe
72192329,20,0,Mr Bob Laxton
72193980,18,2,Mr Bob Blizzard
72191893,19,1,Mr Bill Wiggin
72191179,20,0,Mr Ben Chapman
72190950,20,0,Mr Ben Bradshaw
72192404,19,1,Mr Barry Sheerman
```

```
72194843,19,1,Mr Austin Mitchell
72196586,19,1,Mr Anthony Steen
72192304,19,1,Mr Anthony David Wright
72191781,20,0,Mr Angus Robertson
72196111,20,0,Mr Angus MacNeil
72196775,20,0,Mr Andy Slaughter
72190625,20,0,Mr Andrew Tyrie
72190096,19,1,Mr Andrew Robathan
72192405,15,5,Mr Andrew Reed
72190349,20,0,Mr Andrew Pelling
72191981,20,0,Mr Andrew Mitchell
72192539,20,0,Mr Andrew Mackinlay
72196623,18,2,Mr Andrew Love
72196835,20,0,Mr Andrew Lansley
72195572,19,1,Mr Andrew George
72191279,19,1,Mr Andrew Dismore
72191787,20,0,Mr Alistair Carmichael
72194657,19,1,Mr Alan Simpson
72190985,20,0,Mr Alan Keen
72191202,18,2,Mr Adrian Bailey
72195985,20,0,Miss Kate Hoey
72190972,20,0,Miss Anne McIntosh
72191969,19,1,Lady Sylvia Hermon
72193831,12,8,Hon Lindsay Hoyle
72191191,19,1,Dr Vincent Cable
72192665,17,3,Dr Tony Wayland Wright
72190565,15,5,Dr Rudi Vis
72192205,19,1,Dr Roger Berry
72196865,19,1,Dr Phyllis Starkey
72195526,20,0,Dr Kim Howells
72192799,20,0,Dr Ian Gibson
72191734,19,1,Dr Hywel Francis
72192346,18,2,Dr Evan Harris
72192602,18,2,Dr Doug Naysmith
72192653,19,1,Dr Brian Iddon
72191944,19,1,Dr Andrew Murrison
72192832,15,5,Dr Alasdair McDonnell
72190918,17,3,Dr Alan Whitehead
72191186,17,1,Mr Bill Etherington
72195094,16,2,Ms Margaret Moran
72190588,16,2,Mr Gwyn Prosser
72196888,9,8,Rt Hon Dr Denis MacShane
72190141,14,3,Mrs Jacqui Lait
72192113,6,11,Rt Hon John Spellar
72192965,17,0,Rt Hon Andrew Smith
72191792,17,0,Mr Chris Bryant
72191960,16,1,Mr Andrew Rosindell
72191890,13,2,Rt Hon William Hague
72196428,15,0,Ms Nadine Dorries
72190979,12,3,Mr Shaun Woodward
72191761,14,1,Mr Mark Lazarowicz
72192210,15,0,Mr Lembit Öpik
72193796,9,4,Mr Andrew Miller
72190984,13,0,Mr Geoffrey Robinson
72191018,13,0,Mr Dan Rogerson
72193819,7,6,Rt Hon Paul Murphy
72198297,10,3,Ms Rosie Cooper
72191794,13,0,Dr John Pugh
72192541,5,7,Mr Michael Connarty
72191051,3,9,Mr Malcolm Moss
72191297,6,6,Mr Andrew Selous
```

```
72192689,9,3,Rt Hon Alan Milburn
72190990,10,2,Ms Julie Kirkbride
72190444,8,4,Ms Helen Goodman
72192568,7,5,Mr Nigel Evans
72192302,12,0,Mr Andrew Stunell
72194129,12,0,Rt Hon Michael Jack
72192221,7,5,Mr Roger Godsiff
72192624,12,0,Mr Humfrey Malins
72192550,12,0,Mr Geoffrey Clifton-Brown
72195852,12,0,Mr David Wilshire
72192567,12,0,Mr David Willetts
72194901,12,0,Mr David Tredinnick
72193870,12,0,Dr Lynne Jones
72194002,6,1,Ms Katy Clark
72191110,7,0,Prof Steve Webb
72190041,6,1,Ms Sarah Teather
72194964,7,0,Ms Diane Abbott
72191395,7,0,Mr Nick Gibb
72191540,4,2,Ms Claire Curtis-Thomas
72196488,6,0,Ms Madeleine Moon
72192496,6,0,Mr Mike Hancock
72191956,4,2,Dr Bob Spink
72191990,4,1,Mr Derek Conway
72191771,5,0,Mr Parmjit Dhanda
72190555,5,0,Ms Jo Swinson
72192815,5,0,Mr Martyn Jones
72193797,5,0,Mr John Thurso
72192806,5,0,Mr David Davies
72192365,5,0,Mr Bob Russell
72195963,5,0,Hon Bernard Jenkin
72194854,5,0,Mr Nick Hurd
72191096,5,0,Mr John Robertson
72196808,4,1,Mr David Taylor
72196090,4,1,Mr Chris Ruane
72190169,4,1,Mr Brian Jenkins
72192931,5,0,Sir Michael Lord
72190021,4,1,Rt Hon Thomas McAvoy
72194867,5,0,Rt Hon Iain Duncan Smith
72194123,5,0,Rt Hon Douglas Hogg
72190008,5,0,Ms Lynne Featherstone
72190989,5,0,Ms Fiona Mactaggart
72193058,5,0,Mrs Anne Main
72191275,5,0,Mr Tom Levitt
72192963,5,0,Mr Quentin Davies
72191166,4,1,Mr Mike Hall
72190476,5,0,Mr Jonathan Djanogly
72191287,5,0,Mr James Purnell
72190257,5,0,Mr David Winnick
72190174,5,0,Mr Andrew Turner
72192998,5,0,Hon Nicholas Soames
72196046,5,0,Hon Gwyneth Dunwoody
72193968,5,0,Dr Liam Fox
```

No faxes were sent after August 2006.

Faxes Sent to Parliament 2007

During Feb/March 2007 I successfully sent 1860 faxes to Parliament containing articles about the MI5 persecution. This attracted the attention of the "Fixated Threat Assessment Centre" of the Metropolitan Police, and on 14 March 2007 I met Mr Forfar and Detective Constable Mark Whittle for an interview. I told them I would cease sending further faxes. Whittle said he had an MI5 contact who assured him that MI5 was not, nor had been, undertaking actions against me, and I have no file with them. I did not believe him and told him so. Later I asked Forfar to arrange a meeting with his MI5 contact to resolve our differences, and he refused.

In the records is listed the fax number sent to, the count of successful fax transmissions, the count of failed fax transmissions, and the name of the Parliamentary recipient.

```
72190976,4,1,Sir Peter Tapsell
72190983,0,5,Sir Peter Soulsby
72194866,4,1,Rt Hon Richard Caborn
72192705,0,5,Rt Hon Patricia Hewitt
72193640,0,5,Rt Hon Margaret Hodge
72195952,4,1,Rt Hon Kevin Barron
72194880,4,1,Rt Hon Jane Kennedy
72192639,0,5,Rt Hon Hilary Benn
72190949,0,5,Rt Hon Hazel Blears
72192276,0,5,Rt Hon Dawn Primarolo
72193890,0,5,Rt Hon Alan Beith
72192347,4,1,Mr Nigel Dodds
72193047,5,5,Mr Ian Cawsey
72190209,0,5,Ms Natascha Engel
72196107,1,9,Ms Michelle Gildernew
72193664,4,1,Ms Karen Buck
72192381,0,5,Ms Julia Goldsworthy
72192115,0,5,Ms Helen Southworth
72190977,2,3,Ms Geraldine Smith
72195955,2,3,Ms Emily Thornberry
72196876,4,1,Ms Dari Taylor
72194298,2,3,Ms Celia Barlow
72193847,0,5,Ms Barbara Keeley
72190770,3,2,Ms Ann Coffey
72190926,3,2,Ms Angela E Smith
72192544,2,3,Mrs Rosemary McKenna
72191797,0,5,Mrs Iris Robinson
72192759,2,3,Mrs Betty Williams
72191957,2,3,Mrs Angela Watkinson
72190938,0,5,Mr Vernon Coaker
72196496,0,5,Mr Tobias Ellwood
72195275,1,4,Mr Terry Rooney
72191049,0,5,Mr Stephen Williams
72190922,2,3,Mr Russell Brown
72194358,0,5,Mr Ronnie Campbell
72196828,2,3,Mr Roger Gale
72195400,2,3,Mr Robert Flello
72190667,0,5,Mr Philip Davies
72190971,2,3,Mr Phil Willis
72192545,0,5,Mr Paul Clark
72190974,2,3,Mr Paul Burstow
72191963,2,3,Mr Norman Lamb
72190260,1,4,Mr Nick Clegg
72191468,0,5,Mr Neil Turner
72195015,0,5,Mr Michael Clapham
72193415,2,3,Mr Martin Horwood
72192389,0,5,Mr Mark Oaten
72195220,4,1,Mr Mark Hendrick
72192110,0,5,Mr Ken Purchase
72192522,9,1,Mr Brooks Newmark
72190939,2,3,Mr John Smith
72192829,0,5,Mr John Maples
```

```
72190442,4,1,Mr John Leech
72192969,3,2,Mr John Heppell
72195657,0,5,Mr Jim Murphy
72194812,2,3,Mr Jim McGovern
72192686,0,5,Mr Jim Dowd
72190696,0,5,Mr Jeffrey Donaldson
72194993,4,1,Mr James Plaskitt
72191163,1,4,Mr James Gray
72190903,4,1,Mr Ian Stewart
72190390,1,4,Mr Ian Pearson
72194488,2,3,Mr Ian Austin
72190134,3,2,Mr Huw Irranca-Davies
72191742,0,5,Mr Gregory Barker
72196948,0,5,Mr Graham Stuart
72192691,0,5,Mr Gordon Prentice
72191198,3,2,Mr Gerald Howarth
72190682,0,5,Mr Frank Doran
72194945,0,5,Mr Fabian Hamilton
72194153,0,5,Mr Eddie McGrady
72192718,3,2,Mr Ed Vaizey
72194992,0,5,Mr Douglas Carswell
72190901,1,4,Mr Desmond Swayne
72191979,2,3,Mr David Wright
72191738,4,1,Mr David Heyes
72193606,0,5,Mr David Hamilton
72190910,3,2,Mr David Drew
72193713,2,3,Mr David Crausby
72190328,2,3,Mr David Clelland
72193373,3,2,Mr Crispin Blunt
72195901,2,3,Mr Ben Wallace
72192304,1,4,Mr Anthony David Wright
72191740,0,5,Mr Alistair Burt
72193006,0,5,Mr Alan Campbell
72191202,4,1,Mr Adrian Bailey
72191191,2,3,Dr Vincent Cable
72192665,4,1,Dr Tony Wayland Wright
72198018,0,5,Dr Roberta Blackman-Woods
72191860,0,5,Dr Nick Palmer
72191734,4,1,Dr Hywel Francis
72196820,3,2,Dr Howard Stoate
72192832,4,1,Dr Alasdair McDonnell
72195906,5,0,Rt Hon John Gummer
72190473,5,0,Mrs Laura Moffatt
72192557,5,0,Mrs Angela Browning
72196379,4,1,Mr Michael John Foster
72194952,5,0,Mr Edward O'Hara
72192495,5,0,Mr Barry Gardiner
72192653,5,0,Dr Brian Iddon
72194873,5,0,Sir Stuart Bell
72194526,5,0,Sir Robert Smith
72196805,5,0,Sir Patrick Cormack
72196886,5,0,Sir Nicholas Winterton
72192991,5,0,Sir Michael Spicer
72196094,5,0,Rt Hon Tom Clarke
72191145,5,0,Rt Hon Theresa May
72192702,5,0,Rt Hon Tessa Jowell
72195838,5,0,Rt Hon Stephen Dorrell
72195041,5,0,Rt Hon Stephen Byers
72190559,5,0,Rt Hon Sir Menzies Campbell
72194213,5,0,Rt Hon Sir Malcolm Rifkind
72196825,5,0,Rt Hon Sir Gerald Kaufman
72192566,5,0,Rt Hon Sir George Young
72195600,5,0,Rt Hon Sir Alan Haselhurst
72192211,5,0,Rt Hon Ruth Kelly
72193840,5,0,Rt Hon Peter Lilley
72193816,5,0,Rt Hon Peter Hain
72194405,5,0,Rt Hon Oliver Letwin
72192619,5,0,Rt Hon Nick Raynsford
72195941,5,0,Rt Hon Nick Brown
72195945,5,0,Rt Hon Michael Meacher
```

```
72194884,5,0,Rt Hon Michael Mates
72196901,5,0,Rt Hon Michael Martin
72190360,5,0,Rt Hon Michael Howard
72192528,5,0,Rt Hon Michael Ancram
72194780,5,0,Rt Hon Margaret Beckett
72194841,5,0,Rt Hon Kenneth Clarke
72192565,5,0,Rt Hon Keith Hill
72190377,5,0,Rt Hon John Redwood
79256996,5,0,Rt Hon Jacqui Smith
72192771,10,0,Rt Hon Ian McCartney
72194877,5,0,Rt Hon Harriet Harman
72195734,2,3,Rt Hon Gordon Brown
72190495,1,4,Rt Hon George Howarth
72192428,5,0,Rt Hon Geoffrey Hoon
72195815,5,0,Rt Hon Gavin Strang
72190601,5,0,Rt Hon Frank Field
72196956,5,0,Rt Hon Frank Dobson
72192990,5,0,Rt Hon Francis Maude
72192688,5,0,Rt Hon David Maclean
72195860,5,0,Rt Hon David Davis
72191506,4,1,Rt Hon David Cameron
72195903,5,0,Rt Hon David Blunkett
72192586,5,0,Rt Hon Clare Short
72194881,5,0,Rt Hon Charles Kennedy
72190526,5,0,Rt Hon Charles Clarke
72193823,5,0,Rt Hon Bruce George
72192889,5,0,Rt Hon Bob Ainsworth
72192413,5,0,Rt Hon Ann Widdecombe
72195943,5,0,Rt Hon Ann Clwyd
72190046,5,0,Rt Hon Andrew Mackay
72195930,5,0,Rt Hon Alun Michael
72196943,5,0,Rt Hon Alan Williams
72195856,10,0,Rt Hon Alan Johnson
72195854,9,1,Rev Ian Paisley
72191790,5,0,Ms Vera Baird
72194550,5,0,Ms Theresa Villiers
72190986,5,0,Ms Siobhain McDonagh
72190958,3,2,Ms Siân James
72190864,5,0,Ms Sarah  McCarthy-Fry
72192642,5,0,Ms Sally Keeble
72194581,5,0,Ms Rosie Winterton
72191793,5,0,Ms Meg Munn
72198768,5,0,Ms Meg Hillier
72191157,5,0,Ms Maria Eagle
72192898,5,0,Ms Lynda Waltho
72194837,5,0,Ms Liz Blackman
72191513,5,0,Ms Linda Riordan
72198105,5,0,Ms Kerry McCarthy
72192906,5,0,Ms Kali Mountford
72195000,5,0,Ms Justine Greening
72190991,5,0,Ms Judy Mallaber
72194397,5,0,Ms Joan Walley
72192335,5,0,Ms Joan Ryan
72196045,2,3,Ms Joan Ruddock
72196196,5,0,Ms Jessica Morden
72192148,5,0,Ms Janet Anderson
72192112,4,1,Ms Glenda Jackson
72190489,5,0,Ms Gillian Merron
72194519,5,0,Ms Dawn Butler
72190468,5,0,Ms Claire Ward
72192769,5,0,Ms Christine McCafferty
72191277,5,0,Ms Caroline Flint
72195581,5,0,Ms Bridget Prentice
72191158,5,0,Ms Barbara Follett
72196556,5,0,Ms Anne Snelgrove
72195239,5,0,Ms Anne Milton
72191770,5,0,Ms Ann McKechin
72192233,5,0,Ms Ann Keen
72198598,4,1,Ms Angela C Smith
72190883,5,0,Ms Alison Seabeck
```

```
72190956,5,0,Mrs Sylvia Heal
72192324,5,0,Mrs Sandra Gidley
72195722,4,1,Mrs Maria Miller
72192592,5,0,Mrs Louise Ellman
72190987,3,2,Mrs Linda Gilroy
72190960,5,0,Mrs Julie Morgan
72192755,5,0,Mrs Joan Humble
72193010,5,0,Mrs Janet Dean
72190980,5,0,Mrs Eleanor Laing
72192762,4,1,Mrs Cheryl Gillan
72190378,5,0,Mrs Caroline Spelman
72191898,5,0,Mrs Annette Brooke
72191760,5,0,Mrs Anne Moffat
72192503,5,0,Mrs Anne McGuire
72193935,5,0,Mr William Cash
72191751,5,0,Mr Wayne David
72192417,5,0,Mr Tony McNulty
72192585,5,0,Mr Tony Lloyd
72191947,5,0,Mr Tony Cunningham
72195826,5,0,Mr Tony Baldry
72191943,10,0,Mr Mark Tami
72191769,5,0,Mr Tom Harris
72196491,5,0,Mr Tom Brake
72194919,5,0,Mr Timothy Boswell
72194857,5,0,Mr Tim Yeo
72190461,5,0,Mr Tim Loughton
72192810,3,2,Mr Tim Farron
72195169,5,0,Mr Stewart Jackson
72190367,5,0,Mr Steve McCabe
72192949,5,0,Mr Stephen Timms
72195982,5,0,Mr Stephen Pound
72190584,5,0,Mr Stephen O'Brien
72194953,5,0,Mr Stephen Hesford
72190462,5,0,Mr Stephen Hammond
72196567,5,0,Mr Simon Hughes
72191183,5,0,Mr Shailesh Vara
72196477,5,0,Mr Sadiq Khan
72191747,5,0,Mr Roger Williams
72196187,5,0,Mr Robert Wareing
72192608,5,0,Mr Robert Walter
72196867,5,0,Mr Robert Syms
72192933,5,0,Mr Robert Marshall-Andrews
72194865,10,0,Mr Eric Illsley
72190083,5,0,Mr Richard Shepherd
72192256,4,1,Mr Richard Ottaway
72192170,5,0,Mr Richard Burden
72198319,0,5,Mr Richard Benyon
72195699,5,0,Mr Piara Khabra
72195851,5,0,Mr Philip Hammond
72190788,5,0,Mr Philip Dunne
72190992,5,0,Mr Phil Woolas
72192964,5,0,Mr Phil Hope
72193985,5,0,Mr Peter Viggers
72192356,5,0,Mr Peter Kilfoyle
72191212,5,0,Mr Peter Bottomley
72192775,5,0,Mr Peter Atkinson
72192527,5,0,Mr Peter Ainsworth
72192252,5,0,Mr Paul Truswell
72191184,5,0,Mr Paul Keetch
72191754,5,0,Mr Paul Holmes
72194614,5,0,Mr Paul Goodman
72192433,5,0,Mr Paul Flynn
72191986,5,0,Mr Paul Farrelly
72191961,5,0,Mr Patrick Mercer
72193987,5,0,Mr Patrick Hall
72195665,5,0,Mr Pat McFadden
72193641,5,0,Mr Paddy Tipping
72193955,5,0,Mr Owen Paterson
72194478,5,0,Mr Oliver Heald
72190445,5,0,Mr Norman Baker
```

```
72192561,5,0,Mr Nigel Waterson
72191295,5,0,Mr Nick Herbert
72192683,5,0,Mr Nick Harvey
72192690,5,0,Mr Nick Ainger
72194899,5,0,Mr Neil Gerrard
72195898,5,0,Mr Mohammad Sarwar
72191746,10,0,Mr Mark Simmonds
72194759,10,0,Mr David Gauke
72190978,4,1,Mr Mike Gapes
72190911,5,0,Mr Michael Wills
72190263,4,1,Mr Michael Moore
72191393,5,0,Mr Michael Jabez Foster
72194829,5,0,Mr Michael Gove
72196791,5,0,Mr Michael Fallon
72194903,5,0,Mr Matthew Taylor
72192749,5,0,Mr Martin Salter
72195728,5,0,Mr Martin Linton
72190965,5,0,Mr Marsha Singh
72194935,5,0,Mr Mark Todd
72195969,5,0,Mr Mark Pritchard
72193826,5,0,Mr Mark Prisk
72191709,5,0,Mr Mark Hoban
72190937,5,0,Mr Mark Harper
72191858,5,0,Mr Mark Francois
72194894,5,0,Mr Mark Fisher
72191980,5,0,Mr Mark Field
72192795,5,0,Mr Malcolm Wicks
72192334,5,0,Mr Malcolm Bruce
72191431,5,0,Mr Liam Byrne
72190970,5,0,Mr Lee Scott
72192325,5,0,Mr Laurence Robertson
72191745,4,1,Mr Khalid Mahmood
72191753,5,0,Mr Kevin Brennan
72191759,5,0,Mr Kevan Jones
72190957,5,0,Mr Kelvin Hopkins
72193922,5,0,Mr Keith Vaz
72190975,5,0,Mr Keith Simpson
72190643,5,0,Mr Julian Brazier
72192133,2,3,Mr Jon Trickett
72192590,5,0,Mr John Randall
72196141,5,0,Mr John McFall
72195965,5,0,Mr John Mann
72190779,5,0,Mr John MacDougall
72193806,5,0,Mr John Horam
72192273,5,0,Mr John Hayes
72192676,5,0,Mr John Grogan
72196059,5,0,Mr John Greenway
72192340,5,0,Mr John Barrett
72191743,5,0,Mr John Baron
72192706,5,0,Mr John Austin
72193895,5,0,Mr Joe Benton
72195872,5,0,Mr Jimmy Hood
72193804,5,0,Mr Jim Paice
72191976,5,0,Mr Jim Knight
72192776,4,1,Mr Jim Fitzpatrick
72192696,5,0,Mr Jim Dobbin
72196290,5,0,Mr Jim Cousins
72190024,5,0,Mr Jeremy Wright
72192328,4,1,Mr Jeremy Corbyn
72192728,3,2,Mr Jeffrey Ennis
72194870,5,0,Mr Jamie Reed
72193888,5,0,Mr James Duddridge
72194907,5,0,Mr James Cunningham
72190514,5,0,Mr James Clappison
72196866,10,0,Mr Ivan Lewis
72195492,5,0,Mr Ian Taylor
72191948,5,0,Mr Ian Lucas
72192238,5,0,Mr Ian Davidson
72193705,10,0,Mr Adam Price
72191895,5,0,Mr Hugo Swire
```

```
72191765,5,0,Mr Hugh Robertson
72190346,5,0,Mr Hugh Bayley
72192844,5,0,Mr Henry Bellingham
72192510,3,2,Mr Gregory Mulholland
72190685,5,0,Mr Greg Pope
72195245,5,0,Mr Greg Clark
72190659,5,0,Mr Grant Shapps
72191649,5,0,Mr Graham Brady
72195859,5,0,Mr Gordon Marsden
72198693,5,0,Mr Gordon Banks
72191227,5,0,Mr Gerry Sutcliffe
72196372,5,0,Mr George Osborne
72192879,5,0,Mr George Galloway
72192414,5,0,Mr Gary Streeter
72191154,5,0,Mr Gareth Thomas
72192536,5,0,Mr Fraser Kemp
72194303,5,0,Mr Frank Cook
72192783,5,0,Mr Eric Pickles
72196898,5,0,Mr Eric Martlew
72192090,5,0,Mr Eric Joyce
72192633,5,0,Mr Elfyn Llwyd
72194883,4,1,Mr Edward Leigh
72192875,5,0,Mr Edward Garnier
72190250,5,0,Mr Edward Davey
72192070,5,0,Mr Don Touhig
72192695,5,0,Mr Don Foster
72194803,5,0,Mr Dominic Grieve
72195520,5,0,Mr Derek Wyatt
72193642,5,0,Mr Derek Twigg
72190028,5,0,Mr Dennis Skinner
72190913,5,0,Mr David Watts
72193998,5,0,Mr David Ruffley
72190936,5,0,Mr David Mundell
72192564,5,0,Mr David Lidington
72195814,5,0,Mr David Lepper
72198188,5,0,Mr David Laws
72190357,5,0,Mr David Lammy
72190919,5,0,Mr David Kidney
72195939,5,0,Mr David Heath
72192671,5,0,Mr David Hanson
72192163,5,0,Mr David Evennett
72190952,5,0,Mr David Chaytor
72191772,5,0,Mr David Cairns
72194126,5,0,Mr David Borrow
72192245,5,0,Mr David Amess
72191438,5,0,Mr Danny Alexander
72190904,5,0,Mr Damian Green
72191449,5,0,Mr Dai Havard
72195905,5,0,Mr Colin Breed
72192289,5,0,Mr Clive Betts
72196938,5,0,Mr Christopher Chope
72190214,5,0,Mr Chris Huhne
72191763,1,4,Mr Chris Grayling
72190505,5,0,Mr Charles Walker
72191977,5,0,Mr Charles Hendry
72195388,5,0,Mr Brian Donohoe
72191885,1,4,Mr Boris Johnson
72192329,5,0,Mr Bob Laxton
72193980,5,0,Mr Bob Blizzard
72191893,5,0,Mr Bill Wiggin
72192804,5,0,Mr Bill Rammell
72191179,5,0,Mr Ben Chapman
72190950,5,0,Mr Ben Bradshaw
72192404,5,0,Mr Barry Sheerman
72194843,5,0,Mr Austin Mitchell
72196586,5,0,Mr Anthony Steen
72191781,5,0,Mr Angus Robertson
72196111,5,0,Mr Angus MacNeil
72196775,5,0,Mr Andy Slaughter
72194381,5,0,Mr Andy Burnham
```

```
72190625,5,0,Mr Andrew Tyrie
72190096,5,0,Mr Andrew Robathan
72192405,5,0,Mr Andrew Reed
72190349,5,0,Mr Andrew Pelling
72191981,4,1,Mr Andrew Mitchell
72192539,5,0,Mr Andrew Mackinlay
72196623,5,0,Mr Andrew Love
72196835,5,0,Mr Andrew Lansley
72195572,5,0,Mr Andrew George
72191279,5,0,Mr Andrew Dismore
72191787,5,0,Mr Alistair Carmichael
72191951,5,0,Mr Albert Owen
72194657,5,0,Mr Alan Simpson
72191737,5,0,Mr Alan Reid
72190985,5,0,Mr Alan Keen
72193963,5,0,Mr Adrian Sanders
72195985,5,0,Miss Kate Hoey
72190972,5,0,Miss Anne McIntosh
72191264,3,2,Miss Anne Begg
72191969,5,0,Lady Sylvia Hermon
72193831,4,1,Hon Lindsay Hoyle
72196839,5,0,Dr Stephen Ladyman
72190565,5,0,Dr Rudi Vis
72192205,5,0,Dr Roger Berry
72191967,5,0,Dr Richard Taylor
72196865,5,0,Dr Phyllis Starkey
72195526,5,0,Dr Kim Howells
72192799,5,0,Dr Ian Gibson
72192346,5,0,Dr Evan Harris
72192602,5,0,Dr Doug Naysmith
72190264,5,0,Dr Des Turner
72191944,5,0,Dr Andrew Murrison
72190918,5,0,Dr Alan Whitehead
```

No faxes were sent after March 2007.

Later FTAC tried to obtain my NHS medical records. They lied to my doctor that I had sent 40,000 faxes to Parliament whereas the real number is only 24,272 over ten years which is way below the police figure. They did not obtain my medical records. It is disappointing that they chose to lie on this figure and that they chose to lie that I had no MI5 file when MI5 themselves have admitted I have a file with them. Mendacity seems part of police procedure.

Return to **Main Page**   *The author may be reached by feedback*

My Complaints

Overview

The "Complaints" area of this website contains various challenges and complaints I have made to relevant organisations, such as the BBC, and MI5 (via the Security Service Tribunal and Interception of Communications Tribunal).

The current situation as regards complaining about what I have been subjected to is that all relevant people have denied everything. I consider the whole lot of them to be liars. BBC TV newscasters Michael Buerk and Martyn Lewis have categorically denied (although refusing to do so in writing) the surveillance activity they have been accused of. They are liars - that is the sum and total of it.

Jeffrey Gordon Solicitors

I went to see solicitor Mr Baker of the firm Jeffrey Gordon in Battersea in December 1994, and subsequently wrote to him. There were two issues on my mind. One was the treatment I had received at OCTS primarily at the hands of Steve Mitchell in 1992 as a result of which I had to take two months off sick and have been on medication ever since. I wanted some form of justice for the abuse I had suffered at work and its serious consequences. The other was an incident de-planing from a British Airways flight in Toronto Airport in 1993 when a group of four men laughed at me "if he tries to run away we'll find him." I wanted to use the legal process to identify those four men, who were MI5 agents, although I did not know it at the time.

Mr Baker replied as shown in the first three pages of the following document.

JEFFREY GORDON & CO SOLICITORS

172 LAVENDER HILL
LONDON
SW11 5TG

Tel: 071-228 7050
Fax: 071-223 8241
DX 58555 Clapham Junction

Mr B C Szocik
90 Cavendish Road
London
SW12 0DF

Our ref: BB/TF
Your ref:

13 January 1995

Dear Mr Szocik

BRITISH AIRWAYS

Thank you for your letter of 30 December last with cheque for £50.00 on account of costs.

Having considered the matter further, it appears unlikely that we, as Solicitors, will be able to achieve anymore than you did as far as obtaining information as to passengers on British Airways, given this is confidential.

The only way we could obtain such information by compulsion would be to make an application to the Court for Specific Discovery of this information, but in order to do so, we would have to make out that British Airways were, themselves, a likely party to future litigation. Regrettably, this is clearly not the case as your grievance appears to lie with the four fellow passengers on the flight in question.

Furthermore, even if we were able to obtain this information, it is most unlikely that we would be able to trace the individuals and, indeed, any former addresses given may no longer be applicable. Furthermore, it is highly probable that the individuals are now resident in Canada. In any event, I note you are still unable to particularise the precise nature of your allegations against these men.

Another issue is the lapse of time since this alleged incident ie over eighteen months, so that if you did suffer any damage at the time, this is clearly no longer applicable. Moreover, if proceedings in Slander were to be launched, Legal Aid would not be available to fund them.

/Continued...

Jeffrey Gordon LLB · Commissioner for Oaths

-2-

In short, and having duly reflected on the matter, I cannot advise that from a legal or, indeed, practical cost point of view, you should take this matter any further.

When you originally consulted me, I understood the claim was against former employers or co-workers, but that is, apparently, not the case, and in any event similar considerations would apply to a claim of that nature.

I am sorry to disappoint you with my views, but cannot see a practical way forward in pursuing this matter.

No doubt you will seek alternative legal advice should you take a different view.

Finally, I enclose a note of my firm's professional charges for considering this matter.

Yours sincerely

B R Baker
JEFFREY GORDON & CO

Encl

JEFFREY GORDON & Co
SOLICITORS

JEFFREY GORDON, LL.B
COMMISSIONER FOR OATHS

172 Lavender Hill,
London SW11

VAT No. 235/8000/87

Our Ref: BB/TF

13 January 1995

Mr B C Szocik
90 Cavendish Road
London
SW12 ODF

RE: BRITISH AIRWAYS

To Professional Charges				
for advising you in relation to a potential civil claim, considering law, evidence and procedure and advising against pursuing the claim.				
Fee of			43	00
VAT @ 17.5%	7	52		
			50	52
Less paid on account			50	00
Balance owing				52p

JEFFREY GORDON & CO SOLICITORS

1 LAVENDER SWEEP
OFF LAVENDER HILL
LONDON SW11 1DY

Tel: 0171-228 7050
Fax: 0171-223 8241
DX 58555 Clapham Junction

Mrs B T Szocik
9 Auriga Drive
Nepean
ONTARIO
CANADA
KT2E 7T9

Our ref: SL/TF
Your ref:

31 January 1996

AIR MAIL

Dear Mr Szocik

Following your communication with our Mr Baker, I would repeat my advice that your instructions do not disclose any reasonable cause to action known to law. As a result, I feel it would be wholly improper for us to retain your cheque for £50.00 and hereby return it to you.

Yours sincerely

Sean Longley
JEFFREY GORDON AND CO

Encl

Jeffrey Gordon LLB · Commissioner for Oaths

His advice to not take any action disappointed me. I wrote to him again in Feb 1995 making explicit the connection between the four men on the BA flight and the harassment I had suffered at work and elsewhere, which had been coordinated by an agency I was at that point unaware of, but later became clear was MI5. I went to Clapham Police Station to complain in Easter 1995, although that complaint was not accepted by the police officer, and contemporaneously visited Jeffrey Gordon again, speaking briefly to Sean Longley, who suggested tacitly to me that an intelligence agency might be responsible for the persecution. That led me to think MI5 were behind it, and began a series of posts to internet newsgroups blaming them which have continued ever since.

I wrote to Mr Baker again on 19 Jan 1996 following a telephone conversation in December 1995. The letter was answered by Sean Longley (see page 4 of above multipage document) who said there was no "reasonable cause to action known to law." At that point communications with these solicitors terminated.

Ottawa Civic Hospital and Alan Holdsworth

In October 1996 while living in Ottawa I developed an intensely painful infection for which I went to see my Canadian GP who prescribed codeine. I went to the Civic Hospital on 25 Oct 1996 and subsequently received pills for the infection. I went to the Civic Hospital emergency department again with continuing pain on 2 Nov 1996 and was seen by an English doctor, Dr Worthington. He examined me and found there was nothing physically wrong, it was just an infection.

On that occasion I had to wait quite a long time to be seen by the doctor, and several patients jumped the queue ahead of me. One of them was a tall white male in his fifties with grey hair who was seen in a room in front of me (with the door open) by Dr Worthington, who asked him his name. The man aggressively announced his name was "Tad". Dr Worthington was obviously puzzled, looked at his notes and said, "But your name is Alan Holdsworth isn't it?" to which the man looked very much abashed. I cannot be sure of the name; the first name was definitely Alan, the second name sounded like Holdsworth but I cannot be certain.

The man's name was obviously not "Tad" which was the name by which I was known at work. He was an MI5 agent whom I have seen several times, most recently in December 2001 in Abbeville Road, Clapham when I went to post my subject access request to MI5; also at Ottawa Airport dressed warmly with a woolly hat at the height of summer pacing up and down aggressively to intimidate me; also at a cinema in Streatham when he came in, sat directly in front of me and looked back at me menacingly; also on a KLM flight in 1995 when he stared at me aggressively, at which time he was in the company of a smaller dark haired man, who was also an MI5 agent.

The man is clearly the ringleader assigned by MI5 to organise my persecution, and he was in his fifties in 1996, so I would expect he would have retired by now (2007). He is a dangerous psychopath who should not be working for the Government; his history of aggression towards me, mostly through other people, should have seen him locked up a long time ago, but he is protected by the security service who employ numerous other sociopaths and no such fate will befall him.

I should have challenged the man in the hospital then and there, but my priority was the pain my infection was causing me and I was keen to be seen by a doctor, so I let it go. I wrote to Dr Worthington on 10 Nov 1996.

Dear Dr Worthington,

I am writing regarding my visit to the Emergency Ward on Saturday 2/Nov/1996. During my visit, I witnessed another patient being seen - I cannot remember if it was by you or by another doctor. The other patient was a white male in his 40s or 50s. He gave his name as "Tad" which surprised the doctor who said "but your name is Alan Holsworth isn't it?". I cannot be sure of the surname - it might have been Holworth, or Houldsworth.

"Tad" is not a recognised synonym for "Alan". It is however an abbreviation for "Tadeusz", which is the name I usually go under (my name is Boleslaw Tadeusz Szocik), and "Tad" is what I am known by at work. Holsworth was in one of the rooms at the time, and I was directly outside, so he could see me clearly.

The reason I am worried about this incident is that I have been subjected to harassment for some time now, for example by people shouting outside the building where I live. I believe on occasion I have been followed, and this time "they" (whoever they are) sent this person into the Emergency Ward after me.

On Thurday 7/11/1996 I went to and spoke with a member of staff in Emergency Ward again. She advised me it would be necessary to bring in the police to conduct a search for Holsworth. My question is whether you were the doctor who saw Holsworth; do you remember his full name; and whether, if the police were brought in, the Civic would be able to make available records which would enable the police to establish his identity.

I am sorry to burden you with this because I know you must be very busy, but it would be very encouraging if we could clear up this matter.

Yours sincerely,

Dr Worthington replied a few days later. His response was disappointly negative and brief; he would not give out the man's identity.

Ottawa Civic Hospital

1053 Carling Ave.,
Ottawa, Ontario
Canada K1Y 4E9
(613) 761-4000

761-4347

November 18, 1996

Mr. B.T. Szocik
710-145 York Street
Ottawa, Ontario
K1N 8Y3

Dear Mr. Szocik:

Thank you for your letter dated 10 November. Unfortunately I am not able to clarify or help you regarding the issue in your letter.

Yours sincerely,

J.R. Worthington, MB, ChB, FRCPC
Chief
Department of Emergency Medicine

/hs

I wrote again to Dr Worthington on 9 Sep 1997 having seen a lawyer to pursue the case, but he had nothing further to add.

My First Summons against BBC

On 17 Jan 1997 I wrote a "letter before action" to the BBC, complaining of harassment by BBC newscasters and warning that I would sue the BBC if they did not respond adequately. I sent copies of the letter to Martyn Lewis and Michael Buerk, both of whom had personally spied on me at home while they read the news.

> Viewer and Listener Correspondence
> BBC Villiers House
> The Broadway, Ealing
> London W5 2PA
>
>
> Dear Sirs,
>
> Copies of this letter have also been sent to Martyn Lewis and Michael Buerk.
>
> My reason for writing to you is that I wish to bring a complaint about harassment from the BBC TV News programmes. Since summer 1990 BBC newsreaders have spied on me by looking into my living room at home in Clapham while they read the news. This has formed part of a wider harassment against me, at work and elsewhere. I came to this conclusion both on the basis of facial and verbal expressions of those reading the news in reaction to things happening in my home, and on the basis of other incidents where it was openly stated that this was happening. The actual spying is in my belief carried out by a hitherto unidentified third party, and has occurred in other locations, namely at a neighbour's in Cavendish Road, and in accommodation at Oxford in 1992/93.
>
> You may or may not be aware of some other aspects of the harassment which have been quite unpleasant, namely harassment at my previous and current workplaces by verbatim repetition of phrases spoken at my home and accommodation, harassment in public places by strangers, and harassment during travel by people planted there for that purpose. I believe the current purpose of the harassment is to force me to kill myself to prevent the harassers, yourselves included, from being brought to justice, and last year there were several incidents of people shouting "suicide" at me, which would appear to corroborate that view.
>
> I seek specific answers to the following questions from you;
>
> 1. 1.confirmation or denial to the accusation that you have been watching me (or anyone else) in the manner described at any point during 1990-97;
> 2. if your answer to (1) is a denial, whether you would be willing to make that denial on oath in the form of an affidavit;
> 3. if your answer to (1) is a confirmation, please identify the "unknown third party".
>
> If I do not receive a satisfactory reply to this letter within three weeks of its being sent, ie by Friday 7 February, or if you deny the accusation but decline to do so on oath, then I will issue a summons against you at my local county court (Wandsworth) seeking to compel you to answer the accusation by means of an affidavit.
>
> Yours sincerely,

The BBC informed me that they had spoken to Michael Buerk and Martyn Lewis, and that these two newscasters had categorically denied spying on me. However, the BBC and these two employees have refused to put these denials in writing. Needless to say, I do not accept the denials of the BBC and its employees. I think they are lying. Unfortunately I cannot prove otherwise, and my attempt to "smoke them out" by suing them hit a brick wall.

BBC

6 February 1997
VIEWER & LISTENER INFORMATION

Mr B Szocik
45 Englewood Road
London
SW12 9PA

BRITISH BROADCASTING CORPORATION
VILLIERS HOUSE
THE BROADWAY
EALING
LONDON W5 2PA
TELEPHONE 0161 743 8000

Dear Mr Szocik

Thank you for your letters of 17 January, which have been passed to me for reply.

I am very sorry to hear that you feel your private life is being intruded into, however I can assure you that the BBC would never engage in any form of surveillance activity such as you describe.

Yours sincerely

Beverley Thompson
Viewer & Listener Correspondence

Because the BBC's response was unsatisfactory, in February 1997 I issued proceedings against them for the tort of nuisance, claiming damages.

County Court Summons

(1) Plaintiff's full name address
Boleslaw Tadeusz Szocik
45 Englewood Road
London S.W.12 9PA

(2) Address for sending documents and payments Ref/Tel no.

COPY

(3) Defendant's full name and address Company no.
John Birt, Director-General
BBC Television Centre
London W12 7RJ

Case Number

In the County Court

The court office is open from 10am to 4pm Monday to Friday

Telephone:

seal

This summons is only valid if sealed by the court. If it is not sealed it should be reported to the court.
Keep this summons. You may need to refer to it.

What the plaintiff claims from you

Brief description of type of claim
Nuisance

Particulars of the plaintiff's claim against you

1. On a number of occasions between 1990 and 1997 the BBC TV Newsreaders (including specifically Michael Buerk and Martyn Lewis) spied on me by looking into my living room at my parental home in Clapham while they read the news.

2. The spying caused me to stop watching the television news at home, and therefore caused the tort of private Nuisance, since it interfered with my normal use and enjoyment of my parental home.

3. The spying has also occurred in other locations, namely my accommodations in Oxford during 1992-93, and at a neighbour's house in Cavendish Road, Balham.

4. Plaintiff claims damages for the nuisance suffered limited to 5,000 pounds.

Amount claimed see particulars

Court fee	80
Solicitor's costs	0
Total amount	

Summons issued on

What to do about this summons

You have 21 days from the date of the postmark to reply to this summons
(A limited company served at its registered office has 16 days to reply)
If this summons was delivered by hand, you have 14 days from the date it was delivered to reply

You can
- dispute the claim
- make a claim against the plaintiff
- admit the claim and costs in full and offer to pay
- admit only part of the claim
- pay the total amount shown above

You must read the information on the back of this form. It will tell you more about what to do.

My claim is worth: £5,000 or less ☒   over £5,000 ☐
Total claim over £3,000 and/or damages for personal injury claims over £1,000
I would like my case decided by: trial ☒   arbitration ☐

Signed Plaintiff or plaintiff's solicitor (or see enclosed particulars of claim)
BT Szocik

N2 Default summons (amount not fixed) (Order 3, rule 3(2)(b)) (11.95)   Printed by Satellite Press Limited

Notice of Issue of Default Summons
(amount not fixed)

Plaintiff

B.T. SZOCIK

To the plaintiff('s solicitor)

B.T. SZOCIK
45 ENGLEWOOD ROAD
LONDON
SW12 9PA

In the WANDSWORTH **County Court**

Plaintiff's Ref.	
Date	10 FEB 1997

The court office is open between 10 am and 4 pm Monday to Friday

Please bring this notice with you to court.

Case Number	Defendant(s)	Issue fee	Date of postal service
	B.B.C. TELEVISION CENTRE	50.00	24-2-97

Notes

- The above case(s) was (were) issued today. The defendant has 14 days from the date of service to reply to the summons. If the date of postal service is not shown on this form you will be sent a separate notice of service (Form N222).

  The defendant may either
  - Pay an appropriate amount into court to compensate you. This is called a payment in satisfaction. The court will send you a notice telling you how much has been paid and explaining what you should do next.
  - Dispute your claim. The court will send you a copy of the defence and/or counterclaim and will tell you what to do next.
  - Admit that he should pay you an appropriate amount in compensation but ask for time to pay. The court will send you a copy of the reply and tell you what to do next.
  - Admit liability but make no proposal for payment. The court will send you a copy of the reply and tell you what to do next.
  - Not reply at all. You should wait 14 days from the date of service. You can then ask the court to enter judgment by completing Form N234. If you do not ask for judgment within 12 months of the date of service, the case will be struck out. It cannot be reinstated.

- The summons must be served within 4 months of the date of issue or (6 months if leave to serve out of the jurisdiction is granted under Order 8, rule 2). In exceptional circumstances you may apply for this time to be extended provided that you do so before the summons expires.

- You may be entitled to interest if judgment is entered against the defendant and your claim is for more than £5000.

- Always quote the case number.

Proceedings after judgment

- **You must inform the court IMMEDIATELY** if you receive any payment while a warrant or other enforcement is current and/or before any hearing date

You should keep a record of any payments you receive from the defendant. If there is a hearing or you wish to take steps to enforce the judgment you will need to satisfy the court about the balance outstanding. You should give the defendant a receipt and payment in cash should always be acknowledged. You should tell the defendant how much he owes if he asks.

N205 Notice of issue default summons (amount not fixed) (Order 3, rule (2)(d)(1)) (2.95) Printed by Satellite Press Limited

IN THE WANDSWORTH COUNTY COURT

CASE NO. WT700543

BETWEEN:

BOLESLAW TADEUSZ SZOCIK

Plaintiff

-and-

JOHN BIRT, DIRECTOR GENERAL

Defendant

NOTICE OF APPLICATION

TAKE NOTICE that the Defendant applies for an Order that:-

1. Pursuant to County Court Rules Order 13 rule 5, the Plaintiff's claim against the Defendant be struck out on the grounds that:

    (a) it discloses no reasonable cause of action; and/or
    (b) it is scandalous, frivolous or vexatious

2. The time for serving the Defence be extended until after the hearing of this application.

3. The costs of this application be borne by the Plaintiff in any event.

Counsel will not be attending
Time estimate - 5 minutes

Dated 24 February 1997

Signed *BBC Litigation Dept.*

BBC Litigation Department, BBC White City, 201 Wood Lane, London W12 7TS.
Solicitors for the Defendant.

THIS SECTION WILL BE COMPLETED BY THE COURT

To the Plaintiff

TAKE NOTICE that this Application will be heard by the District Judge

on *Tuesday 6th March* 1997 at *10:00am* o'clock

IF YOU DO NOT ATTEND THE COURT WILL MAKE SUCH ORDER AS IT THINKS FIT

General form of judgment or order	**In the WANDSWORTH County Court**

Plaintiff

BOLESLAW TADEUSZ SZOCIK
45 ENGLEWOOD ROAD
LONDON
SW12 9PA

Case No.	WT700543
Plaintiff	BOLESLAW TADEUSZ SZOCIK
Defendant	JOHN BIRT DIRECTOR GENERAL
Plaintiff's ref.	
Defendant's ref.	EH/LEGAL/RM/3530

Before District Judge WALKER sitting at Wandsworth County Court, 1st Floor Chambers, 76-78 Upper Richmond Road, Putney, London SW15 2SU.

Upon hearing the Plaintiff in person and upon hearing the Defendant's Solicitor

IT IS ORDERED THAT pursuant to County Court Rules, Order 13 Rule 5 the Plaintiff's claim be struck out as disclosing no reasonable cause of action and being scandalous, frivolous and vexatious.

AND IT IS ORDERED THAT there be no order as to costs.

Date Order Made: 6TH MARCH 1997
Order Drawn: 7 March 1997

Defendant

JOHN BIRT DIRECTOR GENERAL
BBC TELEVISION CENTRE
LEGAL DEPT
LONDON
W12 7RJ

The court office at WANDSWORTH COUNTY COURT, 76-78 UPPER RICHMOND ROAD, PUTNEY, LONDON SW15 2SU is open between 10 am and 4 pm Monday to Friday. When corresponding with the court, please address forms or letters to the Chief Clerk and quote the case number. Tel: 0181 333 4351/2

General Form of judgment or order

N24

At the time the Protection from Harassment Act did not yet exist, so I was forced to claim for the tort of private nuisance. The BBC's lawyers cynically sought an order for my action to be struct out as disclosing no reasonable cause of action, and/or being scandalous, frivolous or vexatious. The hearing took place at Wandsworth County Court on 6 Mar 1997. It was an open and shut case; the district judge saw no possibility of my claims being true, and acceded to the BBC's demands to strike out my claim.

My Second Summons against BBC

Instead of appealing the striking out of my first summons, in March 1997 I issued a second, differently worded summons against the BBC. I was encouraged to do this by Usenet participant Paul Janik, who gave me a text to use for a second summons, with the suggestion that it might be more successful than the first. I claimed an injunction to stop the newscaster spying, and minor damages.

County Court Summons

Case Number:

In the County Court

The court office is open from 10am to 4pm Monday to Friday

(1) Plaintiff's full name address
Boleslaw Tadeusz Szocik
45 Englewood Road
London SW12 9PA

(2) Address for sending documents and payments Ref/Tel no.

Telephone:

(3) Defendant's name and address Company no.
Attn: John Birt, Director-General
BBC Television Centre
London W12 7RJ

This summons is only valid if sealed by the court
If it is not sealed it should be reported to the court
Keep this summons. You may need to refer to it

What the plaintiff claims from you

Brief description of type of claim: Nuisance

Particulars of the plaintiff's claim against you

1. The plaintiff is and was at all material times residing at 45 Englewood Road. At some time prior to or during June 1990, persons of unknown identity entered Plaintiff's premises and installed concealed television equipment in said premises.

2. A campaign of harassment was launched against the Plaintiff by the persons of unknown identity, which in part took the form of instigating harassment by BBC TV newscasters (including specifically Michael Buerk and Martyn Lewis) as they read news bulletins, by making direct and personal comments to Plaintiff.

3. The campaign's purpose was to subject Plaintiff to great mental stress and induce mental breakdown. As a result of it Plaintiff did indeed suffer from severe mental strain in 1990-97.

4. In order to avoid the mental strain being caused to him the Plaintiff has been compelled to stop watching BBC TV news. Defendant therefore committed the tort of private nuisance, since normal use of home was interfered with.

5. Plaintiff claims a permanent injunction prohibiting further nuisance, and damages for nuisance suffered limited to £5,000.

My claim is worth: £5,000 or less [ ] over £5,000 [X]

Total claim over £3,000 and/or damages for personal injury claims over £1,000

I would like my case decided by: trial [X] arbitration [ ]

Signed: B Szocik
Plaintiff or plaintiff's solicitor
(or see enclosed particulars of claim)

Amount claimed see particulars	
Court fee	£0
Solicitor's costs	0
Total amount	

Summons issued on

What to do about this summons

You have **21 days** from the date of the postmark to reply to this summons
(A limited company served at its registered office has 16 days to reply)
If this summons was delivered by hand, you have **14 days** from the date it was delivered to reply

You can
- dispute the claim
- make a claim against the plaintiff
- admit the claim and costs in full and offer to pay
- admit only part of the claim
- pay the total amount shown above

You must read the information on the back of this form. It will tell you more about what to do.

Notice of Issue of Default Summons
(amount not fixed)

Plaintiff

BOLESLAN T SZOCIK

To the plaintiff('s ~~solicitor~~)

MR B T SZOCIK
45 ENGLEWOOD ROAD
LONDON SW12 9PA

In the WANDSWORTH **County Court**

Plaintiff's Ref.	—
Date	14 MAR 1997

The court office is open between 10 am and 4 pm Monday to Friday

Please bring this notice with you to court.

Case Number	Defendant(s)	Issue fee	Date of postal service
WT701061	B.B.C TELEVISION CENTRE	£80.00	28-03-97

Notes

- The above case(s) was (were) issued today. The defendant has 14 days from the date of service to reply to the summons. If the date of postal service is not shown on this form you will be sent a separate notice of service (Form N222).

The defendant may either
- Pay an appropriate amount into court to compensate you. This is called a payment in satisfaction. The court will send you a notice telling you how much has been paid and explaining what you should do next.
- Dispute your claim. The court will send you a copy of the defence and/or counterclaim and will tell you what to do next.
- Admit that he should pay you an appropriate amount in compensation but ask for time to pay. The court will send you a copy of the reply and tell you what to do next.
- Admit liability but make no proposal for payment. The court will send you a copy of the reply and tell you what to do next.
- Not reply at all. You should wait 14 days from the date of service. You can then ask the court to enter judgment by completing Form N234. If you do not ask for judgment within 12 months of the date of service, the case will be struck out. It cannot be reinstated.

- The summons must be served within 4 months of the date of issue or (6 months if leave to serve out of the jurisdiction is granted under Order 8, rule 2). In exceptional circumstances you may apply for this time to be extended provided that you do so before the summons expires.

- You may be entitled to interest if judgment is entered against the defendant and your claim is for more than £5000.

- Always quote the case number.

Proceedings after judgment

- You must inform the court IMMEDIATELY if you receive any payment while a warrant or other enforcement is current and/or before any hearing date

You should keep a record of any payments you receive from the defendant. If there is a hearing or you wish to take steps to enforce the judgment you will need to satisfy the court about the balance outstanding. You should give the defendant a receipt and payment in cash should always be acknowledged. You should tell the defendant how much he owes if he asks.

N205 Notice of issue default summons (amount not fixed) (Order 3, rule (2)(d)(1)) (2.95)   Printed by Satellite Press Limited

IN THE WANDSWORTH COUNTY COURT

CASE NO. WT701061

BETWEEN:

BOLESLAW TADEUSZ SZOCIK

Plaintiff

-and-

JOHN BIRT, DIRECTOR GENERAL

Defendant

NOTICE OF APPLICATION

TAKE NOTICE that the Defendant applies for an Order that:-

1. Pursuant to County Court Rules Order 13 rule 5, the Plaintiff's claim against the Defendant be struck out on the grounds that:

    (a) it discloses no reasonable cause of action; and/or
    (b) it is scandalous, frivolous or vexatious

2. The time for serving the Defence be extended until after the hearing of this application.

3. The costs of this application be borne by the Plaintiff in any event.

Counsel will not be attending
Time estimate - 5 minutes

Dated 26 March 1997

Signed

BBC Litigation Department, BBC White City, 201 Wood Lane, London W12 7TS.
Solicitors for the Defendant.

THIS SECTION WILL BE COMPLETED BY THE COURT

To the Plaintiff

TAKE NOTICE that this Application will be heard by the District Judge

on Friday 11th April 1997 at 11:00 am o'clock

IF YOU DO NOT ATTEND THE COURT WILL MAKE SUCH ORDER AS IT THINKS FIT

General form of judgment or order

In the County Court

Case No.	WT701061
Plaintiff	Boleslaw Tadeusz Szocik
Defendant	British Broadcasting Corporation
Plaintiff's ref.	
Defendant's ref.	EH Legal Rm 3530

Plaintiff
Boleslaw Tadeusz Szocik
45 Englewood Road
London SW12 9PA

Before Deputy District Judge Goodchild sitting at

Upon hearing the Plaintiff in person and Upon Hearing the Defendant's Representative

IT IS ORDERED THAT
1. Pursuant to County Court Rules Order 13 rule 5, the Plaintiff's claim against the Defendant be struck out on the grounds that: It discloses no reasonable cause of action
2. The time for serving the Defence be extended until after the hearing of this Application
3. The costs of this Application be borne by the Plaintiff in any event
4. No further proceedings to be issued by the Petitioner against these Defendant's without leave of the Court

Date Order Made: 11 April 1997
Order Drawn: 23 April 1997

Defendant
British Broadcasting Corporation
Litigation Department
White City
201 Wood Lane
London
W12 7TS

The court office at is open between 10 am and 4 pm Monday to Friday. When corresponding with the court, please address forms or letters to the Chief Clerk and quote the case number. Tel:

General Form of judgment or order

N24(A)

Again the BBC applied to have my claim struck out, and again they succeeded. The hearing was on 11 Apr 1997 and one part of the order was to prevent me from suing the BBC again without permission of the court. I do not know if this order had legal validity, because I sued as a litigant in person without legal expertise. The BBC got what they wanted and I was very disappointed. The district judge explained she was making the order to save me money, because each time I sued it cost a fixed sum of £ 80, although the BBC did not seek to recover their costs from me. She suggested that for the action to go ahead I would need some material evidence, such as a tape recording showing a newscaster reacting to what they saw in my house.

Paul Janik was friendly with police and claimed to be in contact with a security service agent. His real motive in encouraging me to sue again was revealed a few days later. I contemporaneously brought a complaint against MI5 to the Security Service Tribunal, who gave my details to MI5, as listed elsewhere on this website. A few days after MI5 got my name Janik posted my name, home address in London and phone number to an internet newsgroup, with the intention of silencing further complaints. It is still in the Google archive. He claimed he got my details from the BBC, but the BBC's solicitor Emma Hovanassian, who dealt with the case and attended both hearings, said Janik had phoned her anonymously, claiming that he was also in legal action with me (which he was not), and she confirmed my name to him, but he already had my name from another source which he did not disclose, which was obviously the security service seeking to silence me.

A letter from MI5

I wrote to the Security Service stating that I wished to bring a complaint against their activities in my life. Here is their reply; "if you believe you have been the subject of inquiries by the Security Service or that the Security Service has done anything else in relation to you or your property, you may wish to apply to the Security Service Tribunal who are able to pursue these points on your behalf."

>
> PO BOX 3255
> LONDON
> SW1P 1AE
>
> B T Szocik
> 45 Englewood Road
> London
> SW12 9PA
>
> 26 February 1997
>
> Dear Mr/Ms Szocik
>
> Thank you for your letter dated 18 February 1997 which has been forwarded to me for a reply.
>
> If you believe you have been the subject of inquiries by the Security Service or that the Security Service has done anything else in relation to you or your property, you may wish to apply to the Security Service Tribunal who are able to pursue these points on your behalf. I am enclosing a leaflet which explains the complaints procedure and provides an address to which you can direct your concerns.
>
> I hope this may be of some assistance.
>
> Yours sincerely
>
> T Denham
>
> T Denham
> for the Director General

Please see further items for replies from the Security Service Tribunal, and Interception of Communications Tribunal.

Security Service Tribunal Denies

In June 1997 the Security Service Tribunal wrote to me regarding the complaint I had brought against MI5 in February. They say,

```
The Security Service Tribunal have now investigated your complaint and
have asked me to inform you that no determination in your favour has
been made on your complaint.
```

The Security Service Tribunal

PO Box 18
London SE1 0TZ
Telephone: 0171-273 4095

Mr B T Szocik
45 Englewood Road
London SW12 9PA

Our reference: SST/97/01
Date: 2 June 1997

Dear Mr Szocik

I write in connection with your complaint dated 28 February which I acknowledged on 13 March 1997.

The Security Service Tribunal have now investigated your complaint and have asked me to inform you that no determination in your favour has been made on your complaint.

Yours sincerely

E R Wilson
Tribunal Secretary

Again, I do not believe their denials. I think MI5 <u>has</u> taken the action against me as described, and is refusing to admit what they have done. To the best of my knowledge, the Security Service Tribunal has <u>never</u> found in favour of a complainant. This tends to strongly suggest that MI5 lies on a routine basis, and the Tribunal can't fulfil its functions in the face of Security Service falsehoods.

Interception of Communications Tribunal Denies

In May 1997 the Interception of Communications Tribunal wrote to me regarding the complaint I had brought in February. They say,

```
The Interception of Communications Tribunal have now considered your
application carefully and have asked me to inform you that their
investigation into the matters you raised has satisfied them that there
has been no contravention of Sections 2 to 5 of the Interception of
Communications Act 1985 in relation to a relevant warrant or relevant
certificate.
```

The Interception of Communications Tribunal

PO Box 12376
London SW1P 1XU

Telephone: 0171-273 4096

Mr B T Szocik
45 Englewood Road
London SW12 9PA

Our reference: ICT/97/06
Date: 7 May 1997

Dear Mr Szocik

I write in connection with your application dated 18 February which was acknowledged on 21 February 1997.

The Interception of Communications Tribunal have now considered your application carefully and have asked me to inform you that their investigation into the matters you raised has satisfied them that there has been no contravention of Sections 2 to 5 of the Interception of Communications Act 1985 in relation to a relevant warrant or relevant certificate.

Yours sincerely

E R Wilson
Tribunal Secretary

Rubbish. They're bugging my house and they won't admit it. The ICT and SST are a sham.

Gagged by BBC Ariel's editor

On 25 June 1997 I wrote to Landmark Publishing Services, who deal with advertising for the BBC's in-house magazine Ariel. I requested they run an advert "BBC Newsreaders Spying on my Home" in the Personal column. They accepted my instructions and payment, and the following advert did indeed run in Ariel's issue of 8 July 1997.

Personal

BBC Newsreaders Spying on my home
http://www.pair.com/spook/

Following the successful placement of this small ad, I wrote again to Landmark on 17 July 1997, requesting they run exactly the same advert for 10 issues, enclosing payment. Unfortunately, the advert did not appear in any further issues of Ariel, because Ariel's editor Robin Reynolds nixed it. Here is an email from Elaine Smith of Landmark dated 26 August 1997.

```
With regard to your E-mail of 22 August 1997 concerning your advertisement in
the Ariel magazine.

I was instructed by Ariel to remove your advertisement from the classified
pages as they were not comfortable with the contents of the Internet address
you supplied. I realise we have placed the advertisement successfully for you
in the past. Unfortunately this time they decided they did not want it
printed.

[snip]

I'm really sorry for the inconvenience I know this will have caused you, but
as you will understand Ariel have the last say in what is printed and what is
not.

Kind Regards

Elaine Smith
Classified Advertising Manager.
```

In my reply to Elaine Smith, I said;

```
I will speak to them directly, I believe their email address is Ariel@bbc.co.uk. As you say, if the
advert went through the first time, then it should have gone through this time without problems. As
I see it, either what is on the website is true (which is my belief) in which case they should
allow it to be published, or else it is symptomatic of delusions in which case again any reasonable
person would recognise it as such and its publication would not be suppressed. After all Britain is
not supposed to have censorship - it isn't a Communist country.
```

I also wrote to Mr Reynolds, Ariel's editor, asking him to reconsider his decision to censor my advert. He replied with the following letter;

BBC

ARIEL
BBC STAFF MAGAZINE

BRITISH BROADCASTING CORPORATION
HENRY WOOD HOUSE
3 & 6 LANGHAM PLACE
LONDON W1A 1AA
TELEPHONE 071-765 3623
FAX 071-765 3646

Mr. B.T Szocik
Apt 407. 145 York Street
Ottawa
Ont KIN 8Y3
Canada

September 26 1997

Dear Mr Szocik

Thank you for your interest in advertising in Ariel. I regret to say that having seen your advertisement in our July 8 issue, and having visited your Web site, I do not believe this is an appropriate notice for the Personal column of a staff publication.

Yours sincerely

Robin Reynolds
Editor

Since a magazine's editor has final say over what appears in the publication, there is nothing further that I can do to encourage Ariel to accept my advert. Mr Reynold's censorship of my legitimate complaint gives the game away a bit, though. The BBC wish people to think of them as truthful and impartial - yet when they are caught harassing one of their audience, they resort to the same censoring tactics characteristic of the regimes they hypocritically condemn.

PRIVATE EYE

Eye Say, and Lord Gnome Answers

My interactions with Private Eye started in May 1995, shortly after I'd started bleating on usenet. I tried to get the Eye interested in my case, as I thought they more than anyone have their finger on the pulse, and would surely already know something about my case. In my first email to them, entitled "pas de bouteille?" (wot no bottle?), I asked if they had the nerve to publish what was known to many thousands of people. Their email flunky answered;

```
Date: Thu, 11 May 95 13:40 BST-1
From: strobes@cix.compulink.co.uk (Private Eye)
Subject: Re: pas de bouteille?

In-Reply-To:
Bottle? Dunno really - but I've passed your mail on to the Ed for his consideration.

Steve Mann
(strobes)
===========================================================
Date: Mon, 15 May 95 12:51 BST-1
From: strobes@cix.compulink.co.uk (Private Eye)
Subject: Re: hello again

In-Reply-To:
Hello yourself...

Thanks for the email. Unfortunately, I can't say whether or not the Eye will do anything with
this... I'm only the messenger. As the only computer-literate peron in the Gnome organisation, I
get to read all the email and then pass it on to the Editor.

Sorry -- not very helpful, I know.

Steve Mann
(strobes)
```

The following year I gave PE another little prod, which yielded the following;

```
Date: Tue, 13 Feb 96 11:38 GMT
From: strobes@cix.compulink.co.uk (Private Eye Magazine)
Subject: Re: Previous communication

In-Reply-To:
Sorry not to reply sooner... we've been swamped with email and I have very little time to answer
it.

However, the editor sees all the email received here and I'm afraid he hasn't expressed an interest
in your story so I can only assume that he feels it isn't for us.

Sorry.
Strobes
```

Given that I couldn't provide the evidence to persuade the Eye of the credibility of my claims, I did the next best thing, which was to take out classified adverts in their "Eye Say" and "Eye Tech" columns. My motivation for doing so is obvious; the Eye is read both by many thousands of ordinary folk, but also makes its way into the homes and consciousness of the UK's political and media elite. It is also a known favourite with "Five". What better way of taking the fight to the enemy?

The first small ad appeared on 10 Jan 1997 in issue 915 in "Eye Say". It ran in that column on 24/1/97 and 7/2/97. On 21/2/97 it ran in "Eye Tech", and on 7/3/97 and 21/3/97 again in "Eye Say".

I then changed the ad's wording to read "BBC Newsreaders Conspiracy", and the new wording ran in "Eye Say" from 4/4/97 issue 921, 18/4/97 to 2/5/97. The word "xenophobic" in the first advert had been intended to convey the sense of exclusion through the bigotry of my enemies, both on the basis of race and mental condition, but it seemed a bit too non-specific. "BBC Newscasters Conspiracy" was a little more immediate, although readers had to actually wade through the website to find out what it was that the newscasters were conspiring to do.

My next effort tried to spice up the text. "MI5/BBC Conspiracy" ran for six issues in "Eye Say", from 5/9/97 issue 931 until 31/10/97. I suppose there is something a little sad about somebody who knows he has mental illness, placing adverts about a conspiracy in which MI5's watchers enable BBC newscasters to personally and directly communicate with him while reading the news. It is pretty sad, but unfortunately it is also true, both in the objective reality we all inhabit, as well as in my own mind.

There followed a hiatus of about a year until I resumed advertising on 2 October 1998. I paid over £200 for six months advertising of the new improved text "MI5 Persecution, BBC Newscasters Spying on my Home". This text ran from issue 960 until issue 972 (19 March 1999) in "Eye Say".

Private Eye's editor Ian Hislop denies knowing anything about my case, as the following email illustrates.

```
Date: Tue, 3 Nov 1998 14:10 +0000 (GMT Standard Time)
From: strobes@private-eye.co.uk (Private Eye)

Sorry to take so long to answer. As soon as the editor
returned from holiday Steve went away. Steve is still away and so I am answering your letter.

I have asked the editor and he knows nothing about any conspiracy between MI5 and the BBC.

Hope this helps.

Mary Aylmer
Private Eye
```

I must say I'm quite surprised he knows nothing; the "Eye" is usually well clued up on what's going on.

Bindman and Partners, Solicitors

As early as the start of 1995 I was in communication with a local lawyer to attempt to identify the "persecutors". In January 1996, on the advice of my psychiatrist, I wrote to Robin Lewis at the well-known London firm of Bindman and Partners. My doctor told me another of his patients was being represented by this firm, and described them as the "underdogs' solicitor".

My three-page letter to Mr Lewis (dated 23 January 1996) went into quite a lot of detail about what had happened at my former employers in Oxford in 1992, and the external-to-the-company stimulus to that harassment. I also described the BA incident in June 1993, and suggested that Mr Lewis's firm could represent me in a legal action, either against my former employers, or against one of the organisations which had been molesting me.

Bindman & Partners
SOLICITORS

275 Gray's Inn Road · London · WC1X 8QF
DX 37904 King's Cross · Telephone 0171-833 4433 · Fax 0171-837 9792

Mr B T Szocik
9 Auriga Drive
Nepean
Ontario K2E 7T9
CANADA

Your reference:
Our reference: **119/RL/LD**
Date: **30 January, 1996**

Dear Mr Szocik

Thank you for your letter of January 23rd which I have read with great care. I regret that I am unable to assist or advise you. I return your papers. There is no fee for my advice and I also return your cheque.

Yours sincerely

ROBIN LEWIS

Encs

PARTNERS
Geoffrey Bindman · Felicity Crowther · Stephen Grosz · Robin Lewis · Naomi Angell · Claire Fazan
Katherine Gieve · Neil O'May · Saimo Chahal · Adrian Clarke · Michael Schwarz · Alison Stanley

ASSISTANT SOLICITORS
Sue James · Judi Kemish · Jon Nicholson · Desmond O'Donnell · Margaret Pedler
Sharon Persaud · Clive Romain

Barristers: Caroline Bates · Caroline Hallissey
Immigration Adviser: Graham Smith · Partnership Manager: Madeline Russell

Regulated by the Law Society under the Financial Services Act 1986

Bindman & Partners
SOLICITORS

275 Gray's Inn Road · London · WC1X 8QF
DX 37904 King's Cross · Telephone 0171-833 4433 · Fax 0171-837 9792

Mr B T Szocik
9 Auriga Drive
Nepean Ont K2E 7T9
CANADA

Your reference:
Our reference: **MISC/RL/LD**
Date: **21 February, 1996**

Dear Mr Szocik

I am sorry that you found my letter of January 30th brusque and insulting. I can assure you that neither was my intention. I am not able to assist you in the matters of which you complain. I return your letters and cheque. I am afraid that I must now regard this correspondence as closed.

Yours sincerely

ROBIN LEWIS

Encs

PARTNERS
Geoffrey Bindman · Felicity Crowther · Stephen Grosz · Robin Lewis · Naomi Angell · Claire Fazan
Katherine Gieve · Neil O'May · Saimo Chahal · Adrian Clarke · Michael Schwarz · Alison Stanley

ASSISTANT SOLICITORS
Sue James · Judi Kemish · Jon Nicholson · Desmond O'Donnell · Margaret Pedler
Sharon Persaud · Clive Romain

Barristers: Caroline Bates · Caroline Hallissey
Immigration Adviser: Graham Smith · Partnership Manager: Madeline Russell

Regulated by the Law Society under the Financial Services Act 1986

Bindman & Partners
SOLICITORS

275 Gray's Inn Road · London · WC1X 8QF
DX 37904 King's Cross · Telephone 0171-833 4433 · Fax 0171-837 9792

Mr B T Szocik
9 Auriga Drive
Nepean Ont K2E 7TP
CANADA

Your reference:
Our reference: **MISC/RL/LD**
Date: **7 March, 1996**

Dear Mr Szocik

I write to you for the third and last time to tell you that I will not accept your instructions. I return, for the third time, your papers and your cheque for £50 and if you wish to write to me again you may do so, but I will not reply. Our correspondence is now at an end.

Yours sincerely

ROBIN LEWIS

Enc

PARTNERS
Geoffrey Bindman · Felicity Crowther · Stephen Grosz · Robin Lewis · Naomi Angell · Claire Fazan
Katherine Gieve · Neil O'May · Saimo Chahal · Adrian Clarke · Michael Schwarz · Alison Stanley

ASSISTANT SOLICITORS
Sue James · Judi Kemish · Jon Nicholson · Desmond O'Donnell · Margaret Pedler
Sharon Persaud · Clive Romain

Barristers: *Caroline Bates · Caroline Hallissey*
Immigration Adviser: *Graham Smith* · Partnership Manager: *Madeline Russell*

Regulated by the Law Society under the Financial Services Act 1986

Bindman & Partners
SOLICITORS

275 Gray's Inn Road · London · WC1X 8QF
DX 37904 King's Cross · Telephone 0171-833 4433 · Fax 0171-837 9792

B T Szocik
45 Englewood Road
London SW12 9PA

Your reference:
Our reference: **NB/AdM**
Date: **26 May, 1999**

Dear Mr Szocik

Thank you for your letter of 25 May 1999. I regret that I am unable to help you at this time.

Yours sincerely

NICK BRAITHWAITE

Robin Lewis's reply was brief in the extreme, and is reproduced on the first page of this multipage document. My reply (dated 11 February 1996) said I was "disappointed to receive your insultingly brusque reply to my letter and would ask you to look again at the matter." To which Mr Lewis replied as shown on the second page of the document. I wrote to him again on 29 February 1996; his reply is on the third page, that he will not communicate further. On 29 March 1996, and again on 21 April 1996, I did again write to Robin Lewis, but he did not reply.

Three years later, on 25 May 1999, I again wrote to Bindmans, following a referral from MIND's legal department. Again I wrote, this time to Nick Braithwaite, with a detailed statement; and again they sent a reply terse to the point of rudeness, shown on the fourth page. On the phone I suggested to Mr Braithwaite that his refusal to take my instructions was due to prejudice against the mentally ill. He spluttered and coughed, and said words to the effect that he usually found that a mentally ill person's complaint would be a product of their delusion.

At the time of writing (April 2000) I have completely given up on the "lawyer option", having tried and failed repeatedly to secure the assistance of the legal profession.

Counter-surveillance sweep by Nationwide Investigations Group

In July 1994 the private detective agency Nationwide Investigations Group conducted an electronic counter-surveillance sweep of my parents' home in London. They checked for radio transmitter devices, and tested the telephone line for attached bugs. They found nothing.

I am afraid that I was unsurprised at their not finding any evidence of covert surveillance. It had been made very clear to me, particularly during 1990-92, that audio, and almost certainly video, surveillance of my parents' home was taking place. But this would not have been made quite so obvious unless the persecutors were confident of their apparatus being undetectable using the technology the police, or a private agency like Nationwide, would be using.

I don't know very much about the surveillance technology that has been used against me, but I understand that devices can be built which switch off on receiving a coded command, and may switch on again after a counter-surveillance sweep has completed; that devices may rapidly alter the frequency of transmission, "frequency-hopping" devices which presumably cannot be detected in a sequential scan of the sort employed by Nationwide; and of course "probe" microphones can be inserted "through-the-wall", although I hesitate to believe our neighbours would permit this.

Our Ref: JW/SF/SE9988
Date: 15th July 1994

Mr B T Szocik
45 Englewood Road
London SW12

Dear Sirs,

RE: ELECTRONIC SWEEP

In accordance with your instructions dated the 12th July 1994 we report as follows.

On Tuesday the 14th July 1994 an agent of this Company departed our offices attending at 45 Englewood Road, London SW12.

Upon arrival our agent carried out an electronic sweep with the use of a Professional 5000 multi-scanner, CCL UHf scanner and a the Guideline telephone tap detector.

Having carried out a thorough ssweep of the premises and the telephone system we are pleased to report that nothing untoward was located.

We trust this information is of some reassurance to you and if we can be of any further help in this or any other matter, please do not hesitate to contact the writer.

Assuring you of our best attention at all times.

Yours faithfully
NATIONWIDE INVESTIGATIONS

JASON WOODCOCK

We paid Nationwide £411.25 (including VAT) for the surveillance sweep, which took them about an hour and a half to complete, using a "Professional 5000 multi-scanner, CCL UHF scanner and Guideline telephone tap detector." As I said above, I don't know very much about these things, so I can't comment on the capabilities or otherwise of this equipment. But clearly the "watchers" are using technology which in 1994 was beyond the detection capabilities of a good private detective agency.

Home Office MI5 Liaison won't comment

I wrote to Jack Straw, Home Secretary, in early 1999, following an article in the Times in which he spoke of his "close monitoring" of the Security Service. My letter asked him if he had "authorised any surveillance or harassment actions against me". He didn't reply himself, but passed on my request to the Home Office's Organised and International Crime Directorate (how appropriate for an international master criminal like myself), and specifically their Intelligence and Security Liaison Unit. They first made a fairly vacuous response; after further prodding, they made a further response, shown here.

HOME OFFICE
Organised and International Crime Directorate
Intelligence and Security Liaison Unit
50 Queen Anne's Gate, London SW1H 9AT

Switchboard: 0171 273 3000

Mr B T Szocik
45 Englewood Road
LONDON
SW12 9PA

1 March 1999

Dear Mr Szocik

Thank you for your letter dated 23 February.

It has been the policy of successive Governments neither to comment on the operations of the Security Service nor to reveal whether they hold information about particular individuals or organisations. To depart from this policy would risk disclosing information that would undermine the Service's effectiveness and this would not be in the public interest. I regret therefore that we are unable to confirm or deny whether you have been the subject of investigation by the Service or that any information is held on you.

If you feel that your communications have been intercepted you may wish to write to the Interception of Communications Tribunal on the attached leaflet.

Yours sincerely

Administrative Officer

So there you are. Zip the lips, lie low and say nuthin. Open government? That'll be the day.

Communications with Security Service Tribunal in 1999

I took some more potshots at the SS-Tribunal in the first half of 1999. The correspondence between myself and the Tribunal Secretary is detailed on this webpage. Ultimately I decided not to pursue another complaint with them, partly from Robin Ramsay's advice (and that of a solicitor I consulted), but mostly because it was rather obvious from Mr Brooks' replies that the Tribunal has no investigative means of its own and is that useless animal, a toothless watchdog.

The Security Service Tribunal

PO Box 18
London SE1 0TZ
Telephone: 0171-273 4095

Mr B T Szocik
45 Englewood Road
LONDON
SW12 9PA

Your reference:

Our reference:

Date: 19 March 1999

Dear Mr Szocik

Further to our telephone conversation today I am pleased to enclose a copy of the leaflet entitled "Complaints against the Security Service". As you will see the leaflet explains the various matters which the Security Service Tribunal may investigate. If you wish to make a complaint you should complete and sign the tear-off section of the leaflet and return it to me at the above address.

I hope you will find this helpful.

Yours sincerely

N Brooks
Tribunal Secretary

Included with this first letter was a copy of the leaflet, "Complaints about the Security Service". This tells you that the Tribunal can order "the service to end its inquiries about you; the service to destroy any records it holds about those inquiries; the quashing of a property warrant; financial compensation". Yeah, right. Look, there's a flying pig, oink-flap, oink-flap.

The Security Service Act 1989

The Security Service Act 1989 commenced on 18 December 1989. It placed the Security Service on a statutory basis and introduced a way to complain about the Service. The Intelligence Services Act 1994 and the Security Service Act 1996 make some changes to the 1989 Act. The relevant provisions of the three Acts are given below. The main points of the 1989 Act are:

1. The functions of the Security Service

The functions of the Security Service are:
- to protect national security, in particular from espionage, terrorism, sabotage and agents of foreign powers;
- to safeguard the economic well-being of the United Kingdom against external threats; and,
- to act in support of the police and other law enforcement agencies in preventing and detecting serious crime.

2. Controls

The Director General of the Security Service, who is appointed by the Home Secretary, must make sure that the Service only obtains information which it needs to carry out its functions and that information is only disclosed for that reason, or for the purpose of criminal proceedings.

The Home Secretary must approve the provisions which allow the Security Service to disclose information which may be used to decide whether someone should be employed, or continue to be employed ('vetting information').

The Secretary of State may also issue specific ('property warrants') which authorise actions relating to property.

3. The Commissioner

The 1989 Act established the Commissioner: a senior judge, independent of the Government, who keeps under review the issue of property warrants and may assist the complaints Tribunal.

4. Establishment of an independent Tribunal

The 1989 Act established a Tribunal comprising senior members of the legal profession. The Tribunal is independent of the Government. Any person can complain to the Tribunal about anything they believe that the Security Service has done to them or to their property.

That person can be an individual or an organisation and a complaint about a person's property may include the place where they live or work.

5. How to apply to the Tribunal

You can apply to the Tribunal for them to investigate whether the Security Service has acted against you or your property, or given vetting information about you to your employer or to someone to whom you have applied for a job.

You should apply on the form attached to this leaflet. Remember, **you must sign the form** and any other document you have prepared as part of your complaint. The Tribunal can only investigate questions relating to the actions of the Security Service.

- Complaints about the interception of communications (postal or telecommunications) entrusted to the Post Office or to a UK public telecommunication system should be addressed to the Interception of Communications Tribunal, PO Box 12376, London SW1P 1XU.
- Complaints about the Secret Intelligence Service and GCHQ, who provide intelligence or perform tasks relating to the actions or intentions of persons outside the British Islands, should be addressed to the Intelligence Services Tribunal, PO Box 4823, London SW1A 9XD.

6. What the Tribunal can do

The Tribunal cannot investigate complaints which relate to actions by the Security Service which took place prior to 18 December 1989, unless the actions were continuing on that date.

When you have lodged your complaint with the Tribunal, they will find out if the Security Service has made you the subject of its inquiries.

If it has, and these inquiries are continuing at the time of your complaint, the Tribunal will determine whether the Service has reasonable grounds for continuing them.

If the inquiries have stopped, they will determine whether there were reasonable grounds for starting them.

If your complaint concerns the disclosure of vetting information, the Tribunal will also establish whether the Service has disclosed such information and, if so, whether the Service had reasonable grounds for believing the information disclosed was true.

If your complaint refers to action against your property, the Tribunal will refer the complaint to the Commissioner.

The Commissioner is required to investigate whether a warrant has been issued under the Intelligence Services Act 1994 against your property and, if one has been issued, to review the Secretary of State's exercise of the power to issue it. The Commissioner will inform the Tribunal of his conclusions.

The Tribunal and Commissioner have full powers to call on any official documents or information they need. To determine whether the Security Service has taken any action against you, or your property, the Tribunal will need to disclose to the Service your full name, date of birth and any address relevant to your complaint. By completing the attached form you are consenting to such disclosures.

Your application will be handled in confidence. A complainant to the Tribunal will not be at risk of prosecution under the Official Secrets Acts in respect of any disclosure of information made to the Tribunal.

7. The outcome of the Tribunal investigation

The Tribunal will advise you as soon as possible of their conclusions.

If the Tribunal or in a case concerning yourself, the Commissioner find in your favour, the Tribunal will notify you and a report will be made of their findings to the Commissioner and to the Secretary of State. They may also order one or more of the following courses of action:
- the Service to end its inquiries about you;
- the Service to destroy any records it holds about those inquiries;
- the quashing of a property warrant;
- financial compensation.

If the Tribunal or Commissioner do not find in your favour, the Tribunal are not permitted to disclose whether the Service has taken any action concerning you, or your property. You will be advised simply that the Tribunal have not found in your favour.

8. Application form

You may ask your solicitor or other adviser to apply on your behalf, but **you must sign the form** and any other document you have prepared as part of your complaint.

Published by Home Office Communication Directorate 1998. HOME/J671411/J

My subsequent letter to Nick Brooks, Tribunal Secretary, dated 25 March 1999, said;

Dear Mr Brooks,

We spoke on the phone last week and you kindly sent a copy of the form, "Complaints about the Security Service".

I have a few questions which I should like to ask you, before I undertake the task of making a formal complaint. As you know I made a complaint in February 1997, and in June of that year the tribunal made a bland and unsatisfactory statement that "no determination in your favour has been made on your complaint". During our phone conversation I expressed the view that the Tribunal was incapable of performing its functions and acts as a whitewashing body for the Security Service. My questions are as follows;

(1)   Has the Security Service Tribunal ever during its existence found in favour of a compaint against MI5?

(2)   Is the Tribunal able to disclose whether "no determination in your favour" is made because MI5 claims to have no inquiries on a subject, or whether it is made because MI5 admits to actions against a subject but claims justification?

If disclosure is not possible for individual cases, then in 1997 for how many cases (out of what total) did MI5 claim justification?

(3)   Is the Tribunal able to investigate information such as British Airways passenger lists, given that these could conclusively prove MI5 involvement? Would the Tribunal be forced to rely on MI5 to carry out such investigations, or would it have some other means of investigating? It might look slightly ridiculous for the Tribunal to rely on MI5 to investigate their own misdeeds.

When I made my previous complaint to the Tribunal in 1997 I gave very little information as to the nature of my complaint. This time I intend to give as complete information as possible; but before I do so, I would ask you to answer the questions above, to outline the "ground rules" for a Tribunal investigation and reporting of its results.

Yours sincerely,

Mr Brooks replied by sending me a photocopy of two pages from the 1997 Report of the Security Service Commissioner, as follows.

The Security Service Tribunal

PO Box 18
London SE1 0TZ
Telephone: 0171-273 4095

Mr B T Szocik
45 Englewood Road
LONDON
SW12 9PA

Your reference:

Our reference:

Date: 6 April 1999

Dear Mr Szocik

I refer to your letter of 25 March to the Security Service Tribunal.

You ask a number of questions regarding the Security Service Tribunal. I enclose a relevant extract of the 1997 Report of the Security Service Commissioner, the Rt Hon Lord Justice Stuart-Smith which may be of interest. This Report was laid before Parliament by the Prime Minister in July 1998. You will note from this extract that Tribunal investigations seek to determine whether the Security Service has made an individual the subject of inquiries and if so, whether there were reasonable grounds for starting or continuing such inquiries in discharging the Service's functions. This extract also explains the notification of Tribunal decisions.

You indicate your intention to submit detailed information for the Tribunal's investigation. I should stress that you had the opportunity to submit such supporting information when you initially complained to the Tribunal in 1997. The Tribunal will only normally re-open an investigation if significant additional information is provided. Upon receipt I will, therefore, submit any supporting information you provide to the Tribunal to determine whether they are content to re-open an investigation into your concerns.

Yours sincerely

N Brooks
Tribunal Secretary

The photocopied pages from the 1997 Report follow.

21. At present while the Act is not yet in force, the police do not use their power under the 1984 Home Office Guidelines in counter-terrorism cases; they take the view, rightly in my opinion, that this is a matter for the Security Service. I hope that this will continue to be the case when the Police Act comes into force on 1st April 1998. There is provision under section 101 of the Police Act for the Secretary of State to issue a code of practice in connection with the performance of functions under the Act. It may be that this is a matter which could be addressed in the Code of Practice.

The Security Service Tribunal

22. Any person may complain to the Tribunal if they are aggrieved by anything which they believe the Service has done in relation to them or their property. Unless the Tribunal consider the complaint to be frivolous or vexatious, they must investigate it to ascertain if the complainant has been the subject of inquiries by the Service. If such enquiries are or have been made, the Tribunal must determine whether the Service had reasonable grounds for making or continuing the inquiries about the complainant in discharging its functions. If the complainant alleges that the Service has disclosed information for use in determining whether he should be employed, or continue to be employed, by any person or in any office or capacity, the Tribunal must investigate whether the Service has disclosed information for that purpose and if so, whether it has reasonable grounds for believing the information to be true. (Schedule 1, paragraphs 1 to 3).

23. Where the complainant alleges that anything has been done by the Service to his property, the Tribunal must refer the complaint to me and I have to ascertain whether a warrant has been issued in respect of property. If it has, then I must determine, applying the principles applied by a court on an application for judicial review, whether the Secretary of State was acting properly in issuing or renewing the warrant (Schedule 1, paragraph 4).

24. Where the Tribunal make a finding in favour of the complainant, they must notify him of the fact and make a report of their findings to the Secretary of State and to me. If I make a determination in favour of the complainant the Tribunal must notify him of this fact. It will be observed that the complainant will not know, if his complaint is rejected, whether no enquiries have been made or nothing has been done to his property, or whether the Tribunal or Commissioner were satisfied that any action taken was justified. In fact the 1989 Act does not permit the Tribunal to elaborate further or disclose whether the Security Service had taken any action against a complainant. Schedule 1 paragraph 5(3) to the Act, provides that "where in the case of any complaint no such determination . . . . is made by the Tribunal or the Commissioner the Tribunal shall give notice to the Complainant that no determination in his favour has been made on his complaint." Furthermore paragraph 4(2) of Schedule 2 of the Act provides that ". . . . the Tribunal shall not, except in reports under paragraph 5(1)(b) of Schedule 1 to this Act, give any reasons for a determination notified by them to a complainant." The ambiguity of the terms in which the notification of the Tribunal's decision is expressed is intentional. If the Tribunal were able to advise a complainant that he or she had not been the subject of Security Service interest, silence or any equivocal answer on another occasion might be interpreted as implying that Security Service activity had taken place. Indeed if legitimate targets, for example terrorists or organised drugs traffickers, were able to circumvent the system by establishing that they were the subject of surveillance by the Service they would be able take effective action to avoid detection which would without doubt increase the threat to life and serious damage to property.

25. Since the Tribunal was established on 18 December 1989 it has considered 275 complaints. 13 cases were still under investigation at 31 December 1997. It will be noted that in all cases neither the Tribunal nor myself have found in the favour of any complainant. A substantial number of complaints made could well have been regarded as frivolous and vexatious and thus not investigated. Since, however, the investigation of such complaints is relatively straight forward the Tribunal have erred on the side of caution and accepted them rather than reject them on this basis. Of the total number of complaints received enquiries made by the Tribunal have revealed that in 36 cases the complainants were the subject of a personal file in the Security Service and 70 cases where the applicant had corresponded with the Service or had been the subject of a vetting disclosure. In some of these cases the action took place prior to the commencement of the 1989 Act but the Service, as a matter of good practice, always disclose any information they hold or have held.

26. Since 1989 I have considered 108 applications in which the complainant has alleged that their property has been interfered with. One was still under investigation at 31 December 1997. Of this total my enquiries have established that in one case only a warrant had been issued.

27. This might lead some to speculate that members of the Service are carrying out operations involving unlawful interference with property, such as the installation of eavesdropping equipment, without first obtaining a warrant from the Home Secretary. Whilst I am not in a position to answer the question categorically, because it is not my function to review operations, from my experience as Commissioner over the past eight years I think I can say that this is not true. I am firmly of this opinion because I have seen the tight managerial control exercised over these types of operations and this together with the technical complexities of some of the operations make it impossible to conceal such activity from management or colleagues. Indeed these operations take considerable time to plan, implement and monitor; an officer's unauthorised action could not go unnoticed. Finally, if the target is a legitimate one within the functions of the Service, then there should be no difficulty in obtaining a warrant.

Investigation of complaints

28. The following information is relevant to the complaints received and investigated by the Tribunal during the year:

Complaints received in 1997	45
Complaints received and investigated during 1997	32
Complaints investigated in 1997 which had been received in 1996	8
Complaints outstanding on 31 December 1997	13

29. No determination has been made in favour of a complainant.

Complaints in relation to property

30. The following information relates to complaints received by the Tribunal which related to property and which were referred to me:

Complaints received and determined during 1997	14
Complaints received in 1997 but not yet determined	1
Complaints received in 1996 and determined in 1997	0

31. I have made no determination in favour of a complainant in those cases completed in 1997.

In particular, the answers the report gives to my questions are; the Security Service Tribunal has NEVER found in favour of a complainant; see sections 29 and 31 of the scanned report. Nick Brooks has confirmed orally over the phone that he has no memory of the Tribunal ever finding in favour of a complainant.

Secondly, the question of whether the Tribunal is able to disclose "no determination in your favour" is because MI5 claims to have no inquiries on a subject, or whether it's because MI5 admits to having inquiries but claims they are justified. The answer to this one is in section 24, which says the ambiguity is intentional; and the Tribunal will in no circumstances give an unambiguous answer of whether MI5 claims or disclaims inquiries on a subject.

In section 27 of the report, SS Commissioner Lord Justice Stuart-Smith says the blanket denials "might lead some to speculate that members of the service are carrying out operations involving unlawful interference with property, such as the installation of eavesdropping equipment, without first obtaining a warrant from the Home Secretary." He goes on to try to deny this speculation. But we've heard from Peter Wright that this went on all the time in the 1960s. So why wouldn't it still be happening now? Of course it is.

The Tribunal Secretary had avoided answering the question from my previous letter, of whether the Tribunal had any independent investigative capacity. So I asked him again.

Dear Mr Brooks,

Thank you for your letter dated 6 April enclosing an extract of the 1997 Report of the Security Service Commissioner. This answers two of the three questions asked in my letter of 25 March.

The third question remains. In 1993 I travelled on a British Airways flight on which there also travelled four men, one of whom stared at me, laughed and said, "if he tries to run away we'll find him". I took this to mean that these were the men who had been pursuing me for some time in the UK. This leads me to ask again the last question in my previous letter;

(3) Is the Tribunal able to investigate information such as British Airways passenger lists, given that these could conclusively prove MI5 involvement? Would the Tribunal be forced to rely on MI5 to carry out such investigations, or would it have some other means of investigating? It might look slightly ridiculous for the Tribunal to rely on MI5 to investigate their own misdeeds.

I would very much hope that some means is available to the Tribunal and Commissioner to investigate possible MI5 malefaction, other than relying on MI5 themselves. When I receive an answer to this question from you, I will work to put together a more comprehensive and detailed complaint for the Tribunal's consideration.

Yours sincerely,

Brooks' reply was;

The Security Service Tribunal

PO Box 18
London SE1 0TZ
Telephone: 0171-273 4095

Mr BT Scozik
45 Englewood Road
LONDON
SW12 9PA

Your reference:

Our reference:

Date: 7 May 1999

Dear Mr Scozik

I refer to your letter of 20 April. I am sorry you have not received an earlier reply.

I am sure you will appreciate that it is difficult respond to your query regarding the Tribunal's investigation of your complaint in advance.

When a complaint is lodged with the Tribunal, it will find out if the Security Service has made the complainant the subject of its inquiries. If it has, the Tribunal will determine whether the Service had reasonable grounds for continuing them. If they have stopped, the Tribunal will determine whether there were reasonable grounds for starting them. To support these statutory functions, paragraph 4(1) of Schedule 2 of the Security Service Act 1989 provides:

> "It shall be the duty of every member of the Service to disclose or give to the Tribunal such documents or information as they may require for the purpose of enabling them to carry out their functions under this Act".

The Tribunal will ultimately determine their investigation of any given complaint on the basis of the information provided and the outcome of their inquiries.

Yours sincerely

N R Brooks
Tribunal Secretary

Brooks doesn't want to give a direct reply to the question, since that would place him in a bad light. So he gives an indirect answer; the tribunal, he avoids saying, has no investigative capacity; there is no mention even of any investigative capacity provided by MI5 themselves; nobody can investigate anything, all the Tribunal can do is ask MI5, and they, in their "Alice in Wonderland" world, can redefine the truth as it pleases them, and dissemble, and lie.

Before deciding not to put another formal complaint before the Tribunal, I asked Robin Ramsay, editor of Lobster magazine, what he thought of the idea of making a complaint to the Tribunal. He replied;

RESPONSE Yes it is a waste of time. They will do nothing.

In a further email he elaborated;

```
As for quoting me on the Security Service Tribunal - if you think my
comments would mean anything, feel free. The problem people have is
this: they almost have to go through the motions of going to the
Tribunal for if they don't they will always be asked, 'Why didn't you
go the proper authorities?'  (This is one of the chief functions of
'the proper authorities'.)
  Robin Ramsay
```

So the sum of the various parts of this story is; DON'T GO TO THE TRIBUNAL. If you do, then MI5 will open a file on you (if you don't have one already). Don't do as I did, do as I say. If you feel a really deep-seated urge to complain, do so first under an invented name, which will make you understand just how useless the Tribunal is, how little information they provide, and how unpleasant it is to know that you have given MI5 a reason to officially open a file on you in their Registry.

Charing Cross police, March 1999

In March 1999, I was phoned at home by Det.Sgt.Richards of the computer crime unit at Charing Cross police station. This followed a number of emails I had sent, using as a return address Chris Tarrant @ Capital Radio, quoting something he'd said in 1994;

```
"you know this bloke? he says we're trying to kill him.
we should be done for attempted manslaughter!"
```

I subsequently communicated with DS Richards, and requested he investigate my allegation against Tarrant; which he refused, in quite rude terms. The following excerpt states;

```
"What I'm concerned about is you sending illegal emails. Your reasoning is
of no interest to me."
```

The following addendum speaks for itself;

```
"I have read your various bits on the internet. I'm afraid there is no
substance or credence to it. It's an absolute load of rubbish. I don't
investigate rubbish. I can't be more blunt or to the point than that."
```

In the years 1990-2003 **I three times requested the police look into the harassment which MI5 have been carrying out,** and each time the police have refused. I spoke to Clapham police in 1995, at which time I had not figured out who was responsible; the officer at the station was polite, but concerned with seeing me off quickly. The second request is documented on this page. The third occasion was in April 2000 when the detective from Houses of Parliament police told me to cease faxing Westminster politicians; with similarly negative outcome.

The obvious lesson is that British police do not willingly investigate allegations against the Security Service; and it's a waste of time requesting they do so.

DS Richards' phone call was **disclosed on the internet** by an anonymous poster, as follows;

```
From: John West
Newsgroups: uk.misc
Subject: Re: recent spats about how to point out faq info
Date: Sat, 13 Mar 1999 21:06:41 GMT
Organization: Fishy Bits
```

```
Lines: 26
Message-ID:
NNTP-Posting-Host: 212.140.72.19

Considering Corley has recently had his collar felt by the boys in blue
following complaints from Capital Radio regarding him forging their e-mail
address in spam e-mails, I don't think he's going to be doing much
spamming.
/\John/\
```

The newsgroup article would have come either from Police or someone at Capital Radio, since no-one else knew of the conversation; and obviously the disclosure was improper. However when I complained to the Information Commissioner, both the Police and Capital denied they had sourced the disclosure, as the following letter shows.

Re: Your complaint with the Metropolitan Police Service.

I refer to our recent telephone conversation about the above and can advise I have now received a response from the Metropolitan Police Service. The audit report shows no inappropriate access has been made to your records and therefore there is no evidence of a disclosure from the police.

As I have received a similar response from Capital Radio, I am unable to proceed any further with your complaint. I understand this will come as a disappointment to you, but as Ms Chandler previously pointed out in her letter of 26 April 1999, this Office has no power other than that given to it by the Data Protection Act 1984.

Also as previously advised, the Registrar's Office does not have the power to ask the Internet Service Provider (ISP) to 'freeze' the information they hold for longer then their retention policy. Although an approach could be made to the ISP, this could prove to be problematic as we have no evidence of a criminal offence, or a breach of Principle under the Data Protection Act 1984, so I have no grounds on which to ask for their co-operation. To request information we would need a warrant from a judge, which would require evidence of a criminal offence, or we could rely on Section 28(3) of the Data Protection Act 1984, but this has to be in relation to a criminal offence also. The decision to approach the ISP, or not, will have to be made by the Compliance Manager who deals with that within the Registrar's Office, and I will advise her of the details of your complaint, so she can decide how to proceed.

I understand that the outcome of your complaint with the Metropolitan Police Service will be a disappointment to you, but due to the lack of evidence, I do not anticipate any further action in respect of this issue.

Yours faithfully

Jane M Kelly
Compliance Officer

Either the Police or Capital would therefore be lying - how unexpected. Although the disclosure was improper, it does not appear to have been illegal and its source remains unknown, so the Information Commissioner could not take the matter further.

Charing Cross police continued to deny making any disclosure, other than to the radio station, as shown in the following letter.

> I reply to your letter dated 25th April 1999. I am aware that you have some concerns over the investigation to which you were spoken to by DS Richards on 10th March 1999. I am aware that you wish to know whether Mr Chris Tarrant has been interviewed by Police. It is not Metropolitan Police Service policy to disclose details of the investigation of crime to those who are not victims and who haven't been charged with any offences.
>
> I am also aware that you are concerned about the disclosure of your conversation with DS Richards to third parties. This has been fully investigated and there is no evidence of any unauthorised disclosure by any police employee. A report has been completed by DS Richards in this respect and forwarded to the Data Protection Registrar.
>
> If you have any further enquires about this matter please do not hesitate to contact me on the above number.
>
> Yours sincerely
>
> *[signature]* DS.
>
> John Foulkes
> Detective Sergeant

My letter had requested the police question Tarrant about his 1994 remarks on "attempted manslaughter" by MI5. Of course, the police refused to ask Tarrant whether or not he had said that.

I reply to your letter dated 7th June 1999. I am aware that you have two further enquiries in relation to your conversation with Detective Sergeant Richards 10th March 1999. I will deal with both.

Firstly you claim that DS Richards stated that the E.Mails were illegal. You have asked me to confirm exactly what legislation was alleged to have been breached. I have been informed that you were told that the E.Mails "could constitute an offence". The offence investigated was an allegation of crime made by Capital Radio. The allegation related to an offence either under either Section 1 of the Computer Misuse Act 1990 or section 43 of the Telecommunications Act 1984.

Your second enquiry concerns unauthorised disclosure of your details by DS Richards to Capital Radio. DS Richards states that he did disclose your details to Capital Radio as you claim. This disclosure is not improper and is within police service regulations.

I hope this information's satisfies your queries.

Yours sincerely

John Foulkes
Detective Sergeant

The alert reader will note from the following letter that DS Richards later claimed he had not described to me my emails as "illegal", which is counter to the reality of the first audio segment on this page. It's disappointing to see this sort of behaviour from the police.

However the lesson I really learn from re-reading these notes is that I have been insufficiently assertive of my rights in real life, rather than merely on the internet. If I had sought to bring a formal complaint against Capital in 1999, the police would have had to question Tarrant; which would have placed him in the difficult situation of either lying to the police, or telling them the truth. It was my mistake not to force the issue with Richards. Obviously the police didn't want to question Tarrant because they knew perfectly well that my allegations were valid; to dismiss as "rubbish" what Richards must have known to be true is despicable.

Correspondence with Keith Hill MP, 1997-99

In early 1997 I went to see my local MP, Keith Hill (Labour - London Streatham), at one of his surgeries, to ask his advice and enlist his support in combating the MI5 conspiracy. He appeared helpful during the meeting, promising assistance to find a lawyer and help with my legal efforts. Unfortunately, a month after the meeting he appeared to have changed his mind, as the following letter shows.

Keith Hill
Labour Campaign Headquarters
Fred Hughes House, 84 Streatham Hill, London SW2 4RD
Hotline 0181 674 1122

Mr B T Szocik
45 Englewood Road
London SW12 9PA

16 April 1997

Dear Mr Szocik,

Thank you for visiting one of my advice surgeries in March and for telephoning my office recently. Please accept my apologies for the delay in writing to you during this busy period.

Unfortunately I do not think that there are any representations which I can usefully make on your behalf at present. I therefore return the documents you showed me for your own records.

Yours sincerely,

Keith Hill

Enc

Hotline 0181 674 1122

Labour

I wrote to Mr Hill a year later, on 20 May 1998, stating that I wished to make a complaint to Police regarding the continuing actions against me, and requesting his help in so doing. He responded a week later;

Keith Hill Labour MP for Streatham

HOUSE OF COMMONS
LONDON SW1A 0AA

Telephone 0171 219 6980 (24 hour answerline) Fax 0171 219 2565

Mr B T Szocik
45 Englewood Road
London
SW12 9PA

Our Ref: SZOC2705.DOC

27th May 1998

Dear Mr Szocik,

Thank you for your recent letter regarding the harassment you feel that you continue to suffer. I am very sorry to hear that the situation has not improved.

However, I have studied your letter and the attachment carefully and still feel unable to be able to assist. I am sorry if this is disappointing, however I am not really sure what I could usefully do.

Yours sincerely

P.P. *Lisa Homan*
Keith Hill MP

REPRESENTING THE STREATHAM CONSTITUENCY IN PARLIAMENT
(including parts of Balham, Brixton, Clapham & Tulse Hill)
Clapham Park, St Leonard's, St Martin's, Streatham Hill, Streatham South, Streatham Wells, Thornton, Tulse Hill & Town Hall

Again I wrote to Mr Hill on 10 November 1998, stating;

I am sure you will remember me from your surgery a year and a half ago, and subsequent letter dated 20/5/98 which is reproduced over the page.

Once again I am asking you if you can help me, particularly in obtaining the passenger list for the BA flight in 1993, where four of my persecutors confronted me. The harassment has restarted over the last two weeks, by "coincidence" as I have restarted faxing your fellow MPs. If these faxes worry my persecutors then they must be having some effect - therefore, I feel encouraged to continue them.

Several of your Parliamentary colleagues have expressed the view that I should be making more of an effort to secure the assistance of my MP rather than presenting the matter to random members of the Commons. I hope you will be more helpful now than on the earlier occasions I contacted you.

His response was in the following terms;

Keith Hill Labour MP for Streatham

HOUSE OF COMMONS
LONDON SW1A 0AA

Telephone 0171 219 6980 (24 hour answerline) Fax 0171 219 2565

Mr B T Szocik
45 Englewood Road
London
SW12 9PA

Our Ref: SZOC1611.DOC

16th November 1998

Dear Mr Szocik,

Thank you for your letter of 10 November.

As you know, I considered very carefully the representations you made to me at an earlier stage and decided that there was no appropriate action I could take on your behalf. I have reviewed the position and can see no reason to alter my decision.

Meanwhile, I have become aware of the fax campaign you are directing at other Members of Parliament. I wish to make it absolutely clear that this course of action will have no effect on my view of this matter.

However, I am conscious of the irritation your behaviour is causing to my parliamentary colleagues. I must, therefore, ask you to stop this practice. Otherwise, I shall have no choice but to make a formal complaint to the police, on the grounds of harassment.

Let me say quite frankly that I shall take this step very reluctantly. I would much prefer you discuss your problems with a counsellor and would be willing to offer you advice on the means of contacting an appropriate person.

Yours sincerely

Keith Hill MP

REPRESENTING THE STREATHAM CONSTITUENCY IN PARLIAMENT
(including parts of Balham, Brixton, Clapham & Tulse Hill)
Clapham Park, St Leonard's, St Martin's, Streatham Hill, Streatham South, Streatham Wells, Thornton, Tulse Hill & Town Hall

I thought it unusual for a British Member of Parliament to involve the Police on the grounds of excessive communication. Being a legal neophyte I sought the advice of a local solicitor, who opined that no case existed for a charge of harassment;

> Dear Mr. Szocik
>
> **RE : YOURSELF AND KEITH HILL MP**
>
> I refer to our meeting yesterday and write to confirm the contents thereof.
>
> You sought my advice on a letter you had received of 16th November 1998 from Keith Hill MP in which he said that unless you stopped your fax campaign aimed at other members of Parliament he would have no choice "but to make a formal complaint to the Police, on the grounds of harassment". I also briefly read through some of the faxes that you had directed at the MP's.
>
> I advised you that from the faxes that I had read that I did not believe that the Police could commence any criminal proceedings against you on the grounds of harassment as I could not see anything that would cause undue stress to the recipients or put them in fear of their safety. However I advised you that Keith Hill MP may be able to pursue the matter through the Civil Courts by way of a civil Injunction against you in order to put a halt to your fax campaign.
>
> On the basis of the information that you provided to me you were not entitled to Green Form Assistance and I therefore enclose my receipted invoice for the initial consultation in the sum of £35.25 including VAT. I advised you that should you need to defend any proceedings in the civil proceedings commenced by Keith Hill MP or any Police action then you may be entitled to legal aid, which amongst other things would depend upon your disposal income and disposable capital.
>
> I take this opportunity to thank you for your instructions in this matter.
>
> Yours sincerely
>
> H.S. BAINS
> BAINS & PARTNERS

In any case, who would I be harassing? Only Mr Hill, or hundreds of Westminster MPs simultaneously? I wrote again on 1 February 1999 to Mr Hill, enclosing my solicitor's advice above. Mr Hill did not respond to the letter.

For my subject access request to Mr Hill's office in 2002, please follow this link.

Data Protection application to Keith Hill MP, 2002

In May 2002 I made a subject access application under the Data Protection Act 1998 to Keith Hill, my local MP. I was interested to see who he had spoken to during 1997-1999, when we were communicating by letter.

Coupled to my data protection application, I asked Mr Hill;

Additionally I ask the non-data-protection question of whether you spoke to the Police about me, about our communications or my faxes to Parliament, either in April 2000 or at any other time. Please identify any such communications.

His response consisted of a computer printout, with covering letter, which are shown here. His letter says he may have spoken to Police about the faxes Parliament had been receiving, but his memory is unclear "at this remove in time".

The data printout spells out that I asked for Mr Hill's assistance against "BBC news readers who are spying on him through the television." It also contains a reference of Mr Hill's office referring my case to Social Services, to whom I am unknown.

Keith Hill Labour MP for Streatham

HOUSE OF COMMONS
LONDON SW1A 0AA

Telephone 020 7219 6980 (24 hour answerline) Fax 020 7219 2565
e-mail: hillk@parliament.uk Website: www.keithhill.labour.co.uk

Mr Tadeusz Szocik
45 Englewood Road
LONDON
SW12 9PA

Our Ref: LH/SZOC001/970739   10 May 2002

Dear Mr Szocik,

Thank you for your letter dated 9th May. I enclose a printout of your details, which are held on my database. I no longer have any hard copies of information relating to your case on file, as due to the lack of storage capacity in my office files are periodically disposed of.

With regards to communications with the police, it is possible that my office spoke to the House of Commons police authorities about complaints received from parliamentary colleagues about the nuisance caused by your faxes. However, I cannot be more certain about the nature of these contacts at this remove in time.

I trust this information responds to your enquiry.

Finally, I am returning your original letter together with your cheque in the sum of £10.00.

Yours sincerely

Keith Hill MP

Cc   Data Protection Registrar
      Wycliffe House
      Water Lane
      Wilmslow
      Cheshire, SK9 5AF

REPRESENTING THE STREATHAM CONSTITUENCY IN PARLIAMENT
(including parts of Balham, Brixton, Clapham & Tulse Hill)

I wrote again to Mr Hill on 13 May and asked him to elucidate; in his response of 17 May he said he was unable to add to his earlier note on this point.

> Dear Mr Szocik,
>
> Further to your letter of 13 May, the "SS" referred to is Lambeth Social Services; and I am unable to add to my earlier note on the police.
>
> Yours sincerely
>
> *Keith Hill*
>
> Keith Hill MP

Date 5/10/2002   **CFL CaseWorker**   Page 1
Full Case/Client Details

SZOC001   Mr Tadeusz Szocik
45 Englewood Road
LONDON, , SW12 9PA
Phone:
Attributes

970739   User Ref: Opened 3/7/1997   Last Update 5/10/2002
         KeyWords   Last Print   Holdover
         SOC.SERV:, PRESENTS CHALLENGING ISSUES:

Came to ask for our support in his case against BBCnewsreaders "who are spying on him through the television".

Letter recived requesting his details from our computer cover letter with print out cc to Data Protection Agency	Closed	5/10/2002
write to const	Closed	4/16/1997
unknown to SS	Closed	4/10/1997
referred to SS	Closed	4/2/1997

Eye Say, 2002

In 2002 I placed an entire year's worth of advertising with Private Eye magazine classifieds, in the Eye Say column. The aim was, as usual, to send the constant reality of MI5 Persecution into the public domain - since MI5 insist that everyone know how clever they are in ruining my life, getting the media to attack me, and trying to physically harm me, then I insist everyone know about their actions also. However, when you describe the illegal actions of the English Stasi to English people, the response is rigid silence.

Issue 1045. The ad merely commented on BBC newscasters spying on my home, aided by MI5 bugs. This is something that continues regardless of any attempt made to complain, since the system for complaints against the Security Service is intended by the Government to have no effect.

Issue 1046. Everyone knows about MI5's actions, in other cases as well as mine, but the basic corruption surrounding British Intelligence guarantees their immunity from justice.

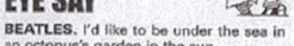

Issue 1047.

Issue 1048. Rat on the English Spies. Reward for information leading to conviction.

Issue 1049.
Peter Krüger's article.

Issue 1050.
Security Service Tribunal (currently Investigatory Powers Tribunal) is an essential element in the web of corruption and lies around the security services.

Issue 1051.
Security Service provides the means, and BBC provides the TV presenters, who spy on their viewer. They say it's "very funny" that the BBC try to harm their viewer psychologically, and MI5 try to harm their target physically, because of course the only people who know about these happenings are those people who can be relied on to disclaim them.

Issue 1052.
Jon Snow the conceited hypocrite.

Issue 1053.
Look at a British agent working. Shouldn't we give them more money to "work"? MI5 pimp England's reputation for their immoral earnings.

Issue 1054.
No, of course they're not blackmailing Snow. He says he refused MI5's money, but he's spying while he reads the news, which makes him a mendacious hypocrite.

Issue 1055. Something wrong with individuals who work for secret police agencies generally, and the English secret police fit the mould by employing psychopaths. The real culprit is the Government for deliberately removing any capability from the oversight machinery.

EYE SAY

EYE THINK WARS ARE CAUSED by our subconscious fear of starvation. LC.

www.sosume.co.uk – CAN YOU HANDLE THE TRUTH?

MI5 PERSECUTION – covert abuse, overt denial. Something Wrong with Stephen Lander's agents. www.five.org.uk/webfaq/#mi5tactics

SATANIC ENGLISH FAMILY put curse on world in February 2002. Box 0555.

SPEECHWRITING by Britain's LEADING PROFESSIONAL, Mitch Murray – see page 34..

THE THINGS you don't know about.

www.nhs-exposed.com – Undercover Medicine. We dare to publish what others dare to hide.

Issue 1056. Corruption pays. The taxpayer gets fleeced.

EYE SAY

SHEFFIELD, 2 MILLION. as a result of Max Clifford, kisses had lost 2 million.

SPEECHWRITING by Britain's LEADING PROFESSIONAL, Mitch Murray – see page 34.

COCAINE AIR.

MI5 PERSECUTION – £1,000,000 per annum for Twelve Years to fund 24/7 persecution. Ten to Fifteen Million Pounds Stolen for their Compensation by Security Service agents from You, the Taxpayer. www.five.org.uk/usenet/#petermc

IT WAS SUNDAY NIGHT. The attack was on Sunday night.

Issue 1057. Lander will never be convicted because the British system is intentionally corrupt.

EYE SAY

DEAR HOME SECRETARY. Children in prison – shock revelation www.mysoapbox.co.uk

KERTEMINDE. Please ring. xxx.

CAPITAINE – thinking of Kylie. ILY. SOUS-FIFRE.

JACK WAS INTRODUCED onto LOOT messageboard by an MI5 agent.

SPEECHWRITING by Britain's LEADING PROFESSIONAL, Mitch Murray – see page 34.

IT WAS murder.

MI5 PERSECUTION – Conspiracy to Harass. Illegal Bugging. Psychological Assault. Lunar Lander's future as a man of many Convictions – www.five.org.uk/webfaq/#whyss

NO really.

Issue 1058. If the Police are institutionally racist, then Security Service is 96% white Anglo.

EYE SAY

AS. As if.

CAPITAINE – thinking of (mother) and missing you. SOUS-FIFRE.

ENGLISH gentleman.

SPEECHWRITING by Britain's LEADING PROFESSIONAL, Mitch Murray – see page 34.

MI5 PERSECUTION – "well, if he wants to be mentally ill and a bloody foreigner to boot, if he goes to the same university as us, then what does he expect?" – www.five.org.uk/usenet/#smid

ARE you?

READ THE DECISION OF THE EMPLOYMENT TRIBUNAL Marietta Farnsworth and Derbyshire County Council – http://homepage.ntlworld.com/bill.farnsworth/marietta.htm

---

Issue 1059. Security Service find staring at a bloke exciting. Very queer behaviour.

EYE SAY

JOHN DOHERTY (Sellotape) Saxophone neophyte still? ron_vaughan@carrotmail.com - or friendsreunited.com

UNLESS...

MI5 PERSECUTION – they introduced Performance related Pay some years ago. Watch website video of Security Service agents Performing gaily for Pay – www.five.org.uk/evidence/#mbeat

GLOBAL WARMING: what you condone when you do not lose you condone when you lose.

JESUS was going to take revenge on MI5 for crucifying him.

SPEECHWRITING by Britain's LEADING PROFESSIONAL, Mitch Murray – see page 35.

MIND THE THOUGHT POLICE. Paul W. Lloyd. Box 0459.

CAN I BORROW your name?

EYE SAY

SADDAM must not be allowed on the climbing frame.

FEED FROM the twisted news spoon! www.thespittingcobra.com

IT WAS MI5

EYE REMEMBER all who died 6th and 9th August 1945 in Hiroshima and Nagasaki.

SPEECHWRITING by Britain's LEADING PROFESSIONAL, Mitch Murray – see page 35.

EYE REMEMBER WHY we had to drop the bombs in August 1945. Thank you Harry.

MI5 PERSECUTION – twelve years of MI5 hate crimes... to what purpose? entertainment? www.five.org.u'

Issue 1060. It's incredible that these things could go on for over a decade, without any check on MI5's behaviour. We are told by the TV and newspapers what a decent society we have, yet it is the same TV and newspapers which have been molesting me and others. Hypocrisy is such a central part of British life.

Issue 1061.

Neither confirm nor deny from MI5. What sort of country is this, that places zero supervision on its secret services, with the results seen for so many years? The Establishment is not a democracy, and elections do not determine how the permanent government behaves.

EYE SAY
WWW.FAXFN.ORG. The Green Belt. You old NIMBYS steal from the young and poor to pollute the world. Geddit? Look up to see.
IRAQI babies are babies.
SPEECHWRITING by Britain's LEADING PROFESSIONAL, Mitch Murray – see page 34.
DON'T ADD ANYTHING onto the message and don't take anything away from the message.
MI5 PERSECUTION. Security Service are afraid to Admit they're behind the Persecution – www.five.org.uk/faxes/sent/#9906A

HEDGEHOG ROLLING CONTEST. In the shadow of the rock during the Fringe. Only surplus Hebridean hedgehogs rolled. Spiky hedgehog haircut prizes.

NO rumaging.

Issue 1062.

Neither confirm nor deny from BBC. When I took BBC to court in 1997 they struck out my action without them even formally denying the charge.

EYE SAY
CAPITAINE: THINKING OF SNAP. With good wishes. SOUS-FIFRE.
SPEECHWRITING by Britain's LEADING PROFESSIONAL, Mitch Murray – see page 34.
MI5 PERSECUTION – BBC Newscasters Spying on my Home, while they Read the News. Understandably, they Refuse to Deny the charge. www.five.org.uk/faxes/sent/#9811B
HELLO MADAM, Frostyface, Yes You! After all this time. Email? Box 1962.

Issue 1063.

Parliament stays silent in face of thousands of faxes. Let's not acknowledge his complaint, let's not investigate what MI5 have been doing. Instead, Westminster politicians complain about the ink expended in printing the faxes.

EYE SAY
MISS SALLY MADDIN is a colourless fruit squashed in terminus to Mr Thomas Burn.
CHERIE'S PORTIA REVIEW. Plus Racing Tips, Sky dinosaur scam – www.buggerbognor.org

EYE EXPOSE – Peter Sutcliffe was eliminated 12 times. Why? www.yorkshireripper.co.uk

JAMES. James.
WWW.FAXFN.ORG – Tell DEFRA fuel poverty simply solved.
SPEECHWRITING by Britain's LEADING PROFESSIONAL, Mitch Murray – see page 34.
MI5 PERSECUTION – over 24,259 faxes sent to Parliament, media etc. during a three year period. Their reaction: Suppression. Rigid secrecy in an "open" society. www.five.org.uk/faxes/
THERE WAS A FACTORY in Germany. 1032. The factory was surrounded by 13 blind mice.

Issue 1064.

English politician Keith Hill tried to incarcerate me for writing to Parliament, and guess what he says now? "Neither confirm nor deny." He can't remember if he did or didn't set the police to imprison me.

EYE SAY
DAVID PHILLIPS – Happy Birthday to the greatest brother in the history of brothers. With all my love – your little brother.
OPEN THE GATES of Wisdom at www.grenvillecroll.com
TONY BLAIR welcomes alien pop bank to Earth: www.the-saucers.com
www.faxfn.org – NOTE TO THE OFFICE of Government Commerce: Go on. Tell us. Which large Government Software Projects have used the PRINCE software methodology – successfully? (Other experiences welcome.)

EYE EXPOSE – Peter Sutcliffe was eliminated 12 times. Why? www.yorkshireripper.co.uk

MI5 PERSECUTION – my elected representative Keith Hill MP cannot remember if he complained to Police to stop my faxes to Parliament. It's easy to forget these things. www.five.org.uk/plaint/#khilla
20/1 WINNER, Dear Charles, Derry, Cherie, Rosbifs letters. www.buggerbognor.org

EYE SAY

MR O'BRIEN is loved and adored by Miss Cutts. Mine, all mine!
CAPITAINE – thinking of Ivan Van Dahl "TRY". Love, SOUS-FIFRE.
OPEN THE GATES OF WISDOM at www.grenvillecroll.com

EYE EXPOSE – Peter Sutcliffe was eliminated 12 times. Why? www.yorkshireripper.co.uk

MI5 PERSECUTION – "if Keith Hill your own MP cannot help no-one else in the House of Commons can." www.five.org.uk/faxes/recv/parliament/#45985629

TONY BLAIR welcomes alien pop band to Earth: www.the-saucers.com

DARKNESS BEFORE DAWN. Two years of unparalleled evil. The machine's response to the fair warning. Now the Sun will rise. CT.

THE ONLY WAY the attack on Iraq would be averted was if there was a coup in one of the host countries. Russia or Turkey. It was Russia.

Issue 1065. So Parliament can't control MI5? Can't, or won't?

EYE SAY

ST JUDE strikes again. Grateful thanks as ever. Praise God!
ONE THING I DO KNOW: that wind is not a violent man.
www.faxfn.org To the Office of Government Commerce: Re. Software Development. We still want to know if any large government IT projects have been successful - and used your methodology. (BTW. Now The Economist magazine is on your case too. Oh dear.)
SCIENTOLOGY AND DIANETICS: for critical opinions, please see www.xenu.net
www.ebnrage.com Transmitting to all countries whatever the political climate. Emergency Broadcast Network. thx1138ebn
EYE EXPOSE – Peter Sutcliffe was eliminated 12 times. Why? www.yorkshireripper.co.uk
MI5 PERSECUTION – England's second biggest open secret of the last decade. www.five.org.uk
BROOMLEIGH Housing Associa-tion - Learn how Broomleigh litigates http://broomleigh.com/ and http://www.broomleigh.com/

Issue 1066. What was the first? We didn't kill her, it was an accident, everyone knows that.

EYE SAY

DEAR '[intentionally blank] Second-hand Bookshops' ironic advertising geenyus (Australian Chaser, Issue 63),Fuck off, wannabe. Eye subscriber, Balmain

EYE EXPOSE – Peter Sutcliffe was eliminated 12 times. Why? www.yorkshireripper.co.uk

MI5 PERSECUTION – Lander leaves security service to become Law Society commissioner. Would you let Brady oversee Ashworth? www.five.org.uk

Issue 1067. British Intelligence Serial-Killer-in-Chief, honoured by an Establishment of equals.

EYE SAY

I'M JUST TRYING to save my soul.
CAPITAINE – thinking of Coldplay and I'm sorry. ILY – SOUS FIFRE.
WWW.FAXFN.ORG – does Government software fail because the Treasury can't cope?

EYE EXPOSE – Peter Sutcliffe was eliminated 12 times. Why? www.yorkshireripper.co.uk

MI5 PERSECUTION - "it doesn't get into his head". Persecutors' response to last week's ad. www.five.org.uk/evidence/#bhpo
WHAT ARE YOU GOING TO DO when the reaper falls? Fearful condem-nation. Wilful confrontation. Painful configuration. Complain.

Issue 1068. Evil English agents paid by the government to follow and abuse.

EYE SAY

HE IS the king of Israel.
www.faxfn.org – the Gateway Software reviews - is the Treasury's head in the sand or up a darker place?
MI5 PERSECUTION – "communicate with Parliamentary Intelligence and Security Committee", suggested an MP. But the weakness in these bodies is inevitable bias. www.five.org.uk/faxes/recv/parliament/#rjackson
AMERICA could nuke em with fuel air bombs.

Issue 1069. How do you complain about criminal actions when the criminals are running the show?

EYE SAY

I'VE GOT BAD NEWS for journalists. Its 1 o'clock in Swaziland – and what about the rest of us?
MI5 PERSECUTION – over 200,000 people have seen my website since 1996. How "inconvenient" for Security Service – fact stranger than myth? www.five.org.uk
SOME PEOPLE ARE CONCERNED that the uranium was 150 miles from the border with Iraq.
CAPITAINE – thank you for being so patient. ILY. Sous-Fifre.

WHO IS DR ADOKO? www.dradoko.com

THE NEW PUBLICITY GURU? www.man-of-letters.co.uk Go on, take a look; read carefully.
380 mighty.

Issue 1070. Fact stranger than myth? Can't guarantee your safety? They threatened, tried and failed, which was unusual - so now they keep trying.

Issue 1071. What is crime anyway? If the British State harms people, is that crime, or shall we redefine the technical rules to legalise what are effectively British Intelligence death squads?

EYE SAY

MRS SIMPSON – I will happily abdicate for you if you wish. Edward R.

BOND BUILDING, Edinburgh. Problems? Want to join forces? Box 0671.

WHAT DID you call me?

WHO IS Dr Adoko? www.dradoko.com

MI5 PERSECUTION – their agents' job for life (and livelihood) is stalking me. Crime pays when redefined as National Security. www.five.org.uk

WHEN HE SANG 'The children will starve and live in fear' his voice sounded cruel.

www.faxfn.org HM Treasury – an apology: while we still think the Gateway Review Process is daft, our last advert was unnecessarily offensive.

IT'S GOOD NEWS you're not a commentary of your conscience.

Orange County Sheriff's Office 2006

As readers will be aware, MI5 sent an agent to masturbate outside the window of my apartment on 1/September/2000. Six years later I was encouraged by the website HollaBackNYC, which deals with sex crimes, to report the criminal activities of MI5's agent to the proper authorities, which in this case meant to Orange County Sheriff's Office which deals with Winter Park, Florida where the crime had occurred. I wrote to them on 22 August 2006 enclosing a CD containing a video of the incident (as shown on the webpage referenced above) and a closeup picture of the MI5 man's face, as follows.

Attn: SEC 11
Orange County Sheriff's Office
10244 E.Colonial Drive
Orlando FL 32802
USA

Dear Sirs

I spoke on the phone with your office today. As stated, I wish to report a crime which occurred on 1/September/2000 around 3.30pm outside my apartment at 1915 Summer Wind Drive, Winter Park, FL 32792. As shown on file britspy.avi on the enclosed CD, a man publicly masturbated outside my apartment window. His face is quite clearly visible on the video recording and an image has been extracted as file britspy.jpg. A childrens' play area is a few yards to the left of the picture, and the man can be seen running furtively away after performing the act. I have not previously reported the crime, but having read the HollaBackNYC webpage which deals with sexual offences I now wish to do so. Currently I live at the UK address given above.

This is not a random incident but part of an orchestrated campaign of abuse by the British Security Service MI5 which has been stalking me since 1990 and continued harassing me while I was living in Winter Park in 2000. Their actions are currently the subject of a lawsuit in the UK brought by lawyers Bates Wells Braithwaite. There was a series of incidents where MI5 agents masturbated publicly until their man was caught on video at which point the events stopped. In early June 2000 an MI5 agent phoned me at home in London UK and feigned an orgasm on the phone. Soon after two men emerging from a nearby house feigned masturbatory noises. On 27/July/2000 a girl took off an item of underwear in exactly the same location as the man a month later, intended by MI5 as an act of sexual abuse. Finally their agent was caught on camera as shown.

This is a serious incident because it wasn't a random pervert outside the window but a paid agent of British Intelligence who have been persecuting me for partly sexual reasons for 16 years. It is known on other occasions that MI5 use American law enforcement to commit their activities while in the US and the man visually appears to be an American so worryingly they may have paid an American agent to masturbate on their behalf.

Please identify a detective who can deal with this material. There may be an issue with the limitation period having expired on this crime but that period may be tolled because it is a continuing pattern of conduct. I look forward to hearing from you. The best way of reaching me is by email on the above address.

A month later I followed the letter up with a phone call to Sgt Richard Mankewich who deals Sex Crimes in Orange County. His emailed reply dated Tue, 26 Sep 2006 was as follows;

Sorry for the delay, we are extremely busy. I believe I viewed that CD last month along with other Detectives. I don't recall actually seeing anyone in the video masturbating. I recall seeing someone's back and then he runs off. In order to prove this crime we need someone to swear to seeing the man's penis.

Sergeant Rich Mankewich
Orange County Sheriff's Office
Criminal Investigations Division
Sex Crimes Unit
Offie: (407) 254-7243
Fax: (407) 254-7244
Email: Richard.Mankewich@OCFL.NET

Because the MI5 Agent was not showing his penis in the video, the Sheriff's Office stated they would not investigate the incident as an act of Public Masturbation. I turned the matter over to their Professional Standards Division, which after investigation issued the following statement;

Dear Mr. Szocik,

On August 22, 2006 you brought to the attention of the Orange County Sheriff's Office an alleged misdemeanor offense which occurred six (6) years prior (September 1, 2000). Sergeant Mankewich responded to you on September 26, 2006, subsequent to a mail correspondence where you provided him video which you maintain corroborates your concerns. Sergeant Mankewich determined the video was of no use in determining that a crime occurred or identifying any perpetrator. Sergeant Mankewich informed you of his conclusion on September 26, 2006.

Further, the offense you allege, as stated previously, is a misdemeanor crime in the State of Florida and the statute of limitations expired one year from the time of occurrence (September 1, 2001). Even if a crime occurred and the perpetrator could be identified, at this point the Orange County Sheriff's Office would not investigate the offense due to the expiration of these time limitations. Your delay in reporting this event was a critical oversight that can not be overstated.

The variety of other issues you address in your correspondence concerning the British government and an alleged conspiracy against you are not issues to be dealt with by the Orange County Sheriff's Office.

Therefore, after reviewing the information you have provided and evaluating the response of the Orange County Sheriff's Office personnel, I have concluded that your concerns were addressed properly. This matter is considered closed.

Thank you,

Commander Matthew J. Irwin
Orange County Sheriff's Office
Sex Crimes Unit
2500 West Colonial Drive
Orlando, Florida 32804

Essentially OCSO took a minimalist view of the crime without reference to the external MI5 aspect. I was unable to convince them to further investigate the case, and even today, somewhere out there, the unidentified and unpunished Masturbating MI5 Agent, who must have been well compensated for his nefarious and perverted activities, continues to ply his dubious trade.

Orlando Police Department 2006

On 17 August 2006 I emailed OPD wishing to report the attempted homicide of 17/Nov/2001 when MI5 agents conspired to kill me in Orlando. They replied the following day requesting I make a police report by phone, which I did on 22 August. You can see OPD's report of the conversation on pages 2-4 of the following multipage TIFF.

ORLANDO POLICE DEPARTMENT

Statement

Case #: 2006-315577

Date of Statement: Month: 8 Day: 24 Year: 2006 Time: 8:30am
Offense: ATTEMPTED HOMICIDE
Date of Offense: Month: 11 Day: 17 Year: 2001 Time: 11pm
Suspect (last, first, middle): SECURITY SERVICE
Location of Offense: LAKE EOLA PARK, ORLANDO FL
District: DOWNTOWN
Person Code: Name: SZOCIK, BOLESLAW TADEUSZ
Age: 39 DOB: 23/MAY/67 Race: WHR Sex: MALE
Address Res.: 45 ENSLEWOOD ROAD LONDON UK
Zip: SW12 7AP Phone: 011 442 08675078

Type of ID shown: ID# if applicable:

I, BOLESLAW TADEUSZ SZOCIK, do hereby voluntarily make the following statement without threat, coercion, offer of benefit, or favor by any persons whomsoever.

PLEASE SEE ATTACHED LETTER AND MATERIALS FOR STATEMENT.

DECLINATION TO PROSECUTE STATEMENT FOR ALL OFFENSES

My signature below means that I refuse to prosecute the person(s) named above for the alleged crime(s) that occurred to me or to the property under my control.
SIGNATURE: _____ DATE: _____

Sworn to and subscribed before me, this 24th day of AUGUST 2006 in LONDON, U.K.
Notary Public ☑ Law Enforcement or Corrections Officer ☐
MY COMMISSION IS Name Key [ ] PERMANENT
Personally Known ☐ Produced Identification ☑
Type of Identification: UK DRIVING LICENSE SZOCI605232BT97SZ

I will testify in court and prosecute criminally. Initials: BTS
Victim's Rights Booklet provided? Yes ☐ No ☑
I swear/affirm the above and/or attached statements are correct and true.
Signature: BT Szocik
Miranda Warning Read? Yes ☐ No ☐
Page 1 of 9

White: State Attorney   Yellow: Records   Pink: Investigator   Green: Victim

MANFRED PHILIPP KUHN
NOTARY PUBLIC LONDON
PHONE +44 20 7470 7131
FAX   +44 20 7470 7132

```
ORLANDO POLICE DEPARTMENT 7.0.4          Date Created: 8/23/2006
                                                  Page:     1
Suspicious Incident/Person                Case No: 2006-315577

Primary Victim:  SZOCIK,BOLESLAW,T,

Date/Time Reported:    8/22/2006 15:06 Hrs.   Dispatch Incident Type:
Date/Time Occurred:   11/17/2001 23:00 Hrs.   SUSPCS INC
Date/Time Between :   11/17/2001 23:00 Hrs.   Unit No:  998
Location Occurred :   431 E CENTRAL BV #907
Cross Street    . . :
Grid: GRID#-1347       Sub-Grid: GRID 1347B        District: D-I1


Reporting Officer :         5878 ASHTON,CHARLENE,M,
Primary Unit Assigned to Investigate: A&B Unit       Apv Ofcr:
Scene Processed by:                                         Event Log NO
Assigned Investigators:              Special Circumstance:

Stat|___| Disp|___| Date|__/__| Invt|____| Asmt Type|___| Date|__/__|
Case Status: Unassigned  Disposition: INACTIVE       DispDate 8/23/2006
------------------------------------------------------------------
Distribution
None


Case Narrative
08-22-2006 at 1506 hours, the victim, Boleslaw Szocik, called the
Information Desk at the Orlando Police Department to report the
following:

Victim stated, on 11-17-2001 at 2300 hours, he was living at the
Post Parkside Apartments located at 431 East Central Boulevard in
Apartment #907.  Victim stated, on this date and time, six or seven
males, possibly white, knocked on his door.  Victim stated these
males were shouting sexual abuse at him, along with statements
concerning prostitution.  Victim stated these males wanted him to
come outside so they could shoot him.  Victim stated he did not go
outside and never saw any weapons.

Victim stated these males were hired by people (NOI) in the United
Kingdom to come over to Orlando to kill him.  Victim did not want to
provide a lot of the case information over the phone but stated he
wanted to send a transcript of this conversation with the suspects
to the Orlando Police Department.

Victim stated he had delayed in reporting this incident, because he
went back to England and contacted attorneys there, but they never
returned his inquiries.

Victim was given the City of Orlando website, in order to print out
a sworn written statement to complete and send to us, along with his
transcripts.

Victim stated, if it is determined a crime has been committed, he
will prosecute.
```

```
ORLANDO POLICE DEPARTMENT 7.0.4        Date Created: 8/23/2006
                                                Page:     2
Suspicious Incident/Person                 Case No: 2006-315577

ca/5878/08-22-2006/1648 hours/n


-----------------------------------------------------------------
                         PRINCIPALS
Victim      : SZOCIK,BOLESLAW,T,
   No.  1     45 ENGLEWOOD RD
              LONDON ENGLAND, SW129PA

   Race . : White      Sex: Male        D.O.B: 5/23/1967 Age: 39
   Height :      "  Wgt:       Hair:    Eyes . . . :
   Build. :              Complexion:    Citizenship:
   Driv Lic #:                      St: Soc Sec #:
   Occupation:           School:        Ethnicity:

       Residence Type  : Other       Residence Status : Non Res
       Extent of Injury: N/A         Special Circumstn:
       Injury Type . . : NA          Injury Type  . . :
       Hospital/Clinic :              Transported by . :
       Statement Type  : Verbal      Related Offenses :    1

VOR: UNK,SUSPECT,, - Stranger
Subject Narrative
Home phone #011442086750873


-----------------------------------------------------------------
Suspect     : UNK,SUSPECT,,
   No.  1

   Race . : White      Sex: Male        D.O.B:             Age:
   Height :      "  Wgt:       Hair:    Eyes . . . :
   Build. :              Complexion:    Citizenship:
   Driv Lic #:                      St: Soc Sec #:
   Occupation:           School:        Ethnicity:

       Residence Type  : N/A         Residence Status : N/A
       Extent of Injury: N/A         Special Circumstn:
       Injury Type . . : NA          Injury Type  . . :
       Hospital/Clinic :              Transported by . :
       Statement Type  : None        Related Offenses :    1

Subject Narrative
Six or Seven possibly white males.


-----------------------------------------------------------------
Offense Number:   1
Crime Code: 0SU09
Statute . : 0                 Attempted/Committed : Committed
Location Type . : Apartment   Criminal Activity . : N/A
Occupancy Code  : N/A         No. Premises Entered:
```

```
           ORLANDO POLICE DEPARTMENT 7.0.4      Date Created: 8/23/2006
                                                          Page:     3
Suspicious Incident/Person              Case No: 2006-315577

Type of Weapon   : N/A            Weapon Feature    . . :
# Adults Present:                 # Juveniles Present :
Entry Method   . : NA             Entry Point . . . . . :
Exit Method  . . : NA             Exit Point  . . . . . :
Alcohol Related  : No             Drug Related  . . . : No
Domestic Crime   : No             Hate Crime  . . . . : No
Computer Theft   :                Just. Homicide Code :
Hom/Ag Aslt Circmst :             Just. Circumstances :
Larceny/Theft Categy:             Counterfeit Type. . :
Counterfeit Status. :             Count./Forg. Amount :
```

****

I Swear or affirm the above statements	Officer Name/ID# (Print)
are correct and true.	
(Signature)_____	
Sworn to and subscribed before me, the undersigned Authority,	
This____day of_____,20____.	
Notary Public |_| Law Enforcement Officer |_| Emp#____ Orlando PD	

The men did not knock on the door, they were shouting from the park. Otherwise the report is accurate from my conversation with OPD. I sent them a detailed notarised report a couple of days later. You can see the cover page of the report on page 1 of the multipage TIFF; the report contained nine pages including a detailed letter, the Ginsberg transcript of the recording of the attempted homicide and the MI5 death threat immediately preceding the attempt. The letter stated that the Seven Men had been instructed by British Security Service to kill me, and that they could be private agents or more probably US law enforcement; that the case would be dealt with by OPD's Assault and Battery unit, and treated as an assault. The letter further stated that the conspiracy to kill had been preceded by rape threats made by MI5 against me, following which I had bought two handguns for self defence, and an internet death threat which I sent with the report. The Seven Men tried to entice me into the park so they could shoot me. After a period of time, they gave up shouting abuse and left the park.

On 26 September 2006 I emailed Sgt Brennan to find out what had happened to the notarised report I had sent, which they had not replied to. Also on 14 October 2006 I wrote to a lawyer Mr Geismar who had been referred by the Orange County Bar Association Lawyer Referral Service instructing him to bring the complaint before the State Prosecutor's office. Geismar found that the State Prosecutor required that the case be forwarded by OPD. He therefore wrote to Orlando Police on 21 October 2006 requesting they investigate. He subsequently spoke to the OPD investigator who could not recommend prosecution based on the age of the case and the lack of concrete evidence to show the identities of the Seven Men hired linking them to MI5.

Sgt Brennan assigned the case to Detective Montford who made no attempt to investigate it and sought to close it without doing any work. I told Brennan I would refer the matter to Internal Affairs if he continued to refuse to investigate, and I followed up with an actual complaint to them on 18 November. Sgt. Joseph J. Windt of Internal Affairs told me his group only investigated internal policy violations and my complaint against Brennan did not disclose any such. I further emailed Brennan on 22 December 2006 requesting information about his investigation since Windt had said they would re-open the case in the event of further evidence coming to light. He replied on 29 December as follows.

> Please forgive my lack of response to your previous request. I certainly did not mean to appear discourteous. I had assumed your attorney, with whom my detective had been communicating, had relayed our findings in the investigation. Detective Montford explained to your attorney that the incident that occurred in our city, at best, is an assault. There is likely insufficient probable cause to prove that case. In the event that sufficient probable cause did exist, Florida State Statute 775.15 (2)(d) requires that prosecution in all second degree misdemeanor cases must be commenced within 1 year of the date of offense.
>
> Of the offenses you have enumerated in your communications, the assault allegation is the only one that falls under the jurisdiction of the Orlando Police Department. Since the time limitation for prosecution of that offense has lapsed, the case is inactive and will no longer be investigated.
>
> SGT Roger Brennan
> Orlando Police Department
> Assault and Battery Unit
> Office (407) 246-2927
> Fax (407) 246-2994

Thus Orlando Police closed the case. When I enquired about records later they only found three pages representing the initial phone report.

Bugsweep by Steadman's team

In February 2006 I asked the reputable firm Lorraine Electronics to recommend a team for a TSCM sweep of my house in Clapham South. They recommended Nick Steadman, who forwarded details of his team as follows;

Background details for Electronic Countermeasures and Security Sweeps

- The three members of the sweep team have over 30 years combined experience in Electronics Countermeasures and Security.
- Our backgrounds include service for Her Majesty's Government, UK Special Forces Communications and British Telecom.
- We use the latest Audiotel computer-aided scanning equipment to detect illicit radio transmissions and we back this up with a thorough physical search. Telephones are physically opened and inspected for any signs of tampering and additional circuitry. Telephone lines are checked for taps and transmitters. If required, discreet security seals can be applied to equipment and mains / telephone sockets. These seals enhance security and reduce time on follow-up sweeps.
- For your 7 room domestic project we would send a two man team and charge a rate of £875 for the day.
- Our findings can be presented in a Report (Charged at £75.00) which contains advice on improving and maintaining a secure environment for all types of sensitive information.

Steadman confirmed by email that his two man team use an NLJD to discover bugs even when they have switched off or are otherwise not operating. He said there would be a charge of £875 plus an additional £75 for a written report. He and another team member turned up on 26 April 2006, and conducted a thorough sweep which lasted some four hours. They conducted a number of sweeps and found nothing. Steadman said he used to work for HM Government conducting sweeps of this sort, mostly at overseas locations; he refused to say which agency he worked for, that they're not supposed to talk about it.

They swept with broadband detector, then with Audiotel spectrum analyzer; on the analyzer he compared scans from different parts of the house, found a lot of harmonics of FM broadcast stations but found nothing suspicious. He said that if the bugs could be switched off remotely, then they would only be detectable by physical search/NLJD; they did an NLJD sweep using Audiotel broom of the entire house and found nothing in walls or furniture. Steadman said he was trained at Audiotel's in house facility; they found nothing on the mains lines or phone lines, or in the phone sockets. He said all he and his associates do is TSCM, they are not subsidiary to some other job. He checked the inside of the TV set and found no extraneous circuitry, or transmissions.

Steadman's report is as follows.

Electronic Countermeasures Sweep

Initial Report

45 Englewood Road

Clapham

LONDON

SW12

Wednesday 26 April 2006

CONTENTS

Part One - GENERAL CONSIDERATIONS

Part Two - TARGET ANALYSIS

Part Three - THE COUNTERMEASURES SWEEP

Part Four - RECOMMENDATIONS

Part One - GENERAL CONSIDERATIONS

Introduction

At the request of Mr T Szocik an electronic countermeasures sweep was carried out at 45 Englewood Road, Clapham, LONDON, SW12 on Wednesday 26 April 2006.

Whilst information can be stolen by other means, information-gathering through the use of electronic eavesdropping represents a real and significant threat. The purpose of this sweep was to satisfy Mr Szocik that the techniques used would significantly reduce the threat from eavesdropping devices, to assess vulnerability to this and other forms of attack, and to make recommendations where appropriate to protect him from risks of this nature.

Scope of the Report

Although this Report is concerned with electronic eavesdropping, observations and recommendations are made with regard to general security matters, where applicable.

Part Two - TARGET ANALYSIS

General Site Considerations

There are suitable hiding places in all areas for bugging devices, microphone cables and tape recorders. Many areas could allow concealment of radio transmitters with large battery packs for extended operation. There is, in all areas, sufficient furniture to permit quick concealment of a small, disposable radio transmitter. Some areas can be overlooked using high power optics.

The main threats are perceived to be from :

Radio transmitters / baby alarms installed within rooms for relaying room conversation.

Tape recorders concealed within rooms for recording room conversation.

Use of cables to carry room conversation, whether by audio frequencies (wired microphone), or by means of a high frequency carrier, to a Listening Post either within the premises or in nearby buildings.

Telephone tapping equipment placed on the line.

Telephone tapping equipment placed between the line and the analogue extension.

Audio modifications made to digital handsets.

Interception of video information on computers / VDU screens.

Specific Considerations

45 Englewood Road is a three-storey Victorian terraced house, linked to its neighbours on both sides. There are voids in the loft and cellar areas where microphones could be easily inserted.

There is no alarm system or CCTV cameras protecting the premises.

Part Three - THE COUNTERMEASURES SWEEP

The following areas were checked :

Room No*	Type	Remarks
G01	Front Room	Full check
G02	Dining Room	Full Check
G03	Garden Room	Full Check
101	Rear Office	Full Check
102	Middle Bedroom	Full check
103	Front Bedroom	Full check
201	Attic Bedroom	Full check

*Room numbers allocated by Team.

Each area was subject to :

Upper band radio frequency scan (10 MHz - 5 GHz)

Low band radio frequency scan (12 KHz - 10 MHz)

Low frequency mains carrier scan (25 KHz - 500 KHz)

Computer-aided scans were made, analysed and electronically examined for any anomalies, and then stored for future reference and comparison. **No hostile transmissions were detected during the inspection.**

Telephone sockets were opened and inspected carefully for any signs of modification.

The downstairs analogue telephone was checked for :

Upper band radio frequency devices

Lower band radio frequency devices

Parallel taps

Infinity taps

Audio modifications

The instrument was tested with both the conversation monitor and Delta V radio frequency detector.

A Non-Linear Junction Detector (Broom) was used to check for concealed electronics, backed up by a thorough physical search.

In addition the front and rear gardens, loft spaces and cellar were all visually inspected.

The TV set in the front room was opened and the circuit board was checked for any extra components.

No radio bugs, hard-wired devices, audio modifications, telephone taps or illicit recording equipment were found during the counter-measures sweep.

Part Four - OBSERVATIONS AND RECOMMENDATIONS

One disadvantage of living in an old terraced property is the direct party wall link to neighbours. Furthermore chimney-breasts, cellar and loft spaces all have voids, which allow access to each other's properties. The saving grace with these locations is that sensitive conversations are rarely held in them.

There is always a risk that a neighbour might use a device which detects conversations through walls. Unfortunately there is no defence against this form of attack other than to ensure that any sensitive conversations are held away from the house.

There may be some merit in installing an alarm system to deter potential attackers from entering the property. The addition of a CCTV camera at the front and rear of the house would complement this.

Contractors carrying out work on the premises should always be escorted.

The ADSL phone line is difficult to intercept due to the combination of speech and data on the same line. We would suggest, however, that a DECT instrument replaces the old analogue telephone in the front room.

Any computers in the house should have short screen saver delay times to prevent any sensitive information being displayed for long periods.

The wi-fi network unit should have access codes changed on a regular basis.

Needless to say, I was disappointed that Steadman's team had found nothing, but it merely shows that MI5 must be using some advanced technology which a competent TSCM operative could not find, even with an NLJD.

Eye Say, 2006-07

In 2006-07 I placed multiple issues of advertising with Private Eye magazine classifieds, in the Eye Say column. Their aim particularly was to try to draw attention to MI5's attempt to kill me in Nov/2001.

Eye Say

PREP SCHOOL QUESTIONS? Talk about your school – talk, ask, buy, sell! www.prep-talk.org

"JUST ONE DROP can cause a major wave." Join survivors making waves by signing this petition KILL BILL vol. 2 The Draft Mental Health Bill www.petitionthem.com/?sect=detail&pet=2183

MI5 tried to kill me on 17 November 2001 – www.mi5.com

Issues 1151-1153. The ad contained the bald statement that MI5 had tried to kill me on 17 November 2001. Originally I wanted the text "www.mi5.com/evidence/#deathsquad" to appear, but Private Eye insisted I not offend MI5 by stating that their death squad had been operating in the United States in 2001.

Eye Say

THE SOCIALIST PARTY aims at building a moneyless world community based on common ownership and democratic control with production solely for use not profit. It opposes all leadership, all war. For information and sample literature write to The Socialist Party (PE), 52 Clapham High Street, London SW4 7UN. www.worldsocialism.org/spgb www.shirtoffmyback.co.uk

CAMERON: The Tory Neil Kinnock, or Westminster's David Brent? SwingaRight.org

SPONSORS WANTED for a British Political Peerage plus tax.

MI5 TRIED TO KILL ME on 17 November/2001 –www.mi5.com/evidence/#ds

Issue 1155-1163. The same but with revised wording.

MI5 TRIED TO KILL ME, 17 November 2001. Resulting legal action cost £30,000 so far; risk losing home. Please help, www.mi5.com (CreditCard/PayPal), Barclays, S/C: 20-21-78. A/C: 80884065.

Issue 1165-1169. A request for help in my legal fight.

Eye Say

www.taintedblood.info Join Our Fight For Justice.

JAMES BOND single-handedly defends Britain's National Security, www.mi5.com/evidence/#britspy

Issue 1174-1179. A reference to the Masturbating MI5 Agent from 2000.

Eye Say

MI5 SUED in Florida Federal Court for assault / attempted homicide, http://www.mi5.com/legal/orlando/orlando.htm assault / attempted homicide.

Issue 1192-1196. Reference to my lawsuit against MI5 in Orlando Federal Court for

Eye Say

MI5 PERSECUTION – mind control torture. "We're not doing this for fun." http://www.mi5.com/evidence/mc/mc.htm simply for fun.

Issue 1197-1201. Mindcontrol torture which the gay MI5 sadists apparently do

BBC Ariel accepts my MindControl Torture advert

In early 2008 I paid £66 for three personal adverts in the BBC's Ariel staff magazine, mainly to see if they would be accepted or if Ariel's current editor would reject them as had Robin Reynolds in 1997. To my surprise not only were they accepted but presumably due to a publishing glitch Ariel printed the ads for six weeks instead of the three I had paid for. They appeared in week 3 (15.1.08) through week 8 (19.2.08). The following advert ran for those six weeks.

I decided against further advertising with Ariel because £22 per issue is quite expensive and I am short of money. I did not know what if any impact the ads were having and I got no feedback from BBC employees on the website so I discontinued the personals.

PERSONAL

MI5 persecution – mind control torture. We're not doing this for fun. www.mi5.com